# Toronto, No Mean City

But Paul said, I am a man
which am a Jew of Tarsus,
a city in Cilicia,
a citizen of no mean city.     ACTS 21:39

# TORONTO

ERIC ARTHUR

# No Mean City

Third Edition

Revised by
STEPHEN A. OTTO

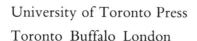

University of Toronto Press
Toronto Buffalo London

First edition
© University of Toronto Press 1964
Reprinted 1964, 1965, 1968

Second edition
© University of Toronto Press 1974
Reprinted 1978

Third edition
© University of Toronto Press 1986
Toronto Buffalo London
Printed in Canada

ISBN 0-8020-5668-7 (cloth)
ISBN 0-8020-6587-2 (paper)

---

**Canadian Cataloguing in Publication Data**

Arthur, Eric, 1898-1982
  Toronto, no mean city
  Bibliography
  Includes index.
  ISBN 0-8020-5668-7 (bound) – ISBN 0-8020-6587-2 (pbk.)
  1. Architecture – Ontario – Toronto – History.
  I. Otto, Stephen A., 1940-  II. Title.
  NA747.T6A76 1986  720'.9713'541  C86-093387-3

---

This book has been published with the assistance of the Canada Council and
the Ontario Arts Council under their block grant programs.

# Contents

PREFACE TO THE THIRD EDITION / vii

FOREWORD / ix

ACKNOWLEDGMENTS / xi

INTRODUCTION / xv

1 The Village and the Ancient Trails / 3

2 'As it was in the beginning ...' / 10

3 A Late-Flowering Georgian / 33

4 Prosperity and Eclecticism / 67

5 Romanesque and Cast Iron / 157

6 Epilogue / 223

NOTES / 233

APPENDIXES
A / The Architectural Profession in the Nineteenth Century / 237
B / Builders and Contractors / 265
C / The Origin of Street Names in Toronto / 272

BIBLIOGRAPHY / 295

INDEX /301

PICTURE CREDITS /313

# Preface

## to the Third Edition

I remember more than twenty years ago receiving a gift of the first edition of *Toronto, No Mean City* and, book in hand, setting out to explore the city in which I had been born. What pleasure there was in seeing parts of Toronto as if for the first time and in sensing the continuity of history that was represented by its older buildings. My gratitude to the late Eric Arthur for this birthright was one reason for undertaking the third edition of this book. His pride in our city and his enthusiasm were inspiring.

Another reason existed in the impressive quantities of information and many new pictures that have come to light since the first edition was published. Newspapers of the nineteenth century now have yielded building reports and construction-tender calls that fill out the decades before the appearance of the *Canadian Architect and Builder* magazine in 1888. From these sources it has been possible to enrich and expand the biographies of Toronto architects in appendix A and to add a new appendix B for builders and contractors. Among the pictures uncovered since 1964 are twenty-five of the earliest photographs of Toronto, found a few years ago in the Foreign and Commonwealth Office Library in London, England; six of those views of 1856–7 are included in this edition. Of particular significance, however, was the presentation in 1979 of the J.C.B. and E.C. Horwood Collection of architectural drawings and related materials to the Ontario Archives. In making his magnificent gift – the largest collection of its kind in Canada and the most valuable donation ever received by that institution – the late Eric Horwood hoped that it would help to strengthen our collective memory of our architectural accomplishments. He would, I think, approve of its extensive use in the preparation of this new edition.

*Toronto, No Mean City* has been the most significant book on the fabric of the city to appear since John Ross Robertson's *Landmarks* was published during the first decade of this century. The interest in older buildings that both books fostered was reinforced by Canada's Centennial in 1967 and the passage of the Ontario Heritage Act in 1975. Although almost twenty buildings have been demolished that existed in 1964 and were illustrated by Professor Arthur, it is not too much to hope that the third edition will foster a renewed vigilance over those buildings that remain.

Edith Firth, to whom Professor Arthur was greatly indebted for her assistance with the first and second editions of this book, has been a partner once again in the preparation of this edition, giving generous encouragement and needed advice. I am very grateful also to Robert Hill and Kent Rawson for making available their extensive research notes on Toronto buildings and architects. They, as well as Marion MacRae, Shirley Morriss, Douglas Richardson, Jack Richardson, and David Roberts, responded to my numerous questions with helpful information and were good enough to suggest many improvements to the appendixes on architects and builders.

Several of the new illustrations could not have been included except for the interest and kindness of Jim Burant, John Crosthwait, Mike Filey, Helen Heward, Donna Ivey, Tom McIlwraith, Rollo Myers, and Joan Winearls. In revising the text, appendixes, and captions I have appreciated the insights and important information provided by Jim Bitaxi, Donald Brown, William Cooke, Pleasance Crawford, Lynne DiStefano, Jim Gillespie, William Greer, Dennis Reid, Thomas Ritchie, Judith Saunders, Roy Schaeffer, Pamela Manson Smith, William Withrow, John Zigur, and Willie Zimmerman. I would be remiss were I not also to acknowledge the co-operation I received from many members of the staff of the Metropolitan Toronto Library and the City of Toronto Archives. I am grateful also to Wayne Daniels, who prepared the index. The Central Records unit of the Department of the City Clerk and the Records unit of the Department of Buildings and Inspections were most helpful in confirming the dates for construction and demolition. Throughout the book inclusive dates for the erection of a building are given where available; where only one date is given, it indicates the first year of substantial construction.

A grant from the Ontario Arts Council that offset out-of-pocket expenses in obtaining the new illustrations for this edition was much appreciated.

STEPHEN A. OTTO
22 February 1986

# Foreword

Too little has been written about the early development of Toronto and the reasons for its growth. When my grandfathers came to live here about one hundred years ago, one from Scotland, the other from what was once known as Lower Canada, Toronto was a city of some sixty or seventy thousand people. At the beginning of that century it was nothing but a frontier village of no more than four or five hundred inhabitants. Today the population exceeds one and a half million, and there is no end in sight.

In writing this book, it was not Eric Arthur's purpose to explain why Toronto has grown so big so quickly or to guess what may happen to it in the years that lie ahead. However, in providing us with this record of the things our predecessors built, often with difficulty and with limited resources, he has given us some insight into their characters. Torontonians have been noted for their drive, energy, and ambition, for a materialistic urge to get ahead. In the process they found time to create some things that were handsome, even beautiful. It is these that should be preserved.

Toronto is no longer exclusively British or colonial in outlook. It is now a cosmopolitan city whose people have come from all corners of the earth. This makes it a much more lively and interesting place to live and provides an atmosphere in which the arts can flourish and develop. Nevertheless, the same characteristics of drive, energy, and ambition are still very much in evidence. We would not wish it to be otherwise.

Some years ago Professor Arthur told me of his plans to write this book about the origins and early architecture of Toronto. He asked me to write a foreword. As one who was born and brought up in Toronto, I was pleased that a man of Professor Arthur's talents was going to write a book about our city, and I was flattered at the thought of being associated with it even in a minor way.

However, our conversation proved to be one of the most expensive experiences I have ever had. Professor Arthur had expressed the wish to include illustrations of the building at 15 Wellington Street West, owned by the firm of which, at the time, I was the senior partner. Shortly after our conversation the building was inspected and found to be unsafe. We were ordered to vacate it. Some of my partners thought that the building should be demolished to make way for a more modern structure. Others felt that this might spoil Professor Arthur's book, on which he had been working for some years. They said that if I were to write the foreword, the only decent thing for us to do would be to renovate the building. This argument prevailed, and the old Commercial Bank building at 15 Wellington Street West has been completely rebuilt from the inside out. It was a costly undertaking.

However, it is a lovely building. Now it will be preserved for many years, and not only within the pages of this book. I am sure all my former partners are pleased with the decision that was taken, for there cannot be many chartered accountants who, in Professor Arthur's words, occupy 'a truly fine building that cannot help but evoke thoughts of Greece and of Byron, Shelley, Keats, and others.'

I hope his labours will inspire others to preserve some of the few architectural gems of earlier times that still remain. One of these is St Lawrence Hall on King Street at Jarvis. A building of a much later period renovated recently is St Anne's Church on Gladstone Avenue, north of Dundas. The interior of this church was decorated by local artists who later became famous as the Group of Seven. In a pulsating, vital metropolis like Toronto, with its ever-changing population, there is a need to be reminded of the things that were created by those who went before us. Professor Arthur's book meets this need admirably.

W.L. GORDON
31 December 1963

St Anne's Church, Gladstone Avenue (1907),
Ford Howland, architect:
one of the most colourful
church interiors in Toronto,
a labour of love on which several of
the Group of Seven painters
left their mark

# Acknowledgments

For a quarter of a century or more this study of Toronto has never been far from my thoughts, and it is inevitable, however much I regret it, that many acquaintances and some old friends who provided information will be forgotten in these acknowledgments. We may have met by chance at dinner, on the street, or in a bus, and, rather as in the stories about subversive characters one reads in the newspapers, an address has been given, a snapshot or a letter has changed hands, and we have parted. The number of such encounters, if not legion, must number hundreds, and they have led more than once to old books, old photographic collections, and not least to old people.

It has been my good fortune to make my investigations into old Toronto at a time when many who are still living remember with enviable clarity the buildings and people of the later nineteenth century that are of vital importance in the story of the city. So many of our ancient landmarks are lost that the architectural historian of even so recent a period as the nineteenth century must frequently feel that he is concerned with some ancient civilization like Pompeii or Herculaneum. Fortunately, he can be brought back to reality by meeting older citizens like William Wadsworth, QC, who remembers vividly having Sunday tea with his mother at the house of her uncle, Colonel Frederic Cumberland, the designer of St James' Cathedral. Even more impressive and more indicative of the youthfulness of Toronto are Mr Wadsworth's records of his great-grandfather Thomas Ridout, who came to Toronto when the population was only fifty. For the interviewer, Max Beerbohm's phrase, 'the intruder from posterity,' cannot help but come to mind.

Few who recall the seemingly venerable walls of old Trinity (1851) on Queen Street would believe that many now living knew its architect, Kivas Tully, who died in 1905. I myself knew and greatly admired W.A. Langton and his brother Hugh, the distinguished sons of the great vice-chancellor of the university John Langton, who acted as intermediary between Cumberland, the architect, and Sir Edmund Head in the building of University College in 1856. It is with rather special pride that I can count the late Dr Needler as colleague and friend. He fought in the Riel Rebellion and was a youth when the Metropolitan Church was built. For him, the melancholy story of Mrs Anna Jameson, who died in 1860, seemed that of a near and dear friend rather than of a figure who appeared briefly on the Toronto stage and left, never to return, in 1837. These are but a few of the men and women in that ever-diminishing band whose memories, only slightly dimmed, recall the buildings and the people of the past century.

Fortunately for the architectural historian, there were others, actually living in the nineteenth century, whose love of buildings was second only to their interest in their neighbours. Where they lived, where they worshipped, and where they worked have been the study of several works. Chief, of course, was Dr Henry Scadding's *Toronto of Old*, followed by the monumental records of John Ross Robertson in his *Landmarks of Toronto*. I am bound to acknowledge my profound obligations to both of them. There are other sources of material cited in the bibliography elsewhere in this volume, but I should like to pay special tribute to the late Percy Robinson, whose *Toronto during the French Régime* first introduced me to a period that I found far from negligible in the evolution of Toronto's urban pattern.

But to return to the present. Many have gone, but there are still Torontonians with no personal memories of the nineteenth century who yet, perhaps by reason of their closeness to it as children, have made a study of early buildings and people of that period the habit of a lifetime. From them the most notable contribution was that of the late T.A. Reed, who published little but left a sizeable collection of photographs to complement the John Ross Robertson sketches in the Metropolitan Toronto Library. Reed was not only an eager collector of Canadiana; he ranked second to none in his love of Toronto.

Less well known, but one who has been tireless in research on my behalf, has been John Songhurst. Mr Songhurst has long been a resident of Toronto and can remember his first interest in buildings as a messenger boy seventy years ago. At the age of seven he received the first volume of the *Landmarks*, and it has been a constant companion ever since. His wife shares his interest, as well she might, having been born in St Lawrence Hall of parents who, like her grandparents, had the custody of the hall in the days of its dignity in the life of the community.

I am particularly indebted to Hugh Robertson, the photographer. His skill is apparent in his work, but had it not been for his interest in the subject and his willingness to work at odd and critical times, many buildings would have perished without record. At various times foundations and friends have contributed towards the cost of photography, and I am happy to express my gratitude to the Architectural Conservancy of Ontario, the Flavelle Foundation, and Harry Kohl.

I am very much obliged to Wallace Bonner of the Toronto Public Library for bringing to life by photography many old maps and hardly discernible pictures; to Uno Prii and Vyt Kvedaris, two young architects, for sketches of similar material; and to Mrs Howard Garfield and Mrs G.E. Edgar for the typing and retyping of these pages.

Professor John Russell of Winnipeg has been a source of inspiration and encouragement over most of the years this book was in preparation, and I can only hope that the book itself may be some sort of requital for his kindness.

I am under various obligations to friends who have provided information on matters of art, technology, or history: to F. de Rege, the consul general of Italy; His Excellency Leo Maynard, the Canadian ambassador to Italy; Dr Emilio Goggio, Alan Jarvis, William Colgate, Mrs Marion Fowler, R.E. Chadwick, L.J. McGowan, George Grainger, and W.E. Fleury.

Finally, there are people and institutions without whom this study of old Toronto would in all probability not have been made. I am chiefly indebted to the president and Board of Governors of the University of Toronto for allowing me sabbatical leave in 1958–9, and to the Canada Council for a very welcome senior grant directed particularly to research into the early architecture of Toronto. I should be remiss if I did not include in these thanks my colleagues in the School of Architecture, whose labours, one must assume, were not lightened by my absence.

The basic material on the origin of street names comes from John Ross Robertson and T.A. Reed, but even their lists left many streets of doubtful or unknown origin. Some yet remain uncertain, but the gap in our knowledge has been greatly narrowed. It is my hope that the publication of the origin of Toronto street names will bring more people to the defence of ancient names when they are attacked by those for whom history has no meaning or importance. Until recently Ann and McGill Streets were not unromantic reminders of Ann McGill, who became the wife of Bishop Strachan, but Ann became Granby as a concession to a long-held Toronto belief that a change of name would raise the tone of a street both socially and morally. Granby, of course, was a marquis. The fact that in 1834 Strachan purchased twenty-five acres north of Gerrard Street out of which he gave the land to the city for Ann, McGill, and part of Carlton Streets carried no weight with Judge Parker, who granted the change. Guy Carleton Wood was Mrs Strachan's brother, and Carlton is misspelled.

I am very aware that there is some presumption in a person of antipodean birth and English education following in the footsteps of Scadding, Robertson, and Robinson as a recorder of old Toronto. My excuse is that the story might well be told again through the eyes of an architect, aided, as his predecessors were not, by photography and the clarity of the modern printed page. At the same time I am very conscious of the fact that the story of its architecture is part of the social history of Toronto and cannot be told without a knowledge of the political and economic history that, through war and peace, boom and depression, gave it character and life.

In that area of knowledge, I must confess my own inadequacy and my very real debt to Miss Edith Firth. She must be held blameless for any of the errors that appear, inevitably, in these pages. The period in which she is an authority covers the early years of York, Upper Canada; I, with the innocence of a fairly new Canadian and an audacity that at times must have left her breathless, have not hesitated to explore the Toronto scene from Louis XIV to Edward VII. Her painstaking reading of manuscripts and her frequent suggestion of clues that led to English architects like Fowler and Soane can never be repaid.

For many years Mrs Harry Davidson has been a tireless research worker and collaborator in the preparation of the material for this book. Many of the illustrations would have remained hidden but for her zeal in pursuing them in odd places, and the section on street names owes much to her patience and persistence. My very sincere thanks go to her.

The writing of a book makes many inroads on the family and social life of the author, and my thanks go to my wife for her sympathetic understanding of the many problems the work imposed.

Last, but by no means least, is my grateful acknowledgment of the generosity of the J.S. McLean and the Laidlaw foundations, which have helped to make the publication of this book possible.

ERIC ARTHUR
Toronto 1963

# Introduction

This architectural history of Toronto has been in the mind of the writer since the time, many years ago, when he first made it a habit of wandering with no fixed objective through the streets of the old town. Thirty-five years ago one could enjoy many thoroughfares that still had about them an air of colonial Upper Canada – a quiet Georgian peace created in part by the low horizontal lines of the two-storeyed, terraced houses. Those streets are now slums or ruins and can be enjoyed, like Ruth Draper with her imaginary garden, only in memory.

But if the architecture is gone, a few individual buildings of an older time remain. The visitor to Paris knows what it is to turn a corner and see a famous monument like the Madeleine for the first time. It is not necessary to leave Toronto to have the same emotional experience; one may have it when one looks north on John from Queen and sees the Grange for the first, or even the tenth time. Osgoode Hall at the head of York and Sir William Campbell's house, which used to close so beautifully the vista of Frederick Street, are not easily forgotten.

The newcomer to Toronto from Europe or Great Britain has probably left a city that was rich in those ancient landmarks that give colour and meaning to history. And there are other newcomers – our own children – for whom the city of Toronto shows few visible signs of its ancient origins or of the various cultural influences that have shaped our architecture since Simcoe chose his capital in York.

In the march of progress we have ruthlessly destroyed almost all our older architecture; street names cherished for a hundred years or more have been altered to suit the whims of the people on the street, and even our most treasured buildings, Fort York, going back to the beginnings of British settlement, have been threatened because the historic soil on which they stood interfered with the curvature of a modern expressway. In our defence it must be said that the loss of a great deal of early building can be laid to more than one disastrous fire in the days when water pressure was inadequate and fire-fighting equipment was primitive. Whatever the reasons for the destruction of our early architecture, the sad fact remains that the buildings worthy of record from the nineteenth century are, for the most part, churches and university buildings whose safety can be reasonably assured. The rest have disappeared, some without a trace.

It would not be the wish of this writer to condone the destruction of our early buildings, but it would be unfair to compare the interest of the people of London or Edinburgh in the preservation of their ancient monuments with the apparent lack of interest of the citizens of Toronto in theirs. Toronto is a growing city under a pressure that could hardly be conceived of in a city in the United Kingdom, where half-timbered houses can stand on High Holborn in London from Jacobean times and Georgian squares remain un-touched by the speculative builder or the financial institution. It has not been so here. What has been saved from wanton destruction or from fire in the last hundred and fifty years is extremely vulnerable in a period of unpre-cedented growth. As a result, the few idealists who tried to save the Cawthra house at King and Bay knew that they stood little chance against the millions of the Bank of Nova Scotia, which required the site for a new head office. We may regret the loss, but we may feel less humiliated if we think of the chances of survival had the same old house stood at the corner of the Hay-market and Piccadilly.

It was partly the architectural gaps in our history that posed for me the question whether to show only buildings of unquestioned merit or to dem-onstrate the taste of the century more truthfully by showing a greater number of buildings of unequal architectural quality. The decision to do the latter was supported also by the fact that while not every reader has access to the John Ross Robertson *Landmarks*, many would be interested in illustrations of historic houses, churches, and other buildings that, on a strictly archi-tectural selection, would be discarded.

I have suggested that we in Toronto are curiously apathetic towards our history in terms of landmarks, street names, and the like; indeed, surely no city in the world with a background of three hundred years does so little to make that background known. Our children are brought up to take pride in the British beginnings of the city, but they have a limited knowledge of that vastly more exciting period when the Senecas had a village on the site, when black-robed priests and French noblemen dwelt at times at the mouth of the Humber and wrote glowing letters home to France of the potential of Toronto as a settlement in the empire of Louis xiv. No pageants recall the great events that took place under the French regime: 1959 passed with little comment on the destruction of Fort Rouillé in 1759, and yet, in the opinion of historians, this was the birthplace of a metropolis that now boasts two and a half million souls. Pierre Roy, the Quebec archivist, was moved to say of Fort Rouillé, 'this is the great city of Toronto in embryo – Paris did not have a more glorious beginning.' In J.E. Middleton's three-volume work on the *Municipality of Toronto*, the French period enjoys a mere ten pages out of a total of over a thousand.

I hope to show in the early part of this book on Toronto that its beginnings are based on use and a road pattern to my mind far more important than that isolated monument Fort Rouillé, housing less than a dozen men. It has become popular to speak disparagingly, or to speak not at all, of the so-called pre-history of Toronto, but from that neglected period we can make more valid comparisons with the birth of Paris in Roman Lutetia and of London in Londinium than that made by Roy.

The comparison, at first sight far-fetched, is between the effect of Roman planning on Paris and London and our present-day use of the location of the old trails. That they are by no means insignificant can be gathered merely from their names – the Don Valley Parkway, the Frederick Gardiner Expressway, and Davenport Road. The most important and the oldest of the old trails followed the Humber. It has disappeared, but its value as a highway to the north has not changed in several hundred years. We replaced it with Highway 400. The monotony of the rest of our street pattern, the gridiron, is a technique of planning that we received as a legacy from Rome via Alexander Aitkin in 1793. It is for these reasons, very real to the architect and the town planner, that the pre-Simcoe period in our history is discussed in some detail.

There is, of course, another reason, and that is the inaccessibility of information for those new and old Canadians who would like to be more familiar with the earliest period. It is to be found chiefly in *Toronto during the French Régime* by Percy Robinson, a book issued first in a limited edition, for many years out of print. In 1697 Father Hennepin dedicated his book on the *New Discovery of a Large Country in America* to 'His Most Excellent Majesty William III,' which Robinson rather slyly suggests 'will not be without significance to those who recall the subsequent devotion of the city of Toronto to that Monarch.' It may well be asked whether our continued devotion to the memory of the House of Orange has not blinded us to the beauty, the tragedy, and the high adventure of the period under the kings of France – the centuries that saw brave men and women bringing civilization into the wilderness, as well as gentlemen explorers, both French and English, with names that rank high in the histories of both countries. Those years saw, too, the arrival of quite a number of rascals of many races, and of dedicated Catholic priests, some of whom were to die at the stake for their faith. All these people knew by reputation the village at the mouth of the Humber and the trails from the north, the east, and the west that led to it. A surprising number knew the site of Toronto from actual experience and left records of their impressions.

To the memory of

ERIC ARTHUR

1898–1982

# 1 The Village and the Ancient Trails

The pre-British story of Toronto is stimulating enough for the people of Canada, but it is a moving, almost a personal one for those of us who call Toronto home. We can still tread the principal path of the great explorers. It is broken, it is true, and is no longer a trail, but the basic elements remain unchanged. With eyes closed to the structures that have appeared only in this century, we can stand where Etienne Brulé stood on a September morning in 1615. To the south he would look on the great lake, its waves sparkling in the autumn sunshine, its farther shore remote and invisible. To that lonely traveller, the first of his race to set eyes on Lake Ontario, the sight must have been no less awe-inspiring than that which, under poetic licence, Cortez saw from his peak in Darien. More so, indeed, because Brulé was far from Quebec in the company of only twelve Hurons, and the vast waters stretching to the far horizon had to be crossed or circumnavigated by canoe.

By then people had occupied this area for more than ten thousand years. The first inhabitants lived by hunting, fishing, and gathering nuts, berries, and such, moving in small family groups from one campsite to another. Through an extensive trading network they obtained precious materials such as copper, shells from the ocean, and useful or decorative stones not available nearby. In the millennium before the birth of Christ, the making of pottery became common. This was followed about 500 AD by the introduction of agriculture: first corn, and later, beans, squash, sunflowers, and tobacco would be cultivated, all of which greatly changed the living patterns of the native people. Their campsites became permanent settlements, which grew in size and population.

Then, for reasons not well understood, sometime before 1600 the inhabitants of the Toronto area, known to us today as the Hurons and Petuns, withdrew to south of Georgian Bay, leaving their former tribal lands empty. Feuding with the tribes of the Iroquois League living south of Lake Ontario

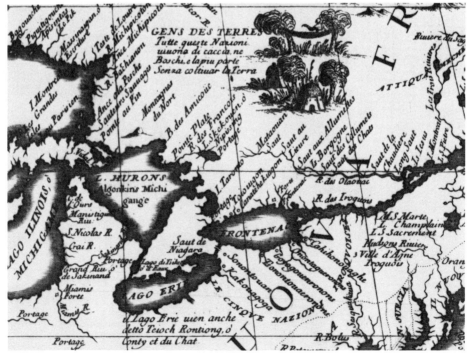

**1.1** Map showing the Toronto Carrying Place or the *passage de Toronto* (from Percy J. Robinson, *Toronto during the French Régime*)

**1.2** A detail of a map of North America by Coronelli, published in 1688 but showing, as did the globe made five years before for Louis XIV, the Seneca villages 'Canatehekiagon' and 'Toioiugon' on 'L. Frontenac' (Ontario), as well as the portage to 'L. Taronto' (Simcoe) continued, however, becoming more intense as the Hurons allied themselves closely with the French, until all-out warfare erupted. By 1651 the Huron Confederacy had been shattered by the Iroquois. Soon after, some Iroquois tribes, including the Senecas, occupied several sites along the north shore of Lake Ontario in an attempt to control the fur trade. These interlopers were dislodged by the French in 1688. Into the empty lands that resulted moved the Mississaugas from their traditional hunting grounds along the southern edge of the Canadian Shield.

Half a century after Brulé gazed across the lake, with the swamps and high clay banks of the Humber behind him, a village could be found on the east bank of the river, within sight of what we know today as the Old Mill. The village was called Teiaiagon. The population of Senecas, and later Mississaugas, would frequently be swelled by white men, most of whom would be free traders. The rest were soldiers and administrators under orders to enrich the coffers of the kings of France and to extend the borders of their empire, or they were members of that smaller band of soldiers of Christ – Jesuits, Sulpicians, and Récollets – dedicated to the goal of the extension of God's kingdom in the wilderness.

Teiaiagon was a trading post, a meeting place for three trade routes – the Indians from the north, the French from the east, and the English from the south. But more important, for it affected the development of Canada, was its strategic location at the southern end of 'le passage de Toronto,'[1] or, to give it its other name, the Toronto Carrying Place, through which travellers went on journeys to Georgian Bay and the Great Lakes – even to the far Mississippi. The Carrying Place was, therefore, not a place so much as a well-defined portage: 'The Carrying Place possessed a permanence very different from casual paths through the forest. It was as old as human life in America.'[2] Canoes and equipment had to be carried from Teiaiagon to the west branch of the Holland River, which provided a storm-free and navigable waterway into Lake Simcoe. The last lap in the Carrying Place between Lake Simcoe and the vast open water of the Great Lakes was the rivière Toronto, which we now call the Severn.

Of lesser importance than Teiaiagon was another village not too distant to be considered with the site of metropolitan Toronto. It was called Ganatsekwyagon by the Senecas who inhabited it, and is shown on the west bank of the Rouge in Father Pierre Raffeix's map of 1688. This, however, is not the first time that the village appears in history: the Sulpician priest the Abbé Fénelon spent the winter there in 1669–70. The name Frenchman's Bay would hardly suggest to the reader the dignity of a Sulpician mission in the reign of Louis XIV, but by that name for the inlet and community near the mouth of the Rouge we do give rather grudging recognition to the presence of a French priest nearly three hundred years ago. The river itself got its name from the deposit of red clay brought down from the banks.

Between the Humber and the Rouge, the Don, which we know today as a sluggish, sewage-laden stream, was once a magnificent river, navigable by canoe for at least five miles and famous, like the Credit and the Humber, for its salmon. From her eyrie on the Castle Frank ridge overlooking the Don, Mrs Simcoe wrote in her diary of the colour and mystery of the scene as the Indian braves speared salmon from canoes at night by the light of flares. Deer abounded in the area, but the fishing, apart from trade, would be additional justification for the settlements of Teiaiagon and Ganatsekwyagon, and between the two there must have been considerable traffic by trail and canoe.[3] The harbour is still there, and great ships come from the far corners of the earth, just as, at another time, the *bateaux* of the French explorers came from Quebec.

As we travel at speed over the Gardiner Expressway and the Don Valley Parkway, we are likely to forget that we are riding on the ancient 'road' system of the Indians, the *coureurs de bois*, and the traders. These were only trails, but how sensible those who blazed them were in their use of the terrain. Much more sensible indeed than was Alexander Aitkin, whose gridiron was imposed on the site of Toronto in 1793 (2.3), ignoring completely the traffic problems to be faced on hills or the unique town-planning possibilities of the ravines. The Indians could have shown Aitkin a simpler way of climbing the Avenue Road hill than by charging it head on.

If to the above we add Davenport Road and Indian Road (an old trail, but laid out as a road by John G. Howard) and allow ourselves the not unreasonable exaggeration of including Highway 400 as the successor to the *passage de Toronto*, we have a network of trails that is built into the fabric of metropolitan Toronto. For that reason we should not accept for the birth of Toronto the building of Fort Rouillé in 1751 – a little structure that had a lifetime of less than nine years and, in 1754, a population of one officer, two sergeants, four soldiers, and a storekeeper. That would be an insignificant and transitory landmark on which to base the foundation of a great city – transitory indeed compared with the immemorial trails. London has its Watling Street as a reminder of the Roman occupation of Londinium; Paris has its rue St Jacques, and posterity may yet realize its debt to those aborigines who blazed the lakeshore, Davenport, and Don trails.

Teiaiagon does not appear again in this story of Toronto, but it will surprise many to know that the location of the village and the Humber are engraved indelibly on a terrestrial globe that once rested in state in the Grand Salon of the Doge's Palace in Venice. It was there in 1875 when Barlow Cumberland reported its existence to Dr Henry Scadding, but it has since been moved to the Biblioteca Nazionale Marciana in the Piazzetta San Marco. The globe was made in 1683 for Louis XIV by the geographer Coronelli. It is three feet, six inches, in diameter, and 'Toioiugon' is distinctly marked, along with the words 'portage' and 'L. Taronto.' It requires no great stretch of the imagination to see the Grand Monarque seated in Versailles reading letters from his administrators in Canada concerning the state of affairs at the *passage de Toronto* and turning to see its location on the globe. When the poet Thomas Moore wrote in 1804

Where the blue hills of old Toronto shed
Their evening shadows o'er Ontario's bed

he may not have known how truly old was the settlement that he visited.[4] He saw it with the discerning eye of the poet, and he felt instinctively its venerability, where contemporary visitors saw only its newness.

The first actual building by methods familiar to Western eyes was the construction of a blockhouse, or *magasin royal*, at or near the mouth of the Humber in 1720. It was one of several at key points on Lake Ontario that were designed by the French to eliminate competition in their trade with the Indians. The one at Toronto was built by the sieur Douville and, according to Percy J. Robinson, was similar to one at Lewiston on the Niagara River. The Lewiston blockhouse was presumably of wood with embrasures for musket fire, and was forty feet by thirty within a palisade. The building of magazines provided the French with only a precarious monopoly in the fur trade and for only a brief period. But for a time it was so successful that profits of the trade at New York declined by almost one-half,[5] to the great chagrin of the English, who countered by building a stone fort at Oswego (1726). The French in turn strengthened their position on the lake by completing Fort Niagara, the stone fortress we admire today at the mouth of the river opposite Niagara-on-the-Lake.

The post at Toronto, a name that, by 1726, had superseded the old 'fort du lac Ontario' and remained in use till Governor Simcoe decided on the more English title of York, in the feverish competition of the time proved to be not a serious contender for the fur trade compared with Oswego, and in 1750 the French were forced to reply with a Fort Toronto erected by the sieur de Portneuf. It stood near the mouth on the east bank of the Humber, and within a few months proved so successful that a second fort was found necessary.

In August 1750 the governor of Quebec, the marquis de La Jonquière, wrote to Antoine-Louis Rouillé, comte de Jouy, the minister of Marine and Colonies in Paris, that the 'house' that the sieur de Portneuf had built at Toronto was too small and that the garrison could easily be overpowered by the Indians, let alone the English. He asked and received permission to build another and larger fort, which he would call Fort Rouillé. So the last of the French forts at the site of Toronto was begun under the supervision of the contractor and master carpenter Joseph Dufaux, and complete in 1751. The fort's location was three miles east of the Humber and was marked, in 1887, by a monument that stands today in the grounds of the Canadian National Exhibition. In keeping with La Jonquière's flattering suggestion to his minister in Paris, a plaque identifies the fort as Rouillé. It was, however, generally described as Fort Toronto or by its full title of 'le fort royal de Toronto.'

By the fall of 1759 Canada had ceased to be a battlefield in the Seven Years' War between England and France. Fort Frontenac had already fallen, and the bastion at Niagara fell to the forces of Sir William Johnson on 25 July 1759 after a siege of nineteen days. The governor-general, Vaudreuil, had given orders for the evacuation and destruction of Fort Toronto if it appeared likely that the fort would fall into British hands, and sometime during the siege of Niagara his orders were carried out by Captain Douville, in charge of the fort. Dr Scadding remarks: 'All that the English or any one else on approaching Toronto, would discover of the once flourishing trading post there would be five heaps of charred timber and planks, with a low chimney stack of coarse brick and a shattered flooring at its foot, made of flagstones from the adjoining beach, the whole surrounded on the inland side by three lines of cedar pickets more or less broken down and scathed by fire.'[6]

It is customary to think of the next thirty years as a blank in the historical continuity of Toronto as a trading centre. Officially, certainly, it had ceased to exist. The French had gone, and the English were slow to realize its potential as a site. General Gage, the British commander at Montreal, issued a proclamation in 1762 declaring the fur trade free to all but forbidding the export of peltries to France. Passes seem to have been issued from Montreal, much as are licences today, to hunt or to trap; among those enjoying such privileges at Toronto was a Monsieur Baby, one of a well-known family from Detroit that had been engaged in the fur trade long before the conquest. His kinsman was the Honourable James Baby, who gave his name to the modern district surrounding Baby Point.

Then there was the family of Rousseau, which helps to fill in the gap between the burning of Fort Rouillé and the arrival of Governor Simcoe. We hear of Jean-Bonaventure Rousseau dit Saint-Jean, living in Montreal, being granted (1770) a licence for one year 'to pass unmolested with one canoe and six men from Montreal to Toronto, with liberty to dispose of his goods and effects as he should occasionally find a market in his passage.' His merchandise consisted of 'eighty gallons of rum and brandy, sixteen gallons of wine,' and gun powder, shot, and balls amounting in value to three hundred pounds lawful money. No wonder that Gage wrote 'Complaints have been made here from Michilimackinac that the traders of Toronto debauch all the Indians from those quarters by selling them rum ...'[7]

At the time of the founding of York, the Rousseaux had been established in Toronto for at least twenty years. Even the Toronto River in contemporary accounts became known as the St John River. The son of Rousseau the trader was that Jean-Baptiste Rousseaux St John (as he spelled the name) who lived in a house near Teiaiagon, who witnessed the 1805 treaty confirming the Toronto Purchase, and who, as pilot on the *Mississaga,* had the distinction of bringing Governor Simcoe and his wife and party safe to harbour on the historic occasion of the founding of York. We remember him in St John's Road in the city of Toronto. Percy Robinson remarks: 'The last Frenchman of Toronto was to welcome a governor who proceeded at once to wipe out all the traditions of the French régime.'[8]

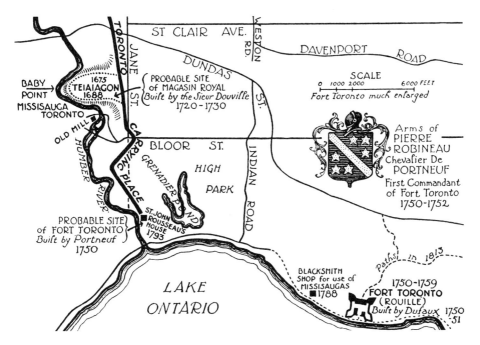

**1.3** Map showing position of the three French posts at Toronto (from Percy J. Robinson, *Toronto during the French Régime*)

**1.4** In February 1757 Captain René-Hippolyte Laforce charted Lake Ontario, and his map included this inset of Fort Rouillé, showing clearly its four bastions and gate facing west. Buildings abutted the walls around a square.

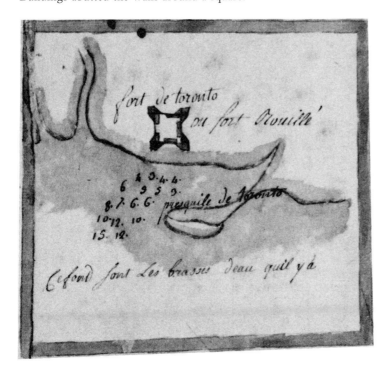

# 2 'As it was
#     in the beginning ...'

When one studies the late eighteenth-century history of Toronto, it is clear that two men played a great part in guiding the destiny of the future city. They were Sir Guy Carleton, the first Lord Dorchester, and Lieutenant-Colonel John Graves Simcoe. History has shone a bright light on the latter, and someone in Toronto daily recalls him in Simcoe Street (once Graves) and John Street, but it was Lord Dorchester as governor-in-chief of Canada who arranged the Toronto Purchase, the first step in the negotiations for a site for the future capital of Ontario. Even if his preference was for Kingston, and Toronto came about only as a compromise, the first step was a significant one. In 1787 Dorchester arranged a meeting between three Mississauga chiefs and his deputy surveyor-general John Collins for the purchase of a rather vaguely described area of land amounting, in the final settlement, to 250,880 acres. The meeting was held at another carrying place, the one on that narrow neck of land between the mainland and what is now Prince Edward County. There, without pressure or hard bargaining as far as one may learn, the site of Toronto was bought for £1,700, along with some barrels of cloth, some axes, and odds and ends 'dear to the heart of the simple savage' – 'In witness whereof, we have hereunto set our hands and seals the day and date above mentioned [23 September 1787] Wabukanyne, Neace, Pakquan (chiefs) Witness present John Collins, Louis Protle, Nathnl Lines *Interpr.*'[1]

Eighteen years went by and another meeting was held, not from any qualms of conscience that the former deal was unjust or that the constitutional owners of the land had been deceived but because the earlier instrument was 'defective and imperfect.' In the interim Neace had died and Wabukanyne had been murdered by a Queen's Ranger in York in 1796. Pakquan did not sign the 1805 treaty, but another Wabukanyne, probably a son, was there to sign with seven chiefs. The treaty was witnessed by J.W. Williams, John Blackenbury, ensign 49th Regiment, P. Selby, and J.-B. Rousseaux. The date of this historic meeting was 1 August 1805 and the place the mouth of the River Credit in Ontario.

The year following the Toronto Purchase of 1787 is not without interest in the story of Toronto. In July of that year Lord Dorchester gave orders for a survey to be made of the land acquired from the Mississaugas, including a site for a new town. The significance of this survey lies in the fact that at so early a date, and some five years before Lieutenant-Governor Simcoe went 'a city-hunting,' the governor in Quebec had decided on the strategic value of Toronto as a town site. His interest in the area arose from a general plan to open up again the *passage de Toronto* from the Humber mouth to Lake Huron, and both Robinson and Middleton agree that, had it not been for the strong views held by the governor-in-chief on this matter, the capital of Upper Canada would today be on Simcoe's chosen site, the forks of the Thames.[2]

Seventeen eighty-eight is also the date of a quite remarkable plan made by Captain Gother Mann commanding the Royal Engineers in Upper Canada. He called it 'Plan of Toronto Harbour, with the proposed Town and part of the Settlement.' As can be seen in the illustration (2.2), the plan includes a central square containing military and government buildings surrounded by a common, which, in turn, is enclosed to the north, east, and west by a residential area. The whole territory is bounded by the modern High Park, Broadview Avenue, and Bloor Street. The old Carrying Place is there, but shown as a road leading to Lake la Clie, a misspelling of lac aux Claies, the name usually given to Lake Simcoe as the former 'lac Toronto' fell into disuse.

The plan is what one might expect of a military engineer and may go back in origin to the gridiron settlements that Roman engineers designed for coloni, or pensioned veterans in garrison towns. In Roman terms, Mann's square of public buildings becomes a forum and the residential squares a setting for the houses of the discharged soldiers. Had his plan been designed for a level site like that of Timgad in North Africa, it might, with some stretch of the imagination, be thought to have merit. The idea of public buildings in a neat British square separated in perpetuity from the residential area by a green common with shade trees and sheep quietly grazing is quite delightful, but fantastic and unrealistic when one considers the rising terrain and the deeply penetrating ravines. These topographical problems would hardly be appreciated in London, where Mann's plan of 'Torento' was forwarded with the colonial correspondence in 1790.

As we approach the last decade of the eighteenth century, several factors emerge that were to affect profoundly the future of Canada and the ultimate decision for the site of Toronto. Until the end of the Seven Years' War (1763) Canada had been predominantly French, and it was only with the American War of Independence that the racial balance of population was to change. Canada then became the natural refuge for those colonists who preferred the British Crown to life in the republic. The number of Loyalists

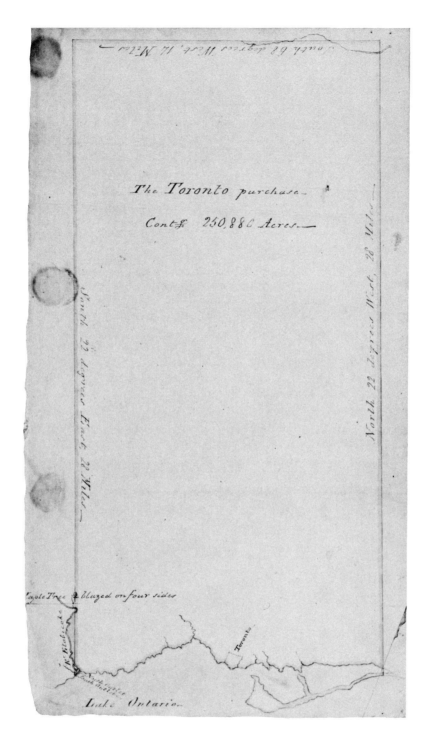

**2.1** The Toronto Purchase (1787). On the lakefront it extended east from the mouth of the Etobicoke River a distance of fourteen miles. Northwards the property extended twenty-eight miles. The total area was 250,880 acres.

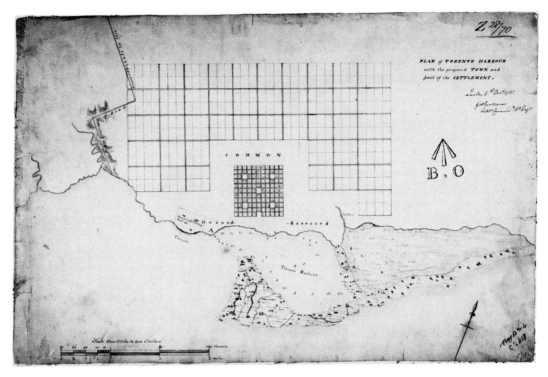

2.2 Gother Mann's plan of 'Torento' (1788)

2.3 Alexander Aitkin's plan of York Harbour, surveyed by order of Lieutenant-Governor Simcoe, 1793

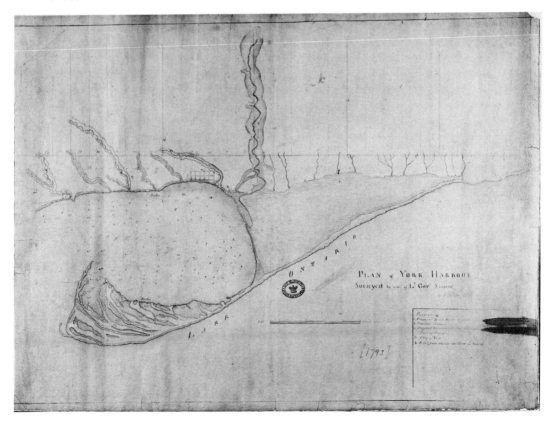

who came north cannot be accurately determined, but there may have been as many as fifty thousand. The majority of these went to Nova Scotia and New Brunswick, but others established thriving settlements in the western part of the old province of Quebec – on the St Lawrence River, at Kingston, in Prince Edward County, on the Niagara Peninsula, and along the Detroit River. Agitation by these settlers for representative government and English law had much to do with the Constitutional Act of 1791, which separated Quebec into two parts at the Ottawa River. Lower Canada, largely French, retained the old system of laws with 'representative institutions added,' while Upper Canada followed the English model.

In 1791 Colonel Simcoe was appointed lieutenant-governor of Upper Canada, and in September of that year he sailed from Weymouth to Quebec in the ship *Triton*, twenty-one guns, accompanied by his wife and two children and 'a Lieutenant Talbot.' (This was the Talbot who, as Colonel Thomas Talbot, was so active in the settlement of southwestern Ontario.) Niagara, across the mouth of the river from the old French fortress, became the temporary capital of the province, and here the lieutenant-governor summoned his first parliament on 17 September 1792.

What impresses the reader of contemporary accounts of this period and of the principal actors was their calm acceptance of a mode of life completely foreign, at any rate for Mrs Simcoe and the children, to that to which they had been accustomed. Plagues of flies of all kinds were encountered inside as well as outside their house because several windows were unglazed. But Mrs Simcoe's diary, far from giving the impression of boredom or suffering of a wife suddenly transferred from a stately home in Devon to the rigours of an encampment in the wilderness, speaks rather of lively dinner parties, gay balls, the joys of riding, and the pleasures of sketching in water colour. Elizabeth Posthuma Simcoe was an unusual woman and an ideal wife for a soldier and proconsul. Only a soldier's wife, and an exceptional one at that, could write from Niagara-on-the-Lake with such equanimity: 'The Governor set out to walk to Burlington Bay [Hamilton], at the head of Lake Ontario, about fifty miles from hence.' 'I sat up all night ... to read Don Guevara & the history of Prince Ctesiphon & some pages of Don Quixote, went to bed in my cloathes at 6, rose at nine, dressed, breakfasted at 10.'[3] There must have been many unusual women in early Canada, but few who, like Mrs Simcoe, took comfort from Sir Joshua Reynolds's *Discourses* or the five volumes of Palladio.

One of the governor's chief concerns was, of course, to find a site for the capital city of Upper Canada. Niagara would not do, if for no other reason that that, in the governor's words, 'under the guns of an enemy's fort is not the place for the capital of a British province.' It would appear that when Simcoe went on his next exploratory trip, he had already made up his mind from available maps as to the most desirable site for the capital. He travelled through the western end of the province, covering the sites of the modern cities of Brantford, Chatham, London, and Detroit. As early as 8 January

1791 he had written in England: 'I propose that the Site of the Colony should be in that Great Peninsula between the Lakes Huron, Erie, and Ontario, a Spot destined by Nature sooner or later, to govern the interior World. I mean to establish a Capital in the very heart of the Country, upon the River La Tranche, which is navigable for batteaux for 150 miles ... The Capital I mean to call Georgina.'[4] All he needed was proof on the ground itself, and he returned to Niagara convinced.

This is not the place to discuss at length the constant friction between the lieutenant-governor of Upper Canada and the governor-in-chief of Canada, Lord Dorchester – a state of affairs that brought about 'the resignation of both of their respective commands in the usual form of "leave of absence." ' Nevertheless, this incompatibility of the lieutenant-governor in Niagara and the governor-in-chief in Quebec had a direct bearing on the choice of a site for Toronto. We have seen that as early as the survey of 1788 Dorchester had shown an interest in Toronto and, by the time of Simcoe's arrival, was supporting Kingston. He would have nothing to do with Georgina on La Tranche, and the blow to Simcoe's enthusiasm and pride can be imagined.

It was in May 1793 that Simcoe, accompanied by seven officers, set off from Niagara in a bateau on a new search for a capital. The party followed the shoreline to the head of the lake, after which they sailed eastwards, to arrive at last in the Bay of Toronto. Writing in 1832, Joseph Bouchette, who surveyed the harbour in 1793, remarked of it: 'I still distinctly recollect the untamed aspect which the country exhibited when first I entered the beautiful basin ... Dense and trackless forests lined the margin of the lake, and reflected their inverted images in its glassy surface ... the bay and neighbouring marshes were the hitherto uninvaded haunts of immense coveys of wild fowl.'[5]

Mrs Simcoe records in her diary of 13 May 1793, 'Coll Simcoe returned from Toronto, & speaks in praise of the harbour, & a fine spot near it covered with large Oak which he intends to fix upon as a scite for a Town. I am going to send you some beautiful Butterflies.'[6] The people of Toronto are often accused of taking themselves too seriously, and indeed there may be some who would resent a light-hearted reference to butterflies in the same note that heralded the birth of the present proud metropolis. It is usually omitted from her famous first comment on Toronto.

From contemporary accounts we learn that the site of Toronto, if we may consider it from the Humber to the Don, was covered with a bush made up, in general, of hardwood trees and poplar with some clumps of evergreen, cedars, and pine. There were also beaver meadows and much swampy ground through which ran a network of streams that are now submerged in the sewer system of the city. Two to survive into this century were the Garrison Creek and the Taddle, which flowed along the west side of Queen's Park and is perpetuated in name by Taddle Creek Road in the University of Toronto grounds.

In the fascinating diary of Mrs Simcoe there are few items as important in the long story of Toronto as the one in which she describes the departure from Niagara and the arrival of the official party in Toronto.

29th of July  We were prepared to sail for Toronto this morng. but the wind changed suddenly. we dined with the Chief Justice [Osgoode] & were recalled from a walk at 9 oclock this Eveng as the wind was become fair – we embarked on board the Mississaga the band playing in the Ship – it was dark so I went to bed & slept till 8 oclock the next morning when I found myself in the Harbour of Toronto, we had gone under an easy sail all night for as no person on board had ever been at Toronto Mr. Bouchette was afraid to enter the Harbour till day light when St John Rousseau an Indian trader who lives near came in a Boat to pilot us.[7]

One would have thought that the first duty of the Queen's Rangers would have been the erection of Government House, but that awaited the arrival of the family. Simcoe's first 'Government House' deserves a mention as much for its previous history as for its unsuitability as the official residence of His Majesty's representative in Upper Canada. Before leaving London, Colonel Simcoe purchased three or four large and small tents that had been among the effects of the late navigator Captain James Cook, and one of these, known as the 'canvas house,' became the Simcoe home for a whole summer and the following winter. Its location 'on rising ground' was close to the Queen's Wharf at the foot of the present Bathurst Street, and not far from what we call the 'Old Fort.' The Honourable Peter Russell[8] was there in August 1793, and wrote his sister in Niagara:

The Governor & Mrs. Simcoe received me very graciously – but you can have no conception of the Misery in which they live – The Canvas house being their only residence – in one room of which they lie & see company – & in the other are the Nurse & Children squalling &c – an open Bower covers us at Dinner – & a tent with a small Table & three Chairs serves us for a Council Room.[9]

It is no wonder that Mrs Simcoe found life more congenial among her old friends at Niagara, which she visited as often as she could.

The year of their arrival in Toronto was an active one for the Simcoes and a momentous one for the future city. Of major importance was the preparation and official approval of surveyor Aitkin's plan for Toronto (2.3), a plan with which we have had to cope for almost two hundred years and with which posterity will have to deal till the end of time. It was, of course, the surveyor's gridiron, which like Captain Gother Mann's and Lord Dorchester's plans ignored completely the very features that give character and beauty to Toronto – the hill and the wooded ravines. But there the comparison ends. Where the two plans of 1788 were grandiose and impractical, Aitkin's was practical but indescribably mean and unimaginative. It consisted of ten square 'city' blocks bounded by George, Berkeley, Adelaide, and Front streets, with the areas from Parliament to the Don and from Peter to the Humber set aside for government and military purposes. North of the future Queen Street, Simcoe laid out a 'range of 100 acre lots which were to be granted as "douceurs" to the officials as compensation for having to come to York.'[10] Lord Selkirk was not alone in suggesting in 1803 that Simcoe had two reasons for preferring York to Kingston – it was partly because Dorchester favoured the latter town and partly because 'York had the advantage of being able to afford lots for all his friends round it.'[11] Edith Firth describes this as an 'ill-natured rumour,' but if true it would be a unique and unflattering foundation for a great city.

It will be seen that in other matters Simcoe was not without imagination, and one wonders whether he ever dreamed that his little plan would some day spread over several thousand acres, that it would climb hills and leap ravines. One can be sure that he did not.

A minor though a colourful event was the changing of the name by royal proclamation from Toronto to York. The sound of twenty-one guns reverberated among the hills, and what shipping in the harbour mounted cannon added to the joyful noise. It was near the end of August 1793, and the capital still contained not a single house.[12]

The newcomer to Ontario must wonder at the number of English names that mark our counties and our townships far beyond Tiny, Tay, and Flos, which immortalize Lady Sarah Maitland's dogs. It was that 'abhorrence of Indian names' (T.A. Reed) or 'the infelicitous mania for tautology of his generation' (Percy Robinson) that caused His Excellency to change Niagara to Newark, Toronto to York, and so to anglicize the map of Upper Canada as to leave no doubt of his loyalty to His Majesty, King George III. Not until 1834, when York became a city, was the ancient name of Toronto, the 'meeting place of the waters,' restored. Various writers have suggested that it was changed because, as far back as 1799, the duke of York, whom Simcoe sought to honour, had ceased to be a heroic figure and was leading British troops from one disaster to another. It was not a popular change: tempers were aroused in council debates, and William Lyon Mackenzie himself was quite opposed to a return to the old name. It is probable that the choice was finally made because of objections to the town's being called 'Little York' to distinguish it from New York.

The last years of the century saw much activity in land clearing and road building but rather less in house building. In 1795 the duc de la Rochefoucauld-Liancourt reported only twelve cottages in York, all of them near the Don.[13] The log house of squared timber that Abner Miles had contracted in August 1794 to build at York for William Jarvis, the provincial secretary and registrar, was not among those that caught the ducal eye. Apparently Jarvis had second thoughts about leaving 'the snugest and warmest cottage in the province' at Niagara, particularly when few other government officials were making preparations to move to the new capital, and Miles did not proceed with the building. Even Governor Simcoe, who lived at the Garrison when he was in York, was slow to set an example, delaying

**2.4** Mrs Simcoe sketched Castle Frank from the east in 1796. The house was reached by a road snaking up the side of the ridge. After the Simcoes' departure Castle Frank was seldom used. It burned in the 1820s after many years of neglect.

**2.5** Plan and front elevation of the lieutenant-governor's house, erected by Captain Robert Pilkington in 1799–1800. The rooms are not named on the original, and only the kitchen and bake oven (right of plan) can be identified with certainty.

**2.6** The York jail of 1799 had a silhouette remarkably similar to that of the lieutenant-governor's house. Rooms A through K were cells, each ten feet by fourteen feet. The jailer and keeper occupied rooms L and M, and slept on turn-up beds in cubicles N and O.

2.5

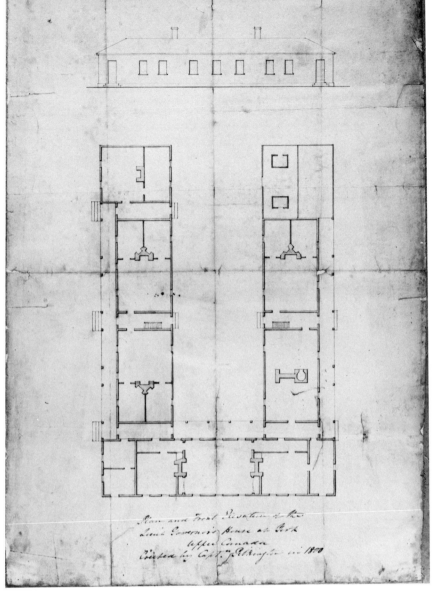

Plan and Front Elevation to the
Lieut Governors House at York
Upper Canada
erected by Capt. Atkinson in 1800

2.6

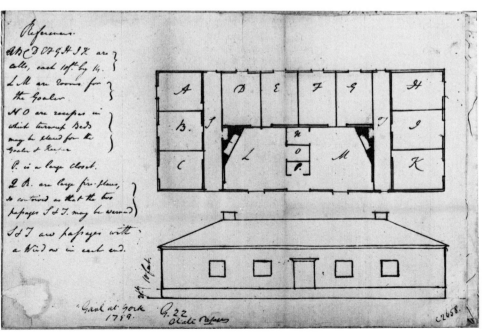

Gaol at York
1759

G.22
State Papers

C2658.

the start of construction on his summer house until late 1795. Two years before, he had obtained in the name of his son Francis two hundred acres of land including a ridge on the west bank of the Don with a superb view to the south down the valley of the river. On it, east of what is now the northern end of Parliament Street, he built the log house, named Castle Frank, in Francis's honour. Mrs Simcoe rightly described it as 'built on the plan of a Grecian Temple,' and to her sketch one looks eagerly for columns that might be Ionic or Doric. They were neither the one nor the other, but were vertical logs sixteen feet high; and the 'cottage' itself was large – fifty feet long by thirty feet wide. Fundamentally Greek as it was in design, its simple construction would make the five volumes of Palladio a rather superfluous reference. Although Mrs Simcoe camped and picnicked at Castle Frank several times while it was under construction during the spring of 1796, it was barely finished when the Simcoes stayed there for almost three weeks in late June and July, before leaving Upper Canada for England, never to return.

In 1795 what few houses existed in York had been hastily constructed of log. It was to be many years in York before the building of houses became a pleasant experience or an economical venture for the home owner. Labour and materials were in such short supply that in 1803, £1,065 (New York currency) was the cost of a two-storey house with four modest rooms on the ground floor. In that year there were only 75 houses in York. By 1809 there were 14 round-log cottages; 11 one-storey and 27 two-storey houses had squared timbers, and 55 houses were clapboarded.[14]

As early as 1800, however, a house was built at the garrison as the official residence of the king's representative in Upper Canada. It was of frame construction to the design of Captain Robert Pilkington, and its first occupant was the second lieutenant-governor, General Peter Hunter. Government House was an unostentatious one-storey structure that served successive governors until 1813, when it vanished in the explosion of the nearby powder magazine. A new Government House was secured by the purchase of Elmsley House, built in 1798 for the chief justice, John Elmsley, at the southwest corner of King and Simcoe streets. Many years later it was succeeded on the same site by a third Government House. Distinguished visitors to the province might stay at Government House; less distinguished – or desirable – guests of the government could be accommodated, at the direction of the chief justice or the magistrates, in the jail erected in 1799 to replace the temporary lock-up for three prisoners that had been ordered built the year before.

Besides these official residences, some records survive of at least four fine private houses, of which one, that of D.W. Smith, the surveyor-general, was hardly surpassed in design by any in the following century. Others were those of Major John Small, Peter Russell, and Mr Secretary Jarvis.

It is little short of a miracle that we have complete records of the Smith house, Maryville Lodge. For over a hundred and eighty years they have passed through wars, fire, and flood and today have a permanent and secure resting place in the Metropolitan Toronto Library. Maryville was really an estate of a size in keeping with the social position of so large a landowner. The Honourable D.W. Smith owned $916^{1}/_{4}$ acres in the township of York of which $116^{1}/_{4}$ acres were south of the modern Bloor Street. Both house and grounds were charming. Two plans of the property exist, the one illustrated (2.7) being the more highly developed. The curving driveway off Ontario Street appears in each, as does the formal garden about the house, but in the other plan in which the fields around Maryville appear, there is a lively 'rivulet' on its way to Lake Ontario and a curving road leading to a large 'well yard' from a gatehouse opposite the eastern end of Duchess, now Richmond, Street.

The house was built of wood, possibly flush boarded, and painted so bright a yellow that the colour gave the house its local name. The design of house, pigeon loft, and out-buildings is so competent that it would be very interesting to know the name of its author. What evidence there is would point to Smith himself as the architect. Books of house designs from the United States would be available to him, and he was, after all, a draftsman and surveyor-general of Upper Canada. In 1797, when Maryville was built, the architect as a professional man had hardly emerged from the building trades in the republic to the south, let alone in Canada. In Massachusetts at that time the architect was commonly called a housewright, and as late as 1805 a book was published in Boston under the joint authorship of 'Asher Benjamin, architect and carpenter and Daniel Raynerd, architect and stucco worker.'

In 1802 Smith returned to England, and the Smith papers show that two years later he was trying to sell Maryville to C.B. Wyatt, his successor as surveyor-general. In April 1805 he wrote to Wyatt: 'I know of no inconvenience my Cottage possesses, having built it at a great expence for my own comforts, and without the smallest view of ever selling it; yet you are not to find it a house finished in the style of Architecture, which is generally so good in England; I mean as to finish in point of Workmanship and materials – tho' no part of it is ten years old.' He went on to say that the plans were not exact, that the drawing room 'is a few inches out of the Square,' and that the 'back part of the house' was different from the plans.

The second house of the eighteenth century of which we have a record is Major John Small's house, Berkeley House, until its demolition in 1926 located at the southwest corner of King and Berkeley streets. Major Small came to Canada from Gloucestershire as clerk of the Crown in the entourage of Colonel Simcoe. In 1795 he acquired at a cost of fifty dollars George Porter's log house, which he enlarged. Porter's lot had been located by the surveyor Alexander Aitkin but was later found to encroach upon the reserve set aside by Simcoe for Government House. Eventually Major Small was able to secure a clear title, and he made further additions to his house that would allow Scadding to describe it as 'one of the usual low-looking dom-

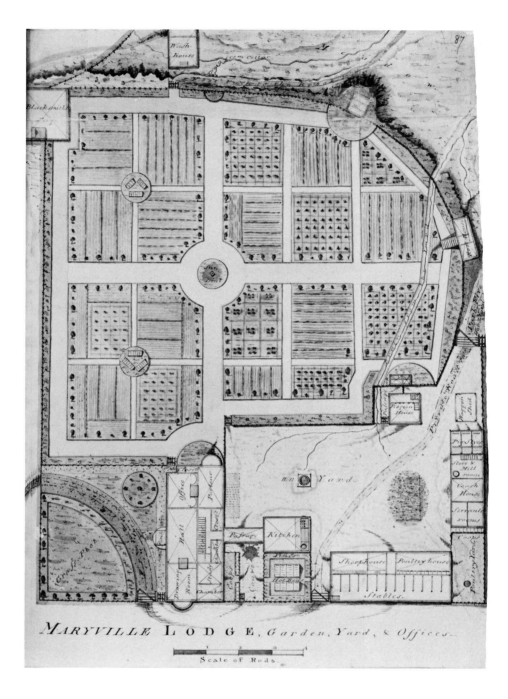

MARYVILLE LODGE, *Garden, Yard, & Offices.*

Scale of Rods.

**2.7** Maryville Lodge as drawn in 1802 by William Chewett shows how a wealthy gentleman lived in York. On the north side of the house are Smith's orchards and vegetable gardens, and to the east his animals, with servants' quarters in the tail of buildings on the extreme right.

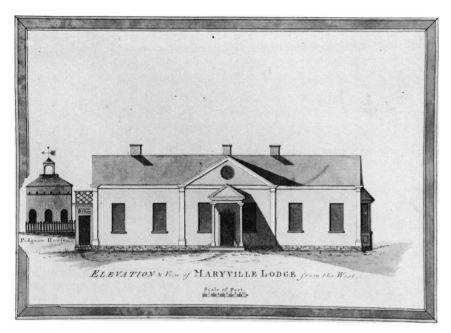

**2.8, 9** Chewett's elevation of Maryville appears in 2.8 and the ground-floor plan in 2.9. The house was built around a small house that the Honourable D.W. Smith bought from John Kendrick in 1796, which appears to have become Smith's drawing-room. As was the custom of the time, his office was in his home. It was entered by a side door clearly indicated on the elevation drawing.

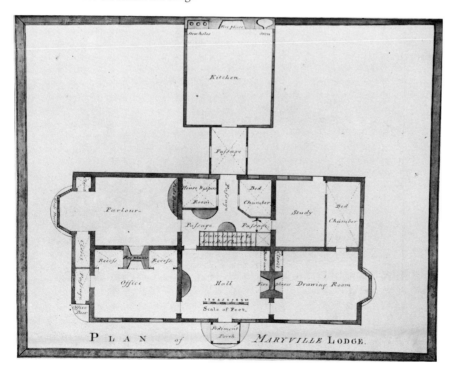

iciles of the country, with central portion and two gable wings, somewhat after the fashion of many an old country manor-house in England.'¹⁵

Berkeley House in our illustration (2.10) shows alterations undertaken by Major Small's son Charles. During this reconstruction the house was stuccoed and the fenestration carried out in the 'Gothic' mode that was fashionable in England in the first quarter of the nineteenth century. Berkeley House in its heyday had thirteen rooms, several of which were as large as eighteen by forty-five feet. The fact that Major Small had killed the attorney-general, John White, in a duel and was acquitted of murder was forgotten by the next generation but was calamitous to the social pretensions of Mrs Small. For a number of years the other ladies of York would not attend parties if it were known that she would be there, and even later when they did, her presence was marked by ugly little scenes, such as the refusal to shake hands.

During the lifetime of the son, Berkeley House was 'one of the great social centres and few indeed are the members of the old aristocracy who have not danced or dined beneath its roof.'¹⁶ It will be remembered by some in the twentieth century as derelict and forlorn, with broken panes and peeling plaster, until it fell before the crowbar of the wrecker.

Among the first houses of York was that at the corner of King and Princess streets, bought by Peter Russell in August 1795 from Christopher Robinson. The following summer Russell, who had become president, or administrator, of Upper Canada following the departure of Colonel Simcoe, asked the carpenter Samuel Marther to produce sketches for enlarging the house into a suitable residence. Work on the additions began in the late fall and had not been completed when, during the night of 25 January 1797, a fire warming Marther's carpenters spread, leaving only the chimneys standing the next morning.

Undeterred, Russell accepted William Berczy's proposal to build a new house facing south at the other end of the property, with a view across Palace (Front) Street to the lake. Construction began in March 1797 and was finished except for the outbuildings when Russell and his sister Elizabeth moved from Niagara the following November. Berczy's design was described variously as 'pretentious,' but not lacking in 'elegance and taste.' We have clues to what it looked like from maps and contemporary watercolours of early York as well as from Russell's accounts. In the nearly identical paintings of York by Edward Walsh and Elizabeth F. Hale, the house appears in the distance as one storey in height with a low-pitched, hipped roof.¹⁷ Across the front of Russell's house are five large windows and an enclosed porch over a central doorway. Initially the building was U-shaped in plan. A sketch in the *Landmarks* based on Dr Henry Scadding's recollections many years later may show the rear elevation of the house seen from King Street or may reflect alterations that made the plan into an H-shape.

There is nothing in the plan or style of the house to suggest why it became known as Russell Abbey. Such a house would have rooms for entertaining

**2.10** Berkeley House, seen shortly before its demolition in 1926, was a gothicized enlargement of Major John Small's dwelling.

**2.11** 'York (Olim Toronto) the intended capital of Upper Canada, as it appeared in the autumn of 1803,' by Surgeon Edward Walsh, 49th Regiment. The view is eastward along Palace (Front) Street. Russell Abbey is seen in the distance, on the left of the largest tree. The first government buildings and the town blockhouse are to the right of the group of smaller trees.

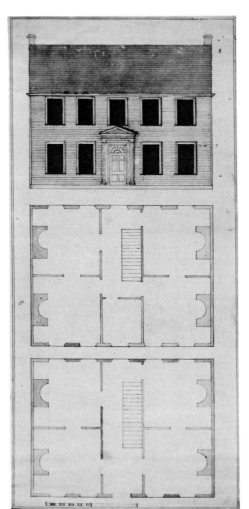

**2.12** William Jarvis may have adapted this plan for his house at York, shipping from Niagara the window sashes and the architrave around the doorway.

**2.13** About 1810 artist Robert Irvine painted some buildings that had been standing for some years west of the town on the lakeshore between John and Peter streets. From left to right they were the residences of George Crookshank and John Beikie, a commissary storehouse by the water, and the Half Way House. Behind the higher sail, troops march towards Fort York; watching the military on parade was a favourite Sunday pastime.

in keeping with the position of the president of the government of Upper Canada, as well as outbuildings for horses, carriages, and slaves. John Ross Robertson writes that 'Peter Russell owned and traded in slaves, despite his vigorous protection of the Indians.' Russell had six black servants, a slave Peggy, her free husband, and their four children, who were also slaves. These were divided between the farm on his hundred-acre park lot and his town house. In the latter he usually had two or three black slaves and the same number of white servants. In 1806 he advertised in the *Gazette and Oracle* 'to be sold, a black woman named Peggy, aged 40 years, and a black boy, her son, named Jupiter, aged about 15 years, both of them the property of the subscriber ... They are each of them servants for life.' Within the memory of many in John Ross Robertson's day 'a pure negress called Amy Pompadour' lived in York who had been presented to 'Mrs. Captain Denison' by Miss Elizabeth Russell.[18] Russell Abbey is remembered today by a shabby bywater called Abbey Lane, off King Street between Princess and Sherbourne streets.

The owner of the fourth fine house, William Jarvis, might have been one of the first officials to settle at York if he had carried through on his plans in 1794 but became instead a notable laggard. In February 1798 he finally took steps to move his home and office from Niagara. After purchasing a lot at the southeast corner of Caroline and Duke streets, now Sherbourne and Adelaide, Jarvis hired Archibald Thomson to build a house. Materials for its construction were secured from scattered places across the province. Lime, hair, and putty came from Thomas Markland in Kingston; boards and planks were ordered from the Hope Mills. James Secord at Niagara supplied planks and barrels of lime. The timber frame for the house may have come from Niagara, which was the source of the sashes and architrave that Christopher Danby crated up for shipment to York. The result could have resembled the elevation and floor plans (2.12) found among the Jarvis papers, now in the Metropolitan Toronto Library.

Our last structures of the eighteenth century, though not the last in date, are the first Parliament buildings of 1796, which stood at the foot of Berkeley Street overlooking the bay. We learn of them in a letter from Simcoe to the duke of Portland, 27 February 1796:

I am preparing to erect such Buildings as may be necessary for the future meeting of the Legislature; the plan I have adopted is, to consider a future Government House, as a Center, & to construct the *Wings* as temporary Offices for the legislature, purposing that so soon as the Province has sufficient Funds to erect its own Public Buildings, that They may be removed elsewhere.

But should the seat of Government be ultimately established on the River Thames ... the *Wings* now erecting ... may be hereafter sold.[19]

Plans for the buildings were drawn by William Graham, master carpenter, who was appointed to superintend their construction. Ephraim Payson, who was the government bricklayer, and David Thomson, the first settler in the township of Scarborough, undertook the work. In the account book of the latter this item appears: 'July 16, 1796: Begun to wall the Government brick houses. 55,000 brick at 17/6 per thousand.'

Construction was well along by 15 March 1797, when the Honourable Peter Russell in a letter to John McGill (commissary, in charge of government buildings) described changes in how the wings would be joined to the projected central section:

Since my last I have had an Opportunity of speaking with Mr. Pilkington [Captain Robert Pilkington], and very much approve of the Alterations he proposes for the Government House. – By these, the two Wings will be 40 by 24 feet and joined to the Body of the House by something like a Colonade ... It is not my intention to Attempt more at present than the two Wings, as before they are finished I may expect to receive final Instructions from home, which will determine me respecting the propriety of entering into so large an Expence as the mansion will assuredly prove.[20]

As a final word, we have another letter from the Honourable Peter Russell, written in York on 9 December 1797 to Lieutenant-Governor Simcoe, still on leave in England:

The Two wings to the Government House are raised with Brick & completely covered in. The South One, being in the greatest forwardness I have directed to be fited up for a temporary Court House for the Kings Bench in the ensuing Term, and I hope they may both be in a condition to receive the Two Houses of Parliament in June next, I have not yet given directions for proceeding with the remainder of your Excellency's plan for the Government House, being alarmed at the magnitude of the expence which Captain Graham estimates at (£10,000) I shall however order a large Kiln of Bricks to be prepared in the Spring.[21]

In 1804 Simcoe's successor, Lieutenant-Governor Peter Hunter, attempted unsuccessfully to obtain assistance from the British government for the erection of newer, larger buildings. At Hunter's request Gother Mann, author of the 1788 Plan of Toronto Harbour and now major-general commanding the Royal Engineers in Canada, estimated that a stone building as large as forty by three hundred feet would cost £15,120. Another design, apparently unsolicited, was put forward by Edward Walsh, showing a house of assembly with a dolphin weather-vane surmounting a dome (2.14). It bears a striking resemblance to one of the unsuccessful proposals submitted almost a decade before in a competition to design the United States Capitol.

When it became clear that a grant would not be forthcoming from the British government and that the brick wings would have to serve some while longer, instructions were given in November 1805 for the construction of a covered way between the two buildings. A year later, in response to

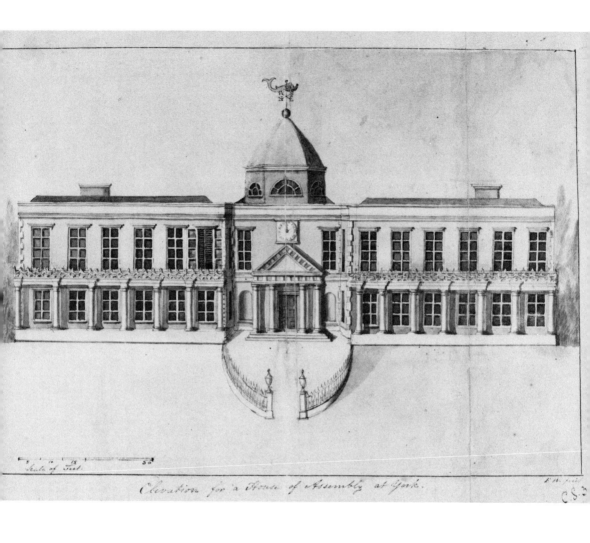

Elevation for a House of Assembly at York.

**2.14** The elevation for a House of Assembly at York, by Edward Walsh, 1804. He estimated that it could be built in brick and wood for less than one thousand pounds sterling. Libraries and the legislative chambers were on the second floor, while banqueting rooms, housekeepers' rooms, and the kitchens were on the ground floor. His provision for four water-closets was decidedly progressive.

complaints by the Speaker of the Assembly that the building was much in need of repair and not fit for the reception of the House, the floor both inside and out under the portico was replaced.[22]

The subsequent history of the legislature may be briefly told. Following the burning of the old buildings in 1813, the members met for one year in the ballroom of Jordan's Hotel, a well-known hostelry on King Street near Berkeley Street. They then moved to the charming low Georgian house of Chief Justice Draper at the northwest corner of Wellington and York, and there they sat until 1820, when a new House arose on the site of the old buildings of 1796. Its life, unhappily, was short, and where the armed might of the United States caused the destruction of the first legislature, an overheated flue marked the end of the second. The year was 1824. For the next five years members occupied the York Hospital – an imposing institution of Georgian design with eight windows across its second storey. They had saved some of the House papers and all of the furniture and the library, but the interior was incompatible with the dignity of the government of Upper Canada, and the intrusion of the legislature on an institution dedicated to the ill in York could not be tolerated for long.

Upper Canada had to wait until 1829 for a well-planned and up-to-date legislative building. The old brick Houses, elegant as they may have been, and their successor were conceived as a symbol of democratic government in an outpost of empire; the new Houses of 1829 were recognizable as public buildings in a young and progressive community. The forest seemed to envelop the old legislature or was never far away; the setting for the new seemed urban and controlled.

Before the departure of the Simcoes for England in July 1796, York must have been a busy place. Under his leadership the ground plan of a village destined to be a great metropolis had been carved out of the wilderness, and Simcoe himself had followed Yonge Street on a survey trip all the way to Lake Simcoe. He did much for Little York, but he was in many ways a visionary with projects in mind even before he left England to assume his post in Upper Canada. Seated in the comparative privacy of his tent, he must have been shocked by the realization of how phantom-like and remote for York were his nucleus of a public library, his society based on the Royal Society, a college, and a botanical garden.

Such symbols of civilization were indeed remote, but in a zoning order of the governor we can detect a vision for York that, even in miniature, would seem to Simcoe to include some of the urbanity and dignity that distinguished cities of the old world like Bath and London. It was, of course, highly impractical and not without an element of snobbery, and is best given in a letter of 1793 (when the Simcoes were still under canvas) written by Richard Cartwright:

You will smile perhaps when I tell you that even at York, a Town Lot is to be granted in the Front Street only on Condition that you shall build a House of not less than 47 Feet Front, two Stories High & after a certain Order of Architecture; in the second Street, they may be somewhat less in Front, but the two Stories & mode of Architecture is indispensible; and it is only in the back Streets and Allies that the Tinkers and Taylors will be allowed to consult their own Taste and Circumstances in the Structure of their Habitations upon lots of 1/10 of an Acre. Seriously, our good Governor is a little wild in his projects.[23]

Governor Simcoe was not there to see his zoning ordinance ignored or the scattered community assume even the semblance of a village, but his faith in the future of the province was a lasting one. On 26 March 1798 he wrote that Upper Canada 'will be with proper & honorable support, the most valuable possession out of the British Seas, in population commerce & principle of the British Empire.'[24]

The Honourable Peter Russell, the owner of Russell Abbey, who headed the government after Simcoe, has been completely overshadowed in the public mind by his distinguished predecessor. We do not think of him as the colourful proconsul or associate him with the pomp of power or the salute of guns. Rather he was the sound administrator (which, indeed, was his title) working for the good of the community of which he considered himself a citizen. Under his wise government speculators and non-residents were kept out of the town lots and a form of zoning was inaugurated to keep the town compact in the face of a tendency, not unknown today, to sprawl in more than one direction.

His achievements are the more remarkable when one considers the isolation of York, the lack of communication except by boat in suitable weather, the reliance on travellers for the mails until 1800. Even then, the service between Montreal and York could count on only four couriers a month in winter and none in summer. 'In 1797 there were no roads connecting York with the older communities in the Province. Thriving settlements were established along the St. Lawrence to Kingston, on the Bay of Quinte and in Prince Edward County, in the Niagara Peninsula and on the Detroit River, all separated from York by vast areas of unsettled bush.' Yonge Street was there, and was indispensable to the farmers bordering it for the transportation of the essential provisions to York, but in spring and fall it was an impassable bog. Under such conditions a not inconsiderable achievement of the Russell administration was the contract in 1799 with Asa Danforth for a road to the east as far as the Trent in the Bay of Quinte. At about the same time a road was begun by the Queen's Rangers, westerly to the Head of the Lake.[25]

The year 1800 has been chosen to close a chapter in the architectural development of Toronto, and to some extent it has not the significance of later dates such as 1834, 1867, and 1900. It was not a year of any note in the government of Upper Canada, but in many ways it represented the end of an era and the beginning of a new one for York. The houses referred to in this section were all there by 1800, and the community had assumed the form of a village, if not of a provincial capital. The population of the town was 403, and while not all, by any means, of the property in Aitkin's ten blocks was occupied, there were enough buildings to give a recognizable pattern to the plan conceived in 1793. It was the opinion of John Bennett, the King's Printer of Upper Canada, writing in 1801, that 'York is just emerging from the woods, but bids fair to be a flourishing town.'[26]

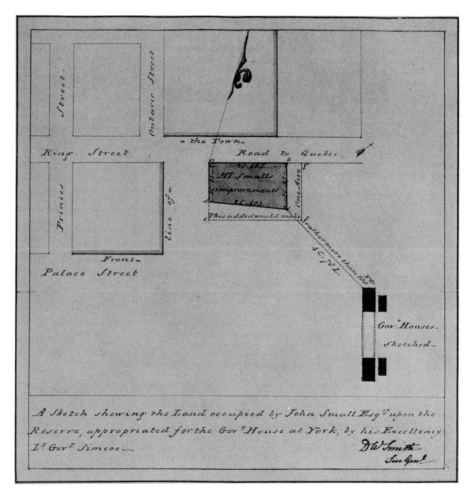

2.15 The legislative buildings, on land reserved by Simcoe at the east end of the original town plot, are shown on this map of 1802 by D.W. Smith. 'Mr. Small's Improvements' included his house, where the executive council met and which later formed the core of Berkeley House. Across King Street from John Small, at the northeast corner of Ontario Street, stood Smith's Maryville Lodge.

# 3 A Late-Flowering Georgian

A grave weakness in Aitkin's plan was that it lacked a focus. Had there been provision for a school, a church, or, more particularly, a village green, the plan of Toronto today would have been different. It also lacked direction, so that when expansion became inevitable, the town grew merely by adding more squares, a practice we have followed ever since except in the labyrinth of Rosedale. Before the original ten blocks were occupied, it had become apparent that the site near the Don was undesirable for a residential district. Visitors to York and the correspondence of the early settlers all tell of the prevalence of the ague, which seems to have been rightly attributed to the miasma rising from a thousand acres of swamp at the mouth of the river. It was also generally agreed that the disease was less frequent in the sparsely settled areas to the west and was unknown on Yonge Street. Hardships and actual suffering can be imagined when it is remembered that until the War of 1812 there were only two qualified civilian doctors in York – Dr William Warren Baldwin, who also practised law and, occasionally, architecture, and Dr James Glennon.

It was therefore an escape from the 'vapours' rather than the inducement of economic or other advantages that led to the movement of population to the west of Yonge Street. As Scadding put it, 'The path of progress was like that of Empire, westward.' It was eventually to be northward, and by 1812 many representatives of the gentry, such as Peter Russell, John Elmsley, James Givins, Aeneas Shaw, and John McGill, had already made extensive clearings on their hundred-acre park lots.

By that time, too, much had been accomplished to give meaning and substance to the life of the town. The civilizing influences of religion, education, and entertainment were at last being enjoyed by a people who were still close to the almost intolerable harshness of life in the early days of York. In 1803 a marketplace was established on the site of the present St Lawrence

**3.1** The house and store of Quetton St George (1807; demolished 1901) at King and Frederick streets. In later years it served as the Canada Company building.

**3.2** The Red Lion Inn (circa 1808; demolished 1889), Yonge Street near Bloor, an important social and political centre for many years

Hall; in 1800 the rector of York, the Reverend George Okill Stuart, was prepared to take pupils, and by 1807 he had established the Home District Grammar School in his house at George and King streets; the Church at York opened its doors for divine service on the site of the present St James' Cathedral in 1807; and in 1809 Quetton St George opened a general store on the ground floor of his very striking house at King and Frederick streets. As early as 1810 York had a bookstore and a subscription library. On the much-needed side of entertainment and relaxation, there were several taverns, and we learn from the *Gazette and Oracle* that Daniel Tiers was in business with his 'Beef Steak and Beer House.'

The architecture of these buildings and their successors for the next thirty years or more was what, for want of a better word, we call Georgian. The great movement that produced the Georgian houses of England in the eighteenth century and later adorned the towns and villages of eastern Canada and the United States finally came to rest in Ontario. Visitors from Great Britain are always amazed to learn how late in date are some of our best old houses. Many were built at a time when taste in England was changing under the pressure of the Industrial Revolution and a series of revivals was taking the place of the traditional manner, with its background of three centuries.

We, too, have had our revivals, but for forty years after the establishment of York we had the kind of architecture that today attracts tourists to Boston or Baltimore and is preserved in those cities by vigilance on the part of an enlightened citizenry. Compared with their ancient architecture, ours was modest in scale and interior fittings, and the area that it occupied was small and vulnerable.

Of the early buildings already mentioned, we have no very accurate record of the 'Church at York' other than that it was 'a plain structure of wood, placed some yards back from the road ... Its dimensions were 50 by 40 feet. The sides of the building were pierced by two rows of ordinary windows four above and four below.'[1] We can appreciate its simplicity in a contemporary American description – 'a meeting house for Episcopalians.' This primitive building served the community until 1818, when Dr John Strachan, who had been its pastor since 1812, induced the congregation to enlarge the church. Tenders were called for lengthening the building east and west with an apse, but for reasons not clear, the nave was widened with a gallery on three sides. The 'new' church was painted an 'azure blue' with white trim and quoins. Here 'used to assemble, periodically, the little world of York: occasionally, a goodly proportion of the little world of all Upper Canada.'[2] For the visitor the church provided quite a few surprising features. For example, the ringing of the bell was sufficiently violent 'sensibly to jar the whole building,' and the habit of one of the early clerks, Mr Hetherington, was 'after giving out a psalm to play the air on a bassoon, and then to accompany with fantasias on the same instrument such vocalists as felt inclined to take part in the singing.'[3]

If the interior of the church was unromantic in design, at least two of the worshippers made up the loss. Sir Peregrine Maitland, the lieutenant-governor, and his wife had both been present on the occasion in Brussels when the latter's mother, the duchess of Richmond, gave the famous ball whose 'sounds of revelry by night' preceded the Battle of Waterloo. They were then unmarried, and their elopement in Paris shortly after outraged the feelings of the duke and duchess of Richmond. They were finally reconciled, and Sir Peregrine's happiness and official career were assured. It is unnecessary to say that the occupants of the lieutenant-governor's pew did not go unnoticed on Sunday mornings in York.

The decade after the War of 1812 saw churches built for Methodists, Presbyterians, Roman Catholics, and Baptists. From what we know of them from contemporary writers and from sketches in the *Landmarks*, they would seem to have been unpretentious little meeting houses of no architectural significance. The Wesleyan Church was built in 1818, about the time of the enlargement of St James'. It stood facing King near Jordan, was forty feet square, and, according to Scadding, the old Anglican church custom prevailed of making the sexes sit separate – the men sat on the east side and the women on the west.[4]

The priest in charge of the first Anglican church at York, and the one who preceded Dr Strachan in that office, was the Reverend George Okill Stuart. His pulpit delivery was curious, marked by 'unexpected elevations and depressions of the voice irrespective of the matter, accompanied by long closings of the eyes, and then a sudden re-opening of the same.'[5] We are, however, more interested in him as the popular and competent tutor to the children of the upper classes as early as 1800 and as the master of the Home District School (1807).

Still standing in 1873 when Dr Scadding saw it was a little building at the corner of King and George streets – one that in its day had served as a school for the children of the earlier inhabitants of York, as the home of the first rector of St James', as general store, and as an inn. The house consisted of two parts, the rectory with its walls of log covered by clapboard, and an appendage in stone 'resembling a small root-house,'[6] which was the Home District School. The establishment continued to function as a centre of education and the home of the rector of St James' until the departure of Mr Stuart for St George's Church in Kingston and the opening of the Blue School under Dr Strachan in 1813. In 1833 this house became the general store of George Duggan, which he shared with his brother, Thomas, a doctor. George was known in the thirties as one of the real characters of York, a jovial fellow who paradoxically was also the coroner. Paradoxically too, he was that George Duggan who would rather ostentatiously leave the church when the Reverend Mr Stuart, as visiting cleric from St George's Kingston, would rise to deliver the sermon.

The house of Quetton St George is one that we would wish to preserve if fate had permitted it to survive. Laurent Quetton was a Royalist officer

**3.3** Gibraltar Point lighthouse (1808–9), seen in a detail from a painting by Robert Irvine, circa 1810, once stood at the entrance to Toronto Harbour but is now inland. It is the second oldest lighthouse remaining in Canada, after the Sambro Island light (1758) near Halifax.

**3.4** York from Gibraltar Point, drawn by James Gray in 1828

**3.5** House of Colonel James Givins (rear view), at the head of Givens Street off Queen Street West (1802; demolished 1891). This famous house ranks number one in the six-volume *Landmarks of Toronto*, ahead even of Castle Frank. When Robertson wrote in 1888, it was considered the oldest building in Toronto. A young lieutenant in the Queen's Rangers, Givins was ADC to Lieutenant-Governor Simcoe and was with him for the historic landing at the harbour of Toronto in 1793.

**3.6** The second Spadina House, the home of Dr W.W. Baldwin (1836; demolished 1866). Like the first Spadina, it stood just east of the Casa Loma steps.

**3.7** The home of Dr W.W. Baldwin, northeast corner of Front and Bay streets (1835; demolished 1889). Rather extravagantly, one would think, the first-floor plan provides for three parlours, a library, and a large closet. All rooms are trimmed or panelled in walnut. The basement plan indicates a kitchen 25 feet by 19 feet, a wine cellar 25 feet by 10 feet, and a meat room 10 feet by 10 feet. The only clue to dining arrangements is a dumb-waiter in the kitchen that served one of the parlours. The sketches would indicate that Dr Baldwin was himself the designer.

in the French army who escaped to North America during the Revolution. Arriving on English soil on St George's Day 1796, he added St George to his name in memory of that occasion. He prospered so mightily as a trader, with agents in Orillia and elsewhere, that by 1809 he was able to move into his 'mansion' at the corner of King and Frederick streets.[7] Robertson stated that 'for its construction he brought the first bricks ever seen in York from Oswego or Rochester,'[8] but he was incorrect. The first brick buildings in York, it will be remembered, were the legislative buildings (1796).

As we see from the illustration (3.1), the Palladian window over the porch is well detailed, and the massive chimneys all give evidence of wide fireplaces and handsome mantels. We have no records of the interiors of houses in Toronto at so early a date, but Poplar Hall at Maitland (circa 1811) can show today mantels of exquisite design, chair rails in the better rooms, and finely proportioned panelled doors. The same can be said of the Barnum House at Grafton (1817) as well as a score of less well-known houses on the Niagara peninsula. When the first series of the *Landmarks* was published in 1894, the house still stood: 'no building is better known, and its removal will take away a landmark from what was once the most important part of town.'

Daniel Tiers, who had operated a beefsteak and beer house in York, was later the owner of the Red Lion Inn. It stood on the east side of Yonge, just north of Bloor, on a piece of property that originally embraced some two hundred acres. We hear of Tiers as early as 1797 on the first list of inhabitants of York and again in 1802, when he subscribed to a fund for the improvement of Yonge Street.

The inn grew in time to be 100 feet in length and had on the second floor a ballroom 40 by 20 feet, with a barrel vaulted ceiling 18 feet high and a fireplace at each end. Looking at the site today, close to that of Britnell's bookshop on the east side of Yonge Street, north of Bloor, it is difficult to imagine its former isolation. As the years went by, it became a great rallying point for farmers; it was a post house for travellers two miles north of the town of York, and the young and the brave would journey there from York and the neighbouring farms for the dancing to which nothing else in York compared. The condition of Yonge Street in spring and summer made driving a nightmare, and dancing was understandably more enjoyable in winter, when parties came in sleighs. The fact that Potter's Field was across the street had no apparent effect on the popularity of the inn or its ballroom, of which the author of the *Landmarks* observes in melancholy mood – 'How many a couple, whose voices are now hushed in the tombs, have whispered soft words in this room.'

The Red Lion was also well known as a rallying place for political meetings, of which the most famous took place when William Lyon Mackenzie was re-elected after his expulsion from the House. On that 'tumultuous' occasion (2 January 1832) as many persons as the floor could hold were

**3.8** Bellevue (1815; demolished 1890/1). The house gave its name to Bellevue Avenue, which runs south from College to Denison Square. Its owner was George Taylor Denison, the first to carry the name, whose son gave the site to the Anglican church and built St Stephens-in-the-Fields at the corner of Bellevue and College. The porch may have been influenced in design by the somewhat older Quetton St George house (see 3.1), which it resembles. The sturdy chimneys remind us that the fireplace beneath burnt logs as a source of heat as well as for the pleasure of the blazing fire.

**3.9** The Town of York, 1813, by George Williams. The boundaries of settlement were New (Jarvis) Street, on the west, to Berkeley Street, and Palace (Front) Street to Duchess (Richmond) Street.

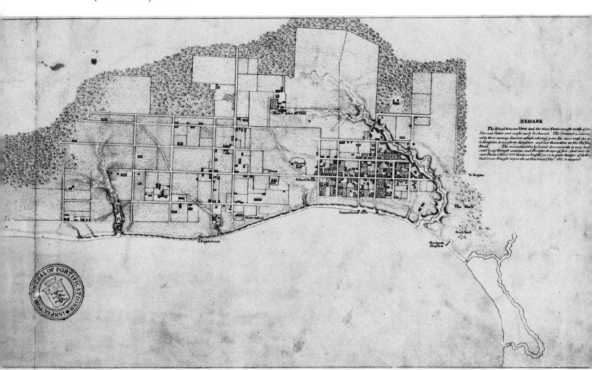

**3.10** The old fort, officers' quarters (1816). Like the majority of buildings in the old fort, this mess building, which could be an attractive farmhouse in any of the older parts of North America, had a friendly domestic atmosphere.

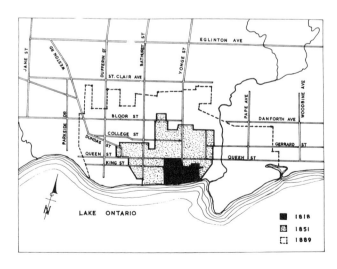

**3.11** Diagram imposed on the plan of Toronto showing three stages of growth: 1818, 1851, and 1889 (redrawn from Griffith Taylor)

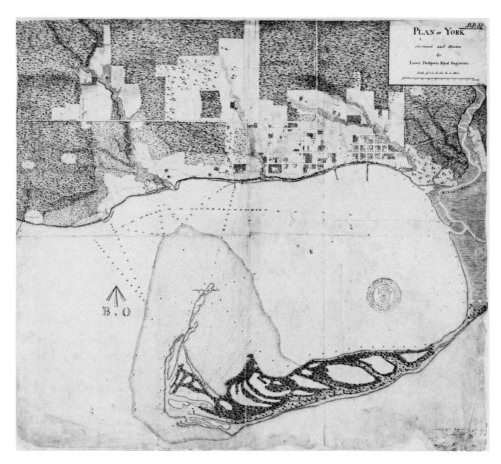

**3.12** Plan of York (detail), surveyed and drawn by Lieutenant George Phillpotts, RE (1818). Phillpotts's map gives us a more realistic picture of York than anything left to us in written description or picture. Lot (Queen) Street strikes boldly off to the west from its junction with 'Young' (Phillpotts's spelling) Street, which passes through dense bush on its way to Holland Landing. The street of real importance was, of course, King, which goes on a diagonal to Kingston on what seems little better than a trail. Aitkin's gridiron had taken form in the checkerboard of houses near the mouth of the Don.

**3.13** Fragment of a plan for Government House, by Sir John Soane (1818)

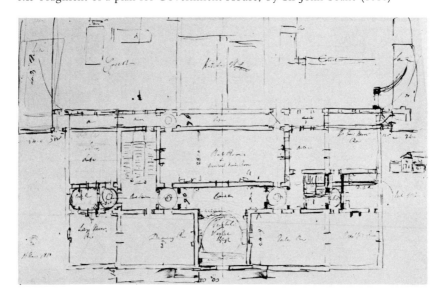

gathered in the ballroom to present Mackenzie with a gold medal and chain and an address. A great honour, too, for Tiers, but when he endeavoured to sell the Red Lion and two hundred acres for four hundred dollars, the amount was thought excessive and the offer declined. There is little doubt, as Robertson suggests, that the success of the Red Lion attracted other businesses and that the Inn itself was the nucleus on which the village of Yorkville was built.

The lighthouse at Gibraltar Point was begun in 1808 and finished in 1809. The point got its name from Governor Simcoe, who saw its location at the mouth of the harbour as being not dissimilar to that of the rock at the entrance to the Mediterranean. Gibraltar Point, as well as Block House Bay, which it shelters, are names that have fallen into disuse. The lighthouse still stands, but mariners are no longer guided by its warning light as they were for well over a hundred years. The structure is 82 feet to the top of the vane, and the walls are 6 feet thick at the base. A curious fact about the design is that the stone cap beneath the lantern, which seems so integral and necessary a part of the shaft, was an addition of 1832 in Kingston stone to the original in Queenston stone.

A house that in 1888 was known as the oldest house in Toronto was that of Colonel James Givins. As a young lieutenant Givins went on Governor Simcoe's famous journey to Detroit and later became his aide-de-camp. The house from the rear is much more picturesque than other houses of the first quarter of the nineteenth century. It was built shortly after Givins's purchase of the property in 1802. The front, which is obscured by trees in the *Landmarks* sketch (3.5), shows a formal elevation with a low pitched roof, a high basement, and two windows on each side of the central door. Of interest to the youth of Toronto who had the privilege of knowing the house in the last century was that it vied with Holyrood Palace in having authentic bloodstains in the floor. Perhaps, indeed, the blood of Rizzio is less authentic than that in the Givins's drawing room, because we know of Mrs Givins's 'surgical skill' and the use of the house for the wounded in 1813. Colonel Givins was a pew holder in St James' from its beginning and is buried in St James' Cemetery.

Unfortunately, no reliable sketch exists of an even more famous house known as 'Spadina,' but Dr William Warren Baldwin's description gives us a good idea of its plan and its symmetrical and generous arrangements. He writes in 1819:

I have a very commodious house in the Country – I have called the place Spadina, the Indian word for Hill – or Mont – the house consists of two large Parlours Hall & stair case on the first floor – four bed rooms and a small library on the 2d. floor – and three Excellent bed rooms in attic storey or garret – with several closets on every storey – a Kitchen, dairy, root-cellar wine cellar & mans bed room underground – I have cut an avenue through the woods all the way so that we can see

**3.14** Residence of the Honourable and Reverend John Strachan, DD (1818; demolished circa 1898), on a site that originally comprised the land bounded by York, Simcoe, Wellington, and Front streets. This residence was popularly called the Palace, and one is not surprised at the question of Strachan's brother from Scotland: 'I hope it's a' come by honestly, John?' From the underpaid schoolmaster and rector in 1813 to the owner of the 'finest house in the town' who 'gave entertainments that outshone those of the Lieutenant-Governor, and rode about in a grand coach with a hemispherical top,' is an ecclesiastical success story that would remind one faintly of Cardinal Wolsey if one did not recall the bishop's marriage to the well-to-do Mrs McGill. When Robertson wrote in 1888, the Palace of the great bishop had degenerated into the Palace Boarding House, and its end came a decade later.

**3.15** The house of Chief Justice Sir William Campbell sat firmly on a site on Duke (Adelaide) Street at the head of Frederick Street from 1822 until 1972. In the latter year many thousands turned out to see it on wheels as it was moved from Adelaide Street to a new and permanent resting place at the corner of Queen Street and University Avenue, just south of the Canada Life Building. The move and the restoration of the house as to structure and furnishings have been made possible through a foundation formed by the Advocates' Society of Ontario. Research on the ground and impressions on the brickwork indicated a semicircular porch with Tuscan columns and pilasters, much earlier than the Greek Doric, which has been scrapped in the restoration.

the vessells passing up and down the bay – the house is completely finished with stable &c and a tolerable good garden, the whole has cost about 1500 £ the Land you know was the gift of poor Mr Willcocks.[9]

This house was destroyed by fire in 1835, when a smaller one was built on the same property. The site was magnificent and lay just east and north of the steps that mark the boundary of the Casa Loma grounds.

It is unlikely that in his later years Dr Baldwin ever climbed the slope that lay below the lofty escarpment on which the house was built. We can be sure that means were found to reach the house by horse-drawn vehicle on an easy gradient and not at right angles to Davenport Road, as we approach the site today. Even so, winter on such an eyrie in the 1830s must have represented a challenge to the fittest, and in January 1844, when he died, we find Dr Baldwin living at the northeast corner of Front and Bay in a house that may well be described as a mansion.

A photograph (3.7) survives, and it will be noticed that the house is of quite traditional Georgian design except for the curious decision of its architect to put the parapet below the cornice and to puncture it with windows. In 1835, there were few laymen and surely no architects so unfamiliar with the elements of classical architecture that the impropriety of a balustrade in so subservient a position would go unnoticed. We must conclude, therefore, that it was done on a whim by Dr Baldwin, who was in this instance his own architect.

The Spadina house of the Baldwins is long forgotten, but the busy thoroughfare of that name will forever be a reminder of a great Torontonian. It is regrettable that the architecture of the modern street is generally poor and out of keeping with the Parisian scale on which Baldwin conceived the roadway from Queen to Bloor Street when he opened the land on both sides for development. Less regrettable, though not greatly to our credit, is our inability to arrive at a common pronunciation for Spadina. The Baldwin family always said 'Spa-deena,' and so it is appropriate that their house and estate should carry this pronunciation today, when the distinctions drawn formerly by some, to say Spa-dina up to College or Bloor and use the more refined Spa-deena in the residential portion to the north, are all but forgotten as well.

In 1811 the loyal colony in Upper Canada would have followed with increasing concern Britain's struggle with France on the continent of Europe. All the same, the fighting was a long way off, and people in York went about their business little thinking that, along with the rest of Canada, they would soon be at war with their neighbour to the south. Following a series of misunderstandings and difficulties, the United States declared war on Great Britain on 18 June 1812.

York was immediately affected, and the population was reduced from over 700 to 625. Lieutenant-Governor Gore, though highly respected in some quarters, was not a fighting man, and as the war clouds gathered in

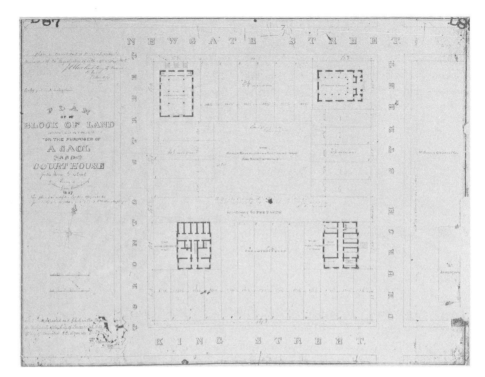

**3.16, 17** The Court House Square, as it was in 1837 (3.16) when surveyed and drawn up by Thomas Young, contained five buildings. Four are shown clockwise from the lower right: the Court House, jail, Wesleyan Methodist chapel, and St Andrew's Presbyterian Church. A fifth, the fire hall and engine house that stood north of the Court House, was left out, perhaps because it was to be relocated. Sufficient credit has not been given to the planners who were responsible for the square, one of the earliest attempts in Toronto at civic design. The jail and Court House on King Street are shown in this 1835 view (3.17), also by Young, looking east towards St James' Church (1831–3). Artistic licence was used in drawing the steeple; it had not been built by the time the church burned in 1839.

**3.18** The second jail (1824–7), built to John Ewart's plans by the contractors Ford and Hayden, was part of York Chambers until demolished in 1957. The yard has grim memories because it was here that Lount and Matthews were executed. By curious coincidence, two architectural families were involved. Storm, the builder of the scaffold, was the father of W.G. Storm, the architect. Joseph Sheard, his foreman, refused on principle to assist in its construction; he would later be the architect for the Cawthra house and, in 1871–2, mayor of Toronto.

**3.19** St Andrew's Church of Scotland, southwest corner of Church and Adelaide streets (1830–4; demolished 1878). John Ewart, the architect and builder, undoubtedly knew of the hold that the Greek revival had on the city of Edinburgh, still referred to as the Athens of the north. As it was usual for Greek-revival architects to adhere closely to archaeological precedent, the problem of fenestration was acute, there being no classical prototype. Circular-headed windows such as those on St Andrew's would definitely be 'against the rules.' The design is heavy, and the transition from the first stage to the next of the spire, which was added in 1841 by John G. Howard, is abrupt.

**3.20** Holland House (1831; demolished 1904), which stood on the south side of Wellington Street between Bay and York, was built by the Honourable H.J. Boulton, the attorney-general, and named after Holland House in Kensington, London, where he was born. The Canadian version, with its Gothic style, resembled John Ewart's designs for the district court house in London, Upper Canada, begun in 1827. Boulton occupied Holland House for only two years and then left Toronto to become chief justice for Newfoundland. The house, which originally faced on Front Street, is of architectural interest chiefly because it represents the transition from the colonial manner to the romantic, which is evident in porch, battlement, and turrets. The south or garden view resembles the castle in miniature, with its circular keep and pointed arches. One would give much to know whether the furniture was contemporary with the medievalism of the exterior.

**3.21, 22** Ontario House, built as a house by Peter MacDougall, converted in 1829 to a hotel that became the Wellington Hotel in 1845, stood at the corner of Wellington and Church streets until 1862. It was sketched by John Gillespie for this lithograph (3.21). The columns were pine logs peeled and planed. In 1837 the proprietor advertised that it was 'newly and beautifully fitted up for the reception of ladies and gentlemen visiting Toronto. The spacious gallery and promenade render it particularly delightful as they overlook the harbour, city and environs.' The view drawn by W.H. Bartlett in 1838 (3.22) shows the building from the fish market on Cooper's Wharf.

3.22

late 1811, he returned to England on leave of absence 'accompanied by his good amiable lady and her menagerie.'[10] Fortunately, as has so often happened in crises in British history, a man with all the qualities of leadership was available to assume command. Major-General Brock could not be made lieutenant-governor as Gore was only 'on leave,' but he was appointed president of Upper Canada with all the powers of the former office, as well as commander-in-chief of the forces.

The seventeenth of August 1812 was a gala day in York. General Brock had returned with his troops after receiving the surrender of General Hull's forces at Detroit; people cheered, and flags flew from every window. But the guns were silent. When the good news reached London a few weeks later, the guns boomed from the Tower, but powder was too precious a commodity to be wasted on salutes in York. Such jubilation as there was was short lived – the death of Brock at Queenston Heights on 13 October was the first major tragedy of the war, and more was to follow.

Historians of the War of 1812 make it abundantly clear that, where York was concerned, our military intelligence was poor, and even though Sheaffe, the new commander-in-chief, expected an attack in the spring of 1813, little notice, if any, was taken of the expeditionary force that was being assembled at Sackett's Harbor on the north shore of Lake Ontario. The American fleet consisted of fourteen vessels mounting fifty guns and carrying some seventeen hundred troops and an undetermined number of marines.

If our intelligence was faulty, so, also, was the enemy's. With a force of four thousand in Sackett's Harbor, it was the original intention to take Kingston and then York, and thus seriously embarrass the British Lake Squadron. Happily for Kingston, a report reached American headquarters that the town was defended by some thousands of British regulars. The report turned out to be quite unfounded, but it was sufficient to divert attention from Kingston to York, which, after all, was the capital of Upper Canada and not to be ignored in the military aims of the war.[11]

On the morning of 26 April 1813 the citizens of York went about their normal affairs quite oblivious of the plans for their capture by a powerful and fully armed enemy. The Reverend Dr John Strachan performed the marriage ceremony for a young couple; merchants such as Quetton St George attended the customers in their stores, and the farmers on the outskirts of the town were busy preparing the land for the spring sowing. There was to be a rude awakening. A lonely actor on the Toronto stage looked out that same evening over the bluffs at Scarborough, and there below him lay the enemy fleet at anchor.

The news was not long in reaching York, where a state of emergency was immediately created by the firing of the signal gun, a summons to the militia that was heard as far away as Markham Township. As one would expect, people's reactions differed as widely as those of Major General Sir Roger Sheaffe, who thought that daylight would allow plenty of time for attack and defence, and of Dr W.W. Baldwin, who 'bundled up his silver' and his black silk lawyer's gown and sent them out of town to a friend's barn. At dead of night, state papers and public money were put in strong-boxes and taken to places of safety. We can imagine the frightened conversations between neighbours as to what was best to do – to stay, with the possibility of being a prey to an undisciplined victorious soldiery, or to go away with what valuables could be carried on foot. In the end it was the part of wisdom to stay and brave the enemy behind one's front door. The empty houses and stores were the ones that were looted.

Prideaux Selby, the receiver-general of Upper Canada, had all the provincial public moneys in his keeping, and he lay dying on that fatal night. Many plans were made to save the public gold. Robertson records an elaborate plot, a scheme of Mrs Selby and Mrs William Allan. According to this apocryphal tale, together they dressed one Billy Roe, the secretary-general's confidential clerk, as an old woman and loaded him, with three bags of gold and a large sum in army bills, into a wagon pulled by an ancient horse. In this guise he drove to the farm of Chief Justice Robinson on the Kingston Road east of the Don Bridge, and there he buried his treasure. After the departure of the Americans he recovered it and delivered it intact before witnesses in the parlour of Dr Strachan.[12] Unfortunately, the reality is more prosaic: the gold was handed over to the Americans.

With daylight, a sleepless people looked out on the harbour and saw the American host, for such it must have seemed, lying at anchor 'close to the south shore of the peninsula in front of the town.'[13] Against the invaders York was practically defenceless. Sheaffe's forces consisted of two companies of the 8th (King's Regiment), a full company of the Royal Newfoundland Regiment, a company of the Glengarry Light Infantry, a bombardier, 12 gunners of the Royal Artillery, 100 Indians, and 300 York militiamen: 700 in all. The odds against York were too great, but the town capitulated only after a brave defence, with loss of life on both sides. For eleven days the citizens suffered the humiliation of seeing the Stars and Stripes fly over the town, and there was burning and looting.

Outstanding among the principals in this drama, a very David in defence of his people, was the master of the Blue School and parish priest, Dr John Strachan. We see him demanding an audience of the American commander to discuss the parole of captured militiamen and the care and feeding of the wounded; and when Major Allan was made a prisoner of war though under a flag of truce, a furious Strachan marched with him 'to the centre of the town in the middle of an enemy column.'[14]

There were others less conspicuous during the occupation but significant in the story of Toronto either in their own right or as the ancestors of succeeding distinguished Torontonians. In the capitulation negotiations John Beverley Robinson, the acting attorney-general, was present to defend the legal rights of the community, and Colonel William Chewett, the father of J.G. Chewett, the surveyor, draftsman, and sometime architect, played an important role at the same meeting. We hear also of Captain John McGill.

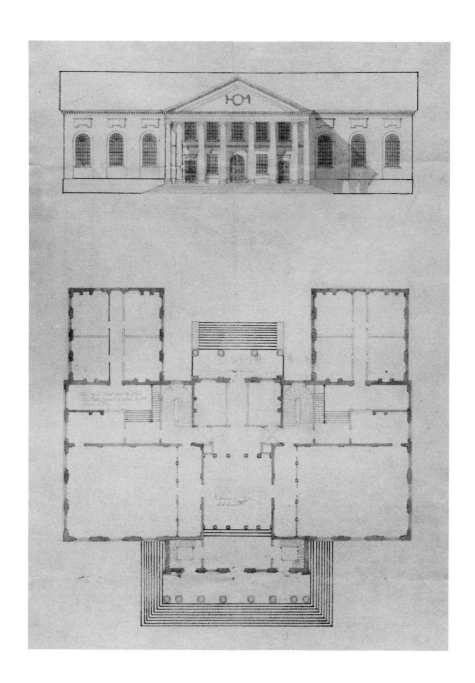

**3.23** 'A Province Building Contemplated at York,' proposed in 1826 by Francis Hall of Queenston. The designs were based on those 'by the late celebrated Adam for a General Record Office for Scotland' but failed to secure the premium offered by the commissioners, which went to Joseph Nixon instead. Hall was a former pupil of the great civil engineer Thomas Telford and was the architect for the 1824 Brock Monument, although he was better known for his work on canals in Upper Canada and the Maritimes.

**3.24** Numbers 23, 25, and 27 King Street West (circa 1835; demolished 1887). The *Globe* moved here in 1853 when the newspaper began daily publication, and left in 1864. The location is now the site of the Commerce Court.

**3.25** Tecumseh Wigwam, northwest corner of Bloor and Avenue Road (1820; demolished circa 1875). The photograph was taken in 1870; the fact that the site is now occupied by the Park Plaza shows how very close behind us is our past. Between 1820 and 1860 the house was famous as an inn and a drinking place for the bloods of York. For many years it was kept by one King, whose son George was hanged for the murder of a stage-coachman. The hitching posts in the photograph of 1870 indicate its former function as a stopping place for the stage and other equestrian visitors. The walls were log (visible behind the stoep), covered elsewhere with clapboard.

**3.26** The second Scadding house (circa 1818; demolished). This log house was built after John Scadding's return to York from England in 1818. It was located across the Don somewhat north of his first house (now in Exhibition Park) on a site approximately that of the present jail. It is said that John's distinguished son, Dr Henry Scadding, used the lean-to on the right as a study while he was a schoolboy at Upper Canada College.

3.25

3.26

**3.27** The Grange, facing Grange Park at the head of John Street (circa 1818). This well-known Toronto house, built for D'Arcy Boulton, Jr, was sketched in the mid-1840s by Henry Bowyer Lane, architect, who was related to the Boultons by marriage and may have had a hand in improvements made to the house at about that time. Originally it stood on a hundred-acre lot, and for many years it enjoyed the proximity of the St Leger race-track, which ran from what is now Dundas Street to the present College Street. The house was increased in size by Dr Goldwin Smith following his marriage to Mrs W.H. Boulton in 1875.

**3.28** The changes made to the Grange by Goldwin Smith were in marked contrast to the taste of his time and consisted chiefly of a new porch in stone, which replaced a nearly identical one of wood, and a library to the west replacing the original 'grapery.' Smith, formerly a professor of history at Oxford, is known to have said once, 'the buildings of every nation are an important part of its history, but a part which has been neglected by all Historians, because the Historians themselves have been entirely ignorant of the subject.'

**3.29** Davenport, the house of Colonel Joseph Wells, on the escarpment east of Bathurst and north of Davenport Road (circa 1821; demolished 1913). Colonel Wells was a hero of Badajos, where Frank Simcoe lost his life. Details in this photograph of the historic house indicate a period later than the 1820s, but fundamentally the house is unchanged. Chimneys, dormers, and window heads have been altered to keep up with the Joneses of the time. The view of the town of York from the lawn must have been unequalled.

**3.30** The Millen Cottage, Bay Street (1826; demolished). Robert Millen came from Belfast and bought himself a lot on the road that led to Teraulay Cottage, the home of Dr Macaulay. In the course of time the dirt road became Teraulay Street and finally Bay; the cottage was demolished to make room for Shea's Hippodrome, and it in turn was razed to make room for Nathan Phillips Square. Millen was a carpenter, and we must admire the loving care that has gone into his doorway (even if the cornice is heavy) and the battlemented rainwater heads. The huge chimney indicates the source of heat and the size of the logs that were burned. The builder of the cottage was, in fact, more than a carpenter, and we are told that the carving on the altar at St Michael's Cathedral was his work.

He was the owner of a park lot east of Yonge, on which he built a house 'on the southerly edge of the forest.' The grounds were once known as McGill Square, but whatever were the owner's intentions, the square was lost with the building of the Metropolitan Church in 1870. St Michael's had occupied the northerly part since 1848, and Robertson suggests that that location was chosen with the expectation of a McGill Square in front as a distinguished and open park for the cathedral.

Accounts differ as to the actual losses in York either from fire or from looting, but C.W. Humphries' well-documented record does not leave the impression of anything like a conflagration or of a disorderly soldiery bent on destruction. Penelope Beikie, whose charming house appears in the *Landmarks*, wrote: 'I kept my castle when all the rest fled; and it was well for us I did so – our little property was saved by that means. Every house they found deserted was completely sacked. We have lost a few things which were carried off before our faces; but as we expected to lose all, we think ourselves well off.'[15]

Jordan Post suffered minor losses; Elmsley House was plundered, and Dr Strachan's appeal to General Dearborn on behalf of Angelica Givins failed to prevent the looting of her lovely house. In American eyes the fact that her husband, Major Givins, commanded a party of Indians put him and his family beyond the pale. In spite of the terms of capitulation, several storekeepers, including Quetton St George and William Allan, suffered serious losses. It is certain that the legislative buildings were burned, although perhaps not on official orders. Nevertheless, this gave Strachan an opportunity to write an indignant letter to Thomas Jefferson in which he referred to the buildings as those 'two elegant mansions.'

There were other losses that were, by comparison, small in size, but their going was none the less grievous. Among them were the Speaker's mace and the carved lion that dignified the Assembly. The mace was returned to Toronto at the centenary celebration in 1934. It was presented to His Honour the lieutenant-governor at the express desire of the president and Congress of the United States. An ignominy hardly to be borne by a British colony was the loss of the royal standard, which is now an exhibit at the United States Naval Academy at Annapolis, Maryland.

Its mission accomplished, the victorious flotilla left the harbour of York, and some years later a street was named, perhaps in requital, for President Madison, the good neighbour.

Recovery was slow for York in the years immediately following the war. The population remained static right up to 1816, but from then on Canada, and indirectly York with it, was to be affected by the grave events in Great Britain that were an aftermath of the Napoleonic Wars. The mother country was then in the depths of an economic depression. Thousands were out of work, and the demobilization of four hundred thousand men had aggravated enormously an already desperate situation. Scotland suffered equally with England, and to its already acute industrial dislocation was added the eviction of the crofters by the great landowners. The conversion of much arable land to deer park was a disaster for the Highland crofters, and many a well-established family in Canada, Australia, or New Zealand traces its history to a family who left Scotland at that unhappy time. Immigration from the United Kingdom to British North America amounted in 1815 to 680; in 1816 to 3,370; in 1817 to 9,797; in 1818 to 15,136, and in 1819 to 23,534.

The population figures for York over the five years to 1820 show growth of more than 70 per cent, to 1,240 persons from 720 in 1816. Yet at the same time the number of houses increased by only slightly more than a quarter, from 117 to 148 dwellings. The influx of immigrants must have caused considerable overcrowding in a community unused to, and unprepared for, such an emergency, and their lot was in many cases extremely hard. One immigrant, in describing his first days in York (about 1819), speaks of sleeping in the upper storey of the Parliament buildings with chalk marks on the floor to mark the area each family could occupy.

An attractive map (3.12) showing the growth of the city by 1818 is that of Lieutenant George Phillpotts of the Royal Engineers. The old centre of population was then bounded by Berkeley, New (Jarvis), Palace (Front), and Duchess, but other sparsely settled streets had been laid out west of Yonge. The area between the present Jarvis and Yonge was largely swamp, though it contained a dozen or more houses and St James' Church. Lot Street (Queen) was laid out as the northerly boundary and ran as far east as Parliament Street.

By 1818 York was only a city in miniature and by courtesy, but the finest architect in England had been asked to prepare plans for some public buildings. We read about them in letters written by William Halton, the provincial agent in London, to Sir Peregrine Maitland. It seems that in June 1818 President Samuel Smith, Sir Peregrine's predecessor, had instructed Halton 'to transmit two different plans of a residence for the Lieutenant Governor: of a building for the accommodation of the two houses of the Legislature and the Courts of Justice; and also of one for the Public Offices of Government.' Halton commissioned two different architects: 'Mr. Soane, Royal Academician and Architect of the Bank [of England],' and Soane's former pupil, David Laing, who was well known, particularly for his designs for the London Custom House. Sir John Soane was a most distinguished architect whose house in London has, ever since his death, been the Soane Museum. Laing's elevation drawings were sent by the November packet, accompanied by an offer to provide one of his own men as supervisor of the work for £120 per annum. His detailed plans were dispatched the following month, with Halton's report that Soane had disappointed and, not having the plans ready, had 'discontinued the subject entirely.' It is possible that the great man was unaccustomed to the North American atmosphere of designing under pressure of time, but he had not been idle. A sketch survives in the Soane Museum that tells the story of a possibly very great building that never left the drawing-board. In any event, after Laing's bill of £157.10.0 was paid, his proposals were set aside. Sir Peregrine continued

3.31 Bank of Upper Canada (1825), at the northeast corner of Adelaide (formerly Duke) and George streets. Seen here a few years before the financial collapse of the bank in 1866, the building suffered many vicissitudes and was once the De La Salle School for boys. It was empty in 1978 when vagrants started a fire that nearly destroyed this landmark. Happily, an award-winning restoration saved the building from demolition.

3.32 Almost certainly the cast-iron lamp standard in front of the bank in 3.31 came from the same mould as one now in the grounds of Upper Canada College.

· ELEVATION · OF · PORTION · OF · PORCH · RAILING · FORMER · BANK · OF · UPPER · CANADA ·
· DUKE · STREET · TORONTO ·

· PANEL · OF · GRAVE · RAILING ·
· ST. MARK'S · CHURCHYARD ·
· NIAGARA – ON – THE – LAKE ·

· FRONT · ELEVATION · OF · WINDOW · BALCONY ·
· HOUSE · AT · 56 · DUKE · STREET · TORONTO ·

· SIDE · ELEVATION ·

DETAILS OF

CAST

IRONWORK

· SCALE · FOR · DETAILS · OF · IRONWORK ·

· VIEW · LOOKING · DOWN ·
· SHOWING · GRATING ·

· METHOD · OF ·
· ATTACHING ·     · SECTION ·
· BRACKET ·

· FRONT · ELEVATION · OF · PORCH · BANK · OF · UPPER · CANADA ·
· SHOWING · POSITION · OF · RAILING ·

· VIEW · OF · TOP ·

DONALD J. REED   MENS. ET DELT. 1931.

**3.33** Details of ironwork on the Bank of Upper Canada and a house at 56 Duke Street, the latter now demolished, were drawn by students in the School of Architecture. The classic porch was added to the bank in 1843 and its fine iron railing three years later, both to designs by John G. Howard.

**3.34** The legislative buildings (1829; demolished 1903) on Simcoe Place (Front Street West) between Simcoe and John streets. Thomas Rogers of Kingston was the architect. The lithography by Currier of a drawing by Thomas Young shows a portico of four columns that was never built – unfortunately for Rogers because its absence exposes a marked difference in scale between the doorways and the windows to the chamber.

**3.35** The interior of the buildings of 1829, photograph circa 1892

**3.36** Plan of the buildings as they were in 1857

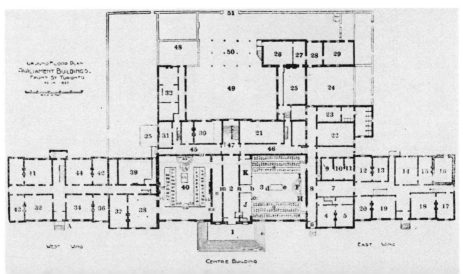

to live at Elmsley House, where necessary repairs were effected, and the brick wings of the old legislative buildings were joined up by new masonry and reroofed to serve another few years.

In a story of Toronto building that recalls so much that is lost, it is a pleasure to be able to point to a house that still stands, even though it has suffered every kind of indignity, not excluding evisceration. The house is that of Chief Justice Sir William Campbell. Sir William came to America as a soldier in a Highland regiment and was taken prisoner at Yorktown in 1781, but two years later he was able to move north to Nova Scotia, where he studied law. At one time he was attorney-general for the island of Cape Breton, a position he held for nine years until his promotion to a judgeship in Upper Canada, where he became an eminent member of the bench.

It is doubtful whether the chief justice's bedroom can be identified in the interior of the house, but a story of his last days is irresistible. His physician, Walter Henry, tells it. Sir William on his deathbed was so weak that he could eat only tidbits; medicines proved unavailing, so the doctor prescribed and provided snipe! 'At the point of the sandy peninsula opposite the barracks, are a number of little pools and marshes, frequented by these delectable little birds, and, here I used to cross over in my skiff and pick up the Chief Justice's panacea. On this delicate food the poor old gentleman was supported for a couple of months: but the frost set in – the snipes flew away, and Sir W – died.'[16] He was seventy-six and the date was 1834. Dr Strachan, now archdeacon, pronounced the funeral oration in St James' Church.

By 1823 the town had grown to 209 houses, 27 shops, and 5 storehouses. It was not until 1828 that it passed the two thousand figure, with a population of 2,235, and was then but six years from its new dignity as a city. The establishment of the Bank of Upper Canada in 1822 and the opening of the Welland Canal in 1829 were concrete evidence of the growing maturity of Upper Canada, and trade and commerce were noticeably stimulated. Evidence of wealth in the hands of a few and a new feeling of security in the province was the building of houses of quite impressive size and of smaller houses and terraces for those of moderate means. The frontier village with its scattered buildings was becoming a memory, and a cohesive community of dignified Georgian dwellings was taking its place.

In the decade before the town of York was incorporated as Toronto, public buildings were constructed at a breathtaking rate. A jail, a court house, and the Bank of Upper Canada came first and might have been followed closely by the new Parliament buildings had the estimates to construct the new scheme chosen by the commissioners not exceeded the five thousand pounds that they had in mind to spend. Other plans were secured, and construction began in 1829. That same year ground was broken for Upper Canada College and Osgoode Hall, plans for both coming from the drawing board of John Ewart. Not to be left behind, the Home District magistrates decided in 1831 to replace the overcrowded York Market with lofty brick buildings that enclosed a large open square. Two years later, across King

Street, the new St James' Church that had been constructed in limestone appeared from behind its scaffolding.

St James' Church deserves a brief mention, especially as it is the one of which, in December 1836, Mrs Anna Jameson, the wife of the attorney-general of Upper Canada,[17] spoke in such unflattering terms: 'A little ill-built town on low land, at the bottom of a frozen bay, with one very ugly church, without tower or steeple ... '[18] As a matter of fact this 'very ugly church' came from the drawing board of Thomas Rogers of Kingston and was by no means unpleasing in design. Unfortunately, the front was never finished, and all Mrs Jameson saw was the rectangular box with the truncated tower. The church was destroyed by fire in 1839, Dr Strachan standing by 'whistling the while as a means of relieving his sorrow.'[19] There was, of course, to be another and then a final St James', the cathedral we know today, but that is later in the story of Toronto.

The building of the Parliament buildings in 1829 was a reflection of the prosperity of the province and the stability of its institutions. Following the burning of the legislature in 1813, the government of Upper Canada had moved from place to place rather like some of those governments in exile that 'made do' with incongruous quarters in the late war. In York, following the fire, we find the legislature first in Jordan's Hotel (hardly in keeping with the dignity of the Crown, incompatible with twenty-one-gun salutes, but not without its compensations), then in 1820 in new buildings, soon also to be destroyed by fire. This was followed by accommodation in the first Toronto General Hospital (or second, if we remember the use of the first St James'), and when that was required for its original purpose, the legislature moved into the court house.

The completion of the new legislative buildings in 1832 on Front Street between Simcoe and John streets would, one would have thought, have terminated this peripatetic existence. However, in 1841 the provinces of Upper and Lower Canada were united and the seat of government was set up elsewhere. Between 1841 and 1849 the buildings were used for university purposes and between 1849 and 1851 as an insane asylum. Their subsequent history included their use for sessions of the United Parliament and as a barracks between 1861 and 1866; finally, the cycle is complete, and we return to them as the legislative buildings of Ontario, 1867–92.

The legislative buildings have gone, and with them the second market, a structure of at least equal significance in the story of Toronto. It was built under the authority of the magistrates in Quarter Sessions in 1831–3, a body always short of funds but one that was the municipal government of the area before its incorporation as a city. Over this building, which housed both municipal government and market, the Quarter Sessions went heavily into debt – so much so that the debt became one of the chief reasons for incorporation and a major embarrassment to the new city government that inherited it. The market cum town hall was the last milestone in the chequered history of York. Only a year away were its new dignity as a city and a return to its old name of Toronto. There would be none then who could conceivably have forecast the greatness of its future.

**3.37** Below Toronto's first City Hall (1831; burned 1849), built to James Cooper's plans, an arcade joined King Street to the market square, which filled the block bounded by King, New (Jarvis), Front, and West Market streets. Butter, eggs, and cheese were sold at the far end, inside the great gateway from Front Street. Butchers' stalls faced inward down the other two sides. In 1841 Thomas Young proposed the addition of a clock turret to the roof over the City Hall, but it was not built.

**3.38** The City Hall and a portion of the market buildings form the left edge of this view westward along King Street about 1845, painted by John Gillespie. Toronto's great fire of 1849 destroyed the City Hall and part of the market, as well as all of the buildings opposite, as far as and including St James' Cathedral. Thomas Young was architect for this church, with its Wren-inspired tower, when it was built a decade before.

**3.39** House of the Honourable William Allan (1828; demolished 1903), in his Moss Park estate on the west side of Sherbourne Street. William Allan came to York in Simcoe's time and lived there till his death in 1853. From then on Moss Park takes some colour from the activities of his son, George William Allan. We read of him as mayor of Toronto (1855), Speaker of the Senate, president of the Royal Canadian Institute, president of the Ontario Society of Artists, chairman of the Art Union of Canada, and president of the Upper Canada Bible Society. The present Allan Gardens owes its existence as a public park to his generosity.

**3.40** Upper Canada College, King Street West (1829–31; largely demolished in 1900), was at more than £17,000 easily the most expensive of any building project undertaken before York's incorporation as Toronto. John Ewart was paid for drawing plans and, when the contractor failed, for building the four boarding houses. These stand, two on each side of the main building, in a lithograph of Thomas Young's 1835 sketch. Visible also are some of the plantings specified in the landscaping plan by André Parmentier of New York.

**3.41** Some shops on the south side of King Street between George and Frederick streets (demolished). Their design would suggest that they were built about 1830.

**3.42** Numbers 69 and 71 Gerrard Street West. This photograph was taken when Gerrard Street was lined with horse chestnuts (like Elm Street) and the houses were still houses. Later, it became known as 'the Village' and the home of silver workers, wood carvers, jewellers, and other craftsmen. They gave place to gift shops and restaurants, and the houses were demolished in 1971.

3.39

3.41

3.42

**3.43** Mud-block house, which stood on Bathurst Street near Sheppard Avenue (circa 1840; demolished). This was once a not uncommon form of construction, which provided a dwelling that was both warm in winter and cool in summer. Such houses abound in Ontario, but in Hogg's Hollow and Willowdale they came to light when moved some years ago for street widening. Moving shook the stucco or the wood siding, either of which is essential as a protection to the mud. The writer once owned a mud block that measured 16 by 16 by 8 inches and was reinforced with pea straw. The late C.W. Jeffery's house in Hogg's Hollow was built of mud block protected by 4 inches of brickwork (see also 4.11).

**3.44** 'Drumsnab,' or the Cayley house (1834), on Drumsnab Road, overlooks the Don Valley near Bloor Street. The original owner and builder was Francis Cayley, who is mentioned by Mary Jarvis as a fellow passenger on a steamboat on Georgian Bay in 1835. Since the sketch was made, a storey was added (in 1856), and the wilderness that once surrounded Drumsnab is now Rosedale. In well over a century of change only the Don has remained constant, and it is no longer that crystal stream in which the salmon leapt in the spring. A feature of the drawing-room known to travellers like Sir James Alexander in 1847 was the mural decoration representing scenes from *Faust* in sgrafitto – drawn, we are told by Sir James, 'with a bold and masterly hand by the proprietor.' A recalcitrant fireplace gives a certain realism to the damnation of Faust, whose features appear strangely through the murk.

# 4  Prosperity and Eclecticism

Both politically and architecturally the year 1834 was a significant one in the story of Toronto. The population had grown to 9,254, and a change had come over its building. There must have been some loyal souls who in that year would have thought of Toronto as 'no mean city,' but there were many who found it, in another sense, indescribably mean. Mrs Jameson had this to say of it in 1836: 'most strangely mean and melancholy. A little ill-built town ... some government offices, built of staring red brick, in the most tasteless, vulgar style imaginable; three feet of snow all around; and the gray, sullen, wintry lake, and the dark gloom of the pine forest bounding the prospect.' 'Two years ago,' she wrote in 1837, 'we bought our books at the same shop where we bought our shoes, our spades, our sugar, and salt pork! Now,' she had to acknowledge, 'we have two good booksellers' shops, and at one of these a circulating library of two or three hundred volumes of common novels.' She felt that a 'reasonable person' might be happy in Toronto if he or she could tolerate the flies and frogs in summer and the 'relentless iron winter.' On another occasion she wrote of the infrequency of the mails: 'It is now seven weeks since the date of the last letters from my dear far-distant home. The archdeacon told me, by way of comfort, that when he came to settle in this country, there was only one mail-post from England in the course of a whole year, and it was called, as if in mockery, "The Express."'[1] Mrs Jameson was a highly educated, talented woman, but her views may have been prejudiced by her unhappy marriage to the attorney-general of Upper Canada.

A sympathetic observer was Dr Henry Scadding, who recalled that in the twenties the intersection of the future Queen and Yonge was so remote from York that travellers found it difficult to locate the few houses in the area, and that it was quite possible to be lost in the surrounding woods and swamps.

Another critic was John Galt, the founder of Guelph and commissioner of the Canada Company, who was inspired to say in his *Autobiography*: 'Everyone who has ever been at Dover knows that it is one of the vilest blue-devil haunts on the face of the earth, except Little York in Upper Canada, when he has been there one day.'[2]

One can have nothing but sympathy for those early critics who complained of the many disagreeable features that are inevitably associated with life in a primitive community – of inadequate heating, smells and lack of sanitation, of wooden sidewalks, muddy roads, and a general lack of those amenities that went with an older and more settled way of life in Great Britain or Europe. These were all practical matters that disappeared with wealth, the organization of the municipality, and the technological developments of the nineteenth century, of which the water closet, designed originally by Sir John Harington for Queen Elizabeth in 1596, was not the least important.

A friendly visitor was Charles Dickens, who, writing to John Forster in 1842, was able to say: 'the town itself is full of life and motion, bustle, business and improvement. The streets are well paved,[3] and lighted with gas; the houses are large and good; the shops excellent ... there are some which would do no discredit to the metropolis itself.' On the obverse side, he was shocked into writing to a friend, 'the wild and rabid Toryism of Toronto, is, I speak seriously, *appalling*.'[4]

T.A. Reed has pointed out that, in the year prior to incorporation, King and Yonge was still

far westward of the town proper, the venture of a store at the [northeast] corner in 1833 being described as 'wild and foolish.' The line of Lot Street (to be called Queen Street in 1842 in honour of Queen Victoria) was the northern boundary, all north of it being laid out in Park Lots, for gentlemen's villas, traces of which still exist in street names, such as Bleecker and Sherbourne, which reminds us of the Ridouts; Jarvis of Secretary Jarvis; James, Elizabeth, Hayter and Teraulay of Dr. James Macaulay and his wife, Elizabeth Hayter (Macaulay had been surgeon of Simcoe's 'Queen's Rangers'); Spadina, Robert, Sullivan, Willcocks, St. George and Baldwin of Dr. Wm. Warren Baldwin and his family; Denison, Bellevue, Borden, Lippincott, Ossington, Dovercourt, Hepbourne and Dewson of the Denisons, and many others of greater or less importance.[5]

On 6 March 1834, by royal assent, the title York was dropped; the ancient name of Toronto was restored, and the town became an incorporated city. To the surprise of many and the disgust of the Tory opposition, the 'rabid reformer' William Lyon Mackenzie was elected mayor. Five wards were created: St Lawrence in the neighbourhood of the market, and four others, St George, St Andrew, St Patrick, and St David, named after the patron saints of the United Kingdom. This nomenclature, with additions, represented the political divisions of the city until 1892, when the numerical system, still employed, was adopted.

When we think of the 153,402 acres covered today by Metropolitan

4.1 The home of William Lyon Mackenzie (1857) at 82 Bond Street was presented to Toronto's first mayor by his admirers in 1859, two years before his death. It stood then, like similar houses throughout the city, as part of a terrace rather than alone. Saved by public-spirited citizens from demolition in 1932 and again in the early 1950s, it is now a museum, furnished in the style of the period.

4.2 The attractive, well-lit kitchen in the basement of the Mackenzie house, with its superb stove – a view looking towards the dining-room

**4.3** John Howard anticipated all that was worst in the Chicago Exhibition of 1893 when, in 1834, he prepared this grandiose design for the open space between the jail and the Court House on King Street. It would have accommodated on the same site a guildhall, court house, post office, public library, merchant's exchange, jail, police office, holding cells, and perhaps several other uses. St James' Church of 1831, which burned in 1839, is on the right.

**4.4** John Severn moved to Yorkville in 1835 and established his brewery in a picturesque group of buildings on a creek northeast of the present intersection of Yonge and Church streets. Scadding noted with approval the galleries on the 'domestic portion' of the structure, from which the 'adjacent scenery' could be appreciated. Further east along the same valley, between Mount Pleasant Road and Sherbourne Street, stood a second brewery belonging to Joseph Bloor. A former innkeeper at the Farmers' Arms near the market square in York, his name is perpetuated in Bloor Street. It was he and Sheriff William Botsford Jarvis who laid out Yorkville as a speculation.

**4.5** Colborne Lodge in High Park (1837) was the home that John G. Howard designed for himself and named after his patron, Sir John Colborne, the lieutenant-governor. It still stands on a knoll overlooking the lake on the great estate that was Howard's munificent gift to the city. The house is a 'cottage ornée,' examples of which appeared in many books of the eighteenth and nineteenth centuries. Their publication met the demand for designs for a house that represented rusticity, nature, and the simple life. The house is open to the public as a museum furnished with many pieces that belonged to the Howards.

**4.6** A large lantern, known to us now only in a photograph, stood on the lawn at Colborne Lodge as late as the 1930s. Decorated with Greek-revival motifs, it must have been used as a guide for visitors arriving at the house, which, even today, can be missed in daylight on modern roads.

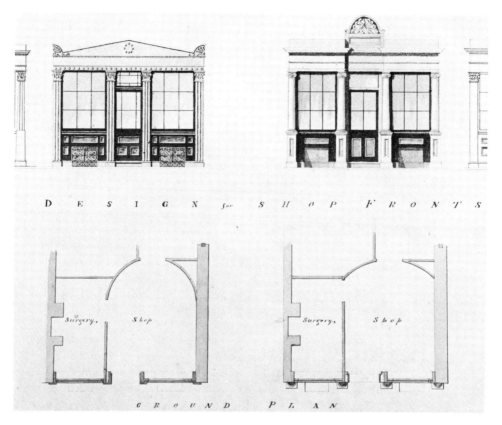

**4.7** Plan for a dentist's surgery and shop by John G. Howard (circa 1835). Until about 1840 the apothecary or chemist served also as dentist – hence the surgery. At a somewhat earlier time barbers often performed minor surgical operations.

**4.8** Three designs for a house by John G. Howard. One would assume that the dining- and drawing-rooms were intended for entertaining on a generous scale and that the large kitchen (20 feet by 13 feet) would serve as a family room for living and eating. By contrast, the four bedrooms were minimal in area. Heating was through coal-burning fireplaces, even in the basement scullery, which was as big as a bedroom. There was no bathroom in the house, but each bedroom would have basin, water jug, and chamber-pot.

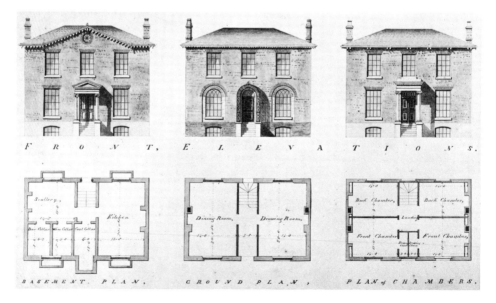

Toronto, it is worth recalling the size of the city in 1834. Its boundaries formed a rectangle described by Parliament Street on the east, Bathurst on the west, the Bay Shore to the south, and a line four hundred yards north of Queen Street at, approximately, the present Dundas Street. Beyond these boundaries growth must have seemed quite visionary, but an open area marked by the present Dufferin Street to the west and the concession line (Bloor Street) to the north was set aside for annexation when sufficiently populated. It was known as 'the Liberties.' The centre of the city was still in the neighbourhood of King and Frederick streets. Lot Street was unopened east of Victoria Street, and on Yonge Street there were few houses and no shops. Roads leading out of the city were still Dundas and Lakeshore on the west, Yonge on the north, and the Kingston Road on the east.

T.A. Reed records also the dire effects of inadequate civic amenities:

There were neither sidewalks, drains nor sewers, no water supply except from wells, no attempt at street lighting, nothing indeed that placed the city above the average of any frontier town. When an enquiry was made into the causes of the cholera epidemic of 1832, a disaster that was repeated in 1834, these primitive conditions were blamed, together with the universal practice of allowing garbage to accumulate on the vacant lots and the curse of strong drink. During these epidemics, business came to a standstill, the streets were deserted, 25 per cent. of the population were attacked and one in ten died.[6]

It would seem paradoxical that a disease-ridden town plagued by flies, and the butt of visiting English of both sexes, would have had the energy and the foresight to press for recognition by the legislature as a city. The fact is that behind this bleak frontier façade were all those elements that are essential to the good life in an organized community. On the wholly physical side were firms in the iron-foundry business, firms with steam sawmills and flour mills, and others that provided the inhabitants with soap and candles as well as 'blue and Poland starch.' On the spiritual side were the churches, of which there were ten; there were the Literary and Philosophical Society, several libraries, and the enterprising Messrs Charles Daly and J.G. Howard, who 'aimed to cultivate the public taste' by arranging loan exhibitions of art.

The Masons had met as early as 1800 and by 1822 had a hall on Market Lane where they gathered 'on every Thursday previous to the full moon.' Several literary magazines appeared and, like their successors for the next hundred years, had their little day and passed away. The Typographical Society was a union rather than a social group, but it was interested in the improvement of the craft and had regular dinners. Joseph Lawrence was its first president. When to these activities we add those groups inevitably connected with the affairs of the ten churches where they worshipped, we have a picture of life quite different from that seen through the eyes of that 'haughty' hypochondriac, Mr Galt, or the lonely and unhappy Mrs Jameson. What we see, in fact, is the present-day great city of Toronto in all its cultural aspects, but in miniature. Even lecture-going, for which Toronto is notorious, was not unknown in 1834. Indeed, it had its own highly organized society under the distinguished sponsorship of Dr Baldwin, Samuel P. Jarvis, Dr John Rolph, James Worts, and John Ewart.

The works of John G. Howard, whose gift of High Park to the city will be remembered long after his buildings have been demolished and forgotten, will be referred to again, but here it is appropriate to include his efforts to influence the cultural life of York. So energetic a man was likely never depressed, but the contrast between London and York, so shocking to Mrs Jameson, must have been equally so for him when he arrived in September 1832 after a journey from England that involved near shipwreck and mutiny with violence.

By 1833 he was the drawing master at Upper Canada College, at a salary of one hundred pounds per annum, and a year later had sufficient position in the local community to be one of the organizers of the Society of Artists and Amateurs. The catalogue of the first exhibition is preserved in the Metropolitan Toronto Library, and there we learn that the new society was under the distinguished patronage of Sir John Colborne and Archdeacon Strachan. Captain Richard Bonnycastle, RE, was president. Rather in reverse of the English custom at cricket, where amateurs are 'gentlemen' and play 'the rest,' the professionals in this first society of artists in Toronto were named but the 'amateurs shall not be compelled to annex their names.' The result was work by Paul Kane, John G. Howard, and others alongside a painting by 'A Lady.' Among the exhibits were 'Lioness and Whelps' and, very daring, 'An idea in Perspective.'

Toronto was apparently not ready for such a society, or the times were out of joint, because only one exhibition, in 1834, was held. In 1847 Howard reorganized the society under the title 'The Toronto Society of Artists.' Hardly more successful than its predecessor, the newly formed group held two exhibitions in the old City Hall and then fell dormant.

The theatre in Toronto has had a chequered career, but its roots go deep into the nineteenth century. The earliest recorded performance was in 1809, when an American strolling company put on *The School for Scandal* in a tavern ballroom. Just before the War of 1812 the favourite place for such entertainments was a tavern known as O'Keefe's Assembly Rooms. We hear of strolling 'Yankee' stock companies visiting York in the twenties, and 'traditions exist of private theatricals in good style at Spadina House and the Garrison.'

Robertson's sketches in the *Landmarks* of several theatres built or 'adapted' between 1820 and 1849 would indicate that the demand for theatrical performances, both amateur and professional, was a lively one. All except one were of frame construction, and had been barns, a Wesleyan chapel, and a carpenter's shop, but only two were destroyed by fire in spite of lighting by candles and construction of a kind that would shock the most casual of building inspectors. The exception in brick was, of course, John Ritchey's Royal Lyceum on King Street, in the rear of what formerly had been Sinclair's Hotel. It opened in January 1849 with a production arranged by the Irish-born actor and impressario T.P. Besnard, known as T.P.B. to a generation of admiring Toronto theatre-goers.

The change that came over the architecture of Toronto about the time of incorporation as a city had nothing to do with the new status of the community, nor was it something that can be fixed by a date. It was a change in taste brought about by the Romantic movement, a movement that was felt most strongly in the Western Hemisphere and left its mark on architecture as well as on literature, painting, and music. Romanticism has been said 'to consist in a high development of poetic sensibility towards the remote, as such. It idealizes the distant, both of time and place. Its most typical form is the cult of the extinct.'[7] We recognize it at this time in St Andrew's church in the style of ancient Greece, and before long we shall see a Gothic St James' and a Romanesque University College. Inspired by books dealing on the one hand with the new science of archaeology or, on the other, with the imagery and beauty of language of Byron, Keats, and Shelley, the lure of Greece was irresistible even in a Presbyterian church. Yet in the confused aesthetic standards of the time, Ruskin and Pugin would have condemned the Greek as pagan and intolerable in a Christian church – only the Middle Ages provided the architecture that pointed to God in pinnacles and soaring spires. For most people the architecture of the Middle Ages suggested piety and the feeling of reverence and awe that went with a dim Miltonian light; and elderly professors dreaming of home could find equally convincing arguments in favour of Gothic as the only style compatible with learning in the new land. We can imagine also the zeal with which they urged their not unwilling architects to give them buildings as remote as possible from the familiar present.

A factor of no little significance in the Toronto story was the arrival of the architect as a professional man. Nothing could be more difficult than judging his first appearance. Clearly, William Berczy and William Warren Baldwin both showed skill in designing buildings, among their many other talents. But neither held himself out as an architect to the same extent as did Edward Angell, who advertised in the York *Observer* of October 1820 that he was a 'House Surveyor and Architect to lay out Building Estate, draw ground plans, sections and elevations to order.' In spite of his royal patron in the person of HRH Edward Augustus, duke of Kent and Strathearn, who was also father of the Princess Victoria, Angell had difficulty securing architectural commissions. The result was that he tended to be occupied with civil-engineering projects like bridges and mills.

Another civil engineer, Francis Hall, was responsible in 1826 for the proposal for 'A Province Building Contemplated at York' and may have had a hand the year before in the design for the Bank of Upper Canada on Duke (now Adelaide) Street. Contemporary accounts said the building would exhibit a combination of Doric and Tuscan orders. It appears today, though, that the plans must have been revised and simplified during construction.

**4.9** Zion Congregational Church, northeast corner of Adelaide and Bay streets (1839; burned 1855). This is a very classical little church, with its Doric columns *in antis* at the porch entrance. It was built of bricks covered with plaster 'made of white marble dust' – a technique not unknown to the Greeks in 500 BC but undoubtedly rare in Upper Canada. The plaster was scored to simulate stone.

**4.10** Three houses, demolished long ago, on Adelaide (formerly Duke) Street near Parliament. The large house on the left, said to have had the year 1845 carved in a stone mounted in one wall, shows old Toronto domestic architecture at its best. It was the house of Jacob Latham, a prominent builder. The semicircular Ionic porch and the balustraded fence contribute greatly to its charm. The middle house was built for Alexander Grant about 1859. The end house at the corner of Parliament Street was Obadiah Stafford's. It might well have been built in the twenties or earlier because Robertson notes that by 1833 it 'presented tokens of age.'

**4.11** House of Dr William Charles Gwynne, Dufferin Street north of Springhurst Avenue (circa 1840; demolished 1917). Dr Gwynne was admitted to the practice of medicine on his arrival in Upper Canada in 1832 and later became a highly respected surgeon and professor at the University of Toronto. The house is of a type not uncommon among Ontario farmhouses, though the French doors are unusual in this climate. The walls were built of sun-dried mud bricks protected by stucco.

**4.12** Beverley House, Richmond and John streets, was demolished in 1913. Almost a century before, in 1817, John Beverley Robinson, then newly married and soon to be appointed attorney-general of Upper Canada, bought D'Arcy Boulton's one-storey brick cottage on a site bounded by John, Simcoe, Richmond, and Queen streets. Robinson enlarged his house by adding a wing to the west, a second floor, and a long verandah across the front, which faced south to Richmond Street. In 1839–40, while he was in England, Beverley House became the residence of the governor-general, Charles Poulett Thomson, who was raised to the peerage while living here and took the title of Baron Sydenham of Sydenham in Kent and Toronto in Canada.

**4.13** Charming cottages, now demolished, on the west side of Bay Street south of College. High land costs and primitive sanitary conditions spelt the end of such housing in Toronto. This photograph was taken about 1930, before Eaton's College Street store occupied the corner opposite.

**4.14** Half Way House, Kingston Road at Scarborough (circa 1850). It was halfway between Dunbarton and St Lawrence Hall. In 1965 the Half Way House was moved to Black Creek Pioneer Village by the Metropolitan Toronto Conservation Authority and was restored as an inn.

**4.15** The former Paisley Shop at 925 Yonge Street (circa 1840; demolished 1961). It would be hard to imagine a shop that offered a more genuine invitation to the customer than did the Paisley Shop. The delicacy of the window detail and the cast-iron columns at the entrance were matched by the elegance of the old silver and glass on display within. The twentieth century has produced nothing to equal it in Toronto.

**4.16** The third jail (1838; demolished 1887), John G. Howard, architect. Built overlooking the bay at the southeast corner of Front and Berkeley streets, it was influenced by Jeremy Bentham's ideas for model prisons. The plan called for three wings radiating from a central core, although only two were completed. The windows in this grim pile remind one of a columbarium, with its niches for urns. If anything, this prison was more terrifying than the old Newgate, whose demolition in 1911 was the cause for general rejoicing in London.

**4.17** The hospital at the new fort, in the Canadian National Exhibition grounds (1840; demolished 1952). Begun shortly after the political unrest of 1837–8 in Upper Canada, the new fort was renamed the Stanley Barracks, after the governor-general, in 1893. Four major buildings within the fort were built in Queenston limestone. Expansion of the midway and car-parking areas at the CNE claimed all but the officers' quarters, which serve today as the Marine Museum and the headquarters of the Toronto Historical Board. The iron gates to the fort, which were made in England, now stand at the entrance to Guildwood Village on Kingston Road.

The occasion for this may have been Francis Hall's resignation as the contractor, long before the building was completed. New plans could have
come from either the obliging Dr Baldwin, one of the bank's directors, or
John Ewart, a York builder who often worked in association with Baldwin
but was quite capable of producing good designs on his own. Ewart arrived
in town before 1820 and was involved one way or another in most of the
public buildings erected in York before the arrival of Thomas Young and
John G. Howard in the early 1830s. They soon secured the greater portion
of architectural commissions in the new city.

As the city grew in wealth and position, buildings arose that called for
the skills of men who were not only master builders but trained in the art
of architecture. By 1844 the editor of the *Star* took note of the city's improvements and found ample reason for optimism: 'What a very slight idea
our friends in the old country have of our fair City of Toronto here in the
far far West. Within these two years we see the stiff, stale appearance of
bygone days, vanishing like ugly phantoms, and ARCHITECTURE in all its fair
proportions stealing coyly from the dark corner in which it has been confined, either by the niggardliness of propriety or stupidity of the building
faculty ... Who shall say what Toronto may not yet be.'[8] Particular praise
was given to the designs of Henry Bowyer Lane, including those for Trinity
Church, called Little Trinity, on King Street East, 'which only wants cut
stone hood mouldings and pilasters to the windows and doors, to make it
a little gem.'[9]

When John Ross Robertson wrote of Trinity in 1898, he described it as
weather-beaten, and the walls 'dingy with the dust and dirt of many years.'
Even then, the district had deteriorated. In our day, it has improved slightly,
but one would go far to find a congregation more loyal to the church they
love. Its congregation may not have been as wealthy as that of Holy Trinity,
but in its great days the Gooderham and Worts families were generous
supporters, and the chief justice, John Beverley Robinson, gave a ten-acre
lot on the Kingston Road for the rector's income.

An interesting tablet records the service of the first pastor, the Reverend
William Honeywood Ripley, who for six years served the church 'without
money and without price.' He was also classical master at Upper Canada
College, and died in 1849 in his thirty-fourth year. For economy's sake the
twenty-four burner gaselier used to be turned low during the sermon, putting
the congregation 'into the hazy mystery of semi-darkness, a condition very
favourable for napping or little social amenities.' The exterior is in the perpendicular Gothic manner, with five aisle windows and a well-proportioned
tower in no need of the spire originally intended for it. A fire in 1960 nearly
proved disastrous, and for a time many must have feared that Trinity would
share the fate of St George the Martyr on John Street.

The Church of the Holy Trinity and its site on Trinity Square have a
romantic history. The site was once occupied by Teraulay Cottage, the home
of the family of Macaulay, which has played no small part in the long history

**4.18** Topographical plan of the city and Liberties of Toronto in 1842, by James Cane, who had been with the British Board of Ordnance before he emigrated to Canada. The built-up area of the city is almost entirely south of Queen Street and east of Spadina. Bloor Street forms the northern boundary.

of Toronto. In 1797 Dr James Macaulay, surgeon of the Queen's Rangers, received a Crown grant of one hundred acres in an area where the principal boundaries were the west side of Yonge, Bloor, and Queen. Early in the century he laid out the southerly portion as a residential subdivision and named it Macaulay town – a 'suburb' of York far removed from the town proper. To provide the community with a centre and focus he built Teraulay Cottage, a house that was to become famous in the social life of York and was destined, nearly half a century later, to be moved bodily to make room for Holy Trinity.

The church was completed in 1847, but only twelve years earlier the land south was known as 'the fields,' and behind, as far as the eye could see, were 'treacherous swamps and tangled forest.'[10] Scadding records that Mr Justice Boulton travelling in his own vehicle took half a day to cover the distance between the Don and Teraulay Cottage. When Colonel John Simcoe Macaulay made a gift of the land necessary for the church, Teraulay Cottage was moved to the corner of the now-disappeared Louisa and the present James Street.

It was in 1845 that Bishop Strachan received a gift of five thousand pounds for the building and maintenance of a church, the only stipulations being that it be called 'the Church of the Holy Trinity,' 'the seats of which to be free and unappropriated forever.' It was also stipulated that three thousand pounds was to be spent on the building and two thousand on an investment for the incumbent. It was not until 1898 that the donor was known to be Mrs Lambert Swale of Settle, near Ripon, in Yorkshire. During her lifetime this unknown benefactress supplied the church with 'silver sacramental plate for public use and smaller service for private ministration,' as well as 'a large supply of fair linen, a covering of Genoa velvet for the altar and surplices for the clergy.'

In 1847 Bishop Strachan published a notice inviting 'the poor families of the United Church of England and Ireland to make the church their own' and another announcing the opening for service of the 'Parochial Church of the Poor of Toronto.' In spite of what they say, these advertisements were not intended to restrict the congregation to a single financial or social group. It was merely that the deed of gift had to be observed, and the Church of the Holy Trinity became the first Anglican Church in Toronto where pews were free. It has also been suggested that the character of Holy Trinity was determined from a fear that many good Anglicans, not appreciating the high pew rents of St James' or the social atmosphere that dominated the cathedral, might have been driven into the bosom of the Presbyterian or Methodist church. In view of the political and emotional atmosphere in the Anglican church in the thirties and forties, one can imagine with what misgivings the congregation of Holy Trinity invited the pew-holders of St James' to worship with them after the disastrous fire to the cathedral of 1849. This *mariage de convenance* lasted for two years, and was not without friction.

**4.19, 20** The Commercial Bank, 15 Wellington Street West (1845), William Thomas, architect. Measured drawings made in 1932 by students in the School of Architecture show how the Greek revival permeated Thomas's design. A long-time owner of the building was the firm of Clarkson Gordon and Company, which sold the building in November 1972 to the Canadian Imperial Bank of Commerce. Today the building is marking time until the properties along the south side of Wellington Street are redeveloped; its demolition would be unthinkable.

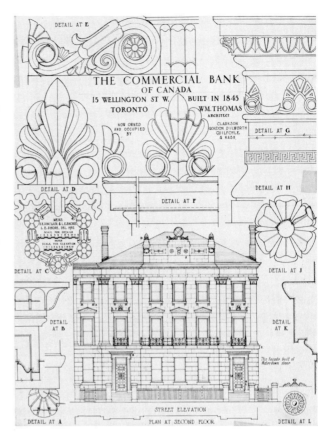

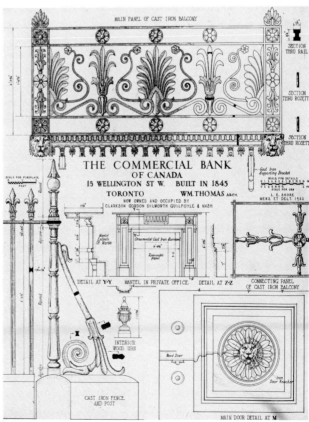

**4.21** Bank of British North America, northeast corner of Yonge and Wellington streets (1845; demolished 1871), John G. Howard, architect. This bank was greatly admired in its day, and its design, according to Scadding, was 'preferred by the directors in London to those sent in by several architects there.' The royal arms over the door, carved by John Cochrane, echoed those on the Bank of England, and the scallop shell on the parapet was a device introduced by Sir John Soane, the architect of the bank in London, to suggest the 'gold-digger's occupation.' Howard also designed the matching wing on Yonge Street of shops with warehouses on the floors above, seen here to the left. It was erected in 1847 for the firm of A.V. Brown, grocers.

4.23

**4.22** Bank of Montreal, northwest corner of Yonge and Front Streets (1845; demolished 1885), Kivas Tully, architect. Built in the manner of a London townhouse or gentleman's club, the bank had commodious quarters on the second and third floors for the manager and his family. To the left is the Custom House of 1873, which replaced an earlier custom house there, also designed by Tully and built in the same year as the bank.

**4.23** Wellington Street, south side, looking east in 1868. From right to left the buildings are the house of F.C. Capreol, a prominent merchant, financier, and railway promoter who lived here from the 1850s to 1874; the Edinburgh Life Assurance building (1858), Cumberland & Storm, architects; and the Commercial Bank (see 4.19, 20).

**4.24** Church of St George the Martyr, John Street (1844; burned 1955), Henry Bowyer Lane, architect. It was built on land given by Mr and Mrs D'Arcy Boulton, Jr, for the 'first west end Anglican parish.' In 1955 a tragic fire destroyed the church except for its graceful tower, which stands today, alone on a green lawn, a picturesque reminder of old Toronto.

**4.25** Methodist Church, south side of Richmond between Yonge and Bay (1844; demolished 1888), Richard Woodsworth, master builder. Even in its later days, when the church was in a rather dilapidated condition, it was still referred to with respect, indeed with reverence, as the mother church of every Methodist congregation in the city. The Methodist Book Room was built on the site, incorporating parts of the fabric of the old building, including the cornerstone. Its contents were found when the Book Room was demolished in 1934.

**4.26** Second City Hall, southwest corner of Front and Jarvis streets (1844; largely demolished 1901), Henry Bowyer Lane, architect. Located across Front Street from the old market, originally it was called the New Market House. The arches flanking the porticoed main doorway led to a marketplace in the rear, and until substantial alterations were made in 1851, there were butchers' stalls on the ground floor. The council chamber and municipal offices were located on the second floor. Although the building was never entirely satisfactory as a city hall, it was not replaced until 1899. The central portion has survived as part of the south St Lawrence Market building, where the very fine rear façade can still be seen from inside the market.

**4.27** Numbers 25, 29, 31, and 33 Lowther Avenue (circa 1875). Yorkville is still a desirable and stable residential district, but nothing remains of the old village as typical as these houses. They do not demonstrate the qualities once found in our old terraces, qualities of rhythm and dignity that were achieved through continuity, but individually they are arresting on a street of rather nondescript houses.

**4.28, 29** Little Trinity Church, King Street East (1843), Henry Bowyer Lane, architect. The first of a trio of Anglican churches by Lane, Little Trinity was followed by St George the Martyr (1844) and Holy Trinity (1846). Carved in two shields that act as terminals to the bold label mould over the main entrance of Little Trinity is the year of its construction.

**4.30** The Schoolhouse (1848), the first free school in Toronto, was the gift of Enoch Turner, a wealthy brewer. It is situated on Trinity Street just south of Little Trinity Church. In 1869 architects Gundry and Langley designed a large addition to the rear of the original building. The school was restored in 1972 and now is visited by children from Metro schools, who attend classes where they sit on old benches, use slates, and experience the atmosphere of a classroom of the mid-nineteenth century.

**4.31** Property of the Honourable John Simcoe Macaulay, who gave the 'most eligible site' in the district, known as Macaulay's Fields, for Holy Trinity. The plan shows Teraulay Cottage and the building lots on adjacent streets in 1845. Anne Street became Alice and then Teraulay; Jeremy was a Macaulay family name.

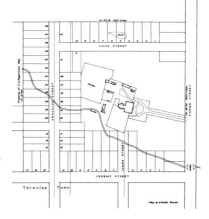

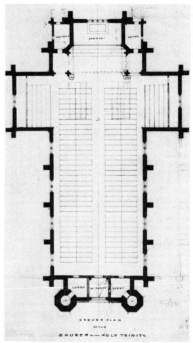

**4.32** Original plan of Holy Trinity (1846), signed by Henry Bowyer Lane, architect. It shows some alterations in pencil, particularly the extension of the chancel into the nave, which was done. The final stone was laid at the top of the northwest turret on 10 May 1847, and the first service took place that year on 29 October, a few days before Lane left Toronto for good.

**4.33** Holy Trinity in 1907, when excavations were being done by hand for Eaton's mail-order building

A competition was held to secure plans for Holy Trinity. After William Thomas had been awarded the premium, Bishop Strachan took the unusual step of setting his designs aside and commissioning Henry Bowyer Lane, assisted by 'three other gentlemen who had studied Church Architecture,' to produce other plans. The result of their united labours looked to John Ross Robertson at the end of the last century 'like some giant entombed' among the lofty factories and warehouses that had come to surround the church, its old rectory, and another house, the home of the Reverend Dr Henry Scadding. This backwater was safe enough, however, compared with the gales of controversy that engulfed the congregation in the 1960s, when a redevelopment of adjacent lands for the Eaton Centre was first proposed. Happily, an accord was reached to preserve the church and bring order, dignity, and nature back to this 'haunt of ancient peace.' Then, when things were looking so promising, a 1977 fire in one of the neighbouring warehouses, which was being demolished, almost destroyed the church too. Today Holy Trinity has been restored to its original glory and sits with confident presence in the centre of a newly created public square.

For almost fifty years the church has been known particularly for a Christmas play that gives pleasure annually to hundreds, and more recently for series of broadcast concerts. It has also had a long tradition of social service to the city. Near the small east door facing the Eaton Centre is a room of considerable interest to students of education in Canada. The story goes back to 1856, when a parochial school designed by William Hay was added to the church, with a classroom for boys on the ground floor and one for girls on the second. There were, apparently, fewer girls, because the space above was divided into classroom and 'winter chapel.' In 1886 a new school was built to replace the old one, and all of the upper floor was devoted to a quite beautiful chapel rarely seen by visitors, with an open timber roof and faded decoration over what was once the altar of the winter chapel.

There would seem to be no continuous link in the work of the Church of Rome between the Mission at the Rouge, with the Abbé Fénelon, and 1801, when it became the custom for French priests on their way to Detroit to hold services in the houses of citizens of York. Sporadic meetings of this kind continued until 1822, when St Paul's was built on Power Street, south of the modern St Paul's (1887) on Queen Street.[11] For some time during the episcopate of Bishop Power, St Paul's was the cathedral church of the Toronto diocese, and adjacent to it was the first Roman Catholic cemetery.

It is pleasant to record that when a 'drive' was made to reduce the debt on St Paul's in 1829, the collectors were the solicitor-general, the Honourable W.W. Baldwin, Simon Washburn, and Lieutenant-Colonel James Fitz-Gibbon, all of whom were Anglicans.[12]

And so, we come to St Michael's Cathedral. One likes to think of cathedrals facing great squares like the Piazza of St Mark's or St Peter's, or being surrounded by landscaped grounds that themselves take on a religious atmosphere quite as pervasive as that within the sacred precinct itself. Eighty years ago St Michael's had such space and trees, but today it is hemmed in

**4.34, 35** Mental Asylum, 999 Queen Street West (1846–9; demolished 1976), John G. Howard, architect; surrounding wall and gates (1851), Cumberland and Ridout, architects. In 1840 design proposals were invited for a prize of thirty pounds for the new lunatic asylum. Howard was the successful competitor, and eventually this enormous structure was built under his supervision. Up to 1900 it was considered the best-ventilated mental institution in North America, though it was a legend that a furnace in the dome drew air and odours from wards through vitreous tile pipes. Instead, the dome contained a large water tank and a quite striking spiral stair to the cupola. Demolition of the building by the Ontario government in 1976, the year after the Ontario Heritage Act became law, was described as 'a collective failure of imagination' and represented a major loss of Toronto's architectural heritage.

**4.36** Oakham House, at the corner of Church and Gould streets (1848), William Thomas, architect. The only other architects of the last century to have lived on this scale were Howard and Cumberland. It will always be a puzzle that Thomas, who could design so well in the Greek-revival manner, would do his own house in a very fake Gothic with heraldic beasts, coats of arms, and carved stone heads. For some time the house was the Working Boys' Home. The interior has, unfortunately, been changed beyond recognition. The building is now part of the Ryerson Polytechnical Institute.

**4.37** Oakham House, the main entrance, once flanked by crouching dogs, which have been taken inside. The carved heads and column capitals flanking the arch are less crisp today, showing the effects on stone of Toronto weather and, perhaps, of ill-advised masonry cleaning.

by streets to the west, south, and east, and on Bond Street by quite incompatible ecclesiastical buildings to the north.

The cathedral has architectural links with the great cathedral at York, England. Two heads flanking the main doorway are that of Paulinus (died 644) on the left and King Edwin (585–633) on the right. Paulinus, the first bishop of the Northumbrians and archbishop of York, was consecrated in 625. In 627 he baptized King Edwin, who built a wooden church and later began one in stone at York. Invisible though also to be found at St Michael's Cathedral are the stone fragments from a pier and a piece of oak from the roof of York Minster, which are contained in a leaden box set in the wall behind the foundation stone.

That exceedingly able William Thomas who designed about a dozen Toronto churches was the architect of St Michael's in 1845. For many years the cathedral remained unfinished, and by the time a tower and spire were to be added in 1865, William Thomas was dead. Although a design was submitted by his son, William Tutin Thomas, who had followed his father's profession, the commission was given to Messrs Gundry and Langley. In the 1890s the Gothic dormers were added, probably at the same time as other work proceeding under the supervision of the architect Joseph Connolly. Dormers on a cathedral roof must be exceedingly rare, and the light that is admitted to the nave is negligible.

The interior of St Michael's is very impressive – columns are light in design and tone and the ceiling is rich with colour – but the visitor who likes to wander down those byways of history that are recorded in plaques and monuments will be disappointed. There are none.

As early as 1791 Colonel Simcoe had discussed with the president of the Royal Society in England the 'desirability of a college of a higher class' in the colony to which he had been appointed. For many years the most modest proposal would have been impracticable because of the sparseness of the population, though Gourlay's scheme (1819) of sending twenty-five students annually to Oxford and Cambridge would have met a very great need. Finally, in 1827 King's College was established by royal charter and endowed with vast areas of Crown lands. Because the charter gave control of the university to the Anglicans, other denominations were resentful and expressed their objections so strongly that the new lieutenant-governor, Sir John Colborne, put a hold on further development of the college until the provincial Parliament could agree on amendments to the charter. Archdeacon John Strachan and the King's College Council had already acquired a large site a mile northwest of York and had commissioned designs for the university from Strachan's friend Charles Fowler of London. In June 1829 Strachan wrote to his architect, 'we have long been anxious for your plans, etc. as well as the model ... I am quite happy to find that you are so much occupied and have the building of Covent Gardens' Market committed to your care.' Fowler had completed the plans in March and sent them off, but the shipping of the model was delayed until the summer. A year later its

4.38 Gundry and Langley's design for the tower and spire of St Michael's, 1865

4.39

**4.39, 40** St Michael's Cathedral, Bond and Shuter streets (1845–8), William Thomas, architect, who contributed so much to Toronto's nineteenth-century architecture. Thomas
designed the cathedral to be seen across the open area of McGill Square to the south.
Although the square was sold to the Methodists, who built the Metropolitan Church there
in 1870 (see 5.101), the two buildings were congenial neighbours. It may have been
that the decorative dormers added to St Michael's in the 1890s were designed principally
to improve its appearance, particularly if the architect Joseph Connolly was involved.
He had a talent, seen also in St Mary's on Bathurst Street, for creating picturesque churches.
Unfortunately, the view of St Michael's suffered when a building connected with Metropolitan Church was erected across the north end of McGill Square.

**4.41** St Michael's Cathedral, the bishop's chair. When William Thomas designed this chair,
he certainly had in mind a prince of the church at a most exalted level. It is unfortunate
that thirty years ago it lost its place in the sanctuary and in the 1960s was removed from the
cathedral. The chair's whereabouts are not known today.

4.40

4.41

**4.42** Bishop's Palace, Church Street (1845), William Thomas, architect. This is one of the best remaining examples of Victorian Gothic. Built in grey Toronto brick with stone facings, it is a very suitable adjunct to the cathedral in the same materials. The central gable with the episcopal arms carved in stone by John Cochrane shows Thomas's mastery of Gothic detail. Heads of the architect and Bishop Power appear as corbels to the arch of the doorway.

**4.43** The Jennings Church, southeast corner Richmond and Bay streets (1848; demolished 1886), William Thomas, architect. Sometime in 1838 'seven members and twenty-one adherents of the United Secession Church of Scotland, met in a carpenter's shop on Newgate [Adelaide] Street' to talk over the formation of a congregation and the building of a kirk. With their first parson, the Reverend John Jennings, they led a peripatetic existence until they built this little Gothic church. A minor miracle was recorded in the early sixties when, in a great wind, a pinnacle fell through the roof, dislodging a nail, which was impaled in a New Testament at Mark 7:25: 'and the winds blew, and beat upon that house, and it fell not; for it was founded upon a rock.'

**4.44** Knox's Church, Queen Street east of Yonge (1847–8; demolished 1905), William Thomas, architect. It replaced a previous church that had burned in May 1847. The architect John Johnston, who had been unsuccessful with his own entry in the competition to design Knox's Church, engraved this lithograph of the winning design by William Thomas, surely a high compliment. Sparks spreading from the fire at Robert Simpson's department store in 1895 destroyed Knox's tower and steeple, which resembled the spire on Thomas's beautiful St Andrew's Church in Hamilton.

arrival in York had not been confirmed, prompting Fowler to write on 5 August 1830, from Gordon Square,

MY DEAR SIR: It is now just twelve months since I forwarded to you the case containing the Model etc. of the proposed university, and I have not yet had any direct intelligence of its safe arrival; but I presume that it is so – If you have not written to me (for I thought it possible that a letter might have miscarried) I attribute it to your being so fully occupied – and to the want of any decision upon the Plans; but if it will not be intruding too much on your time I shall be very glad if you will favor me with some account however brief; for Mr. McGillivray having gone to Mexico, I have now no authentic source of intelligence for Canadian affairs ... To revert to your University, I shall always feel interested to know the progress you make, being aware that you have many difficulties & much opposition to encounter; but which I doubt not your firmness and good judgement will ultimately surmount. [13]

The model was last reported at the Toronto General Hospital on Adelaide Street in 1851, but Fowler's drawings survive in the Horwood Collection at the Ontario Archives. His scheme had been abandoned in the controversy over the charter, which continued until 1837, when the legislators reached a consensus on the necessary changes. Then Thomas Young was asked to prepare plans, only to find that Mackenzie's rebellion and an inquiry into the confused state of the college accounts delayed any laying of the corner-stone until 1842. The event took place on St George's Day, and Henry Scadding tells us that 'a procession such as had never before been seen in these parts' slowly marched up College Avenue to the site of the new university building in Queen's Park, with the soldiers of the 43rd Regiment, bearing arms, lining the route. At a given signal,

The vast procession opened its ranks and his Excellency the Chancellor, with the President, the Lord Bishop of Toronto, on his right, and the Senior Visitor, the Chief Justice, on his left, proceeded on foot through the College Avenue to the University grounds. The countless array moved forward to the sound of military music. The sun shone out with cloudless meridian splendour; one blaze of banners flushed upon the admiring eye. – The Governor's rich Lord-Lieutenant's dress, the Bishop's sacerdotal robes, the Judicial Ermine of the Chief Justice, the splendid Convocation robes of Dr. McCaul, the gorgeous uniforms of the suite, the accoutrements of the numerous Firemen, ... the Red Crosses on the breasts of England's congregated sons, the grave habiliments of the Clergy and Lawyers, and the glancing lances and waving plumes of the First Incorporated Dragoons, all formed one moving picture of civic pomp, one glorious spectacle which can never be remembered but with satisfaction by those who had the good fortune to witness it.

Finally, at the site, the chancellor, Governor-General Sir Charles Bagot, accompanied by the officers of the university and his suite, took his place

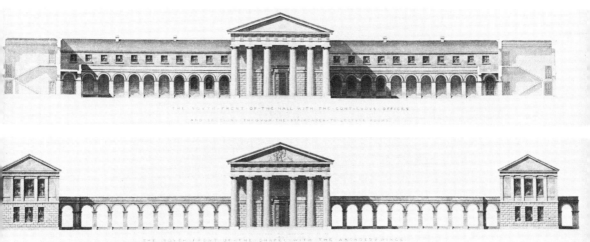

**4.45** University of King's College at York, drawn by Charles Fowler in 1829. He was sufficiently proud of his designs that he exhibited one of the drawings for the college at the Royal Academy in 1830.

**4.46** King's College, Queen's Park (1842–5; demolished 1886), Thomas Young, architect. This Athenian building, intended as the east wing of a group of buildings, occupied a site where the legislative buildings now stand.

in a pavilion erected for the purpose. 'Fronting this was an amphitheatre of seats, ... densely filled with ladies.' Between the pavilion and the amphitheatre the crowd stood.[14]

Architecturally, one feels the cold hand of archaeology in the Greek revival detail of Thomas Young's designs for King's College, and none of the spirit that made the old Commercial Bank so lively a neighbour for everything new or old on Wellington Street. Only a portion of Young's complex of buildings was ever completed. In spite of this he enjoyed the appointment of university architect for seven fat years at the handsome salary of two hundred pounds annually. The additional space needed by the college was secured by pressing the Parliament buildings on Front Street into service as lecture rooms and laboratories. The Parliament buildings were not in use by the government from 1841 to 1849, as the custom of rotating the seat of government for the Province of Canada took the parliamentarians away from Toronto. In 1849, shortly after they returned, legislation was enacted to re-establish King's College on a secular basis as the University of Toronto.

Seven unhappy years then followed before the construction of University College was begun. The first disappointment for the new institution came when it was thwarted in its plans to complete a scaled-down version of Young's complex. Next, the government expropriated its principal building and a large part of its lovely park as a permanent seat for provincial government, a plan that miscarried soon after but that, phoenix-like, would be realized there forty years later. With their university thus dispossessed, professors and students were forced to move from one temporary home to another. They occupied the Parliament buildings again, and also the former King's College building until they were evicted when it, like Victoria College in Cobourg at a later date, was found to be admirably suited to the primitive nineteenth-century requirements of a mental institution.

Of even greater significance than King's College in the architectural development of Toronto was the building of Osgoode Hall. We know that in the nineteenth century the hall went through three stages of construction: in 1829, 1844, and 1857. We have ample documentary proof that Cumberland and Storm were responsible for the last major change in 1857, and there is no longer any doubt that Henry Bowyer Lane was the Law Society's architect in 1844, as John Ewart had been in 1829. Previously the name of the Montreal firm of Hopkins, Lawford and Nelson had entered the story, but from drawings in the Horwood Collection at Ontario Archives it is obvious that they were unsuccessful competitors for the major reconstruction of 1857, who have left us watercolour sketches of the building before the competition and as it might have been if they had received the commission.

Other matters are fortunately not open to question. The Law Society had considered building as early as 1820 with a budget not to exceed five hundred pounds. Nothing was done until 1825, when the government was asked for a grant in aid and the members were able to pledge two thousand pounds towards the erection of the building. The first site selected was Russell Square (eventually the site of Upper Canada College), but that was abandoned in favour of the present property, which the society purchased from the attorney-general, John Beverley Robinson, for one thousand pounds.

The east wing was begun in 1829 and finished in 1832. The architect, John Ewart, was allowed none of the Gothic whimsy that marked the court house he built overlooking the forks of the Thames in the distant London District. Osgoode Hall was described by John Ross Robertson as 'a plain matter-of-fact brick building' two full storeys plus an attic story in height. One year after John Ritchey, the builder, completed the east block, 'twenty-four comfortable bedchambers' were added in a wing to the west where today we find the great library. Following Mackenzie's rebellion the authorities responsible for billeting troops in Toronto could not overlook such accommodation, and the Law Society was willing, naturally, to make a contribution to peace, order, and good government. In June 1838 it leased Osgoode Hall for two years as barracks.

The soldiers stayed until 1843, leaving the building in some disarray as they departed. A claim for damages was made and, as the *Star* reported, 'The Law Society no sooner received the £480 awarded them for the injuries done to this beautiful building by the military, than they commenced improvements instanter.'[15] In August 1844 the Law Society's building committee approved designs by Henry Bowyer Lane for a new west wing, for an impressive stone portico applied to the east wing to create a balanced composition, and for a Palladian loggia and dignifying dome that dressed up the existing range of chambers and offices between the wings.

An entry in Howard Colvin's *Biographical Dictionary of British Architects, 1600–1840* has given rise to confusion of Lane with another architect having the same surname. The closing date for Colvin's monumental work precluded his taking notice of Henry Bowyer Lane, who was born in 1817 or 1818, probably on Corfu in the Ionian Islands, where his father was posted as an officer in the Royal Artillery. His architectural career had barely begun by 1841, when, following an apprenticeship in the office of an unknown but accomplished English architect, he embarked for Cobourg, Upper Canada. There he was welcomed by D'Arcy Edward Boulton, an old friend from Blundell's School at Tiverton in Devon, and by George Strange Boulton. Lane was related to the Boultons through the marriage of two of his aunts to leading members of the English branch of the proud family of Boulton of Moulton. Nor did Lane lack other Boulton patrons when he decided in April 1842 to leave Cobourg for Toronto. John G. Howard recorded the occasion in his journal on 15 April: 'W.H. Boulton, Esq., introduced Mr. Lane, architect, wishing me to take him in partnership, but I declined.'

William Henry Boulton was a member of the Law Society's building committee in 1844. Although Howard was busy enough that year with many small jobs as well as the gigantic project to build the Lunatic Asylum, which we now know as 999 Queen Street, it is likely that he declined to

**4.47** Osgoode Hall, the principal façade

**4.48** Osgoode Hall gate and fence (1866), William G. Storm, architect. This superb 'iron palisade' was cast in a Toronto foundry from moulds made in Scotland. The entrances to the Law Society's grounds have been called 'cow-gates,' as they kept out the cows that sometimes wandered the streets of Toronto in the 1860s and had to be kept off the lawn.

**4.49** Osgoode Hall. A rare view taken by the photographers Armstrong, Beere and Hime a few months before the domed centre section was demolished in 1857. It shows John Ewart's east wing in the foreground to be not as deep as the other wing, designed in 1844 by Henry Bowyer Lane, who was also responsible for the porticos on both wings and for the dome and loggia that dressed up an existing central section.

**4.50** Osgoode Hall, Court of Queen's Bench

**4.51** Osgoode Hall, landing of the stair in the east wing above the entrance hall (see 4.52). The glass dome projects into a hallway in the 'attic' above and draws its light from windows and skylights there.

**4.52** Osgoode Hall, the entrance hall in the east wing. A door on the left leads to the Benchers' dining-room.

4.53 Osgoode Hall, the west side of the gallery that surrounds the rotunda on the second floor

4.54 Osgoode Hall, the Great Staircase

4.54

**4.55** Osgoode Hall, the Great Library (1857–60), Cumberland and Storm, architects. This perspective drawing by W.G. Storm looks west. The impressive plaster work was done by the Toronto firm of Hynes Brothers. A portrait of Sir John Beverley Robinson rather than the pier glass shown here was placed over the fireplace.

**4.56** Osgoode Hall, view from upper rotunda. Scadding was so right when he wrote that this view reminded him of a Genoese palace. Sunlight from the roof and the sides adds a radiance to the interior and emphasizes the perspective of halls and staircases leading from it.

**4.57** Osgoode Hall, the Great Library, looking east towards a memorial of the First World War

enter the competition to design the additions to Osgoode Hall, for reasons rooted in Lane's special advantage.

In 1857 a major reconstruction took place in Osgoode Hall in which the central section was changed beyond all resemblance to the building of 1844. Cumberland and Storm were the architects, and few were more competent. Like their confrères in the rest of the English-speaking world, they were eclectics who could design in Gothic, Greek, or Roman as the mood indicated or the client demanded. Books of classical designs were available to them, and yet the design they produced for the centre has the same faults as its predecessor. It is true that the main cornice is continuous, but the band course and the base below ignore the wings, and the new windows are totally unrelated to the old. In short, the new centre is a frontispiece that seems to have been inserted without apology or acknowledgments of any kind to the graceful pavilions of 1829 or 1844.

Of the new front, this writer wrote in 1952 that 'the impression one gets of the centre part is French, against wings that are as British as St. Paul's Cathedral.'[16] Subsequently, Professor Henry Hitchcock confirmed that impression by showing views of Osgoode against the garden front of the palace at Versailles. The similarity of fenestration, the high parapet, and the urns silhouetted against the sky were quite striking.

Behind most of the new façade on the second floor is the Great Library. Thought of only as a room, it is one of the finest in Canada. Cumberland or Storm may have read in the copy of Britton's *Architectural Antiquities* in five volumes, which the architects borrowed from the society's library, of the so-called magic of the double cube room in the Queen's House at Greenwich and at Wilton. They went one better in proportions almost equal to a triple cube. The Great Library is 112 feet long by 40 feet wide and 40 feet to the top of the vaulted ceiling. Detail, generally, is classic, but the architects' catholic taste permitted them the luxury of a flamboyant fireplace of colossal scale and doubtful historic parentage. Two criticisms may be levelled against the library. As a reading room it takes the full glare of the sun, and as a library it was not designed to house books. Oak bookcases of a later period cut the great Corinthian pilasters off in their middles or their necks in a way that would horrify the Man of Taste.

Of the same date as the library are the ground-floor vestibule, stairs, and rotunda, all of which are so competently handled as to give the sense of space one would associate with a much larger building. Scadding was not exaggerating when he likened the interior to a Genoese Renaissance palace.

The traditional hall of the French (and Ottawa) courts of justice is the 'salle des pas perdus.' No footsteps are lost in the halls of Osgoode. A tile is used of unpleasant colour, pattern, texture, and design, and the visitor, awed by the ever present majesty of the law and the classical grandeur that surrounds him, is appalled by the noise he makes. It is rather like the cloppety-clop of the horses in Grofé's Grand Canyon Suite.

With all its faults, Osgoode Hall ranks highest, in the estimation of this

**4.58** Kearnsey House, 591 Yonge Street at Dundonald Street (1843; demolished 1904), John G. Howard, architect. Kearnsey was built by William Proudfoot, who retired in the 1830s from his business at King and Frederick streets, selling 'wines, groceries and dry goods, wholesale and retail,' but continued from 1835 to 1861 as president of the Bank of Upper Canada. Even from the photograph one gets the impression of a large house, but it had a drawing-room (75 feet by 25 feet) that has not been approached in size by any house in this century.

**4.59** Numbers 109 to 111 Elizabeth Street (demolished 1974). There can have been few cottages in Toronto with the classical pretensions of this one. The walls were a dazzling white, and the well-detailed windows and dormers a bright green. Equally pleasant was the play of light and shade under the eave. Was there always a store below?

**4.60** Store of George Keith and Son, 124 King Street East (1849; demolished 1968), John G. Howard, architect. In its later days the store was remarkable only for the very Greek detail of its doors, which could be seen when closed, and the name on the threshold of the original owner, Thomas D. Harris, an ironmonger. This was Harris's second store; his first was destroyed in the fire of 1849.

**4.61** Normal School and Model School, Gould Street, Cumberland and Ridout, architects. We will see Cumberland in his Greek mood later; we now see him thumbing through some history of architecture from Roman to Gothic, using both in the Normal School (1851–2; demolished 1963). An old photograph taken in the 1850s shows a building two storeys high, the fine Roman centrepiece crowned by a cupola in appropriate classical detail. Practice teaching took place in the Model Grammar School (1857; demolished 1963) on the left, under its own small cupola and lit by large south-facing windows.

**4.62** Normal School. Perhaps to show the architects' virtuosity, the auditorium was Gothic (with cast-iron arcading) from the beginning. In the fast-moving building program of Ryerson Polytechnical Institute, which took over the buildings in St James' Square, the beautiful little auditorium was razed in 1963 before public opinion could be roused. Today only a portion of the façade of the Normal School stands, something like a surrealist painting, with bricked-up rear and unglazed windows as a focal point on the campus.

**4.63** Normal School. In the remodelling of 1896 the heavy attic storey was added, the pediment raised, and the cupola converted into a fearsome thing – half classic, half Gothic.

**4.64** Toronto, Canada West, from the top of the jail (1854), by Edwin Whitfield. A nice Georgian town with an esplanade, and its waterfront as yet undefiled by railways or industry. Whitfield added spires to St James' and St Michael's cathedrals, seen on extreme left and right, even though both churches would have to wait several years before these steeples were built.

**4.65** William Cawthra house, northeast corner of Bay and King streets (1852–4; demolished 1946), Joseph Sheard, architect. The foundation of the Cawthra fortune was a frame store at the corner of King and Sherbourne streets. There in 1806 Joseph Cawthra advertised the contents of his apothecary's shop, which went far beyond the seemingly irrelevant articles in the modern drugstore. He had, he announced, a wide variety of patent medicines 'just arrived from New York' and, in addition, twenty thousand Whitechapel needles, forks, scissors, cognac, shoes, hats, and 'a few Bed-Ticks.' The house of his son William was one of the best examples in Toronto of Greek-revival architecture. When it was demolished to provide a site for the head office of the Bank of Nova Scotia, Anthony Adamson, the distinguished architectural historian who is descended from Joseph Cawthra, tried to have the stonework dismantled for re-erection somewhere else but was able to save only sundry fragments of columns and ornaments, which now stand as a 'ruin' in his Rosedale garden.

**4.66** County of York Court House, 57 Adelaide Street East (1851–2), Cumberland and Ridout, architects. Cumberland could turn his hand to a variety of historical styles, and this was one of his attempts at Greek. The front is austere, heavy, and forbidding, and not helped by the alteration of the wings that once supported the central mass. One thinks immediately of the suggested epitaph for Sir John Vanbrugh, the architect of Blenheim Palace – 'Lie heavy on him, Earth, he laid many a heavy load on thee.' The Arts and Letters Club of Toronto met for several years earlier in this century in the old assize courtroom. Certainly strange quarters for such a club, but there the members built the 'great fireplace,' and there in 1913 they entertained Sir Wilfrid Laurier. Many of Toronto's most distinguished citizens have belonged to this club, now located in St George's Hall on Elm Street (1891; Edwards and Webster, architects, with additions by Sproatt and Rolph).

**4.67** A view of Adelaide Street (south side), looking east from Toronto Street. On the right is the Wesleyan Methodist Church (1832; demolished 1870) at the corner of Adelaide and Toronto Streets. It was the predecessor of the Metropolitan Church at Shuter and Church streets. Adjoining the church is the County of York Court House (1851), showing the wings, which have been sold as separate properties and have gone their own ways, architecturally speaking.

writer, among the historic buildings still left to us in Toronto. It cannot be entirely sentiment or a sense of history that draws one to it, because strangers have admired it. Is it because Osgoode is something of an anachronism, a relic of a distant past reposing peacefully on its equally ancient lawns? Osgoode is already dominated physically by surrounding colossi, but it will never be dominated spiritually. We are left with the conclusion that Osgoode Hall has a personality sufficiently persuasive and powerful to overcome in the spectator any adverse conclusions he may have reached on solely architectural grounds. To submit to such a conclusion in defiance of aesthetic judgment is in the nature of a confession, especially for an architect, but this writer is prepared to accept it.

In none of its building periods does Osgoode show evidence of the eclecticism or the romanticism that, it was suggested, were characteristic of the period 1834–67. In the whole history of architecture, dates of political significance rarely coincide with the beginnings or the ends of movements in architecture, but in a general way, ours in Toronto do. We are examining the period when a quite shameless eclecticism was the order of the day and our most successful architects had two or three styles readily on tap. When in doubt, as Cumberland may have been on the Normal School (1851), it was considered evidence of his virtuosity rather than his lack of conviction that he provided a Roman exterior for a Gothic interior. This was an exciting period in nineteenth-century taste, with styles ranging all the way from Greek to late Gothic.

It was equally exciting politically in ways not always conducive to civic expansion. Toronto bore the brunt of the Rebellion of 1837 in Upper Canada, which culminated in the battle of Montgomery's tavern and the expulsion and exile of the city's first mayor, William Lyon Mackenzie. So serious a political upheaval must have caused many prospective builders to wait for better times, and three years later another blow was to affect the prestige of the city as the centre of government and to create an atmosphere of uncertainty that was to last for many years.

In both Upper and Lower Canada there had long been disaffection because of the presence in each of vested interests and the domination of the ruling officialdom – the so-called Family Compact in Upper Canada and the Château Clique in Lower Canada. In Upper Canada a principal source of irritation was the assumption by the Executive Council, and by John Strachan in particular, that the Clergy Reserves amounting to one-seventh of the lands granted in every township were the exclusive property of the Church of England. Whatever may have been the intention of the Act of 1791, which set aside these lands for the 'Protestant Clergy,' this term could by 1834, indeed long before, be taken to embrace more denominations than the so-called Established Church, and it was not unnatural that these outsiders should demand a share of so valuable a prize.

Lord Durham was sent by the British government to report on conditions in the country and to suggest ways of improvement. The result was the famous Durham Report, in which he recommended the union of the two

**4.68** Toronto General Hospital, Gerrard Street (1853–6; demolished 1922), William Hay, architect. The workmen had scarcely finished building the hospital when this Notman photograph was taken. It shows the large balconies where patients might enjoy fresh air or, depending on one's point of view, risk the menace to health that the *Upper Canada Journal* found in the 'miasmata' of the neighbouring Don. Later, several additions and a mantle of ivy would obscure Hay's picturesque composition.

**4.69** The Mechanics' Institute (on the left: 1853–5; demolished 1950), Cumberland and Storm, architects, and St James' Parochial School (1851; demolished 1904), Cumberland and Ridout, architects, at Church and Adelaide streets. The institute is better remembered as the first Toronto public library, opened in 1884. Externally, it was an undistinguished essay in the Renaissance manner. The parapet is fussy, and the juxtaposition of arches of varying diameters on the ground floor was anything but a happy arrangement. The parochial school ceased to operate in the 1870s and the building was then the home of the Protestant Episcopal Divinity School, which later became Wycliffe College and relocated in Queen's Park.

provinces at once, the ultimate union of all British North America, and the granting of full self-government in domestic affairs. The union of the two provinces was achieved by the Act of Union (1840), and so it was that in 1841 Upper and Lower Canada became the Province of Canada under a governor-in-chief in the person of Lord Sydenham.

With tempers still high in both the old capitals, a new centre of government had to be found on neutral ground, reasonably remote from both Toronto and Quebec, and Kingston was the choice. Lord Sydenham wrote: 'Toronto is too far off, and exposed to many moral inconveniences.' But Kingston was found to be small and consequently inconvenient for the purposes of government. By 1844 we find the capital in Montreal, which was equally central and could provide all the amenities of a metropolis of forty-four thousand people. The political climate, however, was such as to make it an uneasy seat for the legislature of the United Provinces, and in a few years it was to prove untenable as a capital.

In 1849 the Parliament of Canada passed by a large majority what was known as the Rebellion Losses Bill, which made broad provisions for compensating citizens of Lower Canada for losses incurred during the rebellion of a decade earlier. A cry was easily raised by the Conservative minority that this was to reward rebellion. An angry mob burned the Parliament buildings, and Her Majesty's representative, the governor-in-chief, Lord Elgin, was actually stoned as he fled in his carriage. His offence in their eyes was that he gave the royal assent to the bill, although he had done so on the ground that in domestic affairs the Canadian Parliament must be supreme. In September of the same year Montreal ceased to be the capital of the United Provinces.

The union was clearly not a solution to the political problems of the two provinces, but in so far as the capital was concerned, a modus vivendi was established after 1849 by which the seat of government alternated between Toronto and Quebec.[17]

When one thinks of the sensitivity of the building industry to the faintest of political breezes in the present century, one cannot help but marvel at the courage of Toronto investors between the incorporation of the city and federation in 1867. Many of our most important public buildings were erected in that period, and fewer of comparable significance were built from 1867 to 1900 except the third City Hall and the legislative buildings. The years that saw the greatest activity in construction were those between 1852 and 1857, when money was 'poured out like water upon the building of the Grand Trunk and Great Western Lines.' This was 'a period of speculative mania which sent governments, municipalities and corporations into a wild rivalry of expenditure and extravagance.'[18] In the decade following 1852, railway mileage increased from 12 to 1,974 miles.

Further prosperity came about through a reciprocity treaty that Canada negotiated with the United States in 1854. The treaty gave Canadian natural products free entry into the American market. For both provinces this was a boon that reached its peak during the Civil War of 1861. The treaty was terminated by the United States in 1865, but during the decade in which it was in force, trade between the two countries was both extensive and profitable for Canada.

The same period saw the rise of our banking institutions and the fall of several. The competition for business that had previously been waged between the Bank of Upper Canada and the Bank of Montreal as far back as 1822 was intensified by the arrival on the Toronto scene of other banks all anxious to share in the general prosperity. Competition between Toronto and Montreal was never so keen both for business in general and for government business in particular. Before Confederation there were in all eleven banks established with a Toronto head office: the Bank of Upper Canada (1821), the Home District Savings Bank (1830), the Agricultural Bank (1834), the Farmers' Joint Stock Banking Co (1835), the Bank of the People (1835), the Toronto Savings Bank (1854), the Bank of Toronto (1855), the Colonial Bank of Canada (1858), the International Bank (1858), the Royal Canadian Bank (1864), and the Canadian Bank of Commerce (1866). In addition, there were at least nine banks with head offices elsewhere that operated branches in the city in this period.

A feeling of security brought about by unprecedented prosperous conditions in the business community permitted money to go into many civic improvements, and some of our best buildings date from this time. St Lawrence Hall (1849), St James' Cathedral (1850), the Normal and Model Schools (1851), Trinity College (1851), the seventh Post Office (1851), the Toronto Exchange (1855), University College (1856), St Paul's, Bloor Street (1858), and Yorkville Town Hall (1859) all belong to this period, and all but four still stand.

St Lawrence Hall and Market was an ambitious project combining a hall for public gathering with a frontage on King Street and a covered market extending for two hundred feet to Front Street at the rear. The first City Hall had served its purpose and had disappeared in the great fire of 1849, which destroyed much of the old town. The new buildings covered the site of the former municipal seat and assembly hall, as well as that of the old market buildings, most of which were untouched by the fire but were demolished the following year.

The ravages of this famous fire of 1849 may detain us for a moment. It destroyed from ten to fifteen acres of domestic and commercial building in an old and densely populated section of the city. It started in some frame buildings, including stables off George Street, and before it was extinguished by the combined efforts of a poorly equipped fire department and a 'smart' shower, had covered an area bounded by George and Church, King and Adelaide. At its height the flames could be seen from St Catharines. Apart from houses, the following buildings were destroyed: St James' Cathedral, the old City Hall and its wings facing King Street, the offices of two leading newspapers, the *Toronto Mirror* and the *Patriot*, and several stores, taverns,

**4.70** Wellington Street East opposite Berczy Park, looking east, photographed by Armstrong, Beere and Hime, 1857. The Toronto Exchange is in the centre. Beyond it, across Leader Lane, is Hutchison and Company's building, which survives today as the home of several of the city's better restaurants. In the distance can be seen the gable of the Ontario House (3.21, 22) at Wellington and Church streets.

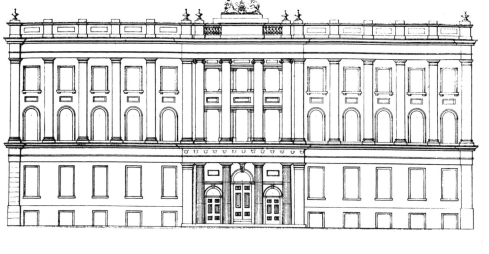

4.71

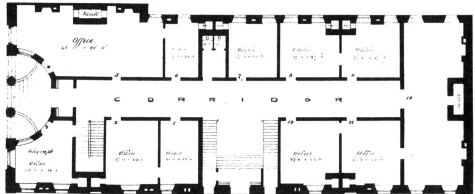

4.72

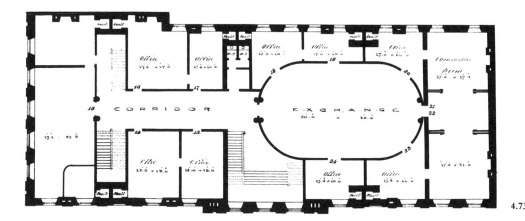

4.73

**4.71, 72, 73** The Toronto Exchange, at the corner of Wellington Street and Leader Lane (1854–6; demolished 1941), James Grand, architect. This was a fine classical building with an equally distinguished plan. The east elevation is shown in 4.71, the ground floor in 4.72, and the second floor in 4.73. The Toronto Board of Trade was located here until it moved into its new building at Front and Yonge streets in 1891.

**4.74** St Patrick's Market, 234–40 Queen Street West (1854; demolished 1912), Thomas Young, architect. In 1836 D'Arcy Boulton, Jr, presented the city with property on Queen Street, with a depth to a lane of 123 feet, on condition that the city build a market and that it be maintained as such forever. The gift was accepted and a frame market erected. Later it was replaced by this building, which, although small, had a powerful Vanbrugh-like scale.

**4.75, 76, 77** St Basil's Church and St Michael's College, St Joseph Street (1855–6), William Hay, architect. A comparison of the original plan (4.75) and the photograph of the actual buildings (4.76) shows many points of departure. The promise of the original plan with its beautiful cloister and court was not realized. It faded even further with the demolition in 1971 of the wing along Bay Street, visible on the right of the photograph. Hay was a versatile architect who designed such different buildings as Yorkville Town Hall (4.114) and the old General Hospital (4.68). Since he did both church and college, it is difficult to explain or excuse the crudity of the junction between the two. The church has, however, a delicately detailed interior of great beauty (4.77).

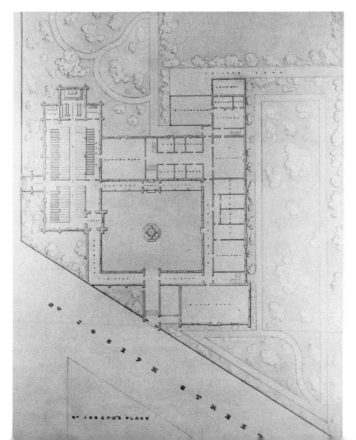

4.76

4.77

**4.78** St Lawrence Hall, decorative swags. Theatrical masks alternate with the Prince of Wales feathers, swords, and bugles in stone, all carved by John Cochrane and his two brothers. When the Cochranes emigrated from Scotland in May 1845, the Perthshire *Consitutional* regretted their need to leave to find work, but said 'Their works will preserve their memory among the citizens of Perth.'

**4.79** A ball in St Lawrence Hall, 1862, in honour of the governor-general, Lord Monck, and Lady Monck

**4.80** St Lawrence Hall, King and Jarvis streets (1849–50), William Thomas, architect. This old photograph shows the hall before its sad decline in the later nineteenth century. Lyman Brothers, druggists, occupied the ground floor in the west wing, while the Toronto Tea Company was located in the east wing. In 1967 the hall enjoyed a major, and deserved, restoration costing nearly two million dollars, paid for by government and private supporters. The building is the home of the National Ballet of Canada, and the Great Hall remains a centre for banquets, lectures, political meetings, and celebrations, just as it was in the nineteenth century.

**4.81** The south end of the Farmers' Market behind St Lawrence Hall, as it was in 1888. St James' is in the distance.

and warehouses. Tin roofs were common in Toronto at the time, but many had wood shingles, one of which, as a flaming torch, ignited some wood-work on the cathedral tower.[19]

A brief list of social events and lectures for which the St Lawrence Hall was a centre in its heyday reads very much like a month of entertainments in Toronto today. On the musical side we hear of the Toronto Philharmonic Society, the Toronto Vocal Musical Society, and the Metropolitan Choral Society. In 1857 citizens heard Handel's *Messiah* in Toronto for the first time. Jenny Lind, 'the Swedish nightingale,' sang before a crowded house (tickets one price, three dollars) in 1851, and over the years the hall echoed to the voices of the great in their generation: Mme Patti came more than once. In his *Recollections and Records* W.H. Pearson tells of being present at Miss Lind's great concert in 1851. Tickets were sold by Nordheimer's, and the crowd was so great that the store was barricaded and protected by the police. It came as a surprise to Pearson to hear Miss Lind sing 'Coming through the Rye' with a slightly foreign accent. On a number of occasions anti-slavery meetings were held, and twice citizens were able to see '*Uncle Tom's Cabin* – a panorama.' Sir John A. Macdonald and the Honourable George Brown could always fill the hall, and, not surprising in a Toronto audience, so could G.W. Stone on 'Electro Biology,' or Professor Daniel Wilson, who spoke on 'Primitive Sources of Historic Truth.' The latter was unable to finish, and everyone returned a week later.

Toronto is equally well known for the immediate response of its citizens to charities, especially in emergency. In 1868 a ball was held to raise funds for distressed fishermen in Nova Scotia, and a Christmas dinner in the same year was given in the hall to 'the boys and girls of the Protestant Home and to the little arabs of the streets.' The Dominion of Canada was one year old.

St Lawrence Hall ranks among the finest of our nineteenth-century build-ings. Its story is well known from the time of its building in 1849–50 to the present. Not so familiar is the fact that William Thomas had proposed a similar or identical design in 1845 for a building to replace the first City Hall as soon as the second City Hall was completed. Cutbacks in spending, however, were the likely cause of a delay in construction until the great fire levelled the first City Hall, when the insurance settlement was available to help build Thomas's design. Architecturally, the hall is in the true Renais-sance tradition. The front is stone, and the iron balconies, of exquisite design, are cast. Rare, indeed, in Ontario is the fine carving on stone that in St Lawrence Hall is to be seen in Corinthian capitals, swags, and sculptured heads. These are the work of John Cochrane and his two brothers, who emigrated in 1845 from Scotland to Toronto. Sad to relate, John died pre-maturely, only a few weeks after St Lawrence Hall was completed.

In 1967, to mark Canada's centennial, restoration of the building was undertaken. The auditorium that saw gay balls and was familiar with the voices of Sir John A. Macdonald and Mme Patti and the music of Haydn and Handel once again sounded to concerts and assemblies. In addition, the building has become the home of the National Ballet of Canada. Today the social and cultural activities that take place in St Lawrence Hall are a vibrant and authentic echo of the York Town Hall, later the first City Hall, that once stood on the same site.

Even the most casual reader of the history of Upper Canada since Governor Simcoe will appreciate the influence of Englishmen (predominantly graduates of Cambridge University) in the social fabric and the government of the province. It was because of their influence in the community that King's College was built, and it was doubtless their unanimous wish (it was a regulation) that Unitarians and Jews be debarred from membership on the faculty or the governing council. Bishop Strachan was its president. As the population increased and its character changed, it was inevitable that politicians and citizens should ask why education at its highest level was dominated by one denomination to the exclusion of all others, especially as the institution was maintained by public money.

On 30 May 1849 the end came. By an act of the provincial legislature, in which the university was remodelled under the style, no longer of King's College but of the University of Toronto, it was enacted 'that there shall be no Faculty of Divinity in the said university, nor shall there be any professorship, lectureship or teachership in the same.' As John Ross Robertson noted, 'The remodelled university was to be an absolutely secular institution. So it became, and so it has remained ever since.'

Bishop Strachan was in his seventy-second year, and would seem to have met defeat for the first time. 'Deprived of the university, what is the church to do? She has now no seminary in which to give a liberal education to her youth.' Elsewhere, he referred to the 'destruction of the University ... a calamity not easy to bear.' Nothing daunted, he decided to go to England carrying with him a petition to the queen praying that Her Majesty would 'be graciously pleased to grant a Royal charter for the incorporation of an university, to be established on this clear and unequivocal principle': adherence to the Church of England.[20]

On Wednesday, 10 April 1850, Bishop Strachan left Toronto for England on the steamboat *America* carrying with him a petition with 11,731 signatures. While there he was given a sympathetic ear by all those most likely to support him in his mission. Lord Grey, the secretary for the Colonies, Sir Robert Peel, the prime minister, and the duke of Wellington all promised that his 'arguments in favour of a Royal charter would receive every consideration.' However, not unaware of the situation in Upper Canada, the imperial authorities deemed it 'impolitic for the time being' to grant the request, although two years later they did so.

In the absence of the bishop and with confident expectation of the success of his mission, Anglican churchmen from all of Upper Canada gathered in Toronto to raise money for the project, the new university with a faculty

**4.82** Trinity College, south front facing Queen Street West (1851–2; demolished 1956), Kivas Tully, architect. A drawing of Tully's original proposal exhibited at the Paris Universal Exhibition of 1855 showed a wing on the west, never carried out, that was as long and ornate as the front. Presumably the intention was to create a quadrangle. It remained a source of regret to the architect throughout his life that, for reasons of cost, the building stood on a terrace surrounded by a grass embankment, visible in this photograph of circa 1857, instead of a stone parapet wall.

**4.83** Trinity College, the entrance gateway on Queen Street (1903), Darling and Pearson, architects

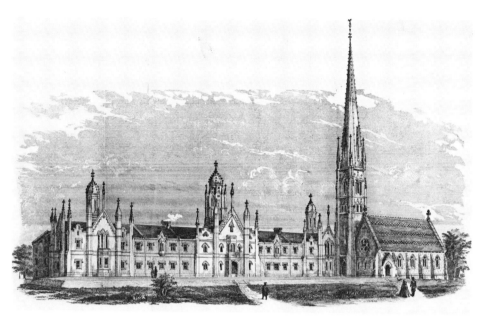

**4.84** Trinity College, the chapel as proposed by William Hay in 1858. Over twenty-five years later, in 1883, a chapel finally was built, but Frank Darling was the architect.

**4.85** The seventh Post Office, Toronto Street (1851–3), Cumberland and Ridout, architects. In this century the building was occupied for a time by the Bank of Canada and, more recently, by its present owners, the Argus Corporation, who probably saved it from the wreckers. It was said in the contemporary press to be modelled after the Temple of Minerva.

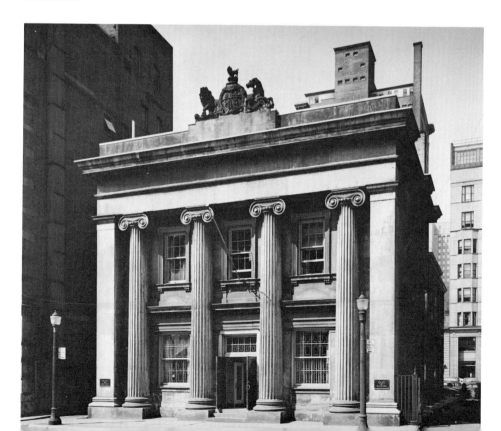

4.88

4.89

**4.86** St James' Cathedral, King Street East at Church (1850–2), Cumberland and Ridout, architects. In the custom of the time the cathedral was the subject of an architectural competition that attracted entries from eleven architects in Canada and the United States. The winning design was that of Frederic Cumberland, who by the time construction was underway was in partnership with Thomas Ridout. This early photograph, likely taken before 1860, shows that the monies available had been exhausted before the tower or a decent fence could be built.

**4.87** Another old photograph of St James', showing the triforium or gallery (since removed) and a column of free pews down the centre aisle

4.86                                    4.87

**4.88** St James', a noble Gothic edifice, in its full glory about 1905. The spire was completed in 1873 to plans by Henry Langley. Its clock was paid for by public subscription and is maintained by the city. It is disturbing that the pinnacles on the buttresses around the apse have been removed within the last few years. In the background can be seen the crowning cupola on St Lawrence Hall, which also contains a public clock.

**4.89** St James' Cathedral, the nave

of Divinity and a charter in the best tradition of Anglican education.

Money was forthcoming in cash, land, and bequests, the largest being a bequest from Dr Burnside of $24,000. In 1851 a small competition was held to choose the best designs for a building that was to be the first stage of Trinity College, to cost not more than $32,000. The two contestants were Kivas Tully and the firm of Cumberland and Ridout. We have no record of the jury of selection, but they did well to choose Kivas Tully. It must have been no little satisfaction to the jury and the university that the construction tender of Messrs Metcalfe, Wilson, and Forbes was for $31,380! But governing bodies change over the years, and a later council seems to have felt under no obligation to Tully. Frank Darling was appointed architect to the fabric, and it was under his direction that the Convocation Hall (1876), chapel (1883), and the west and east wings (1889 and 1894) were added. Long before Darling, in fact in 1858, another architect appears on the scene – let us hope with the best of reasons and on the most ethical grounds! He was William Hay, whom we shall later meet as the author of the Yorkville Town Hall. He prepared a sketch of a completed Trinity, with particular emphasis on a chapel in a style some centuries earlier than Tully's Gothic. It was not built, but one cannot help feeling sorry for Tully, who lived to see his brain-child developed by others. He died in 1905. At the same time, the wonder is that the original Trinity College seemed to be all of a piece, without, as we remember it, a single discordant note.

When the college moved to its present location on Hoskin Avenue, its governing body showed singular lack of imagination in demanding of Darling and Pearson that the new building be a replica of the old, but in stone. Tragic, in a different sense, was the decision of the city to demolish the old building, on Queen Street West at the head of Strachan Avenue, in 1956. The college grounds are still there, but vulnerable for building purposes, like all parks in Toronto.

Scadding has little to say of the 'University of Trinity College' but much of interest regarding the property. The college grounds occupied the lower part of one of the original park lots, which was called Gore Vale in honour of the lieutenant-governor of that name. 'Vale denoted the ravine which indented a portion of the lot through whose meadow-land meandered a pleasant little stream. [The University's] brooklet will hereafter be famous in scholastic song. It will be regarded as the Cephissus of a Canadian Academus, the Cherwell of an infant Christ Church.'[21] Where the brook crossed Queen Street by a steep mound, a blockhouse once commanded the western approaches to York, and a well-trodden path led to it across the common from the garrison. Scadding in his day saw many changes, but he would hardly have believed that, in fewer than a hundred years since he wrote (1873), the college would be razed, the mound made low, and the vale exalted. His Cephissus no longer meanders, but runs in a common sewer into Lake Ontario.

One of the most interesting buildings left to us of the nineteenth century, the seventh Post Office, was built in the exciting decade 1850–60. It was exactly contemporary with St James' and was designed by the same architects. By a curious coincidence, the very different functional requirements of the post office, the branch bank, and the inn produced the same façade and a marked similarity of plan. The side door on the main front usually indicated the business entrance to the bank or post office (or the bar in the case of the inn), while the more generous central entrance was reserved for manager or postmaster and family, who lived above. In the seventh Post Office, living quarters above were reached by a side door in the lane to the south, an exception to the usual rule.

This very striking little temple on Toronto Street was designed by Cumberland and Ridout in 1851. It was by a happy chance that in 1959 a group of businessmen who could afford the luxury of lowness in a skyscraper age were able to save it from the wrecker. The interior has been completely changed, but we know something of the old ground floor. 'The large public hall, with enriched oak and plate-glass letter-box, had three compartments, intersected by Doric columns, with delivery windows and a separate entrance for ladies. The building, which cost £3,500, reflected credit upon its architects, and also upon the contractors.'[22]

To round out the story of the post offices, there was the eighth, which once sat so proudly at the top of Toronto Street, by all odds the finest street in Toronto. It had all the charm of a street in some capital city in Europe. People unknowingly sensed its quality – businessmen were unhurried; motor cars hardly exceeded the pace of the carriages of half a century ago, and the buildings on both sides of the street had about them that dignified venerability that commands immediate respect. Today Toronto Street is 'the street that died,' and the eighth Post Office has been replaced by a federal building that ignores the axis of the street.

The courage and energy that had been characteristic of the people of St James' in previous catastrophes were again manifest after the total destruction of the cathedral in 1849. Never, however, had the congregation been so divided as to the form the building should take or even where it should be placed. Among the various schools of thought was that represented by the dean himself, Dr Grasett, who would sell off the King Street frontage for commercial purposes and build the cathedral on Adelaide Street. Another faction was quite happy to augment the insurance money sufficiently to build a parish church and hall on the foundation of the old cathedral.

By June 1849 the Adelaide Street group was sufficiently strong in the vestry to authorize an international competition for a new cathedral. John G. Howard drew up the conditions that named the jury of award, Messrs Howard, John Johnston, and Thomas Young, and offered prizes of seventy-five, fifty, and twenty-five pounds. About seven weeks later the competition was over; Frederic Cumberland was placed first, John Ostell of Montreal second, and Kivas Tully third.

By that time it was common knowledge that a majority of the vestry had

**4.90** The Rossin House, later the Prince George, southeast corner of King and York streets (1855–7; burned 1862; rebuilt 1865; demolished 1969), Kauffman and Bissell, architects. Apart from the sheer size of this hotel (it had 252 bedrooms, not all of which were finished at first), its design was notably innovative. A reinforcing grid of walls and chimney stacks permitted the masonry to be less massive, and for the first time in a Toronto building, much use was made of iron. When critics branded the structure 'a mere shell; very little better, in point of strength, than a house of pasteboard,' John G. Howard came to its defence. The real proof of its stability came, however, in November 1862, when the building burned and the walls stood unbraced for two winters of the three that passed before rebuilding began.

**4.91** From the roof of the Rossin House (see 4.90), looking north, one of thirteen views forming a panorama taken in early 1857. In this remarkable photograph small wooden cottages on Boulton (now Pearl) Street in the foreground contrast with the magnificence of Ritchey's Terrace on Adelaide Street. The *Globe* said that these latter houses, put up by John Ritchey in 1855, were probably the best ever built in a row in the city. Those on the ends differed from the rest in being red rather than the fashionable 'white' brick. Sir Allan MacNab, then premier of Canada, who was required to live in Toronto during 1855–6, leased one house in Ritchey's Terrace for himself and a second for his daughter and her new husband, Viscount Bury. Visible in the background is the east wing of Osgoode Hall.

**4.92** Houses for J. Lukin Robinson, Front and Windsor streets (1855; demolished), Cumberland and Storm, architects. During a development boom in the mid-1850s Robinson opened Windsor Street between Front and Wellington. This terrace of substantial houses on the west side of the street was matched by an identical row on the other side, recalling the tasteful elegance of a London square. Unfortunately, Robinson's plan faltered when the nearby railways altered the character of the neighbourhood and it became an industrial area.

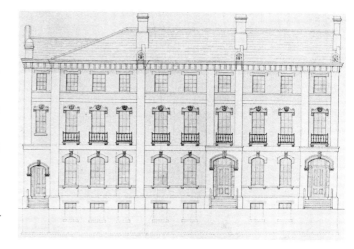

**4.93** Sword's Hotel, Front Street between Bay and York. In 1844 Knox College occupied the new terrace of four houses, built for Captain Thomas Dick, a prosperous steamboat owner. When Knox moved eleven years later, the building became Sword's Hotel. In 1862 Captain Dick took over management of the hotel himself, renaming it the Queen's. Major improvements were made throughout the century by a number of architects. Until the Queen's was demolished in 1927 for the construction of the Royal York, it was renowned for its distinguished clientele, its elegance, and its excellent cuisine.

**4.94** Masonic Hall, later the Canada Permanent Building, on the west side of Toronto Street (1856–7; demolished 1962), Kauffman and Bissell, architects. A huge building in its day, it dwarfed the seventh Post Office to the south. The design was rather hard Gothic and might lead one to think the walls were iron. Actually they were not, but the ground-floor front was cast in Charles Vale's Atlas Foundry, as were the window sashes and inside shutters. This must represent a very early use of the metal window in North America. Originally, there were four shops on the ground floor.

**4.95** Chapel of St James-the-Less, St. James' Cemetery, Parliament Street (1860–1), Cumberland and Storm, architects. This is Gothic revival at its best, in a setting worthy of the building. The material covering the spire today is the only jarring note in an otherwise harmonious composition. In 1844 John G. Howard laid out the cemetery, which is of considerable historic interest as the burial place of such Toronto citizens as Dr Alexander Burnside, Dr Henry Scadding, William Thomas, and Frederic Cumberland. The various stages in the development of architecture in the nineteenth century can be read in the form and lettering of the headstones, which are made from materials ranging from sandstone to cast iron. Colonel Sir Casimir Gzowski is interred in a vault in the style of a minor temple on the Nile.

**4.96** St Stephen's-in-the-Fields, at the corner of College and Bellevue (1858; burned 1865; rebuilt), Thomas Fuller, architect; Gundry and Langley, architects for rebuilding. St Stephen's was the gift, both of site and structure, of Colonel R.B. Denison, the owner of nearby Bellevue. Bishop Strachan laid the foundation stone 'with an offering of corn, wine and oil.' Fuller's church had a brief life of seven years, but the fire that destroyed it left the walls relatively stable. With a break in its history of only one year, during which the congregation met in the house of Frederic Cumberland, the rebuilding was complete in 1866.

**4.97** The second St Paul's Church, Bloor Street East (1858–60), George K. and Edward Radford, architects. This commission was won in competition and is the only major work of the Radford brothers during their time in Toronto in the second half of the 1850s. Later, from 1874 to 1892, George would become the partner of the well-known New York architect Calvert Vaux. Dwarfed though it is, old St Paul's is a charming little Gothic church that would be a matter of pride in any English village. It has no equal among Toronto churches of the nineteenth century unless it be St James-the-Less by Cumberland and Storm on Parliament Street. Happily, enlargements to St Paul's in 1890 by Gordon and Helliwell and in 1903 to designs by E.J. Lennox respected the spirit of the original structure.

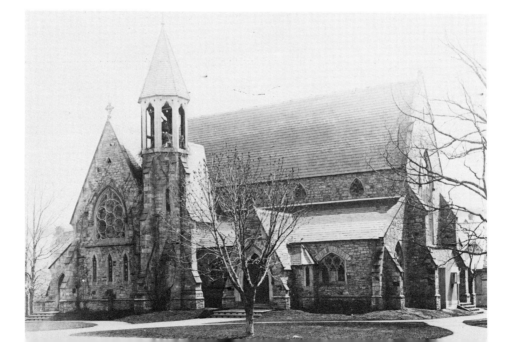

voted for the north or Adelaide end of the site and the leasing of 238 feet on King Street east of Church. The citizens of Toronto became aroused. A meeting of protest was held in the City Hall, and a resolution was passed against leasing the land. There can be few comparable examples of public interference with church government, particularly where a cathedral was involved, and a flurry of vestry meetings followed. Out of it all emerged a resolution rescinding all previous decisions involving the leasing of land but confirming Cumberland's appointment as architect.

At first his instructions were to build on the old foundations, which were close to Church Street, but these in turn were rescinded in favour of a motion putting the cathedral in the centre of the property. This was regarded by some as a cunning scheme to prevent the sale of land at all points of the compass and gives us an idea of the distrust that still existed of the powerful faction that favoured the Adelaide site.

It was not until 1 July 1850, nearly fifteen months after the fire, that the way was cleared for reconstruction to begin.[23] Only five thousand pounds remained of the insurance money when all bills had been paid, but five thousand additional was raised through the sale of pew subscriptions and other sources, and with this sum Cumberland agreed to design a 'usable' but not a completed cathedral. Our Gothic churches had one thing in common with the perpendicular medieval churches of England, and that was a picturesque skyline broken whenever possible by pinnacles and finials. In respect of these St James' was a shorn lamb until 1873–4, when the tower and spire, the transepts, and the pinnacles and finials were all completed. The church clock, the gift of the people of Toronto of all denominations, was installed in 1875 and is still maintained by the city.

An old photograph (4.87) shows the nave before the removal of the triforium or gallery. Such an arrangement provided many more pews, which in St James' were a source of revenue even in the first church.[24] Several unusual features will be noticed in the photograph. The pews in the foreground are of a puritanical severity, with board seat and a rail at shoulder-blade level. Contrary to what one would expect, only the Presbyterians, with their padded pews, showed any regard for comfort in the churches of Upper Canada. An unusual sight today in the photograph is the central row of pews of chesterfield size with an aisle on each side. Unusual also is the placing of the organ pipes at the main, south entrance to the cathedral instead of the more common location in the chancel above the organist and choir. (In the cathedral of today, some pipes are in the chancel.) The Church of England was never as particular as the Church of Rome in the matter of orientation, that of placing the church on an east-west axis with the altar at the east end. St James' breaks all the rules by being on the north-south axis with the sanctuary in what Robertson calls 'the least ecclesiastical of all points of the compass,' a location that in medieval times was considered 'the residence of Satan himself.' It should be noted that the orientation of St James' was set by the building committee.

For those who, in the manner of Sacheverell Sitwell, like to explore old churches, St James' has much to offer. A famous bishop, Dr John Strachan, and a great dean, Dr Grasett, are buried in the chancel. Gathered from the graveyard that once adjoined the cathedral are headstones in English and Latin going back many years. In the south porch is one of the best from the point of view of design and beauty of lettering, that of the Honourable Thomas Ridout, the surveyor-general (1829), and adjoining, one of the most tragic, that of his son John Ridout, who served as a midshipman in the provincial navy and on discharge 'commenced with ardour the study of law, and with the fairest prospects, but a Blight came' and he died on the morning of 12 July 1817. The 'blight' was a duel with pistols fought near Yonge and Grosvenor between young Ridout and his former friend Samuel P. Jarvis.

Tragic, too, was the end of that William Butcher of Walpole in Sussex whose stone is also in the south porch: 'whilst actively engaged in making a scaffold for the spire [he] was precipitated from a height of seventy feet ... and was taken up dead, October 31st, 1839. Aged 27 years.' Butcher was engaged on that wooden spire on the third St James' that became a torch in the great fire of 1849.

Rather unique among the gravestones of Upper Canada is that of the Such family in Latin and Greek, now in the east porch. The inscription is too long to translate here, but a line like 'fuit (o vox lugenda) fuit!' immediately seems to call for the English equivalent. 'He was, oh grievous word, he was!' sounds so much less of a lament than the original. And then there was Mary Remington Such, that 'Puellula rarissimae formae.' The date is MDCCCXXXII. The family of Such came from Rookery Hall, St Mary Cray, in Kent.

Inside the cathedral, memorial stones and brasses are all of historic interest, and quite a few represent a high standard of design and workmanship. The writer admired for many years the one erected by the officers of the Toronto garrison in memory of Colonel Sir Casimir Gzowski KCMG (1813-98), aide-de-camp to the queen. It is in brass on the east wall of the nave.

St James' Cathedral is built of Ohio stone and brick – that curious Toronto brick that starts life as a rather bright yellow and enters old age as grey as the most venerable inhabitant. The cathedral's predecessor, St James' Church of 1831, had been constructed with blocks of Kingston limestone. With other limestones from the Niagara escarpment at Hamilton, Thorold, or Queenston, it was used for the better class of buildings in Toronto until the late 1840s. Some structures combined both, like King's College of 1842, where the foundations were of Kingston stone, while the material for the walls came from Hamilton.

Ohio stone was imported into the province as early as 1845 to rebuild much of the core of the town of London after it had been levelled by fire. Two years later John Worthington of Toronto opened the first quarries in Ohio for Buff Amherst and Berea sandstones. These were worked easily,

**4.98** University College. This bird's-eye drawing, exceptional in the history of Toronto architecture during the 1850s, shows off the buildings, and particularly their patterned slate roofs, to great advantage. The gloominess of the north-facing quadrangle, as it is known, following Oxford custom rather than that of Cambridge, where it would be called a court, has been compounded at times by the planting of trees.

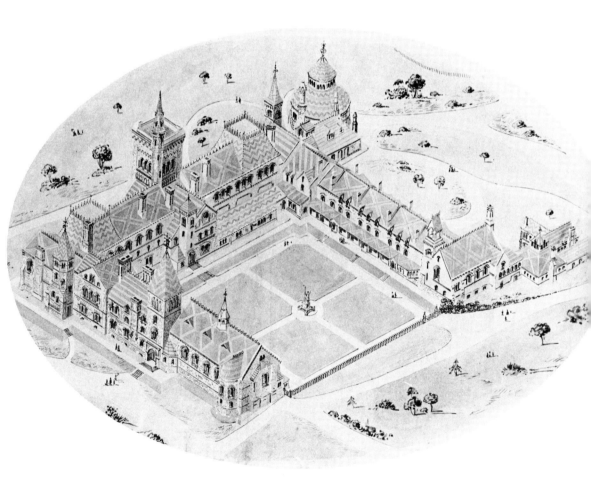

**4.99** University College, University of Toronto (1856–9; burned 1890; rebuilt), Cumberland and Storm, architects. This view, which was William G. Storm's diploma piece when he became a founding member of the Royal Canadian Academy in 1880, points to the major role he had in the design of the building. It shows also a portion of the beautiful grounds laid out by Edwin Taylor, a pupil of Sir Joseph Paxton, to create an appropriate setting for the building and for true learning.

**4.100** The Oxford Museum, Oxford, England (1854), Deane and Woodward, architects. Undoubtedly this building influenced Cumberland and Storm's designs for University College.

**4.101** University College, south façade as restored by David B. Dick after the 1890 fire. Only the western part, seen here to the left of the tree, was untouched by the conflagration.

**4.102** The stonecutters for University College stand outside the architects' office, the sign on which stated that there should be 'No Admittance Except Business.' The office was entered through the doorway seen at the foot of the smaller tower on the left side of 4.101.

4.103 University College, a window in the south wall, photographed by Dean Ellis in 1889

4.104 University College, the main entrance, photographed by Dean Ellis in 1889: still today one of the most photographed pieces of architecture in Toronto. The iron gates at the entrance are hardly visible, but they, like the ornamental strap hinges on all doors, are of the finest craftsmanship.

4.105 University College, the cloisters in the quadrangle

**4.106** University College, a newel in the east staircase

**4.107** University College, the atrium

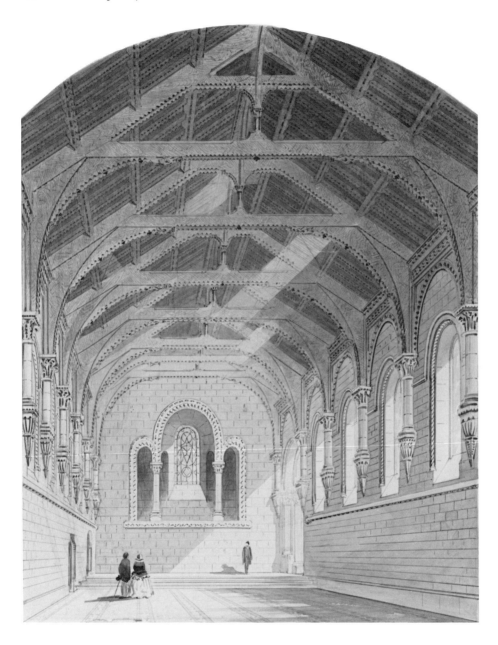

**4.108** Convocation Hall at University College, seen here in a masterful 1850s perspective view by the architects, was at the north end of the east wing of University College before the fire. In the 1890 restoration a number of smaller rooms were built here.

came in a variety of warm colours, and could be shipped conveniently by water. They soon replaced the native limestones for building and were used extensively in St Lawrence Hall, the seventh Post Office, and the County of York Magistrates' Court House. Sometimes, as in St James' Cathedral, only the window surrounds, cornices, and carved portions were of Ohio stone. The foundations and walls were other materials, such as pressed brick from the Yorkville works opened just in time to supply the contractors for the Rossin House hotel (1855) or the rough-faced Georgetown stone from which University College (1856) is built.

John Worthington was a remarkable individual who began his career in Canada as a mason on the construction of the Kingston City Hall. Scarcely a dozen years later he was the largest contractor in Toronto, employing 350 men during the building season. Besides his Ohio quarries he developed lime works at Limehouse, near Georgetown, and was Frederic Cumberland's partner in the Toronto Patent Pressed Brick Company. With his brother James he was awarded the contract to build University College from plans provided by Cumberland and his partner, William George Storm.

One has only to look at any part of University College to say of the architect with Scadding, 'here was a man after the heart of Wykeham and Wayneflete.' Even a person with a taste so eclectic as was Frederic Cumberland's must have had some architectural manner in which he enjoyed working more than another, and in the entrance hall to University College one feels he was not only enjoying himself; he was revelling in it. From the beginning he had his difficulties, not so much with his client, the vice-chancellor, as with the governor-general, Sir Edmund Head.

Before preparing the design, and with the support of the university authorities, Cumberland had visited England at a rather momentous time in the history of the Gothic revival. The most important building in England in 1856 was the Oxford Museum. The architect was Woodward, but Ruskin became interested and hoped to get the whole Pre-Raphaelite brotherhood to work on carving. 'I hope to be able to get Millais and Rossetti to design flower and beast borders – crocodiles and various vermin.' Cumberland knew Ruskin, and there is every reason to believe that he was profoundly affected by what he saw and heard at Oxford. The silhouette of the college is markedly similar to that of the museum – even to the chemistry department, isolated in a chapter house because of its odours and its intrusion on a building sacred to the humanities.

Having absorbed all that he could from Oxford and burning with a zeal for the architecture of the Middle Ages, second only, we can imagine, to that of Ruskin, the high priest himself, Cumberland prepared a scheme for University College in Toronto. Our knowledge of its fate comes from a letter of the vice-chancellor of the university, John Langton (father of W.A. Langton, the architect), who wrote to his brother in England:

The site being chosen, Cumberland drew a first sketch of a Gothic building, but the Governor would not hear of Gothic and recommended Italian, shewing us an example of the style, a palazzo at Siena, which if he were not governor-general and had written a book on art, I should have called one of the ugliest buildings I ever saw. However, after a week's absence the Governor came back with a new idea, it was to be Byzantine; and between them they concocted a most hideous elevation. After this the Governor was absent on a tour for several weeks, during which we polished away almost all traces of Byzantine and got a hybrid with some features of Norman, of early English, etc., with faint traces of Byzantium and the Italian palazzo, but altogether a not unsightly building, and on his return His Excellency approved.[25]

Vice-Chancellor Langton took upon himself the responsibility of dealing with the architect and the governor-general with as little consultation with Dr McCaul, the principal, as possible. He did not trust McCaul and had nobody to back him up 'except the professors who from hatred of McCaul stick to me like bricks but without much power.' In a later letter we find the trusted professors adding to his difficulties: 'their demands for space were however outrageous and, at last, it was only by telling them, as the Governor authorized me to do, that if they did not moderate their expectations, he would stop the building altogether, that I succeeded in making a compromise.'[26] The chairman of the Board of Governors of the University of Toronto today might read of Langton's plight with sympathetic understanding.

But the real enemy was the governor-general, Sir Edmund Head. Unknown, apparently, to the vice-chancellor or to the architect, the governor-general had assumed that teaching in the college was to be on a purely tutorial basis, and it was with extraordinary perspicacity that he discovered that certain rooms shown on the plans were called 'lecture' rooms. This was the last hurdle but one, and was met by Langton through the simple device of 'scratching out the words lecture room, and erasing all appearance of seats for the students.'

The final hurdle was a serious one, and one that might have had disastrous consequences for a building now regarded with admiration and affection by graduates and undergraduates alike. Every possible concession seemed to have been made to the vanity of the governor-general, and it was, probably, with a lighter heart than he had felt for some months that Langton authorized Cumberland to stake the building on the ground.

But here an unexpected difficulty arose. It seems that His Excellency had all along thought that the south front was to face the east (west?), and nothing would satisfy him but so it must be, and, under his superintendence, we proceeded to measure and stake out; Cumberland's face exhibiting blank despair for it brought his chemical laboratory where no sun would ever shine into it, his kitchens, etc., into the prettiest part of the grounds, and several other inconveniences which His Excellency said could be easily remedied. However, there stands on the ground an elm tree, a remnant of the old forest, with a long stem as such trees have and a little bush on

**4.109** The City (Don) Jail on Gerrard Street East (1858; partially burned 1862; rebuilt), William Thomas and Sons, architects. Because of a fire during construction, the jail did not open until 1865. It is an impressive building in the manner made famous by Piranesi the etcher and by George Dance the younger, who designed Newgate prison. Compared with the grimness of Newgate, the City Jail is a friendly building in spite of rustications, vermiculated quoins, and barred windows. Interesting elements in the design are the flanking ventilators rising out of the roof, unfortunately now removed, which might well have come from the hand of the great eighteenth-century English architect Sir John Vanbrugh. One might criticize Thomas here for the weakness of the crowning cornice and pediment and for the complete lack of connection between the central mass and the flanking wings.

**4.110** King Street East, south side, looking towards Yonge Street from the foot of Toronto Street in 1857. A decade before this photograph was taken, the Albert Buildings on the left had just been completed and the shops reminded the *British Colonist* of the quadrant on Regent Street, London. Probably William Thomas was the architect. The Adelaide Buildings, seen here beyond Brown Brothers book bindery and stationery warehouse (founded in 1856 and still in business today but under another name) and the adjacent shop of John Cawthra, were in 1844 one of Thomas's first commissions after his arrival in Toronto.

**4.109**

**4.111** The City (Don) Jail, main doorway. It is unlikely that convicted law-breakers were introduced by this door, but if they had been, it would have had a sobering effect. When the Ontario government proposed in 1977 to demolish the building, there was a public outcry prompted in part by a poster that pictured this doorway. Subsequently, the government decided that the jail would be spared and, after eventual renovations, would be back in use.

**4.112** West Presbyterian Church, later Disciples Church, Denison Avenue near Queen (1861; demolished). One would like to know the name of the architect who designed this very attractive church, and to have known the house on the right, of which we get only a glimpse.

**4.113, 114** Yorkville Town Hall, later St Paul's Hall, on the west side of Yonge between Yorkville and Scollard streets (1859–60; burned 1941), William Hay, architect. 'The singular Hotel de Ville ... has a Flemish look. It might have strayed hither from Ghent' (Scadding). The coat of arms of the village (4.113) displayed symbols of the trades of the first councillors – a beer barrel with an S (John Severn, the brewer); a brick mould with an A (Thomas Atkinson); an anvil with a W (James Wallis); a jack-plane with a D (James Dobson), and, centre, the head of a steer or heifer, the mark of Peter Hutty, the butcher. When Yorkville was amalgamated with Toronto in 1883 as St Paul's Ward, the council chamber was used as a public library and continued in that capacity until a library was built on Yorkville Avenue in 1907. In its last days the hall was the armouries of the Yorkville Company of the York Rangers (now the Queen's York Rangers, 1st American Regiment).

**4.115** Oaklands, the residence of Senator John Macdonald, Avenue Road Hill (1860, 1869), William Hay, also Gundry and Langley, architects. It is regrettable that we have no record of the interior furnishings of this distinguished Victorian house. It is now given over to the use of staff at De La Salle School. The rise in Macdonald's fortune and the increase of his family, which eventually would number a dozen children from two marriages, can be traced in the house. The earliest part on the left is the work of William Hay in 1860. Nine years later Gundry and Langley designed an addition, seen on the right, that included a landmark tower. Early this century, before Oaklands became a school, a Miss McCormick, who was connected with the agricultural-implement family of that name in the United States, owned the house. The porte-cochère and bay windows date from her time.

**4.116** Drygoods warehouse of John Macdonald, 21–7 Wellington Street East through to Front Street (1863; demolished 1966), Gundry and Langley, architects. Built a decade after the publication of Ruskin's *Stones of Venice*, the original building was spoken of with admiration by all contemporary writers. It was a delightful little Venetian palazzo five windows wide, west of the centre line. This photograph shows the building when it had doubled in size (1878; Langley, Langley and Burke, architects) and a very obvious twentieth-century alteration had been made above the cornice in place of a roof with dormers.

**4.117** Pendarves, the house of Frederic Cumberland, St George Street north of College (1857–9). Cumberland was his own architect for this large house. It has no particular style and might as well be classed as mid-Victorian. At one time the grounds extended to College Street and were spacious. The internal arrangements of the house made it admirably suited for entertaining on a large scale. From 1912 to 1915 it was the official residence of the lieutenant-governor of Ontario. It is now the property of the University of Toronto and used as a centre for international students. In this photograph the Forestry Building is shown (left) where it stood until 1958, when it was moved bodily farther up St George Street.

**4.118** House at 112 Gerrard Street East (circa 1860; demolished 1959). Even in disrepair this was Victorian architecture in its gayest mood. The house faced south, and the shadows cast on grey stucco added greatly to the pattern of undulating eave board, the 'Gothick' cusping below the bay windows, and the protecting roof over the verandah.

the top of it, not unlike a broom with its long handle stuck into the ground, and it soon became evident that the tree would fall a sacrifice. This he would not permit and when I hinted that it would certainly be blown down before long, he told me it was the handsomest tree about Toronto (as it certainly is one of the tallest), and politely added 'but you Canadians have a prejudice against trees.' He then stalked off the ground followed by his ADC. I thought Cumberland would have thrown the whole thing up that day, he was so annoyed, but we took up the stakes and staked it out our way with the south front facing the south, and by a little stuffing and squeezing we got the tree into such a position that it may be saved but with the almost certainty that, when it is blown down, it will take some of the students' quarters with it. It is some comfort that that will occur before Tom [the writer's eldest son] is old enough to go to college, or I should be uneasy in stormy nights. However I bless that tree and hope its shadow may never be less for it got us out of [the] scrape. When the Governor paid us a visit next day he was quite satisfied and complimentary, and in congratulating us upon the safety of the tree he said to Cumberland with that impertinence which governors-general can so well indulge in, 'For I am sure you can never put anything up half as pretty.'

It would only be human for the chancellor of Trinity, the Lord Bishop of Toronto, to smile with contentment as the stories regarding the birth pangs of the 'godless' institution reached him in his comfortable medieval quarters on Queen Street.

But the story of University College is not yet fully told. On the night of 14 February 1890 a college servant carrying a tray of lamps stumbled and fell on the stairs in the southeast corner of the building. The kerosene was immediately ablaze; the whole of the east wing was destroyed, as well as the library of over thirty thousand volumes, the museum, and the administrative offices of the college; only the west part of the building, including the Croft Chapter House, the residence, and the dining hall, remained intact. Professor Keys once told the writer that he appeared before a committee sadly estimating the losses to the library and announced himself as one of the great benefactors of the college: he had seven hundred volumes out in his own name. The fire was a disastrous one, but there was never a doubt as to the need for immediate rebuilding. Government and friends came to the rescue, and the college was restored in the manner we know it today. The architect was David B. Dick. For reasons that are not clear he was chosen over William George Storm, who had outlived Cumberland and who begged the university in vain to be allowed to restore their masterwork.

For Cumberland and Storm, any satisfaction with University College was offset somewhat by their failure to secure the first prizes for their entries in the 1859 competition for the parliamentary and departmental buildings at Ottawa. It recalled a similar disappointment five years before, when the government had abandoned plans to build Parliament buildings and a Government House to designs by Cumberland and Storm on the lands expropriated from the University of Toronto. The decision not to locate the capital of Canada in Toronto was met with protest and a number of clever attempts to reverse matters, including twenty-five remarkable photographs of scenes of the city's streets and public buildings that were sent to the British government, and rest today in the Foreign and Commonwealth Office library. The *Globe* noted Messrs Armstrong, Beere and Hime at work on this portfolio in February 1857.[27] Well might the *Builder,* a distinguished London architectural magazine of the time, write, 'We were really not prepared to find Toronto so well worthy to be regarded as a city and a capital, as it appears to be.'[28] Nevertheless, early in 1858 it was announced that the queen had chosen Ottawa as the capital.

The decades that followed the building boom of the fifties and sixties were to be far from negligible in the history of architecture in Toronto, but they produced few comparable buildings. Romanticism in its Gothic form was to make sporadic appearances well into the twentieth century and to take its final dramatic bow in the reconstruction of the Houses of Parliament in Ottawa, a superb group of buildings by a Toronto architect, John Pearson. I am aware that there have been Gothic buildings since, but they have lacked the magic that makes St James' Cathedral, St James-the-Less, old St Paul's on Bloor Street, Little Trinity, or the Archbishop's Palace on Church Street so unquestionably part of the Toronto scene. Not all the architecture of the period can be described as indigenous, but where the term can be applied to a building, it is no small tribute to its creator.

One would like to leave the reader who is willing to explore Toronto with a long list of historic buildings ending with the year of Confederation. Nearly all have been demolished, but enough remain to give a romantic glow to many an undistinguished street. The explorer will remember that the buildings he sees were part of a great movement that swept Britain and the United States before we were affected in Canada. He will look at old St Paul's first of all as a fine piece of architecture wonderfully well built, but he will also remember, with its architect, the village churches and cathedrals of England that inspired it. He may also remember Sir Walter Scott and the influence that he must have had on a movement that was in many ways a literary one. In similar mood he will admire the old Commercial Bank on Wellington – a truly fine building that cannot help but evoke thoughts of Greece and of Byron, Shelley, Keats, and others whose poetry was part of the movement itself in its beginnings. It is appropriate for our interested explorer to dream over what he sees of Old Toronto before Confederation; in the period that follows he must be more alert. Architecture itself was awakening from a long sleep.

**4.119, 120** These small photographs show a few of the many sculptured keystones on the Ontario Bank, some of which are now to be seen in the grounds of the Guild Inn, Scarborough.

**4.121** Ontario Bank, northeast corner of Wellington and Scott streets (1861; demolished 1964), Joseph Sheard, architect. The Ontario Bank had its main office in Bowmanville when it built this building for its Toronto branch. The commission was one of the last that Joseph Sheard undertook before he retired in favour of his son-in-law, William Irving, who in 1874 extended the building six bays to the north in an identical style. It was a very good example of the type of bank that suggested opulence and security, and used the Italian palazzo as a model. Much later in New York, architects like McKim, Mead and White used the same model for banks, clubs, and other buildings.

**4.122** The royal arms, which were sent out from the home office of the Royal Insurance Company in Liverpool to adorn its building in Toronto (see 4.123). Originally placed above the cornice, the carving was moved later to sit over the main door.

**4.123** A view of Yonge Street, east side, looking south from Colborne Street in 1868. The building in the foreground was on the corner of Colborne and Yonge. William Thomas was the architect, and the wholesale drygoods firm of Ross, Mitchell and Company was the first owner. The Bank of Upper Canada was located here when it failed and closed its doors in 1866. The following year the newly chartered Bank of Commerce altered the building, to plans by Gundry and Langley, as its first head office. Also visible in the photograph, at the corner of Yonge and Wellington, is the building of the Royal Insurance Company (1861; demolished 1960), William Kauffmann, architect. It has a royal coat of arms carved in stone above the cornice and faces John G. Howard's Bank of British North America of 1845.

**4.124** Bank of Toronto, northwest corner of Wellington and Church streets (1862–3; demolished 1961), William Kauffmann, architect. A palazzo type of bank headquarters not quite as rich in detail as the Ontario Bank a block away. This photograph was taken by Notman, probably in the seventies, when Georgian houses abutted the bank's premises. The Ontario House (3.21, 22) once looked across the bay to the Island from this corner.

**4.125** Willing and Williamson, 12 King Street East (1863; demolished), William Kauff-mann, architect. The photograph was taken about 1873. Kauffmann was responsible for extensive alterations undertaken a decade earlier for Thomas Haworth, a hardware merchant. Seen here are the resulting cast-iron shopfront and the pattern formed by vertical and horizontal rods below the windows, in a masterpiece of simplicity. This is the kind of little shop that in London would be 'by appointment' and would have an exclusive business with the gentry. Everything is delightful – the 'strap work' on the inside blinds would today be a collector's piece, and the lettering might be 1771 instead of 1871, when Willing and Williamson succeeded Adam, Stevenson and Company. G. Mercer Adam, the author of *Toronto Old and New*, was a partner in this latter firm.

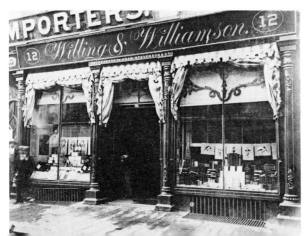

**4.126** Queen's Wharf lighthouse, Fleet Street at Lakeshore Boulevard (1861; moved 1929), Kivas Tully, architect. No longer a beacon for ships on the lake, the old lighthouse is one of the few relics of the past that we have had the foresight to preserve solely for the pleasure of viewing it. We see it today on a well-kept lawn, but this seemingly frail tower knew snow and rain and the force of equinoctial gales for three-quarters of a century, and its light was never known to fail.

# 5  Romanesque and Cast Iron

In the evolution of taste over one hundred years, the last phase, which takes us to the end of the nineteenth century, might seem to the casual observer in Toronto to be hardly worthy of study. He would be wrong, because even a marked deterioration in taste is not uninteresting, and what there was of clutter in the flocked and claustrophobic drawing-rooms of the well-to-do was offset by architectural movements of great significance. A new and virile architecture that was to culminate in the Toronto City Hall (1889) was in the making, and even the seventies showed an awareness of the possibilities of cast iron in the construction of buildings – a technique that was to lead to the skyscrapers in steel that are now a commonplace in the urban scene. The same seventies saw the arrival on the Canadian artistic scene of the Ontario Society of Artists. Meeting first in 1872 in the house of J.A. Fraser at 28 Gould Street, the society is without doubt the oldest society of its kind in Canada. The seventies also saw an art school with a provincial grant established over a store at 14 King Street West. By 1912 the school with such humble beginnings became the Ontario College of Art.[1]

For the new architecture that was in the making, we owe a lasting debt to Chicago. In the eighties of the last century almost all architectural creative activity in North America was concentrated in that city. Where a cold, classic academism had settled on New York and the eastern seaboard, the atmosphere of Chicago was charged with curiosity and experiment in all matters pertaining to building – particularly with cast iron and the seemingly limitless vistas opened up by the electric elevator. From this period a dozen or more architects have left their mark on the modern movement in architecture, and no work on the history of the movement is complete without a record of the achievements of Jenney, Richardson, Burnham, Root, and Sullivan, whose pupil was Frank Lloyd Wright.

**5.1** The Golden Griffin, 128–32 King Street East (circa 1850; demolished 1970). Shop seems an inadequate word for the spendid emporium seen in this Notman and Fraser photograph of 1873. Its even more splendid and defiant golden griffin that presided over the chaos of the sidewalk below was reported in a newspaper of 1869 to sit upon a base 'decorated with a stained glass transparency displaying the words "Golden Griffin."' Presumably the sign could be illuminated from behind. A few years later a fourth storey was added to the building when Messrs Petley and Petley acquired the business from Hughes Brothers.

**5.2** King Street for two blocks on either side of Yonge Street contained most of Toronto's higher-class stores during the second half of the nineteenth century. In this Notman and Fraser photograph of 1884, which looks west from the foot of Toronto Street, the sign on the photographers' own building ('Notman and Fraser Photographers to the Queen') is visible to the left of Robert Walker's Golden Lion (5.3).

**5.3** The Golden Lion, a well-known drygoods store at 33–7 King Street East (1867; demolished 1901), William Irving, architect. In 1846 Robert Walker moved his business into a new stone building on the site (4.110). During 1867 it was replaced by this structure, which, architecturally, was remarkable for the large areas of glass in the lower floors and for the lightness of the mullions that divided it. Some stone from the earlier building was reused in the two upper stories. The lion on the parapet is every bit as rampant as the one that once stood in a similar location on the London house of the duke of Northumberland.

**5.4** The northwest corner of King and Yonge streets in 1868

5.5 College Avenue (now University Avenue) from Queen looking north to Queen's Park. The street was laid out as an approach to King's College. In 1833 John G. Howard designed the entrance gates and gatekeeper's lodge seen on the left in this view of circa 1868. The lodge was demolished in 1896.

5.6 A toll-gate, long since demolished, at Yonge and Marlborough streets, photographed in the 1870s

**5.7** House of Joseph Gearing, Yonge Street at the corner of Carlton (circa 1864; demolished). Gearing was a successful builder, with Deer Park Church to his credit in 1870. His is likely to have been one of the last Georgian houses erected before taste changed so significantly that Police Station 4 (5.24) could be built without public ridicule. There are, of course, signs of uncertainty in the design of the house. The cornice and corbels don't seem right, and the chimneys are small and mean. But these are details that hardly detract from a pleasant grouping of houses and business offices.

**5.8** Gooderham and Worts Distillery, Mill Street (1859; burned 1869; rebuilt), David Roberts, Sr, architect and engineer. After a fire the building was rebuilt in 1870 and was not greatly different from its predecessor. Much has been written recently of the industrial and commercial buildings of the nineteenth century in England. This distillery and the McLaughlin Flour Mills (5.9) show how high was the standard of design in Toronto. In this example we might criticize the smallness of the windows and the consequent lighting conditions for workmen within, but considered just as a building (as, of course, no critic would dream of considering it), the Kingston limestone walls are impressive, the gable end well proportioned, and the strong bands tying the window sills give the building an almost Florentine look – especially if one can ignore the dormers.

**5.9** McLaughlin Flour Mills, on the west side of Bay Street at the Esplanade (1893; burned 1904), Charles J. Gibson, architect. It is doubtful whether there are craftsmen today who could do such a superb job of brickwork. The wall itself is well done, but the lower arches and corbelling are not inferior to the best in countries like Holland and Germany. The design itself is well worthy of notice and ranks with the best of the industrial buildings of the nineteenth century – a field we are just beginning to appreciate.

The architectural excitement that was generated in the midwest was bound to be felt in Toronto. Travel by rail was not difficult, and an entirely new means of communication was available through the architectural magazines that made their appearance in the last quarter of the century. We can be sure that the professional appetite for illustrated architectural literature was as insatiable then as it is today and that English and American magazines were eagerly sought and thoroughly perused. By 1888 the demand in Toronto was sufficient to warrant the monthly publication of the *Canadian Architect and Builder*.

While there was much poor building in the last quarter of the nineteenth century, there was much that was good. The poor can hardly be defended, but to a point it can be explained. One has to remember, despite the newer currents mentioned, the comparative isolation of Toronto in, say, 1875 from such large traditional centres of architectural activity as London, Paris, or Berlin – even Chicago was 525 miles away, and a severe depression was in the making. Our local architects, like their predecessors, had been brought up in the Classical and Gothic schools, and even though they must have been vaguely conscious that the machine was going to affect their ancient craft as it had already affected industry, they could not know whither it would lead, or how.

Such a revelation is not, as a rule, for the anonymous practitioner but for the genius. Of these there were several in the nineteenth century, but the potential of the machine through the mass production of building materials and of well-designed everyday things was not revealed to us until architects like Gropius, Le Corbusier, and Mies van der Rohe appeared in Europe in the late twenties of this century. Today we cannot excuse the flashy products of the automobile and consumer-goods industries on the grounds that we know no better or that the products of the machine are necessarily ugly. A thousand machine-made objects prove such a statement to be false. Very different was the position of the designer in the groping years of the late nineteenth century, when too often products of the machine, the handicraft industry, and building were, alike, ugly. But even if the mediocre dominated, there were fine buildings, large and small, that even today we look on with admiration and respect. They were undoubtedly inspired by the magazines through which the architect found himself in a new world with ever-widening horizons. Without stirring from his office, he could become familiar with the latest buildings in Europe or the United States, and compared with his library of ancient monuments, these were alive, of his day, and of immediate concern.

Of the buildings that he would see illustrated, the ones that would strike him most forcibly would be, as we have said, from Chicago. The Chicago Movement took two forms, both of which were to find an echo in Toronto. The first sprang from the office of an architect named H.H. Richardson and the second from a realization of the potential of cast iron as a building material. Richardson was keenly aware of the humdrum and frequently shoddy building that was going on about him, and he sought a substitute.

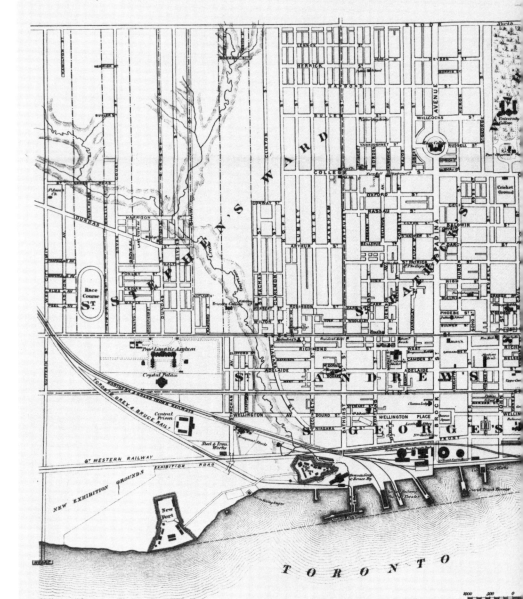

MAP OF

WILLING

Booksellers

Drawn by A.T. COTTERELL, C.E. Toronto.

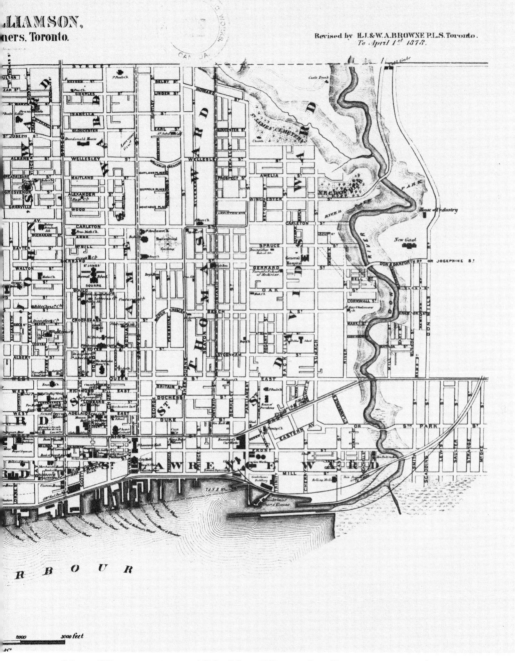

5.10 Map of Toronto, 1878, published by Willing and Williamson (see 4.125)

WEST ELEVATION

**5.11** Wellesley Public School, St Vincent (Bay) and St Alban's (Wellesley West) streets, (1873; enlarged 1876, 1882, 1887; demolished 1962), William George Storm, architect. The growth of the city is reflected in the building of schools and in the several enlargements to this one. The additions, carried out by the firm of McCaw and Lennox and later by E.J. Lennox practising on his own, were of a piece with Storm's original building. The Sutton Place Hotel is on the site today.

**5.12** The Necropolis, Winchester Street east of Sumach (1872), Henry Langley, architect. A very interesting group of buildings as an entrance to an equally interesting old Toronto graveyard. Its name means 'City of the Dead.' In a study of taste the gravestones should not be neglected, as each phase in the architecture of the nineteenth century finds an echo in lettering and design in our older cemeteries. For such a study St James' Cemetery and the Necropolis provide the best examples.

**5.13** Church of St Andrew, southeast corner of King and Simcoe streets (1874–5), William George Storm, architect. This romantic but powerful design, with obvious vernacular influences from the kirk in Scotland, has no equal in Toronto as an example of the 'picturesque.'

5.12

5.14 Robert Marshall's bookstore, 49 King Street West (1880; demolished 1966), showing the arms of the city of Glasgow. It may be true that a Scot is never at home except when he is abroad, but Robert Marshall was still a proud Glaswegian. The arms tell us of 'The tree that never grew, / The bird that never flew, / The fish that never swam, / The bell that never rang.'

5.15 Store of J.H. Greenshields, grocer, 300 King Street East (opened 1878; closed 1956). One could hardly ask for more refinement, charm, and colour than were to be found in the interior of this store. In its latter days Greenshields managed it with the help of a woman bookkeeper, but he recalled the 1880s, when his father had ten assistants to serve the drovers and farmers attending the market behind St Lawrence Hall, as well as the carriage trade.

5.15

He found it in the Romanesque architecture of northern Italy, which in his hands became part of the vernacular architecture of the United States. Richardson had a genius for material, and it was part of his genius that he saw an affinity between the rubble walls of northern Italy and the traditional stone walls of his own country. They were rugged, masculine, and unaffected, and his Marshall Field store showed his contemporaries that the eternal qualities of proportion, scale, and rhythm were attainable even in a purely utilitarian building. When Louis Sullivan saw the Marshall Field store, he said, 'stone and mortar here spring to life and are no more material and sordid things – an elemental urge is there.'

Richardson had many admirers both in the United States and in Canada. His architecture, and even that of his imitators, stood out like rocks in the urban sea of insincere and trivial building that characterized his period. In Toronto nothing for a mile around comes close to the scale of the third City Hall, which is a good example of the Richardson manner; and the legislative buildings in Queen's Park, a less successful example, reduce almost to insignificance their loftier, younger neighbours.

The story of the City Hall is a chequered one, but one that in the end produced a really great Toronto building. The story starts with an international competition in 1885 in which fifty architects submitted designs for a court house to cost not more than $200,000. Nothing came of it because the space requirements were far in excess of the sum of money allowed for building. When, nothing daunted, the city held a new competition the following year, fourteen architects competed. Edward James Lennox of Toronto, always known as E.J., submitted the winning scheme, and while he was a long way from seeing the City Hall built, he was not from then on to be diverted from that ultimate goal. It is true that there are points of similarity between his scheme and the Pittsburgh Court House of 1884 by Richardson, of which Lennox was no doubt aware, but a comparison of the two would dismiss any suggestion of copying.

The first stumbling block, and it was a real one, was again one of cost. The foundations of the court house were put to tender and came out at $111,000, a financial burden not to be borne in an ultimate building to cost less than twice that sum. And so, while the city waited for the next municipal election, the excavation, which should have echoed to the sound of workmen on the foundations, resounded instead to the voices of happy children – the site had become an ice rink.

In the interval the city fathers decided that what Toronto needed was not a court house only but a city hall as well, and in 1887 Lennox was asked to prepare drawings for a building to combine both functions. He did so, and superbly. The eventual cost of $2,500,000, a figure well in excess of the target set by the city, was explained by Mayor John Shaw on opening day, 18 September 1899:

Why people will spend large sums of money on great buildings opens up a wide

**5.16** The eighth Post Office, Adelaide Street East (1871–3; demolished 1960), Henry Langley, architect. This Second Empire building, which sat with such dignity at the head of Toronto Street, is no more. It might be thought fussy by some, with its picturesque roof and its rows of columns, but the most severe critic would agree that it was in scale with the neighbouring buildings and that it had a presence that one would associate with the government of Canada. The royal arms over the main door are now preserved on the south side of Lombard Street, behind the Federal Building, which now stands on the site.

**5.17** Toronto Street, looking north. This is the street that died, seen here a few years before the demolition in 1960 of the eighth Post Office, standing at the head of the vista. On the left is the seventh Post Office and, next to it, the Masonic Hall, known also as the Canada Permanent Building. Further along still, the Excelsior Life Building, designed by E.J. Lennox in 1914, is not unworthy of old Toronto Street. Today a parking garage and some banal modern buildings set the tone on Toronto Street.

**5.18** A.R. McMaster and Brother drygoods warehouse, Front Street west of Yonge (1871; demolished 1962), William Irving, architect. So unlike the very functional warehouses of today, in which brick walls enclose a space, was the building in the Second Empire style erected for McMaster. Known as the Minerva Building, it was damaged in the 1904 fire but was rebuilt and extended in the same style to twice the original size.

**5.19** Bank of British North America, northeast corner Wellington and Yonge streets (1871), Henry Langley, architect. It is interesting to compare the three banks built after the manner of an Italian palazzo to give the appearance of opulence and vast resources. The Bank of Toronto and the Ontario Bank have gone, but the Bank of British North America survives, its main door now on Yonge Street rather than Wellington, where it was until 1903. The building has been cleaned and renovated since this photograph was taken.

**5.20** The new Grand Opera House, south side of Adelaide between Yonge and Bay streets, from the *Canadian Illustrated News* (1874; burned 1879; rebuilt; demolished 1920). Two architects, Thomas R. Jackson of New York and the Toronto firm of Lalor and Martin, claimed credit for the design of this building when it opened in 1874 under the distinguished patronage of the Marquis and Marchioness of Dufferin and Ava. In honour of His Excellency, who was a descendent of Sheridan, the first play performed was *The School for Scandal*, with Mrs Charlotte Morrison as Lady Teazle. The engraving indicates a building of quite frightening scale and proportions.

**5.21, 22** Custom House at the corner of Front and Yonge streets (1873–6; demolished 1919), R.C. Windeyer, architect. This building, like the eighth Post Office (5.16), belongs to that period of architecture known as Second Empire. When it was demolished, a wrecker sold fragments to a collector who assembled them without rhyme or reason in a façade (5.22) that used to stand opposite the old City Hall. Rome has many examples of this kind of pilfering, but it was usually better done.

**5.23** The corner of Bay and Front streets, 1876, showing the change in direction as Front Street approaches Yonge, now incorporated as a graceful curve in the façade of the Dominion Public Building.

**5.24, 25** Police station and fire hall, Dundas Street east of Parliament (1878; demolished 1956), Stewart and Strickland, architects. In a study of taste over a century of building, examples that are characteristic of a period cannot be left out. The flower of Toronto architecture is not to be found in Police Station 4. The small garage with the fancy Dutch gable would appear to be older than its brash neighbour to the east. A keystone is shown in the small photograph.

field of thought. It may, however, be roughly answered that great buildings sym-
bolize a people's deeds and aspirations. It has been said that, wherever a nation had
a conscience and a mind, it recorded the evidence of its being in the highest products
of this greatest of all arts. Where no such monuments are to be found, the mental
and moral natures of the people have not been above the faculties of the beasts.

After such a statement from the chief magistrate there were few with the
temerity to put themselves on the moral level of the beasts and question the
cost of the building.

    The City Hall is built in a combination of brown New Brunswick sand-
stone, used for trim, and a rose sandstone from a quarry near the forks of
the Credit River that provided stone for the legislative buildings and much
of St George Street. It is a stone that takes a rugged face, and was popular
with architects who saw some kinship in it with the masonry of northern
Italy. The exterior of the hall is striking and greatly impressed the international jury that met to judge the designs submitted for the new City Hall
in 1958.

    It is, however, difficult to enthuse over the interior. The entrance hall is
spacious but without distinction, and the council chamber is just a room off
a corridor. The entrance for the mayor and distinguished guests is through
a passage in which two can walk abreast with difficulty. One can only assume
that even in 1890 the Romanesque did not lend itself to the interiors of
rooms for modern use, or that the prototype was much too far from Queen
and Bay for serious study.

    Obviously, a study of nineteenth-century building in the capital city of
Ontario would be incomplete without a reference to its Parliament buildings.
How they came to be as dull as they are is, perhaps, the saddest story ever
told when architects meet and the talk is of competitions.

    An international competition for the legislative buildings in Queen's Park
was held in 1880, and thirteen architects competed, seven being Canadian
and six American. The jury consisted of the Honourable Alex Mackenzie,
W.G. Storm, and R.A. Waite, an architect living in Buffalo. As a result of
the competition, Darling and Curry were placed first, Gordon and Helliwell
second, and Smith and Gemmell third. Each indicated a price that was higher
than the government estimate of funds available, and an extraordinary decision was reached. The first- and second-prize winners were both asked to
sharpen their pencils and prepare working drawings and specifications. This
they did at considerable expense, with Gordon and Helliwell submitting a
price of $542,000 and Darling and Curry $612,000.

    Somewhat discouraged by these figures, the province allowed the work
to lapse until 1885, when 'the Buffalo individual,' as Waite became known
in architectural circles, was asked by the government to decide between the
two architectural firms. In the intervening five years the 'unspeakable' Mr
Waite had found favour with the government both as a person and as a
poker player, and it did not come as a surprise when, in 1885, he announced

that neither design was suitable and that (to quote the *Canadian Architect and Builder* 1890) 'he was the only architect on this continent capable of carrying out such important work.' His offer to design the building was accepted, and $750,000 was thought to be a realistic price in view of the previous tenders of around $600,000.

Under Waite's direction the building actually cost $1,227,963; before he left town, he also designed the head offices of Canada Life and the Bank of Commerce.

One can understand public and professional admiration for such Romanesque monuments as our City Hall and Trinity Church, Boston, but one would hardly have predicted that the same manner would seize the popular imagination in house building. Yet such was the case in Toronto, where many streets in the Annex and much of St George Street are still silent evidence of a period in the history of taste that led us to northern Italy by way of Chicago. Of the houses inspired by Richardson that are left to us, the York Club is probably the most striking. Outside, the walls are a combination of brickwork, ashlar, and rock-faced masonry, which would be formidable indeed were it not for the free-flowing lines of the carving in appropriate places and the harmony of colour among stone, red brick, and bright green copper.

The club was originally a Gooderham house, and it is inside that one is conscious of a more human scale, the warmth of natural wood, and of well-proportioned rooms. Standing in the hall or the reading room, one does not feel the presence of the original owner and his family so much as of those humble craftsmen who wrought with such skill and apparent delight the woodwork in mantels, stairs, and trim in a variety of woods. It is unlikely that after 1892 there was much call for their talents – the machine had overtaken and displaced them.

This writer is not likely to forget the first of three occasions when he had the pleasure of dining at the York Club with Frank Lloyd Wright. Students had been invited to meet the great man, and they stood entranced as he touched mouldings with his hand and recalled as in a dream the days of his youth sixty years before in Chicago. In whatever city we met subsequently, he spoke with affection of the club at the corner of St George and Bloor.

At the same time that Richardson was leaving his mark on the vernacular architecture of the United States, his contemporaries were exploring with equal vigour and greater daring the potential of cast iron as a structural material. Cast iron had been used in Great Britain and elsewhere on bridges, railway stations, factories, and other structures since the late eighteenth century, but the invention of the electrically driven elevator in 1853 suggested a new use for the material in buildings taller than had been dreamt of up to that time. It was not until the seventies and eighties of the century that intensive reconstruction of the Loop in Chicago saw the incipient skyscraper of ten or twelve storeys with a skeleton, and sometimes a façade, of cast iron. In his book *Space, Time and Architecture* Dr Siegfried Giedion states

**5.26** Numbers 502–8 Parliament Street (1879), Victorian domestic architecture in its most exuberant mood. Each door once represented the entrance to a house with spacious rooms, high ceilings, and abundant light. Perhaps from a shortage of cash, the south wing with the mansard roof was not repeated to the north.

**5.27** A group of houses on Spruce Street (1887). Were it not for the dormers, one might be looking in the dusk at a stable on a noble estate in provincial France. This is not row housing at its best, but it contributes something to an otherwise uninteresting streetscape.

**5.28** Police court, station, and fire hall, Court Street (1876; demolished 1961), Harper and Son, architects. Replacing an earlier fire hall where land in the public square had been 'reserved for The Engine House' (3.16), this rather grand building had a policeman's library and billiard room on the third floor.

that iron had been used for such purposes from 1850 to 1880 and reached what he called its 'classic height' in the Paris Exposition of 1889.

An examination of the structural skeleton of downtown Toronto office buildings and warehouses would show quite a number to be in cast iron, and where alterations are made to existing buildings, columns in that material are still frequently employed. The only example in Toronto, where both the structural system and the façade were of cast iron, was the Royal Canadian Bank building at 36–8 Front Street (5.75). It was an unpretentious building passed daily by hundreds without a glance, but historically it was a landmark in a development that was sociological as well as technological. It was through experiments in iron in simple buildings like this that we arrived at those fantastic towering structures in steel that, in each decade of our century, have risen so high in the sky that Frank Lloyd Wright's mile-high building seems not outside the bounds of engineering ingenuity. Socially, such monsters are to be condemned for their disastrous effect on traffic and municipal services and for the sunless, windy canyons that they create in congested urban areas. The lowness of the old Post Office on Toronto Street, which is now an office building, is, unfortunately, something that not everyone can afford. Even so, it is an interesting commentary on our time that the first or second floor in a building of 1851 would be considered more desirable than the twenty-second in a new skyscraper.

Like its famous predecessor, the Crystal Palace of 1851 in London, the Toronto Exhibition building of 1858 was of iron and glass (5.72). In view of the rigours of the Toronto climate it is not surprising that the influence on our architecture of either exhibition was slight, if not negligible. Windows continued to be of normal height and span until we come to 1893 and a quite unusual clothing store called Oak Hall (5.74), which once, quite jauntily, faced St James' Cathedral. This remarkable building was constructed in 1893 in cast iron and glass, the glass being in the largest sheets to enter Canada at that date. According to the author of *Toronto Illustrated*, the fourteen ladies on their pedestals were cast in bronze, while the fifteenth, on the topmost pediment, appeared to have come to life, Pygmalion-like, and to be about to take off. Indeed, in the latter days of Oak Hall the ladies became more than an embarrassment to the city. When one fell like a lethal bronze missile on King Street, her sisters were all removed, without even a Potter's Field to mark their resting place.

Decorative ladies aside, the building might well be considered a landmark in the evolution of the office building in North America. It demonstrated a daringly light structure in cast iron, in which respect it was the forerunner of the steel framework of the modern skyscraper. The all-glass façade is a commonplace today, but in 1893 it would have caused a sensation. The demand for daylight in the office building was recognized in Chicago in the 1880s, but the bay window as a device to direct light still farther into the recesses of the room beyond was not tried in commercial buildings until the

5.29    5.30

**5.29** Consumers' Gas Company building, 17–19 Toronto Street (1876, 1899), Grant and Dick, architects. Most of the decorative parapet, which included datestones, was removed many years ago. After his partnership with Robert Grant ended, David B. Dick had his offices on the top floor of the older part on the left. When called upon by the Consumers' Gas Company to enlarge their building twenty-five years after his first commission, he produced a harmonious and sophisticated addition.

**5.30** Dominion Bank, southwest corner of King and Yonge streets (1878–9; demolished 1913), William Irving, architect. What might be seen as the first claim in an ongoing contest among banks to construct Toronto's tallest building was this five-storey head office of the Dominion Bank, which had been founded in 1869. James Austin, the first president of the bank, also headed the Consumers' Gas Company from 1874 to 1897.

**5.31** The third Spadina House at 258 Spadina Road (1866), seen here before 1912, when a third floor was added. In 1866 James Austin acquired the eighty-acre Spadina estate between Davenport Road and St Clair Avenue from William Willcocks Baldwin, a grandson of Dr William Warren Baldwin. To make room for a new house, the Baldwins' Spadina of 1836 was demolished. The only signs remaining of it are in the basement and a handsome eight-panelled door with sidelights under an elliptical arch that was undoubtedly the former front door. It is the back entrance to the present Spadina, which, surrounded by almost six acres of the original estate, today is owned jointly by the Toronto Historical Board and the Ontario Heritage Foundation.

**5.32, 33** Spadina House. This is the Victorian house par excellence, with none of the clutter seen in contemporary interiors like the Gzowski house (see 5.34). The drawing room is large and well proportioned, with a mantel in white marble at each end. The billiard room has an Art Nouveau frieze and was built in 1898 by James Austin's son, Albert William. He was responsible also for the fine porte-cochère, conservatory, and terraces added in 1907 to designs by the New York architects Carrère and Hastings. His daughter, Mrs Kathleen Austin Thompson, and her family made generous gifts to ensure that Spadina would be preserved as a museum open to the public.

5.33

5.34 House of Colonel Sir Casimir Gzowski, Bathurst Street (1858; demolished 1904). This house was typical in design of the large houses of the late fifties. The interior is seen here about 1890 and represents an accumulation of knick-knacks, family photographs, and pictures gathered over half a century. The billiard room also served as the art gallery.

**5.35** Restaurant of George S. McConkey, 27–9 King Street West (1880; demolished 1929). In 1894 the members of the Ontario Association of Architects moved for their dinner meetings from Webb's to McConkey's. The latter was described as 'more elegant' and the resort of *le beau monde*.

**5.36** Terra-cotta panel on a house of circa 1880, now demolished, on Carlton Street opposite Allan Gardens. This is a rather special example of terra cotta in Toronto, but smaller panels were very common in houses of the period. Strangely enough, they seem to have stood the test of time better than the terra cotta of the twentieth century, which has deteriorated badly on buildings like the Toronto General Hospital.

**5.37** Victoria Orange Hall, at the corner of Queen and Berti streets (1885; demolished 1971), E.J. Lennox, architect. There can be no doubt that Lennox was an important architect in Toronto. Casa Loma is something hard to live down, but the old City Hall and this building are among his best works. The Orange Hall has been neglected by critics but had great charm. Especially in the morning sun the east side was a symphony formed by the rhythmic play of arches combined with carefully disposed accents in a rising scale of brick piers. It is clear that there were brick craftsmen in 1885.

**5.38** The Manning Arcade, 22–8 King Street West (1884–5; demolished 1962), E.J. Lennox, architect. A robust piece of design by the architect of the old City Hall, with well-lit offices. Of interest is the three-dimensional effect obtained by placing the bay in a deep, sculptured recess in the façade. Something similar was also seen in the old head office of the Bank of Nova Scotia on King Street West (see 5.96).

Reliance Building of 1894. If Oak Hall were still on the old stand on King Street, it would be a place of pilgrimage for architectural historians.

Its proprietor was a Canadian senator, the Honourable W.E. Sanford, who, starting in Hamilton in 1858, eventually owned a chain of Oak Halls in the province – all dealing in clothing. Only a very modern, progressive firm would build such a building, and this is further confirmed by former customers who recalled with pleasure that, with every suit of clothes, they received a pea-shooter as a bonus.

The number of buildings with a cast-iron skeleton and a façade of the same material designed to simulate stone are rare in North America, but buildings of a certain age that show a façade of brick or stone are quite frequently supported internally by wood or iron columns. An inspection of buildings on the south side of Front Street between Church and Jarvis tells the whole story of construction from the primitive wood post and beam to iron columns of several sections supporting beams in iron or wood. Only the fact that they have been there so long explains their existence, in contravention of modern safety codes for downtown buildings. We shall not see their like again. The wood on the upper floors of 81 Front Street East is as odorous as sandalwood, but its odour comes from nearly a hundred years of contact with rope, caulking, and canvas, which are the principal stock in trade of the former occupant, Tom Taylor and Co, the ships' chandlers. The old pine floors polished smooth by use, the supporting wooden posts, and the elderly employee sitting cross-legged as he bound a sail – all gave the impression of a scene long antedating the age of steam. The rear of the store once serviced ships when the waters of the harbour came up to the Esplanade.

The change in materials from cast iron to steel was not heralded by any fanfare of trumpets when the first building in Toronto with a structural steel skeleton was erected in 1889. At the time it may have seemed like a natural and inevitable step that made no visible change in the façade of buildings, but neither the builders nor the general public could have foreseen a time when the same construction would produce literal skyscrapers in Toronto, whose top floors sometimes are obscured by clouds.

The building that marked a turning-point in Toronto and opened a new vista with seemingly unlimited possibilities in the field of technology was the old Board of Trade headquarters at the corner of Yonge and Front streets (5.77). The spectator would find it an unusual but not particularly impressive office building with a curved front and conical roof. He could not know that behind the mask of brick and stone was a structural skeleton of steel. We know it from the records, and several years ago we saw the columns and beams laid bare by the wrecker. Like so many Toronto buildings in the nineteenth century the Board of Trade was the result of an international competition. Out of a field of seventeen, half of whom were Canadian architects, Messrs James and James of New York were declared the winner

**5.39, 40, 41** Bank of Montreal, Front and Yonge streets (1885–6), Darling and Curry, architects. In the background are the bank towers that have succeeded this 'banking house,' as buildings of this generation could be called. Replacing an earlier bank of 1845 (see 4.22), this Beaux Arts design is opulent and impressive, befitting a bank head office. As with the 'old lady of Threadneedle Street,' one thinks of it as feminine, marvellously well preserved, and still gracious in spite of a modernistic clock, catchy signs, and new, unsuitable doors. These replaced massive and beautiful doors that gave assurances of security (5.40). The interior is shown at closing time (5.39). Henry Sproatt, the architect of Hart House, was one of the draftsmen who worked on this building. The stone sculptors were Holbrook and Mollington.

**5.42, 43** St Mary's Roman Catholic Church, west side of Bathurst Street at Adelaide (1885), Joseph Connolly, architect, with spire by A.W. Holmes (1904). The combination of Connolly and Holmes produced an outstanding church that sits with distinction at the end of the vista of Adelaide Street. This can be more readily appreciated on foot, since the traffic planners have ordained that for motorists Adelaide Street is a one-way street running eastward here. Surrounded today by a neighbourhood where large numbers of Portuguese-born Roman Catholics live, this church is the centre of the community. The interior is one of the finest in Toronto. It is full of colour and light, right up to the splendid timber roof, whose ridge is sixty-five feet from the floor.

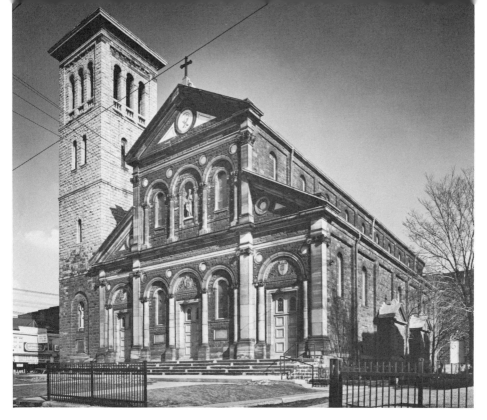

**5.44, 45** St Paul's Roman Catholic Church, Queen and Power streets (1887), Joseph Connolly, architect. This church was a rather courageous attempt at a design in the Italian Renaissance manner in a city where nearly all churches were Gothic. It is not entirely successful, but it deserves a better setting, which it once had. The interior is quite the most beautiful church interior in Toronto, and because of it the church should appear in any list of buildings worthy of preservation.

in April 1889. Professor William R. Ware of New York was the adjudicator. In its latter years it was the head office of the Toronto Transportation Commission.

In a brochure published by the Robert Simpson Company we read that 'the opening of Simpson's handsome new structure designed in the fashionable Romanesque style was an event of 1894.' A store had been on the site since 1881, when Robert Simpson shocked Toronto sensibilities by flagrantly illustrating women's corsets in his newspaper advertisements and by exposing his first woman clerk to no one knew what perils by employment on the second floor. By 1893 Simpson had extended his property on both Queen and Yonge, and a new building was begun. Columns and beams were of steel, but one year after the opening in 1894, the store was destroyed by fire. Undaunted, Simpson proceeded with a new building of steel construction six storeys in height. With very inadequate building by-laws to guide him but with the lesson learned from the previous fire, columns and beams were encased in concrete and floors were made fire resistant. Of considerable interest to the architectural historian are the dates carved in stone on the pilaster capitals on the Yonge Street side. They show the growth of the store from 1893, when building started, to 1895, when the floor area was doubled, and on to later years.[2]

A number of other buildings run neck and neck for the honour of being the progenitors of modern construction in steel, but they show no particular use of the material to distinguish them from the earlier Board of Trade or the Robert Simpson store. Greatly daring for their time in Toronto, however, were the steel roof trusses that spanned the Armouries (1891) on University Avenue (124 feet) and the Manufacturers' Building (1902) at the Canadian National Exhibition (108 feet), both now lost to view. The spanning of the Armouries with such a truss was not impressive compared with that of the Galerie des Machines (1891) in Paris, where the span was 150 meters, but both were part of an exciting period when the covering of great spaces without intermediate supports stirred the imagination of architects and engineers in Europe and America. These experiments with space would seem, in historical perspective, to have made a greater contribution to modern technology than did the skeletal frame of the incipient skyscraper of the same period.

In spite of the excitement aroused by steel in the construction industry, many Toronto buildings in the nineties continued to be built on the ancient principle of the bearing wall, and one important office building remained faithful to cast iron. The Independent Order of Foresters' building (also called the Temple Building) marks the end as well as the beginning of an era (5.79). It was the last tall office building to have a structural frame of cast iron, but its architect, George Gouinlock, introduced features that were strikingly new in 1895. In the whole history of architecture few measures had been taken for the protection of human life from fire, and the taller buildings grew, the greater became the hazard and the more urgent the need.

In the Temple Building, which would be known as a 'prestige' office building in the language of today, cast-iron columns and beams were protected by concrete; floors were of fire-resistant tile construction, and, earlier than any similar building in Canada as far as I can discover, both doors and windows were encased in metal. It was in much the same style as its neighbour the City Hall, and was four years old when the latter was opened in 1899.

In the midst of this period when architects in Toronto were so deeply concerned with the bones of their buildings in cast iron, reinforced concrete, and finally in steel, there intruded a movement that was largely concerned with decoration. It is perhaps an exaggeration to call the scattered examples of Art Nouveau in Toronto a movement, but they are important to us in a discussion of nineteenth-century taste in that they indicate for the first time an awareness of contemporary art in Europe among architects whose previous concern had been largely with creative activity in the United States.

Earlier than Art Nouveau was the Arts and Crafts movement in England, founded by William Morris. For him and his disciples the artist was an indispensable member of society, and the so-called minor arts, such as weaving, typography, furniture-making, pottery, and stained glass, were as important to the well-being of the community in their civilization as were painting and sculpture.

Against such a background, it is not surprising that the Art Nouveau designers, holding identical views, should all owe a debt to Morris. They, too, were concerned with surface decoration and with the crafts, and while later the artist-designers turned architect and became increasingly concerned with architecture and engineering, it is for decoration and the crafts that they are best remembered. The Art Nouveau designers differed fundamentally in outlook from Morris, however, in that theirs was an 'anti' movement, discarding everything that was historical or traditional in origin and looking to the future, while Morris turned to the Middle Ages for inspiration. He was 'anti' only in that he rejected the machine and all its works and sought a new Jerusalem in industrial Britain, where men, once again, would take joy in creative work and the product of their hands.

From the Pre-Raphaelites, who were contemporary with Morris, the Art Nouveau designers inherited the idea of the human female as the 'girl-woman,' virginal and frequently emaciated, with flowing hair and an expression more often of melancholy than of any other human emotion. In St Paul's Church on Avenue Road, Gustav Hahn shows such figures (5.76). Their clothing may conceal either emaciation or a robust female form, but the expression on the face of 'Joy' would not indicate that joy was an emotion any more to be desired than Goodness and Temperance, which her sister maidens solemnly portray.

Important to Art Nouveau, indeed all important, was the 'line,' which could be 'melodious, agitated, undulating, flowing or flaming' and might appear for its own sake, as a line, or as the curling tendrils of a plant. In the St Paul's ceiling we see the former in the vertical lines of the drapery and

**5.46** The old City Hall and Court House (1889–99), E.J. Lennox, architect. Seen here from Osgoode Hall, this is certainly the best known and probably the best loved of the old buildings in Toronto. Built of sandstone from the Credit River Valley and from New Brunswick, Lennox's masterpiece is the best example in Toronto of the manner of building made popular by H.H. Richardson of Chicago in the eighties – especially evident in the Allegheny County Court House in Pittsburgh, on which construction had begun in 1884. The legislative buildings and much of the Annex show the same influence.

**5.47** Old City Hall. This perspective sketch in watercolour, made in 1889, was intended to persuade the voters to support a referendum increasing the budget for the project. Some details, such as the top of the tower and the prominence given to the clock, were changed during the long period the building was under construction.

**5.48** Old City Hall. A rare construction photograph showing the building in 1894 or 1895 from the corner of Queen and Albert streets. On the left, small shops along Queen Street are still standing while the colossus rises behind them. Stonecutters' sheds and the skylit workshops and offices for the project can also be seen on the site.

5.49 Old City Hall, looking up Bay Street. This silhouette was finer before the gargoyles that served as waterspouts at the level of the clock in the tower were removed.

5.50 Old City Hall, the east doorway on James Street leading into that half of the building used for municipal offices. Where the words 'City Hall' appear here among the decorative stone below the windows, on the west side of the building 'Court House' is carved above the doorway.

5.51 Old City Hall. E.J. Lennox, the architect, worked his name into the scrollwork of a frieze. A lifelike portrait found among the grotesques in the arched main entrance is thought by the architectural historian Douglas Richardson to be Lennox.

5.52 Old City Hall, the council chamber, showing the robust mayor's chair and dais that Lennox designed for this setting

5.53 Legislative buildings, Queen's Park (1886–93), R.A. Waite, architect. The hipped roofs in the links between the centre and the wings are hardly appropriate in the general massing of the building, but in the reconstruction after the fire of 1909 in the west wing, a gable roof with stone dormers was substituted. Already in this nineteenth-century photograph there are signs of the fussy Victorian flower-beds that had their origin in the gardens behind Windsor Castle and mar the approaches to the Parliament buildings in the capital cities of countries throughout the Commonwealth. While red Credit Valley sandstone was used originally, it has been necessary to use stone from New Brunswick quarries near Sackville in later additions and repairs.

5.54 University Avenue, looking south from the legislative buildings. This Notman photograph shows a heavily wooded city of 'dreaming spires.' The motor car had not arrived, and the citizen could enjoy the city on foot or in a horse-drawn vehicle. The heavy turreted building on the right is the old Toronto Athletic Club, which is now part of the Ontario College of Art. Just as Orde Street is closed today, so all east-west streets below College Street were stopped on the avenue by a gate or fence. Both University Avenue and College Street were university property, and a twelve-inch strip on College involved legal and financial negotiations before Eaton's store, now College Park, could be built.

**5.55** Toronto Athletic Club, 149 College Street (1891–4), E.J. Lennox, architect. This building had an indoor swimming pool in the basement and a gymnasium on the top floor. The club was short lived, closing in 1898. During its use subsequently by the federal government, Central Technical School, the police department, and today by the Ontario College of Art, the interior was largely changed, but the outside has remained untouched.

**5.56** Upper Canada College, Avenue Road (1889–91; demolished 1958), George Durand, architect. Awarded second prize in the Toronto Court House competition of 1886, George Durand of London had the opportunity three years later, in the new buildings in Deer Park that he designed for Upper Canada College, to show how much he had been influenced by Richardson and, perhaps, by Lennox.

**5.57** Gooderham Building, Front and Wellington streets (1892), David Roberts, Jr, architect. This well-known building stands on the site of an earlier and blunter flat-iron commonly called the Coffin Block. Here George Gooderham presided over his many business interests, including the Bank of Toronto, of which he was president. Its head office (4.124) was located immediately north, across Wellington Street, on the site of the famous Ontario House (3.21, 22).

**5.58** The York Club, north elevation

**5.59** The York Club, exterior from the southwest

**5.60, 61, 62** The York Club, formerly the residence of George Gooderham, at the corner of
St George and Bloor streets (1889–92), David Roberts, Jr, architect. The club's motto
is 'Let's harbour here in York,' from *3 Henry VI*, and is said to have been quoted by
Lieutenant-Governor Simcoe in May 1793 as he stepped ashore on his first visit to York.
The main entrance, on St George Street (5.60), is enriched by carving by Holbrook and
Mollington. Inside, the entrance hall with its fireplace (5.61) and the former drawing-room
(5.62), now a reading-room, are opulent. The house is a splendid example of the Romanesque manner made popular in the 1880s by the American architect H.H. Richardson.

5.62

the uplifted lines of the angel's wing. In its broader form are the formal and symmetrical dark ribbon outline of the dress and the intricate convolutions of the plant tendrils in the adjoining areas of the vault. Peter Selz says of the Art Nouveau designer, 'If he used a flower, it was not the ordinary garden or field variety, but rather the languid, exotic hothouse plant whose long stalks and pale blossoms he found exquisite.'[3] It was just such a plant that Hahn used to form a rhythmic pattern of lilies on both sides of the nave. The beauty of the angel figures with their lilies rising into the un-adorned area of the vault is given added emphasis and dignity by the jux-taposition of the over-all decoration of the tendrils in the triangular spaces. The lily motif itself is so highly conventionalized that in the gloom of the church the flowers appear at first sight as candelabra.

It is interesting to be able to record of a ceiling painted in the early 1890s that the artist, Gustav Hahn, was alive until 1962 and could still talk about his handiwork.[4] When employed on the decoration of the ceiling, Hahn was the chief designer for a firm of decorators, Elliott and Sons, who specialized in church work and had built up a practice going back a decade or more. The donors of the work at St Paul's were E.R. Wood and W.K. Doherty. The ceiling is not as well known as it might be because it was the custom of the church (along with United and Presbyterian and some Anglican churches in Canada) to keep the doors locked on weekdays. The building is now a theatre and community centre.

For the professional historian, Victorian architecture covers the sixty-odd years between the accession of Victoria in 1837 and her death in 1901, but to close the century we are going to look at a more restricted period covering the last years of the old century and the early years of the seventh Edward. In it are those delightful, light-hearted, exuberant buildings that remain to enliven many a street where the architecture of an earlier time has disappeared.

For the most part, our Victorian architecture consists of houses, either single, double, or in rows, and nearly always distinguishable by fretwork porches, bay windows, and gay gables. In the evolution of architectural design, 'gingerbread' has little to contribute, but the gingerbread was but a veneer on a basic structure that we are only now beginning to appreciate. In a study of nineteenth-century taste we can view the decoration as a re-flection of the gaiety that is popularly believed to have been characteristic of life in the nineties. It may teach us nothing, but it may well cause us to wonder to what excesses a later generation may go in reaction to the gutless geometry of so much of our modern domestic architecture.

The lesson we can learn from the Victorians as we could from the Geor-gians is illustrated by the success with which they created an atmosphere of urban amenity through repetition, a sense of space through enclosure, and a human scale. These qualities in the street architecture of a city were known to the ancients; they provide the charm and the urbanity of so many towns in Britain and on the Continent, and once they distinguished the streets and squares of old Toronto. Yet much of the building done in the second half

5.63 Victoria College, Queen's Park (1889–92), W.G. Storm, architect. This was Storm's last great commission, and he died before it was quite finished. Today the grime of nearly a century and the remains of vines that covered this building a decade ago make it hard to appreciate the rich contrasts of banded stone and tile roofs that distinguished Storm's robust design.

5.64 The University of Toronto Library (1891), David B. Dick, architect. The west façade shows a rather incoherent design, which has not been improved by a 1950s addition to the north. Faults of the original are made up for in part by the beauty of the dominating tower and the graceful entrance, which resembles that of Kelso Abbey, founded in 1128 in Scotland. This photograph by Notman is found among the firm's superb collection of portraits and buildings of the nineteenth century, now the property of McGill University. The negatives number some 350,000.

**5.65, 66** Benvenuto, on the west side of the Avenue Road hill (1888–91; demolished 1931), A. Page Brown, architect. This was the residence of S.H. Janes, the successful real-estate promoter who laid out the area we know as the Annex, bounded by Avenue Road, Bathurst Street, Dupont, and Bloor. The house was built of grey rock-faced Kingston stone (still to be seen in a wall on Avenue Road south of Edmund Drive), with very handsome red-glazed roof tiles, which are now on a house built for R.A. Laidlaw at Roche's Point, Lake Simcoe. The lodge and the gates (5.66) lasted long after the house had been demolished. For a time the lodge was a tea-room. The gates with their piers were moved to a property at 40 Burton Road, Toronto. They were made while Mr Janes and his family were in Italy, and there are no finer examples of wrought iron in Canada.

5.67 Benvenuto, a bedroom

5.68 Benvenuto, the dining-room

of the century was large-scale speculation, and the architects of the period and their clients could not have been unaware of the attractiveness of the Georgian houses they were destroying in the search for sites.[5] Such houses can be seen in a photograph (5.103) of 1875 taken from the top of the Metropolitan Church tower. Even at so late a date Toronto was a Georgian brick town of single, double, and row houses along tree-lined streets. The single houses were also united in design, by a common material, brick, a uniform pattern of window, a common cornice line, and the distinguishing feature of the framed doorway or porch.

Repetition of a dwelling or a commercial unit on a street of 'infinite' length like Yonge Street would be boring to a degree, but the repetition of a single house, even if bizarre in design, on a street of limited length can give pleasure. This is especially true where the vista is terminated by a building or, what is all too rare in modern Toronto, where the ultimate in enclosure is achieved by a square or a cul-de-sac. We still have streets where the Victorian rhythm of bay windows, whimsical porches, and fretted gables seen through elms or flowering chestnuts can give real aesthetic enjoyment, an enjoyment that can never be evoked by the dreary lines of strawberry boxes in our newer subdivisions or by the serried ranks of ranch houses in the more salubrious areas developed for the well-to-do.

Space as an emotional experience within a building or formed by a complex of buildings was known to the Victorians, but it is something vital to architecture that we have lost in the meantime. It is recognized as an indispensable principle by all reputable planning authorities and may yet return as a fundamental truth in civic design. In our haste to turn our backs on everything that was old, we ignored so delightful an element in eighteenth-century planning as the building terminating a vista – a feature, now suspect as 'vista mongering,' that appears in many places in the Victorian street pattern. Osgoode Hall at the end of York Street or old Knox at the head of Spadina can be compared with the unsatisfactory modern terminations of Toronto Street at Adelaide or Harbord Street at St George.

Important as were the repetition of a unit to form terraces and the concept of space that produced culs-de-sac and squares, a third quality was necessary to complete the urban picture. That was the human scale that characterized our architecture, both domestic and commercial. The amalgam of all three plus walls of brick or stucco and the shade trees for which Toronto is famous are what give so many of our residential streets their restfulness, their sparkle, and their charm. When one contrasts the older residential districts in Canadian cities with ours, one feels instinctively that the architects and builders of the past in Toronto have produced something that, in many ways, might be called indigenous. Scores of our old streets, whole neighbourhoods indeed, could exist nowhere but in Toronto, while University Avenue and Bloor Street could be found anywhere in the United States.

An event that had a devastating effect on architecture and town planning in North America was the Chicago Exhibition of 1893, a year, in Toronto,

**5.69** Thorncrest, house of G.P. Magann, on Dowling Avenue at the lake (1889–90; demolished circa 1921), David Roberts, Jr, architect. A large house for Toronto, Thorncrest had a fine site, which after the First World War became part of the park south of Lakeshore Boulevard. The photograph is not a good one, but it illustrates many features in the building that had their origin in Chicago – the rambling plan that takes advantage of the lake view, the rugged masonry, the outdoor covered space. Frank Lloyd Wright's work in the United States demonstrated the same 'hovering planes' over deeply recessed areas, and some of his earliest houses share other characteristics of Thorncrest.

**5.70** Numbers 18–24 Soho Street (1888), an extravaganza involving richness of detail and modelling, kept under control by the strong horizontal ridge of the slate roof

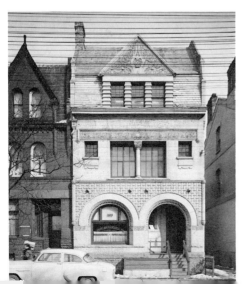

**5.71** House of Dr G.R. McDonagh, 329 Church Street (1888; demolished circa 1970), E.J. Lennox, architect. The architect for the City Hall lavished much care on this townhouse for Dr J.E. Graham, who lived a few doors north at the corner of Church and Gerrard streets, but Dr McDonagh was the first occupant. The Richardsonian manner of the old City Hall shows in the basket-weave brickwork, carving, and dormer.

**5.72, 73** The First and Second Crystal Palaces. There were few buildings in the world in the nineteenth century to equal the Crystal Palace of 1851 in Hyde Park, but several similar great glass and iron exhibition halls followed in Canada and the United States. The first Crystal Palace (1858), Fleming and Schreiber, architects, was on a site due south of the dome of the Lunatic Asylum on Queen Street. Like the great Crystal Palace of Hyde Park, our first palace was moved in 1878 to a new site in the present Exhibition Park, just south of the Dufferin Gate, without mishap and with maximum salvage. A ground floor was put under it and a cupola was added. The architects for the second Crystal Palace were Strickland and Symons; it was destroyed by fire in 1906.

**5.74** Oak Hall, 115–21 King Street East, opposite St James' Cathedral (1893; demolished 1938), George R. Harper, architect. In its heyday this was a famous clothing store, but it was chiefly remarkable for the lightness of its structure and the breadth of glass at all levels.

**5.75** Royal Canadian Bank, 36–8 Front Street East (1871; demolished 1961), Smith and Gemmell, architects. To the purist there is something quite revolting in a façade of iron simulating stone, but one has to remember the period and its problems. Actually, we are looking at a form of construction that was the precursor of the steel structures of today. The architect was prepared to use a comparatively new material, but he fell back on Renaissance forms, perhaps in deference to his client.

**5.76** St Paul's United Church, 121 Avenue Road (1886), Smith and Gemmell, architects. The Art Nouveau decoration on the ceiling, painted by Gustav Hahn in 1890, makes the very beautiful nave unique in Canada, if not in North America. The ribs in the vaulting are cast iron.

**5.77** North side of Front Street at Yonge. Here in one short streetscape are three of the most ambitious buildings of the nineteenth-century city, seen just before demolition in the 1960s shattered the integrity of this view. On the left is the A.R. McMaster warehouse (5.18) of 1871, rebuilt and doubled in size after the 1904 fire. Beyond, at the corner of Yonge Street, the Bank of Montreal (5.41), which escaped the fire, enjoys the unmatched setting created by a small open space along Front Street. Across from the bank is the Board of Trade Building, built in 1889–91 to plans by James and James, English architects who had established themselves in New York. Today only the Bank of Montreal remains.

**5.78** Confederation Life Building, northeast corner of Richmond and Yonge streets (1890–91), Knox, Elliot and Jarvis, architects. One of the most important commissions of its day, it was awarded after a competition. When built, this was considered the last word in office buildings, although thick bearing walls and mill construction did not mark it as a very progressive structure. During a recent renovation the building suffered a fire that might have resulted in demolition except for a heritage-easement agreement with the city. Regrettably, the renovations have not restored the towers, which contributed so much to the building's appearance and to Toronto's skyline.

**5.79** Temple Building for the Independent Order of Foresters, at the corner of Bay and Richmond (1895–7; demolished 1970), George W. Gouinlock, architect. The movement started by H.H. Richardson resulted in a number of Romanesque-revival buildings in Toronto, of which this was one of the best. It was the headquarters for the fraternal insurance organization headed in the 1890s by Dr Oronhyatekha, an Iroquois born on the Six Nations reserve near Brantford. Said the *Globe* at the time the building opened in 1897, 'the surrounding buildings are dwarfed into comparative pygmies.' There was a 'roomy bicycle stable' in the basement.

**5.80** The Armouries, at the corner of University Avenue and Osgoode Street (1891; demolished 1963), Thomas Fuller, architect. This is the work of the architect of St Stephen's-in-the-Fields (4.96) more than thirty years later. During the interval he had designed the Ottawa Parliament building (in partnership with Chilion Jones), and in 1881 he was appointed the Dominion Architect. Like all armouries in North America, this one was built in the style of a fortified castle, with battlements and dungeon-like windows in the towers. The Armouries was, however, no dead exercise in mediaeval archaeology; it had life and nobility.

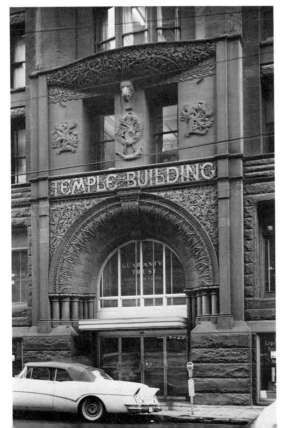

**5.81** Temple Building, detail of stone carving. The architect worked with conviction, and his stone-carvers were skilled in their craft. A portion of the carving below the moose head, which was the symbol of the Foresters, has been preserved in the gardens of the Guild Inn, Scarborough.

when Lennox was working on the City Hall and David Roberts had just finished the house for George Gooderham at the corner of St George and Bloor. The committee in charge of the exhibition had on it a group of architects who represented, in almost equal numbers, the virile and creative local school and the powerful neoclassical school of New York and the eastern seaboard. The vote on which rested the whole character of the exhibition was in favour of the latter, and the result was a White City of Roman buildings on Roman streets about a lake on which American citizens could be ferried on gondolas from one exhibit to another.

No exhibition has ever had more influence on a nation, and Canada was inevitably affected. The buildings themselves were transitory, but they were the inspiration in Toronto alone for such permanent monuments as the Union Station, the now-demolished Bank of Toronto at King and Bay, the Princes' Gates, the Registry Building, which once stood on the site of the new City Hall, and numerous temple-like branch banks and public libraries. Even the schools of architecture were affected, and the popularity of the Ecole des beaux arts in Paris reached an all-time high.

It was not a period in our architectural history, either here, in Great Britain, or in the United States, that we can recall with pride. It would be an understatement to say that it lacked the fire of the Classical revival of the nineteenth century. Our forefathers of the eighteen-sixties in Toronto had books illustrating in line the orders of architecture and the great buildings of antiquity, but when the head office of a bank had to be designed, there were no models from the remote past and few that were contemporary. The situation was very different in the early twentieth century. A flood of illustrated magazines presented the architect with somebody's recent solution to every possible building type, and architecture became rather drearily imitative.

Happily for this writer, the Classical revival that followed in the trail of the White City was slow in reaching Toronto, and what it produced, both good and bad, is of the twentieth century – and consequently, outside the boundaries of this book.

**5.82** The Second Union Station, Front Street west of York (1873; demolished 1927), E.P. Hannaford, architect. The great train shed and station of 1873 with its three towers can be seen here, sandwiched between a second, lower shed along the water's edge and, in the foreground, the lofty extension that joined the station to Front Street in 1893–5, Strickland and Symons, architects. This newer part provided more generous passenger waiting areas and a shopping arcade.

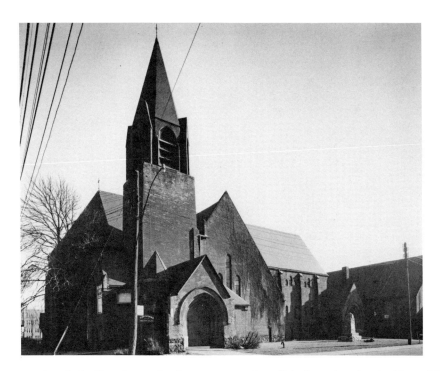

**5.83** St John's Church, Portland Street (1892; demolished 1963), Eden Smith, architect. Known as the Garrison Church long after the soldiers had left the Stanley Barracks, this church and its predecessor saved the troops the fatigue of marching to St James'. The Ontario government still owns the adjoining Victoria Square, which is the graveyard of four hundred soldiers and early citizens, among them children of Sir John Colborne.

**5.84, 85** Robert Simpson Company store, southwest corner of Queen and Yonge streets (1895), Burke and Horwood, architects. The land on which it was built was part of an area bounded by Yonge, Richmond, Bay, and Queen streets that was deeded to 'the Presbyterians' by a rich landowner and tanner, Jesse Ketchum. In 1894 the church held all that property except for the frontage on Yonge Street, which it had sold. Knox Church on Spadina Avenue still receives ground rent from a far from negligible piece of land beneath the Robert Simpson store. The five bays on Yonge Street south from Queen Street, on the right in 5.84, and the seven bays west of the corner date from 1895. The Yonge Street frontage was extended four bays south to Richmond Street in 1912. Seen on Richmond Street are the dapple greys and their drivers (5.85) ready for the signal to leave with their deliveries – an impressive sight until 1928, when horsepower displaced the horses.

**5.86** The Queen Street entrance of the T. Eaton store is seen from Knox Church before Simpson's expanded on to the church site. Today an elevated pedestrian bridge crosses between Eaton's and Simpson's at almost exactly this point.

**5.87** Harbord Street Collegiate, between Euclid and Manning avenues (1890–2; demolished 1930), Knox and Elliot, architects. Few high schools of the nineteenth century can have been so well lit and elegant as this one in a Flemish Renaissance style, with its large windows, turrets, and more than twenty gables. The central tower, like that on the Confederation Life building by the same architects, enriched the skyline for only a brief period. After being struck by lightning in 1916, it was taken down to a point just above the arched trio of openings. The rest of the building was in poor condition when it was demolished and replaced in 1931.

5.84

5.85

5.86

**5.88** House of John Miller, 33 Murray Street (1898; demolished 1963), Charles J. Gibson, architect. Miller was a journalist at one time on the staff of the *Mail and Empire*. The house is said to be a copy of one that he admired in Brussels, but it is more likely to have been the result of his extensive travels in the Near East and the Holy Land. The house is gone, but it was always rather tantalizing to pass it. One expected veiled ladies of the household to sun themselves on the upper balcony or to take a brief walk on Murray Street as a poor substitute for the casbah in Marrakeech.

5.90

**5.89** Massey Hall, Shuter Street (1893–4), Sidney R. Badgley, architect. When the building was opened, the *Canadian Architect and Builder* criticized the exterior as being 'about as aesthetical as the average grain elevator' and branded the Moorish decoration of the interior as pretentious and tawdry. Nevertheless, the hall has been a favourite of several generations of musicians and concert-goers because of its outstanding acoustical properties. The architect, a Canadian living in Cleveland, had designed dozens of large churches throughout the American midwest and was experienced in creating spaces where sound would carry clearly without echo.

**5.90** The Moorish room in the Massey house at the northeast corner of Jarvis and Wellesley streets, originally the home of Arthur R. McMaster and today a popular restaurant. The room was built to the designs of George M. Miller for Mrs Lillian Massey Treble in 1899–1901. Doubtless it was inspired by the decoration of the Massey Music Hall. The rooms are decorated in blue, red, and gold, but even a photograph suggests the Edwardian soirées where the ladies smoked with long cigarette-holders and the men drew on hookahs while someone read passages from the diary of Lady Hester Stanhope.

**5.91** Loretto Abbey, Wellington Street near Spadina (1897; demolished 1961), Beaumont
Jarvis, architect. The abbey was part of a complex that included fragments of Vice-Chan-
cellor Jameson's house as well as spacious rooms built in the 1850s for the Widder family.
The exterior in a red pressed brick was unworthy of the interior, which was quite fine.
In its later years the abbey became a Jesuit seminary.

5.92

5.92, 93 Holy Blossom Temple, Bond Street, now St George Greek Orthodox Church (1895), John Wilson Siddall, architect. Recently restored, the exterior to-day differs from this photograph only in having less-bulbous domes and a picture in the tympanum of St George slaying the dragon. The interior has lost nothing in the change of congregations. Brilliant panels of saints in the sanctuary and the winged figures in the pendentives make a striking contrast with the simple whiteness of the walls. Explorers such as Sitwell or church-goers such as Samuel Pepys would find this little bit of Byzantium on Bond Street an interesting and colourful discovery.

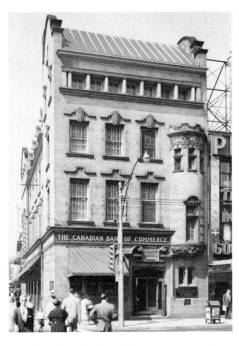

5.95

**5.94** Canadian Bank of Commerce, northwest corner of Yonge and Bloor streets (1898; demolished 1972), Darling and Pearson, architects. The design of this bank was not at all in the usual style of Darling and Pearson, but they could hardly escape the Art Nouveau manner that was the vogue in Europe. The exterior presented as fine a bank as any in Toronto. The interior was less interesting, but what evidence there was of Art Nouveau was scraped away in 1960 in an attempt at modernization. The Toronto Ladies' Club was on the second floor.

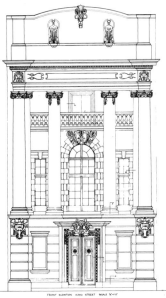

**5.95** The Toronto Club, Wellington and York streets (1888), Darling and Curry, architects. The club was estabished in 1837, a date that justifies its claim to be second in age only to the Philadelphia Club on this continent. Its continuous minutes go back to 1842, when rooms were secured in the British Coffee House, on the site of the present Toronto-Dominion Centre. In 1864 the club had acquired its own building at 77–9 York Street, where it remained until its present quarters were erected. It is difficult to give it an architectural label. In a way it is the history of architecture from Jacobean to Georgian times – all held together by the skill of the architect. Rooms in the club are spacious, with liberal use of wood panelling and broad fireplaces.

**5.96** Bank of Nova Scotia, 39–41 King Street West (1902–3; demolished 1969), Darling and Pearson, architects. Covered with a patina of soot and guano, the old building was difficult to photograph. It was interesting, if only for its sculptured façade, the wall deeply recessed behind the Ionic columns. Those were the days (as in the Manning Chambers) when it was not necessary that every foot of floor space should be remunerative. For many years the building was used as a downtown public library.

**5.97** King Edward Hotel, Victoria Room (1902). Modern architecture in Toronto has so far failed to produce a hotel dining-room with anything like the flair and gaity of this one. The secret of the room's success is the decorative plaster work, which reflects credit on the designer and craftsmen who executed it. The late Mrs H.J. Cody distinctly recalled meeting a Mr Edward Colonna of Montreal who was said to be the designer.

**5.98** Number 70 Wellington Street West (1905; demolished), Wickson and Gregg, architects. This excellent office building was built at a time when the Art Nouveau movement was sweeping Europe and Great Britain. Characteristic features are to be seen in the detailing of the lower windows, and of the doors in particular. The stone carving is vigorous and obviously the work of a master craftsman, not a few of which there were eighty years ago in Toronto. The weighted strings hanging from the cornice oscillate in a breeze and seem effectively to discourage pigeons from roosting on the ledges of the façade at any level. They are also quite decorative in themselves.

**5.99** Church of the Redeemer (1878–9), Smith and Gemmell, architects, and Renaissance Centre (1981–2), joint venture of the Webb Zerafa Menkes Housden partnership and Page and Steele, architects. A transfer of density rights from the church to the tall modern building behind gave the congregation the monies needed to restore their building and to renew their commitment to worship at the crossroads of Bloor Street and Avenue Road.

**5.100** Knox College (1873–5), Smith and Gemmell, architects. This not undistinguished building stands in the circle at the head of Spadina Avenue, north of College Street. In its day it has served as college, armouries for the Toronto Regiment, and as a penicillin plant for Connaught Laboratories. The circle antedates the building and was once known as Crescent Gardens. It was intended as a park under a deed that, on certain conditions that were not met, gave the land to the city. The offer was never taken up, and in 1873 the property was sold by a daughter of Robert Baldwin's to John McMurrich, for ten thousand dollars.

**5.101, 102** Metropolitan Church, Queen Street East (1870–3; burned 1928; rebuilt), Henry Langley, architect. How excellent was the photography of 1880, and how beautiful were the church grounds! The parterre in front has gone, and the park to the north has been sacrificed for Sunday-school and church offices. The Metropolitan suffered a fire in 1928 and was rebuilt in a simplified form by J. Gibb Morton, architect. The cast-iron fence surrounding the church grounds, erected in 1875, was taken down in 1961. It and the fence at St James' were scrapped on the offer of the city to maintain the grass in perpetuity, an extraordinarily short-sighted bargain. Enclosure is resented in Toronto, and the lawn in front of Osgoode Hall behind the Law Society's recently restored fence is one of the few survivors.

5. 102

**5.103** Toronto from the tower of Metropolitan Church, looking south from Queen Street (circa 1875). This remarkable photograph of a Georgian town must date from before 1878, because in that year old St Andrew's Church, on the left, was demolished. Toronto's historical buildings were often needlessly destroyed, but the real loss is seen here. Today on every street individual buildings are in competition with one another; in 1875 we had order and dignity, tree-lined squares and rows of houses like Alma Terrace of 1855 on Richmond Street in the centre of this view. Any house in the foreground would do credit to Beacon Hill in Boston.

**5.104** Collier Street: sunlight and shadow, the feeling of space and security through enclosure that has disappeared from the modern street. We no longer have residential street architecture – only houses.

# 6 Epilogue

The reader has come on a long and, I hope, not too arduous journey since we looked behind the palisades of the ancient village at the end of the well-trodden *passage de Toronto*. We were there in spirit when the lieutenant-governor and Mrs Simcoe sailed into Toronto harbour, and we heard with pride the salute of guns that heralded the founding of York, the capital of Upper Canada. We saw the town prostrate before the guns of the American flotilla in 1813, and we saw it rise again, in two critical decades, as Toronto, the incorporated city.

Toronto never looked back, and it is with reluctance that one leaves the story of its architecture at the threshold of the twentieth century. It has been said more than once in our story that architectural periods cannot be confined by dates, but socially and politically the year 1900 seems to suggest the end of an era with more than usual finality, and the century that followed we can leave with confidence to the chronicler who will, almost certainly, write at the turn of the second millennium. It is a sobering thought that he may be one of my own students, at this moment a callow youth in his freshman year. If we have overlapped into his territory, it is because we could do nothing to prevent the Victorian merging with the seventh Edward; Art Nouveau did not expire on the last day of the old century, and architectural practice continued in its gentlemanly, if sometimes pedestrian course, blissfully unaware of the industrial and technological revolution that lay ahead. The young architect of today who is part of a highly organized office will find it difficult to believe that in 1900 AD architects wrote their specifications by hand, that drawings were laboriously copied and hand coloured because blueprinting was still unknown, and that jobs and clients were visited in horse-drawn carriages.

If we found Toronto great where we left it, our future chronicler will write of a greater and more illustrious city, a metropolis known and respected throughout the civilized world. In his day the *passage de Toronto* will have become a legend, hardly credible in a provincial capital boasting superhighways, underground railways, an airport of international importance, a great university, and a harbour to which ships come from the far corners of the earth.

In the march of progress every vestige of our nineteenth-century heritage will have disappeared, and only University College, Osgoode Hall, the old City Hall, St Lawrence Hall, and a few churches will remain. Even for them, fire is the ever-present menace, and it is not inconceivable that by 2000 AD all the nineteenth-century buildings dealt with in this book will be one with Nineveh and Tyre.

Much as we may regret the loss of buildings, we have an even greater heritage about which Toronto is peculiarly apathetic. Of the 1,900 acres of ravine we once enjoyed, 840 have been filled for factories, roads, and houses. No ravine and no park is absolutely safe from pressures as widely diverse as the government of Canada and the speculative builder. In an atmosphere always charged with emotion – of wounded soldiers needing beds or of undergraduates urgently needing desks – we gave Kilgour Park to the federal government for Sunnybrook Hospital and a botanical garden to York University. In 1962 St James' Square disappeared completely in the enlargement of Ryerson, and the 'several acres' that Jesse Ketchum gave as a children's park in Yorkville have dwindled to the dreary pavement of the school that bears his name. Only in the nick of time did the city at last prevent a rash of speculative building in the ravines, and two or three apartment buildings are there now as permanent reminders to posterity of the need for eternal vigilance.

Periodically, there is talk of a school in Howard's High Park. The project will come up again and, almost certainly, will be based on a claim for physically handicapped children. In short, sponsors will be found for a school based on the most laudable and humane principles, and our withers will be most cruelly and unnecessarily wrung.

We show no particular maturity, in either the press or the public, in our stewardship of the natural resources with which we have been endowed. Only in the Metro development of the Island have we seen leadership of the highest order, but even as I write, the pressure for a bridge, for motor cars, cottages, and apartment houses assumes dangerous proportions. A natural, beautiful island would do much to offset our profligate gifts of parkland for institutional purposes on the mainland.

Posterity will rightly judge that we were unworthy of University Avenue, which, one hundred years ago, was a tree-lined thoroughfare with more dignity than it has today. Twice in the last few years the monuments that pepper the avenue have been taken down, but no one has asked in the press why several of them should be put back again. No one has asked why so puerile a piece of sculpture as the stunted Tommy and the dog-like lions should continue to represent the Sons of England, or why the trend should be perpetuated of turning the central strip into a Valhalla for the deceased chief executives of Hydro. Many objections can be raised to design control, but where bad art and politics combine to belittle a great civic avenue, a fine arts committee of unquestionable integrity and authority would seem necessary.

Forty years from now, our chronicler will look with some bewilderment at these pages. Unless we are greatly mistaken, the intervening decades will produce architecture that will have all the attributes of greatness except a human scale. He will look at canyons of office buildings, multi-storey university buildings, and skyscraper apartment houses that will be the homes of thousands. By contrast, he will notice that, in spite of unashamed eclecticism and lack of conviction on the part of an earlier generation, we once had an architecture where man was the measure in the greater, as in the humbler, thoroughfares. He will find it difficult to believe that the pursuit of old buildings could be fun and an absorbing hobby. Will he find loveliness in old churches, old houses, or even old warehouses, or will age and the patina of age be synonymous with obsolescence? The sand-blasting of the old Bank of Montreal, the porches of St James' Cathedral, Trinity College, and the Metropolitan Church would indicate that such a point of view is not without its adherents, even in 1963.

Through the ages, many books have been written about great cities, but pride and love for the city of one's birth or adoption have never surpassed Cicero's 'civis Romanus sum' or St Paul's boast that he was 'a citizen of no mean city.' It is in that spirit that this book has been written, but admiration and affection should not blind us to the all too blatant ugliness of large areas of Toronto. We not only have ugliness in urban and suburban areas, but as a distinguished Canadian once said to me of Danforth Avenue, 'I am sometimes convinced that we have even a cult of ugliness in Toronto.' The desecration of Toronto Street and the entire absence of design in a civic sense of the filing-cabinet façades on both sides of University Avenue would indicate that we are in no position to cast the first stone at those who preceded us.

Our worst streets are those Victorian and Edwardian thoroughfares where bad design and poor maintenance give an impression of sordidness and decay. King, Queen, Dundas, and much of Yonge are such streets, and their ugliness is not improved by their stretching, seemingly, to infinity. Where they also presented a grim façade to our worst slums, we have gradually made improvements by subsidizing low-rental housing estates, but only the fringe of a vast degenerate area has so far been touched. It is the opinion of this writer that we have far-sighted planners with able staffs in both the city and Metropolitan Toronto, but without public support they cannot themselves create the kind of political climate that demands the large-scale rehabilitation of blighted urban areas. Boston, Hartford, Baltimore, and San Francisco, to mention only a few American cities, are seeing such citizens' and planners' dreams turn into reality.

Since 1852, when the railways were allowed to ravage the waterfront and leave on their flanks an unplanned mess of roundhouses, warehouses, factories, and slums, Toronto has turned its back on the lake. We still have an Esplanade, but no longer is it a place for promenade, for seeing ships at anchor, or for Easter parades. Today the pedestrian is rare on the Esplanade. Trucks and trains have taken his place, and the lakefront has receded beyond sight. The migration to Parkdale did not escape the railway, but the move to Bloor opened up a new residential area. Then came the Annex, Rosedale, Moore Park, Bayview – always with green fields and singing birds beyond, and the seeds of decay behind.

One would like to think that, with Bayview, we had reached the limit of unplanned escapist growth, and that there were great schemes afoot for the rejuvenation of the old city, not merely for business but for leisure and urban living. When one thinks of London, Paris, or New York, one is conscious only of the *urbs*, the great city. In the judgment of posterity it may not be to our credit to be remembered only as the city of suburban homes.

The young in every generation are critical of the old, but to understand the architecture of the past sixty years in Toronto one has to remember that fifteen of them were lost in war and the Great Depression. The modern movement as we understand it today did not spring fully born on Toronto soil from the head of Le Corbusier or of Mies van der Rohe. It took root slowly in a field unprepared, and often resistant to it. Most of our older architects who now command the largest commissions were trained under a Beaux Arts system that gave them a familiarity with Georgian and Gothic architecture, which they regarded not so much as history but rather as a reservoir of design material. The best of these offices gradually saw the light, and their work changed as graduates in their employ were given greater freedom to design. Even in the last decade younger firms have started practice and have demonstrated their skill in buildings of great distinction. The possibilities for employment in Toronto have attracted young architects from every province as well as from the United Kingdom and the continent of Europe. At present their influence is slight, but as their opportunities increase and their confidence grows, we can expect new colour and vitality in the local architectural scene.

The construction of a monumental building like Toronto's new City Hall must be an elevating and exhilarating experience for the community that watches its growth. It must have been so for London and Rome, where old men could boast that they saw St Paul's or St Peter's rise in all its solemn majesty from the seething human tide at its base to the serenity of the loftiest cross. Such an event is rare in the life of a city or a nation, and the whole populace rejoices in its presence.

It is now common knowledge that 520 architects from 44 countries submitted designs for Toronto's new City Hall and that a Finnish architect, Viljo Revell, was the successful competitor. In the conditions of competition there was a statement that must have given all competitors much thought and doubtless influenced Revell even before he put pencil to paper. It was this:

In the eighteenth century city, the cathedral and the town hall frequently dominated the urban scene both physically and spiritually. Our present City Hall is largely overshadowed by commerical and financial buildings, but it still dominates by its presence. It differs in that respect from those centres of civic administrations in North America where the 'hall' is just another office building. One of the reasons for this competition is to find a building that will proudly express its function as the centre of civic government. How to achieve an atmosphere about a building that suggests government, continuity of democratic traditions and service to the community are problems for the designer of the modern city hall. These were qualities that the architects of other ages endeavoured to embody in the town halls of their times.

They were qualities, too, that Revell was able to embody to a remarkable degree in his design, which will become the very symbol of government at the municipal level.

Where the City Hall for Toronto of 1844 lay just outside the shadow of St James', the present one will dominate the whole city – not that it 'vaunteth' itself unnecessarily, but the ramification of services and the multiplicity of departments of the modern city hall demand a building of truly monumental dimensions. Far reaching in its influence on architecture and momentous in the future history of Toronto, the new City Hall, like a spring in the desert, will give life and beauty to wide areas about it. Another decade will see the rehabilitation of the south side of Queen Street, now in all its decrepitude, a renaissance of the whole arid area between Hagerman and Dundas, and a rejuvenation of the ugly warehouses to the east. No city anywhere has, in a century, devoted so generous an amount of urban land for its public square, and the international competition for the building itself focused the attention of the entire world on the corner of Queen and Bay streets in Toronto.

The City Hall will be unquestionably a landmark in the architecture of the city, but it can also be a beacon in the development of Canadian painting, sculpture, and a wide range of skills and handicrafts. In one of the studies prepared for the Royal Commission on the National Development of the Arts, Letters, and Sciences of 1951, mention is made of the extent to which artists are employed on government buildings in all European countries. So civilized a custom has not yet reached North America, except in the Depression years, when painters and sculptors were employed on low-rental housing estates in the United States. Many artists got their start on those projects and were able, through WPA, to give pleasure to hundreds of thousands of people.

There is, of course, ample evidence from historical times, the Renaissance in particular, when all public buildings, churches, and palaces were enriched by the greatest artists with mural painting and sculpture that today are priceless national treasures. Those were the days when the town hall was a symbol of everything that was good and significant in municipal life, and its presence added stature not only to the burgher but to the city and the nation. Such, once, was the Cloth Hall at Ypres, and such still are the town hall and the guild halls of Brussels, but happily one does not have to seek examples only from the distant past. There is at least one modern city where the town hall takes second place to none in the ancient world for the sheer beauty of murals in paint and mosaics, for sculpture, furnishings, and landscaping, and that is Stockholm, the capital of Sweden. Won in competition like Toronto's City Hall, the design of the town hall in Stockholm has captured the imagination of the Swedish people as no building has in several centuries, and today, forty years after it was built, it still attracts thousands of tourists annually from many countries. The same is true of Oslo, and the same could be true of Toronto. Only yesterday, I saw that the City Hall had risen high above the surrounding board fence, and from the seventh floor of a Bay Street office building the staff could see the great central column and the tremendous sweep of the curved enclosing walls. It will be a supremely great building in terms of function and the monumentality of its public spaces, but one would like to forecast that it will also be an edifice where citizens, for centuries, can see all that was best in art in this generation. It is a challenge for the artists of Canada, but no greater than for the artists of much smaller, less rich, and less populated Sweden. This writer is confident that they will meet it.

It was a happy coincidence that, as these lines were written, so signal an event as the solemn laying of the commemorative plaque by Mayor Nathan Phillips had taken place and that nothing humanly predictable could delay the completion of the City Hall by 1965. Taller buildings will be built before the end of the century here and elsewhere in North America, but there will be no comparable or no more renowned city hall. One hundred and seventy-two years are as nothing in the life of a city, but in that brief span we have seen Toronto grow from the small military establishment that mounted guard on the lives of the lieutenant-governor, his family, and council, whose only protection for two summers and a hard winter was flimsy coverings of a canvas tent. The journey from that tiny hamlet set precariously on the edge of the wilderness to the proud metropolis of today is a record of achievement hardly to be equalled in history. The new City Hall is the very embodiment of that achievement and is at the same time a portent of greatness to come. Our chronicler of the second millennium will describe a still more illustrious metropolis, but its heart and head will still be at the corner of Queen and Bay.

6.1 Toronto City Hall and old City Hall. Symbols of the best moments of civic government, these two buildings are exceptional architectural achievements. Any substantial alterations to either should quite properly be resisted.

AFTERWORD

Twenty-three years have passed since Eric Arthur set down his pen at the end of his Epilogue. From it, we know that he looked upon the then-uncompleted fourth City Hall with considerable pride, both as a citizen of Toronto and as the chairman of the jury that had selected Viljo Revell's design. The building was opened to the public by Governor General Georges Vanier on 13 September 1965. Sadly, the architect Revell was not present; he had died a few months before.

It is said in Arthur's Epilogue that the City Hall would be 'unquestionably a landmark in the architecture of the city.' If it has not proved as municipal offices to have been 'a supremely great building in terms of function,' it has contributed significantly nevertheless to how Torontonians have seen themselves during the last two decades and to the pride expressed by boosters of 'the Liveable City.' Although the building has not been filled with painting and sculpture – in part because City Council became faint-hearted about spending the taxpayers' money on such 'frills' – the purchase of Henry Moore's *Archer* and its presentation to the city by Mayor Philip Givens and a group of private citizens has led to the Art Gallery of Ontario's acquisition of one of the world's finest collections of that sculptor's works.

In urging the necessity of a fine-arts committee of unquestionable integrity and authority, Eric Arthur spoke convincingly to our time: many of our great public spaces recently have been diminished by less important art-works. Still pertinent too is his warning that we must be eternally vigilant if we are to overcome our rather sad record of allowing parks and other public spaces to be built upon. For example, in the last two decades we have seen pass into private ownership the greater part of the market-square reserve of 1803; the land has now been developed for luxury condominiums. Un-fortunately, the nearby park named for the colonizer and architect-builder William Berczy, which may have been intended to replace the reserve, was created through the demolition of many of the city's finest commercial buildings of the nineteenth century.

Yet Torontonians can take some satisfaction from the fact that Professor Arthur is likely to be wrong in predicting for the turn of the next century that, 'in the march of progress, every vestige of our nineteenth-century "heritage" will have disappeared, and only University College, Osgoode Hall, the old City Hall, St Lawrence Hall, and a few churches will remain.' The list almost certainly will be much longer, although it will include over-zealous renovations that destroy much of the original character of some buildings. We have this to fear in connection with the old City Hall, now approaching the end of its interim use for the courts and likely to be altered for the purposes of one level or another of municipal government.

We may expect too, although not welcome, yet another battle to protect Fort York from insensitive roadway construction around its perimeter. On the eve of the two-hundredth anniversary of the founding of York and the establishment of the fort designed to protect the town, there is some irony in the number of times, particularly during this century, that the citizens of the city have been called upon to protect the fort. It would be encouraging, and a sign of our maturity as a community, if this next time the defenders included large numbers of citizens from throughout the metropolitan Toronto area. In a world where Toronto, as we have seen, was not born great, there must be an effort to achieve greatness rather than to assume that it will be thrust upon us.

# Notes

CHAPTER ONE: THE VILLAGE AND THE ANCIENT TRAILS

1 Confusing for the ordinary reader of the period, and not a little confusing for map-makers of the past, was the fact that, until the eighteenth century, the word Toronto was used to refer not to the mouth of the Humber but to 'le lac Toronto,' which was Lake Simcoe.
2 Robinson *Toronto during the French Régime* 2
3 Scadding *Toronto of Old* 228; Dr Scadding recalls a time when he himself, in the course of an hour, speared twenty heavy salmon in the Don.
4 Ibid, 22, 'The poor lake-craft which in 1804 must have accommodated the poet, may have put in at the harbour of York. He certainly alludes to a tranquil evening scene on the waters in that quarter.'
5 Robinson *French Régime* 80
6 Scadding *History of the Old French Fort at Toronto* 22
7 Robinson *French Régime* 147
8 Ibid, 8

CHAPTER TWO: 'AS IT WAS IN THE BEGINNING ...'

1 Great Britain, Treaties *Indian Treaties and Surrenders* (Ottawa 1891) I. 34
2 Middleton *Municipality of Toronto* I. 143. The site is now occupied by London, Ontario.
3 Mary Quayle Innis, ed *Mrs. Simcoe's Diary* 89
4 Cruikshank, ed *Correspondence of John Graves Simcoe* I. 18
5 Bouchette *British Dominions in North America* I. 89
6 Mrs Simcoe is addressing the lady in England to whom her diary record was sent weekly. This extract is given in Firth, ed *Town of York* 213; see also Innis, ed *Mrs. Simcoe's Diary* 95.
7 Firth, ed *Town of York* 213. See also Innis, ed *Mrs. Simcoe's Diary* 101.

John Ross Robertson has raised the point that Mrs Simcoe's statement implies that, as Colonel Simcoe had been to Toronto, he cannot have been on board, but that is quite unthinkable in the story of Toronto.

8  Simcoe's original Executive Council was composed of James Baby, Alexander Grant, William Osgoode, William Robertson (not sworn in, and did not sit), and Peter Russell. Members of his Legislative Council were James Baby, Richard Cartwright, Alexander Grant, Robert Hamilton, John Munro, William Osgoode, William Robertson (who did not take the oath), and Peter Russell.

9  Firth, ed *Town of York* 10

10  Ibid, xxxvi

11  Ibid, 253

12  Middleton *Municipality of Toronto* I. 72

13  Rochefoucault-Liancourt *Travels through the United States of North America,* I. 269

14  Firth, ed *Town of York* lxxvi

15  Scadding *Toronto of Old* 199

16  Robertson *Landmarks* s I. 98

17  Mention of the paintings suggests a note on the topographers whose work sometimes sheds so bright a light on life in early Canada. Many were military men for whom the ability to sketch landscape or features in it would be a valuable accomplishment. Others, like Mrs Simcoe, Mrs Jameson, and Miss Anne Langton, were talented women with an English education that may well have included drawing perspective and watercolour. The topographers cannot be said to have contributed much to the development of painting in Canada. Their work was largely documentary and of interest to the student of social history rather than the history of art. For the most part they worked in a period prior to the invention of photography, and without them we could only guess at the appearance of Yonge, King, or the waterfront in York. Quite the most prolific of the topographers was William Henry Bartlett, who was commissioned by the London publisher George Virtue to gather material in Canada for a book on Canadian scenery. The book appeared in 1842, and while many plates deal with scenery, not a few illustrate street scenes and the buildings of the time.

18  Robertson *Landmarks* s I. 123

19  Public Archives of Ontario, Simcoe Papers, IV. 201. See Firth, ed *Town of York* 24–5.

20  Firth, ed *Town of York* 39–40

21  Ibid, 46

22  John McBeath's estimate for repairs approved by Francis Gore, Lieutenant-Governor; in Public Archives of Canada, Upper Canada Sundries, RG 5, A-I, 5, pt 2, p 2219, 27 Nov 1806

23  Richard Cartwright to Isaac Todd, Kingston, 14 Oct 1793; in Firth, ed *Town of York* 22

24  Cruikshank, ed *Correspondence of the Hon. Peter Russell* II. 128

25  Firth, ed *Town of York* lx–lxii

26  Ibid, 242

CHAPTER THREE: A LATE-FLOWERING GEORGIAN

1  Scadding *Toronto of Old* 116
2  Ibid, 122
3  Robertson *Landmarks* s 1. 503, 504
4  Scadding *Toronto of Old* 95
5  Ibid, 139
6  Ibid, 184
7  As a French immigrant he received a large tract of land in the émigré settlement north of York, now called Oak Ridges. Here a number of royalists had been given contiguous lots by the British government.
8  Robertson *Landmarks* s 1. 19
9  William Willcocks was Dr Baldwin's father-in-law. See Firth, ed *Town of York* 306.
10  Scadding and Dent *Toronto, Past and Present* 50
11  Humphries 'The Capture of York'
12  Robertson *Landmarks* s 1. 12
13  Humphries 'The Capture of York'
14  Ibid
15  Ibid
16  Walter Henry *Trifles from my Port-folio* (Quebec 1839) II. 112
17  R.S. Jameson, attorney-general (1833–7) and vice-chancellor (1837–54) of Upper Canada
18  Jameson *Winter Studies and Summer Rambles* 17
19  Robertson *Landmarks* s 1. 506

CHAPTER FOUR: PROSPERITY AND ECLECTICISM

1  Jameson, *Winter Studies and Summer Rambles* 17, 67, 64
2  Galt *Autobiography* I. 334
3  An English visitor writing to the *Christian Guardian* in 1834 reported that 'upwards of two miles of King Street is flagged and paved with stone.'
4  Charles Dickens *American Notes*; quoted in John Forster *Life of Charles Dickens* (London: Household nd) 123
5  Reed 'The Story of Toronto' 205–6
6  Ibid, 206. Accurate statistics for this period are difficult to establish, but in 1832 probably out of a population of 5,502, there were 535 cases of cholera and 205 deaths.
7  Geoffrey Scott *The Architecture of Humanism* (London: Constable 1924) 39
8  *Star* (Toronto) 20 Nov 1844, p 2, col 2
9  Ibid
10  Robertson *Landmarks* s 4. 317
11  In 1826 there were only seven Roman Catholic priests in the whole of Upper Canada.
12  Robertson *Landmarks* s 4. 317
13  Strachan Papers, Metropolitan Toronto Library

14 Scadding *Toronto of Old* 322–3. The long quotation Scadding took from *Curiae Canadenses*.

15 *British Colonist* (Toronto) 27 Aug 1844, p 3, col 1

16 C.H. Armstrong *Honourable Society of Osgoode Hall* 55

17 Toronto, 14 Nov 1849–22 Sept 1851; Quebec, 22 Sept 1851–20 Oct 1855; Toronto, 20 Oct 1855–24 Sept 1859; Quebec, 24 Sept 1859–20 Oct 1865; Ottawa, 20 Oct 1865–

18 Middleton *Municipality of Toronto*, ii. 557–8

19 F.H. Armstrong 'The First Great Fire of Toronto'

20 Robertson *Landmarks* s3. 7

21 Scadding *Toronto of Old* 356

22 Robertson *Landmarks* s 1. 163

23 F.H. Armstrong 'The Rebuilding of Toronto after the Great Fire of 1849'

24 When the stone St James' of 1830 was built, the price of pews was set at 'twenty-five pounds currency.' Pews could be rented, but they were also sold by auction.

25 Langton, ed *Early Days in Upper Canada* 292

26 Ibid, 284

27 *Globe* 3 Feb 1857, p 2

28 *Builder* (London) 15, n 735 (7 Mar 1857)

CHAPTER FIVE: ROMANESQUE AND CAST IRON

1 Of greater significance for Canada, if less for Toronto, was the founding of the Royal Canadian Academy and the National Gallery in 1880. Among the many laudable aims in the charter of the academy were 'the encouragement of design as applied to painting, sculpture, architecture, engraving and the industrial arts, and the promotion and support of education leading to the production of beautiful and excellent work in manufactures.' The Royal Academy's first president was Lucius O'Brien. He was educated at Upper Canada College and is remembered by a simple brass tablet on the walls of the nave of the little mud-brick church at Shanty Bay, the village of his birth on Lake Simcoe.

2 R.E. Chadwick, past president of the Foundation Co of Canada, was in Toronto as an engineer in 1906. He had the distinct impression that the columns supporting the Yonge Street wall of the Robert Simpson Co were 'carried on cantilevers; this arrangement being in anticipation of a future subway, and of so arranging things that the subway authorities might be argued into putting a station in the store.'

3 Selz *Art Nouveau* 16

4 Mr Hahn died in September 1962 at the age of 96.

5 At the same time there were those unscrupulous speculators who left a legacy of congested housing, the deplorable conditions of which were not drawn to public notice until the report of the lieutenant-governor's committee was issued in 1934. The task of eradication and rebuilding as a municipal responsibility has proceeded ever since, but will not be completed in this generation.

# Appendix A

The Architectural Profession in the
Nineteenth Century

Clearly, Dr W.W. Baldwin was several years ahead of his time when in 1834 or thereabouts he delivered a lecture from notes found today among his papers in the Metropolitan Toronto Library, urging that an architectural society be formed. To his audience, which could have contained several builders, masons, and carpenters but no more than three or four architects, he said, 'much now rests in your hands as embarked in the profession of architects and builders to improve greatly the stile, stability, salubrity and accommodation of our buildings in this city – either by forming an architectural society independent of the Mechanics' Institute, or as a branch of it – the object of this society I suggest should be to encourage by honorary notices, either by medals, premiums or public votes of approbation, those architects who may distinguish themselves in the execution of the works they undertake.'

For lack of interest or other reasons, no society was formed in the 1830s. Quite possibly the idea was not considered again until 20 June 1849, when Sandford Fleming recorded in his diary that ten surveyors and engineers had met in the office of Kivas Tully on King Street in Toronto to discuss forming a professional association. We recognize as architects several of those who attended, including Tully, John G. Howard, and Frederic Cumberland. It would be satisfying to know that only fifteen years after the Institute of British Architects had been created, a similar body had come together in Canada. Instead, however, these ten professional men went well beyond their particular interests to establish the Canadian Institute, which was one of the most important intellectual forces in Canada before Confederation and continues today as the Royal Canadian Institute.

Our story resumes almost a decade later, in March 1859, when the Association of Architects, Civil Engineers and Public Land Surveyors was established at Toronto. There were members from all parts of the old Province of Canada (the present-day Ontario and Quebec), and it met monthly in pursuit of 'the establishment of a tariff of charges ... the collection and exhibition of Works of Art, Models and Drawings ... and the meeting together at stated times for the consideration and discussion of subjects that might be of interest to the Association.' In 1860–1 William Thomas was the president, while Thomas Gundry, William Hay, William

Kauffmann, Joseph Sheard, William Tutin Thomas, and John Tully (a brother of Kivas Tully), all of Toronto, held some of the other offices.

Surprisingly, the founding of this first organization was followed within a few months by the establishment of a second body, headquartered in Ottawa. Known by the cumbersome title of the Association of Public Land Surveyors and Institute of Civil Engineers and Architects, it was formed in response to the intense favoritism in the Public Works Department and the handling of the Parliament buildings competition. For almost three years the Toronto and Ottawa associations existed side by side, until, at Kingston in January 1862, they came together as the Association of Surveyors, Civil Engineers and Architects. In Montreal the following May another meeting took place to choose the officers, examiners, and members of council. From Toronto, Frederic Cumberland, William Kauffmann, Cyrus P. Thomas, and John Tully were elected. Unfortunately, the report of this election is the last that has been found for the association. No doubt its fate will be known some day: probably it had been dormant some years before the next attempt was made, in 1876, to found an architects' association.

Once again, the organizing meeting took place in Toronto, although Frederick James Rastrick of Hamilton was in the chair. A new group of architects was involved, including Edmund Burke, Frank Darling, William Irving, Henry Langley, James Smith, and Hamilton Townsend. The province of Ontario was to be the geographical constituency of the new association, but it was intended 'to correspond with an Architects' Association which now exists in Montreal, in order, if possible, to effect an amalgamation of the two.' These efforts succeeded, since in 1877 Rastrick was able to send a copy of the constitution and by-laws of the Canadian Institute of Architects to Charles Barry the younger, who in turn presented it to the library of the Royal Institute of British Architects. This unique document may be found there today. Again, however, the association seems to have folded rather quickly, sometime after 7 February 1878, when E.J. Lennox presented several books to the institute's library.

We feel some sense of history repeating itself in the meeting held on 3 October 1887 at the office of W.G. Storm at 28 Toronto Street to inaugurate the Architectural Guild of Toronto. Those present were Edmund Burke, George Curry, Frank Darling, Arthur Denison, David Dick, Grant Helliwell, William Storm, Walter Strickland, and Hamilton Townsend. Members arranged to dine fortnightly or monthly. At the fourth dinner sixteen architects met in the St Charles restaurant on Yonge Street and agreed to discuss subjects of professional interest, to foster friendly criticism of one another's work, to secure better public recognition, and to raise the standards of professional ethics. Any architect in Toronto was eligible if elected by a majority of four to one.

By 1889 the need for an association with a broader base than the guild was obvious, and on 21 March of that year the first meeting of the Ontario Association of Architects was held. The association was later incorporated by act of the legislature on 13 August 1890, and W.G. Storm RCA, became its first president. There were 154 founder members. As the association increased in numbers and in influence, the importance of the guild diminished until, in 1898, its members disbanded in favour of the Toronto chapter.

It was due to the initiative of members of the guild that the government of Ontario was persuaded in 1890 to establish a Department of Architecture in the School of

Practical Science, University of Toronto. That year Henry Langley's son Charles entered the course, after a year in engineering; he became the first graduate of the department in 1892. His instructors were C.H.C Wright (later head of the department and then of the School of Architecture in the University of Toronto) and Cesare Marani.

Until 1890 the only way in Ontario to obtain the training necessary to become an architect was through apprenticeship to a practising architect. This lasted five years typically but sometimes was shorter, depending on the student's previous experience, such as training in drawing or civil engineering. As early as 1832 the Toronto Mechanics' Institute (founded only eighteen months before) offered drawing classes at the urging of John Ewart. That same year another drawing school in York, conducted by a Mr Young, was advertised. Probably this was the architect Thomas Young, who later taught mechanical and ornamental drawing in the district school, at Upper Canada College, and in classes offered under the auspices of the Toronto Society of Arts. The society existed as one of the bright spots in the cultural life of Toronto during the late 1840s, counting among its leading members William Thomas, John G. Howard, Kivas Tully, John Johnston, William Tutin Thomas, and Thomas Young.

In 1849 a number of 'working mechanics' in Toronto had requested the House of Assembly to establish 'a Provincial School of Art and design where youths intended for various Artistical and Mechanical Businesses could be prepared for entering with advantage upon their Apprenticeships.' Although this petition did not succeed, the idea was taken up with added interest by the Board of Arts and Manufactures of Upper Canada shortly after it came into being in 1857. William Hay and his former pupil Henry Langley were active on the committees, which, until the board was disbanded at Confederation, reported regularly but without immediate result on the need for a school of art and design.

The organization of the Ontario Society of Artists in 1872 gave the necessary impetus to the founding four years later of the Ontario School of Art, now the Ontario College of Art. Architects James Smith and Frank Darling were members of the society and took a particular interest in the school. Smith also played a leading part in the establishment in 1880 of the Royal Canadian Academy, which counted Henry Langley and W.G. Storm as well as Smith among its five architect charter members.

The founding of the Ontario Association of Architects (OAA) was complemented by the appearance of a monthly journal, the *Canadian Architect and Builder*, in 1888. For the next twenty years it reported fully on things of interest to members of the profession. It is wrong to assume, however, that this was the first Canadian periodical devoted to architectural subjects. That honour belongs to the *Canadian Builder and Mechanics' Magazine*, which was published monthly in London, Ontario, in 1869–70 by architect Thomas W. Dyas and his partner Henry Wilkins, a stone-dealer and sculptor. After a year or so this pioneering publication ceased, and no copies of any issue are known to have survived.

From 1899 to 1908 the columns of the *Canadian Architect and Builder* followed the founding and activities of the Architectural Eighteen Club. It came into existence among eighteen angry architects when, following the examinations for membership in the OAA, certain new members were chosen whose marks were lower than those of some who were refused admission. One of the latter entered suit against the

**A.1** Toronto Architectural Guild at Long Branch in August 1888. Back row (left to right): Robert J. Edwards, William R. Gregg, John Gemmell, Henry J. Webster. Middle row: Edmund Burke, William A. Langton, Henry Langley, Henry B. Gordon. Front row: William George Storm, S. George Curry, Norman B. Dick, James Smith.

association and was clearly not satisfied with the defence that he and some others were young and could afford more time to qualify. It is pleasing to report that several older architects shared the indignation of the younger.

Until 1908, when its differences with the OAA were reconciled, the Eighteen Club held cosmopolitan exhibitions and lively meetings, ignoring completely the parent body. Its finest hour came when its members were permitted to appear before the Senate of the university, with Sir Charles Moss, vice-chancellor, presiding. Their complaint was that the university course in architecture did not prepare the student for architecture and that the university would do the profession a service by conducting external examinations for students working in offices. It is recorded that Sir Robert Falconer, the president of the university, 'took the representations very seriously' and organized a series of courses in which 'eighteen professors participated.' Today, many Ontario architects have taken a degree at one of the three university schools of architecture in the province. All who seek the professional designation of architect must register for courses offered by the OAA and can do so only after becoming properly qualified.

The headquarters of the OAA are in that well-known Toronto building at 50 Park Road, designed by John B. Parkin in competition with other architects. It is a very different affair from the office that was at 94 King Street West, which for the sum of $254.41 was furnished in 1900 with 'a Morris chair, a velour cushion, a Japanese rug, a fixed seat (probably for visitors), Michelangelo's "Moses," and two cuspidors' (Raymond Card *Ontario Association of Architects*).

Biographies follow for many of the architects and landscape architects practising in Toronto during the nineteenth century. Some of their more important commissions are noted; generally these date no later than the turn of the century and are located in Toronto. For other commissions, particularly those undertaken during the twentieth century, reference may be had to the *Dictionary of Canadian Biography*, the *Inventory of Buildings of Architectural and Historical Importance* kept by the Toronto Historical Board, or to the materials gathered by the Architectural Conservancy of Ontario, Toronto Branch, and kept at the Fine Arts desk in the Metropolitan Toronto Library. *The Biographical Dictionary of Architects in Canada, 1800–1950*, which is in preparation by Robert G. Hill, will be most helpful when it is published.

The year cited for each building on the list below is the first season of substantial construction, and will often differ from when the building was designed or was opened. To avoid repetition, the works are listed under the partner whose name occurs first in the title of the partnership.

**Angell, Edward** fl 1820–4
A real-estate agent and building surveyor in London, he took up a Crown appointment in Nevis in the West Indies about 1815. When in 1820 ill health forced him to seek a more moderate climate, he came to York armed with recommendations from HRH Edward Augustus, duke of Kent, and advertised himself as an architect. A blot on his military record caused Sir Peregrine Maitland to refuse him a grant of land as compensation for his outlay in building a bridge across the Don River near its mouth. In 1824 Angell returned to London, where he founded the Canada Land Agency.
1821 Toronto Mills for Francis W. Small
1822 York Subscription Bridge over the Don River

**Badgley, Sidney Rose** 1850–1917
After studying with R.C. Windeyer, he opened his own office in 1876 in St Catharines, where he practised until moving to Cleveland in 1887. There he became well known, particularly for his church commissions throughout the American Midwest and Canada, through which he developed his expertise in acoustical design. Hart Massey selected him to design Massey Hall (1893), the construction of which was supervised by G.M. Miller.

**Baldwin, William Warren**, MD Edin 1796 1775–1844
Dr Baldwin settled in York in 1802. Shortly after, in response to an acute shortage of lawyers in the colony, the lieutenant-governor deemed Baldwin and a few others qualified to practise law. In addition to medicine and law Baldwin occasionally turned his hand to architecture, at which he seems to have been a talented amateur. He built Spadina House in 1818 and resided there until it burned in 1835, when he replaced it on the site with a smaller house in stucco and built a large brick home in York.
1818 First 'Spadina' house
1824 Home District Court House and Jail, King Street (with Ewart)
1826 Unexecuted design for new Parliament building, York
1833 Additions to Osgoode Hall, Queen (Lot) Street West
1835 Baldwin's own house, Front and Bay Streets
1836 Second 'Spadina' house

**Berczy, William** 1744–1813
A remarkably talented artist, writer, and architect, who was born Albrecht Moll in Wallerstein, Bavaria, he spent much of his time in Upper Canada from 1794 to 1804 trying to secure the success of a colonizing venture among German-speaking settlers whom he had recruited. Like Dr Baldwin he depended for his living on other sources besides architecture.
1797 Russell Abbey, Front (Palace) Street East
1802 Bridge over the Don River at King Street East
1802 House for Major James Givins, Queen (Lot) Street West
1803 House for Thomas Scott, Wellington (Market) Street East
1803 Christ Church, Montreal

**Bird, Eustace Godfrey**, ARIBA 1870–1950
Born in Barrie, Ontario, to a former officer in the Royal Engineers stationed in Hong Kong and his Chinese wife, he was a pupil of Strickland & Symons and W.G. Storm before leaving for England in 1892. There he worked in the office of T.E. Colcutt and qualified as an associate of the Royal Institute of British Architects. Coming home in 1894, he formed a partnership with Eden Smith, with offices in Toronto and Barrie. He worked for Carrère & Hastings in New York from 1899 to 1906, returning then to Toronto, where until the First World War he was their associate on several projects, including additions to Spadina for Albert Austin (1907), the Bank of Toronto at King and Bay Street (1912), and the banking hall of the Royal Bank at King and Yonge Streets (1913).

**Boultbee, Alfred E.** 1863–1928
The third son of Alfred Boultbee, who was the member of Parliament for East York, and grandson of William Boultbee, a land surveyor who trained with John G. Howard, the younger Alfred Boultbee, known to his friends as 'Pet,' spent a year in the Klondike during the gold rush. While his architectural practice began about 1890 when he left the office of W.G. Storm, his twentieth-century work is better known, particularly his domestic buildings. The South Rosedale houses at 22 Chestnut Park and 35 Crescent Road, the latter with its charming circular swimming-pool in Doric order, are good examples.

**Brown, [John] Francis** 1866–1942
Brown was born at Lévis while his father, Quarter-Master Sergeant J. Brown, RE, was stationed at the Quebec Citadel. In 1870 the family returned to England, but Brown returned to Canada twelve years later. He trained in the Toronto offices of Edwards & Webster and was active in the Architectural Draughtsmen's Club and the Architectural Eighteen Club. Many of his drawings are preserved today in the library at the University of Calgary.
1889 Board of Trade Building, Yonge and
       Front Streets; supervisor of, for James
       & James of New York

1894 Chester Baptist Church, Don Mills
       Road
1898 East Toronto Baptist Church, Gerrard
       Street East

**Brunel, Alfred** 1818–87
An English-born civil engineer, he arrived in Canada in the early 1840s and settled in Kingston, where he was unsuccessful in competitions to design the City Hall and Queen's College there, and Brock's Monument at Queenston. Moving to Toronto in 1853 as assistant engineer for the Ontario, Simcoe and Huron Railroad Union Company (later Northern Railway of Canada), he was closely associated with F.W. Cumberland. He was also city engineer in 1859–60 and undertook occasional architectural commissions, like a shed and fence near the lodge at College Avenue (now University Avenue) and Queen Street in 1860. Whether he was related to the great engineer Sir Isambard Kingdom Brunel remains uncertain.

**Burke, Edmund** 1850–1919
Born in Toronto and educated at Upper Canada College, he began his apprenticeship in 1865 with Gundry & Langley under the watchful eye of his uncle, Henry Langley. Eight years later Langley formed a partnership with his brother, Edward Langley, and Burke. The firm was one of the most successful in the city for two decades until Burke left in 1892 to take over the practice of the late W.G. Storm. The patronage of many merchant princes and Baptist congregations followed him, as did as the business of the Lorne Park development company in which he had an interest. In 1894 Burke was president of the Ontario Association of Architects. That same year he formed a partnership with J.C.B. Horwood that lasted until Burke's death. Drawings for most of the projects for which he was responsible during his long career are in the Horwood Collection, Ontario Archives.
*Langley, Langley & Burke* 1873–84: see Langley
*Langley & Burke* 1884–92: see Langley
*Edmund Burke* 1892–4
1894 Robert Simpson store, Yonge and
       Queen Streets

*Burke & Horwood* 1894–1909
1895  Robert Simpson store, rebuilding after fire
1895  *Globe* building, Yonge Street at Melinda
1899  Toronto Conservatory of Music, College Street at University Avenue
*Burke, Horwood & White* 1909–19
1911  Hudson's Bay store, Vancouver
1913  Methodist Book and Publishing House, now CITY TV, Queen and John Streets

**Chadwick, [William Craven] Vaux** 1868–1941
The son of Edward Marion Chadwick, a lawyer and the author of *Ontarian Families*, he attended Upper Canada College and was articled briefly to his father before forsaking law and entering the office of R.C. Windeyer to train as an architect. He began his practice in the mid-1890s and about 1900 formed a partnership with Samuel Beckett (1869–1917) to design a variety of houses, banks, clubs, factories, and churches. Both partners were members of the Architectural Eighteen Club and served as officers in the First World War, in which Beckett lost his life. A lasting memorial to the firm is the Lawrence Park district, for which Chadwick & Beckett acted as planners and designed many of the earliest houses.

**Chewett, James Grant** 1793–1862
A son of William Chewett, the deputy surveyor-general for Upper Canada, he was educated at Dr John Strachan's school at Cornwall. After obtaining an appointment in the surveyor-general's office, he trained under his father and became deputy head in 1832. Following his resignation in 1841, Chewett managed his family's interests in property, including the Chewett Block at King and York Streets designed in 1833 by John G. Howard, and served as the first president of the Bank of Toronto.
  More a draftsman than an architect, Chewett participated occasionally in design competitions but often received more credit than was due to him for supervising the construction of buildings to plans by others, particularly before the first professional

architects settled in York early in the 1830s.
1831  Unexecuted designs for York Town Hall and Market
1831  St James' Church, King Street, supervised construction

**Connolly, Joseph** 1840–1904
Irish-born and trained in the Dublin office of J.J. McCarthy, 'the Irish Pugin,' Connolly practised briefly in Limerick before immigrating in 1873 to Toronto, where he formed a partnership with Silas James, a land surveyor. By 1877 he was on his own, specializing in the design of churches for a large number of Roman Catholic congregations throughout Ontario. On his death his practice was taken over by A.W. Holmes, who had trained in his office in the 1880s.
*James & Connolly* 1873–7
*Joseph Connolly* 1877–1904
1877  Our Lady of the Immaculate Conception, Guelph
1885  St Mary's Church, Bathurst Street
1887  St Paul's Church, Power Street
1890  St Michael's Cathedral, redecoration and alterations

**Cumberland, Frederic William** 1820–81
Born in London, he was apprenticed to William Tress, a civil engineer, and then held a series of important positions on the engineering staffs of two railways and at the Chatham and Portsmouth dockyards. By the time he immigrated to Canada in 1847, he was not only well qualified but was well connected too through his wife's relations, the Ridouts. His appointment as engineer for the County of York soon after he arrived likely came through their influence, and in 1850 his first partner was the younger Thomas Ridout, newly qualified as a civil engineer. When this arrangement ended in 1852, Cumberland and W.G. Storm formed one of the most important Toronto architectural firms of the nineteenth century. It was dissolved in 1863, although for some years before, Cumberland had been giving the Northern Railway, of which he was managing director, most of his time. Many of Cumberland & Storm's drawings and related specifications are in the Horwood Collec-

tion, Ontario Archives. The University of Toronto Archives also holds some drawings for University College, presented by J.C.B. Horwood in 1922.

*F.W. Cumberland*
1850  St James' Cathedral, King Street
1857  Pendarves, Cumberland family home, St George Street
*Cumberland & Ridout 1850–2*
1851  Seventh Post Office, Toronto Street
1851  York County Court House, Adelaide Street East
1851  Normal School, Gould Street
*Cumberland & Storm 1852–63*
1853  Magnetical Observatory, university grounds
1853  Mechanics' Institute, Church and Adelaide Streets
1855  Houses for J. Lukin Robinson, Windsor Street
1856  University College
1857  Osgoode Hall, new central section
1858  Edinburgh Life Assurance, Wellington Street West
1859  Unexecuted competition designs for Ottawa Parliament buildings
1860  Chapel of St James-the-Less, Parliament Street

**Curry, [Samuel] George** 1854–1942
A native of Port Hope, he began his practice with Frank Darling in 1880. Curry left the partnership a dozen years later, shortly after Henry Sproatt and John A. Pearson joined the firm. Subsequently he formed partnerships with F.S. Baker, 1895–8; Henry Sproatt and Ernest Rolph, 1906–8; and W.F. Sparling, 1910–17. In the intervening years he practised on his own. He was president of the Ontario Association of Architects in 1892. Recently, a store building at Queen and Yonge that Curry & Baker designed for Philip Jamieson (1895) has been visible again with the removal of a modern metal screen. Buildings of the twentieth century associated with Curry are Postal Station F, Yonge and Charles Streets (1905), and the National Club, Bay Street (1906).

**Darling, Frank** 1850–1923
Son of a rector of the Church of the Holy Trinity, he trained with Henry Langley upon graduating from Upper Canada College and Trinity College. In 1870–3 he worked in the London offices of G.E. Street and Arthur Blomfield. Returning to Canada, he joined Henry Macdougall in a partnership, the first in a series that spanned his career, with the exception of two brief periods in the 1870s. For forty-five years Darling was the architect to Trinity College and certain Anglican congregations in Toronto. He also had the Bank of Montreal and the Bank of Commerce as long-standing clients. On the nomination of the Royal Institute of British Architects he was awarded the Royal Gold Medal for Architecture in 1915.
*Macdougall and Darling 1874–5*
*Frank Darling 1873, 1875–8*
1876  Trinity College, Convocation Hall, Queen Street West
1879  Home for Incurables, Dunn Avenue
*Darling & Edwards 1878–9*
*Darling & Curry 1880–91*
1880  First-premium unexecuted design, Ontario Parliament buildings, Queen's Park
1885  Bank of Montreal, Yonge and Front streets
1888  The Toronto Club, Wellington and York streets
1889  Victoria Hospital for Sick Children, College Street
*Darling, Curry, Sproatt & Pearson 1892*
*Darling, Sproatt & Pearson 1893–6*
1894  House for A.D. Patterson, 10 Elmsley Place
*Darling & Pearson 1897–1923*
1898  Parkdale Curling Club, now Masaryk Hall, Cowan Avenue
1898  Bank of Commerce, Bloor and Yonge streets
1900  Holwood, for J.W. Flavelle, Queen's Park
1902  Bank of Nova Scotia, King Street West
1903  Gates, Trinity College, Queen Street West at head of Strachan Avenue
1916  Parliament buildings, Ottawa

**Denison, Arthur Richard** 1857–1924
One of thirteen children of Colonel Richard Lippincott Denison, he was born at Dover Court, the family estate north of Queen

Street and west of Ossington Avenue. After attending Upper Canada College and Royal Military College, he was a student in the architectural office of Stewart & Strickland. During Denison's career he had partnerships with John Falloon, George A. Stewart, George W. King, F.L. Fellowes, and George E. Stephenson.

*Stewart & Denison 1881–6*
1884  St Andrew's-by-the-Lake, Toronto Island
*A.R. Denison*
1887  Argonaut Rowing Club boathouse, foot of York Street
1890  Ossington Avenue Police Station
*Denison & King 1891–3*
1891  Athenaeum Club, 169 Church Street

**Dick, David Brash** 1846–1925
He studied at the Edinburgh School of Design and then worked in the offices of Scottish architects W.L. Moffatt and Peddie & Kinnear before emigrating in 1873. A partnership from 1874 to 1876 with Robert Grant, an established builder, brought him into contact with the Consumers' Gas Company, which was a major client throughout his career. When the partnership with Grant ended, Dick practised on his own for a quarter-century until his retirement, achieving particular distinction with his buildings at the University of Toronto, including the restoration of University College after the 1890 fire. He was a founding member of the Toronto Architectural Guild and president of the Ontario Association of Architects in 1893. Retiring to England in 1902, he died there and is buried at Woking, Surrey. His drawings are in the Horwood Collection, Ontario Archives, except those related to the university that were given by J.C.B. Horwood in 1922 and are now in its archives.
1876  Consumers' Gas offices, 19 Toronto Street (with Grant)
1881  House for William Mulock, Jarvis Street
1886  House for W.J. Gage, Bloor Street at Walmer Road
1888  Wycliffe College, Hoskin Avenue
1890  University College, restoration after fire
1891  University of Toronto Library

1894  William Davies slaughterhouse, Front and Beachell streets
1899  Consumers' Gas offices, 17 Toronto Street

**Dick, Norman Bethune** 1860–95
He studied in the office of Smith & Gemmell and briefly with architectural firms in Cleveland, Kingston, and St John, NB, before returning to Toronto. He was a well-known sportsman and fond of sailing.
1880  Granite Curling Club, Church Street
*Dick & Wickson 1890–5*
1890  Hazelton Avenue (Olivet) Congregational Church
1891  Oddfellows' Hall, Yonge and Gloucester streets

**Durand, George F.** 1850–89
A native of London, Ontario, he trained there under William Robinson and in Albany, NY, with Fuller & Laver. Returning to his home town in 1877, he became the leading architect in southwestern Ontario before his untimely death. The commission to design Upper Canada College came through the Honourable George Ross, minister of Education, who represented a London-area constituency in the legislature. Most of those drawings by Durand that survive are in the Moore-Murphy Collection, University of Western Ontario.
1886  Second-premium unexecuted design, Toronto Court House
1889  Upper Canada College, Deer Park

**Edwards, Robert James** 1854–1927
Born and raised in Barrie, he opened his first office there in association with Frank Darling of Toronto. When it proved unsuccessful he left, to spend five years in Winnipeg and Port Arthur before settling in Toronto in 1886. With Hiram J. Webster, his partner from 1886 to 1896, he designed the St George's Society Hall on Elm Street in 1890.

**Elliot, John Harlock** c 1862–1925?
The son of a well-known Toronto dentist who invented the rotary snowplough, he attended Upper Canada College. Some of his architectural training was in the Chi-

**A.2** Letterhead of Knox and Elliot (circa 1889). The buildings in this florid but fashionable design by John H. Elliot are representative of the firm's elegant and original style, developed during the five years the partners practised in Toronto before moving to Cleveland.

cago office of Burnham & Root, where he met Wilm Knox. Together they opened a Toronto office in 1888, with Elliot likely taking charge of design. The Confederation Life building, won in competition, stands as the firm's crowning achievement in Canada. In 1892 both Knox and Elliot returned to Chicago to assist Henry Ives Cobb with work related to the 1893 Columbian Exposition, following which they re-established their practice in Cleveland. Elliot retired in 1925, a decade after Knox's death.
*Knox & Elliot* 1888–9, 1890–3: see Knox
*Knox, Elliot & Jarvis* 1889–90: see Knox

**Ellis, James Augustus** 1856–1935
Born in Meaford, Ontario, he began his practice in West Toronto Junction, as that area was known before amalgamation with the City of Toronto in 1909. He designed the Disciples Church at Keele and Annette Streets (1891) as well as many schools, factories, and houses.

**Engelhardt, Heinrich Adolph** 1830–1907
Born in Muhlhausen, Prussia, he immigrated to the United States in the 1850s, where he worked as a landscape gardener, and to Canada in 1870. He had commissions in Belleville, Brantford, and Port Hope before his appointment in 1874 to lay out Mount Pleasant Cemetery, Toronto, where subsequently he was the superintendent until his retirement in 1888.

**Ewart, John** 1788–1856
Born in Tranent, East Lothian, Scotland, he worked as a builder in Scotland and London before emigrating about 1816. Within three years he had settled at York, Upper Canada, where he combined building design and contracting, the former sometimes in association with Dr W.W. Baldwin. After 1830 Ewart continued as a successful contractor and supplier of building materials but seems to have left the preparation of plans to the trained architects who had begun to arrive. In time he came to be wealthy and much involved with interests like the Mechanics' Institute and St Andrew's Church.
1822 St Paul's Roman Catholic Church, Power Street
1824 Home District Court House and Jail, King Street East
1827 Middlesex District Court House, London
1829 Upper Canada College, King Street West
1829 Osgoode Hall, Queen Street West
1830 St Andrew's Church, Church and Adelaide Streets

**Fleming, Sir Sandford** 1827–1915
Usually remembered as an outstanding civil engineer, in the early part of his career he combined land surveying with architectural drafting and design. His diaries record the making of perspective drawings for Kivas Tully and F.W. Cumberland to help them secure commissions. The Crystal Palace designed by Fleming with his partner, Collingwood Schreiber (1831–1918), was as much an engineering as an architectural accomplishment.
1847 Competition designs for Knox's Church, Queen Street
1858 Crystal Palace, King Street West at Strachan Avenue

**Fowler, Joseph Ades** 1850–1921
A native of Brighton, England, he came to Toronto about 1872. Almost twenty years later it was said that over two thousand private residences had been erected to his plans, in addition to public buildings, factories, and the like. He developed a considerable practice in southwestern Ontario in the late 1880s through a branch office in Woodstock operated in partnership with Thomas Cuthbertson.
1881 Parkdale Town Hall, Dunn Avenue and Queen Street
1881 Brockton Village Hall, Dundas Street West
1888 Moulton Ladies' College, Bloor Street East

**Fuller, Thomas** 1823–98
Fuller came to Toronto in 1857 from Bath, England, with several years' experience in England and Antigua. He remained here only two and a half years before moving to Ottawa to oversee construction of the Parliament buildings, a commission won with his partner Chilion Jones. Fuller remained there until 1865, when he went to Albany, NY. Four years later he and Augustus Laver secured a commission for the New York State Capitol, and in 1871 they won the first premium for designs for the San Francisco City Hall and Law Courts. Laver went to California to supervise construction, which dragged on for several years, leaving Fuller to struggle with the frustrations of the Capitol job as it became bogged down. The building was unfinished in 1875 when it was taken out of his hands and redesigned by a trio of eminent American architects. He returned to Canada in 1881 to take up an appointment as Dominion Architect. In the succeeding fifteen years he created a presence for the government of Canada through more than 140 public buildings, such as post offices and armouries, on main streets across the country.
1858 St Stephen's-in-the-Fields, Bellevue Avenue at College Street
1891 Armouries, University Avenue

**Gemmell, John** 1850–1915
Gemmell came to Canada as a child from Ayrshire, Scotland, was raised in Toronto, and received his professional training in the office of James Smith. In 1870 he formed a partnership with Smith that ended with Gemmell's death forty-five years later, a record exceeded only by that of Gordon & Helliwell.
*Smith & Gemmell* 1870–1915: see Smith

**Gibson, Charles J.** 1862–1935
Although born in Quebec City, his early
years until 1870 were spent in England.
Gibson received his architectural training in
New York City. Back in Toronto by 1885,
he practised with Henry Simpson in 1888–
90 and then went on his own once more.
1892  St John's Church, Norway, Woodbine
       and Kingston Road
1893  McLaughlin Flour Mills, Bay Street at
       the Esplanade
1898  House for John Miller, 33 Murray
       Street

**Gordon, Henry Bauld** 1854–1951
A Torontonian by birth, Gordon trained
under Henry Langley before striking out on
his own in 1877. Two years later he and
Grant Helliwell formed a partnership, from
which they both retired in 1931 after more
than five decades in practice together.
Church commissions formed a large proportion of their work. Gordon served twice,
in 1896 and 1908, as president of the Ontario Association of Architects.
*Gordon & Helliwell 1879–1931*
1879  West Presbyterian Church, now St
       Stanislaus' Roman Catholic, Denison
       Avenue
1880  Second premium, Parliament build-
       ings, Queen's Park
1887  Bathurst Street United Church, now
       also Bathurst Street Theatre, Bathurst
       and Lennox streets
1890  Church of the Messiah, Avenue Road
       at Dupont Street
1890  YWCA, now Elmwood Club, Elm
       Street
1898  Presbyterian Church of the Covenant,
       now Hare Krishna, Avenue Road at
       Roxborough Street

**Gouinlock, George Wallace** 1861–1932
Although born and educated in Paris, Ontario, Gouinlock was trained in Winnipeg
with architects Barber, Bowes & Barber. By
1888 he was in Toronto and had a brief
partnership with George W. King. Gouinlock was a skilled designer, as evidenced
by the Temple Building, which was won in
competition. Until the First World War
he was architect to the Canadian National
Exhibition and designed the Edwardian

buildings that contributed to the image, on
which it still trades, as a 'Great Fair.' Of
these buildings, the following survive: Arts
and Crafts, Firehall, Horticultural, Music,
and Press, as well as the Gooderham
Fountain.
1895  Temple Building, Richmond and Bay
       streets
1908  Canadian Birkbeck building, 10 Ade-
       laide Street East
1913  North or library wing, Parliament
       buildings, Queen's Park

**Goulstone, George T.**
No record exists of any building by him in
Toronto, as he left early to practise in the
United States. He was one of the founder-
members of the Architectural Draughtsmen's Club (1886) and is remembered with
gratitude in the School of Architecture of
the University of Toronto as the donor of a
scholarship that bears his name.

**Grand, James** 1819–71
Born in Upper Edmonton, Middlesex,
England, he came to Quebec City in 1849
with the Royal Engineers. Three years
later he moved to Toronto, where he
worked in the office of Cumberland &
Storm. In practice for himself in 1854 and
in partnership during 1855–6 with Edward
Osborne, Grand retired in 1857 to become
a building surveyor and land agent. The
early 1860s found him in Chicago and
Guelph before he returned to Toronto and
rejoined the Royal Engineers' office. In
1869 he resumed his own practice, which
at his untimely death was taken over by
Henry James and George Lalor. One of
Grand's sons was a founder of Grand &
Toy, the stationers.
1854  Toronto Exchange, Wellington Street
       East
1856  Sword's Hotel additions, Front Street
       West (with Osborne)
1870  Fire Hall, now St Charles Tavern,
       Yonge near Grenville Street (jointly
       with William Irving)
1871  Schools, King and Parliament streets
       and Bathurst and College streets

**Gray, James Wilson** 1861–1922
Came to Toronto in 1885 from his native

Edinburgh, where he had attended the University of Edinburgh before apprenticing in architectural offices there. In partnership with Alan Macdougall in 1886–7, he practised on his own thereafter. In 1899 he was responsible for alterations to the ground floor in the Confederation Life building at Richmond and Yonge. He also designed the present Knox Presbyterian Church, Spadina Avenue (1909), where he served as a deacon and later as an elder.

**Gregg, Alfred Holden** 1868–1945
Toronto-born, he attended the Model School, Jarvis Collegiate Institute, and the Toronto Art School, now the Ontario College of Art. Gregg learned his profession working for his brother, William R. Gregg, whose partner he became in 1894. He also obtained some experience in architects' offices in Boston and New York in 1887–8. In the United States again early in the century, he returned to Toronto in 1904 to form a partnership with Frank Wickson that lasted until Wickson's death in 1936.
*Gregg & Gregg* 1894–1904: see W.R. Gregg
*Wickson & Gregg* 1904–36: see Wickson

**Gregg, William Rufus** 1851–1930
Born in Belleville, son of the Reverend Professor William Gregg, he trained in the office of Smith & Gemmell from 1871 to 1876. He was in practise by himself from 1882 to 1924, apart from a decade spanning the turn of the century, when he and his brother, Alfred H. Gregg, worked together.
*William R. Gregg*
1884 Thomas Alison house, College and Ross streets, moved c 1922 to face Ross Street, later Dora Hood Book Room
1891 Westminster Presbyterian Church, Bloor Street at Park Road
*Gregg & Gregg* 1894–1904
1904 Eclipse Whitewear Building, King and John streets

**Gundry, Thomas** 1830–69
English-born, he was established as an architect in Toronto by mid-1859. Three years later he and William Hay were in partnership for a brief time before the lat-

ter's return to Scotland, after which Gundry teamed up with Hay's former pupil, Henry Langley. Drawings for a few of their projects, mostly churches, are in the Metropolitan Toronto Library and in the Ontario Archives. Gundry served on the committee of the Association of Architects, Civil Engineers and Public Land Surveyors for 1860–1. He deserves to be better known.
*Gundry & Langley* 1862–9
1863 Warehouse for John Macdonald, Wellington Street East
1865 St Michael's Cathedral spire, Bond Street
1865 St Stephen's, Bellevue Avenue, restoration after fire
1865 St Peter's Church, Bleecker and Carlton streets
1867 Queen's Hotel, Front Street, additions
1868 Government House, King and Simcoe streets
1869 Oaklands, John Macdonald home, Avenue Road, additions

**Hall, Francis** 1792–1862
A native of Clackmannan, Scotland, he trained as a civil engineer under Robert Bald and worked for a decade in the office of the great Thomas Telford during the time the Menai Bridge was being designed and built. Hall came to Canada in 1823, attracted probably by plans to build a Welland Canal, and settled at Queenston. The few architectural designs that can be attributed to him date from the period before 1827, when he moved to Nova Scotia to supervise the building of the Shubenacadie Canal. The balance of his career appears to have been spent working on canals, roads, and railways in both Upper Canada and the Maritime provinces.
1824 Unexecuted design for suspension bridge over the Niagara River
1824 First Brock Monument, Queenston
1825 Unexecuted design for Bank of Upper Canada, Adelaide (Duke) and George streets
1826 Unexecuted design for a Province House at York

**Harper, George Robinson** 1843–1910
In 1868, following his apprenticeship in the office of William Irving, he joined with

his father, John Harper, one of Toronto's early and successful builders, as Harper & Son, architects. After the elder partner's retirement about 1881, George carried on under his own name until his death.
*Harper & Son* 1868–81
1876 Police Court, Station, and Fire Hall, Court Street
*George R. Harper* 1882–1910
1891 Deer Park Sanitorium for Dr Donald Meyers, Heath Street West
1893 Oak Hall store for W.E. Sanford, King Street East

**Hay, William** 1818–88
Hay was born at Cruden, near Peterhead, Aberdeenshire, Scotland. Before he was recruited in 1846 by George Gilbert Scott to oversee construction of the cathedral at St John's, Newfoundland, he worked for the prominent Edinburgh architect John Henderson. There is evidence that at the time Hay might have been thinking of coming to Toronto. Instead, he spent at least three years in the Atlantic provinces and Bermuda, and did not settle in this city until 1852. He returned to Scotland a decade later, leaving behind a large number of well-designed buildings and the architectural descriptions which he appears to have ghost-written in G.P. Ure's *Handbook of Toronto* (1858). From 1872 until his death Hay lived in a house called Rabbit Hall at Portobello on the Firth of Forth and was engaged in the restoration of St Giles' Cathedral. The work was made possible by the large bequest of William Chambers, a publisher. A bas-relief medallion of Hay may be seen in a vestibule of St Giles'.
1853 Toronto General Hospital, Gerrard Street East
1855 St Basil's Church and St Michael's College, St. Joseph and Bay streets
1856 Parochial schools, Holy Trinity Church, Trinity Square
1856 House of Providence, Power Street
1858 Unexecuted design for Trinity College chapel, Queen Street West
1859 Yorkville Town Hall, Yonge Street
1860 Oaklands, house for John Macdonald, Avenue Road

**Helliwell, Grant** 1857–1953
From an old Toronto family that had a

brewery and distillery on the Don from 1821 to 1847, he attended Jarvis Collegiate. It is possible he trained in the office of Langley, Langley & Burke and met his future partner, Henry B. Gordon, there. A founding member of the Architectural Guild, Helliwell was president of the Ontario Association of Architects in 1901.
*Gordon & Helliwell* 1879–1931: see Gordon

**Holland, William** c 1850–99
Born in Newfoundland, he was trained to be a carpenter like his father. To the partnership he formed in 1881 with architect Thomas Kennedy and land surveyor Archibald McVittie, both of Barrie, he brought practical experience in the Toronto building trades. At its peak the firm had three or four branch offices. Holland seems to have been in charge of the one in Collingwood from 1882 to 1886, before returning to Toronto. Few buildings can be attributed to him after his connection with Kennedy ceased in 1889.
*Kennedy, McVittie & Holland* 1881–3: see Kennedy
*Kennedy, Gaviller & Holland* 1884–5: see Kennedy
*Kennedy & Holland* 1885–9: see Kennedy

**Holmes, Arthur W.** 1863–1944
Working in G.E. Street's London office was good training for Holmes, who, following his arrival in Toronto in 1886, became Joseph Connolly's draughtsman. During the 1890s he was in partnership with Albert Asa Post, specializing in church work. In the twentieth century he became the pre-eminent architect for Roman Catholic commissions in the Toronto area.
*Post & Holmes* 1891–7: see Post
*A.W. Holmes*
1904 St Mary's Church spire, Bathurst Street
1907 St Helen's Church, Dundas Street, Brockton
1912 St Ann's Church, Gerrard Street East
1914 Holy Name Church, Danforth Avenue

**Horwood, John Charles Batstone** 1864–1938
Descended from a long line of Newfoundland builders, he was born at Quidi Vidi,

near St John's. Apprenticed to Langley, Langley & Burke from 1882 to 1887, he went to New York in the early 1890s to work for Clinton & Russell. On his return to Toronto in 1894, he became Edmund Burke's partner, just in time to apply what he had learned about fire-resistant construction to the rebuilding of the Robert Simpson store after it burned. Department-store design remained a specialty of the firm, which made several later additions to Simpson's and counted the Hudson's Bay Company as a major client. When the Eighteen Club was formed, Horwood became a member while Burke took the part of the Ontario Association of Architects. In spite of this their partnership endured. In 1909 Murray White became a partner in the firm. In 1919 it was renamed Horwood & White, and it continued under this name until 1969, when the senior partner, Eric Crompton Horwood (1900–84), who had taken over from his father in 1938, retired.

A permanent memorial to J.C.B. and E.C. Horwood and to their profession exists in the architectural drawings and related materials that Eric Horwood presented in 1979 to the Ontario Archives. Containing over thirty thousand items documenting the work of more than fifty architects, many of whom worked during the nineteenth century, it is the largest and richest collection of its kind in Canada.

*Burke & Horwood* 1894–1909: see Burke
*Burke, Horwood & White* 1909–19: see Burke

**Howard, John George** 1803–90
Born John Corby in Bengeo, Hertfordshire, he attended school in nearby Hertford. When only fifteen he went to sea for two years before apprenticing as a carpenter and joiner. In 1824 he was articled to William Ford, a London architect who soon after married Corby's sister. Three years later Corby himself was married to Jemima Frances Meikle, who later would greatly assist her husband in his architectural practice, often undertaking the tedious work of copying specifications. In 1832 they immigrated to York, Upper Canada, and he changed his name to Howard.

As one of the earliest trained architects here, and with the added advantage of an appointment as drawing master at Upper Canada College, Howard contributed greatly to the appearance and form of Toronto in the 1830s and 1840s. The Lunatic or Mental Asylum on Queen Street West, for which he won the commission in competition, was his major work. There were important commissions elsewhere as well. By 1855 he was virtually retired from practice, was about to stop his teaching at Upper Canada, and had been replaced as city surveyor, a part-time post he had held since 1843. The balance of his life was spent writing his memoirs and as forest ranger for High Park. Following his wife's death in 1877 he erected the monument to her there that is surrounded by part of an iron fence that once enclosed St Paul's Cathedral, London.

Howard placed himself in the forefront of the city's benefactors with his gift of 120 acres of High Park in 1873 and the bequest of his home, Colborne Lodge, and a further 45 acres. The park has been augmented by municipal acquisition to 406 acres today. Howard was an associate of the Royal Canadian Academy in 1880 and was made a member shortly before he retired from the academy in 1882. Today his papers, including his surviving architectural drawings and office daybooks, are in the Metropolitan Toronto Library. Colborne Lodge and many of his paintings are in the custody of the Toronto Historical Board.

1833  Chewett's Buildings, King and York streets
1833  Entrance gates and lodges, King's College
1837  Colborne Lodge, High Park
1838  Third Jail, Berkeley Street
1841  St Andrew's Presbyterian Church spire, Church and Adelaide streets
1841  St Paul's Anglican Church, Bloor Street East, Yorkville
1842  Court House and Jail for the Johnstown District, Brockville
1843  Kearnsey House, Yonge and Dundonald streets
1843  St John's Anglican Church, York Mills
1844  St James' Cemetery grounds plan, Parliament Street
1845  Bank of British North America, Wellington Street East at Yonge
1846  Mental Asylum, Queen Street West

**Howland, [William] Ford** 1874–1948
Indentured to Langley & Burke in 1891, he
later gained experience in New York, returning to Toronto in 1904 to share in
the work of rebuilding after the fire of that
year. He designed St Anne's Church on
Gladstone Avenue in 1907, and soon after,
he and Charles Langley began a large practice in banks, churches, and houses that
continued until 1941.

**Hynes, James Patrick** 1868–1953
His older brothers had Toronto's leading
plastering company in the late nineteenth
century. Hynes is shown in directories as a
draughtsman or student in the offices of
Kennedy & Holland, Darling & Curry, and
Strickland & Symons between 1885 and
1889. In the twentieth century he was responsible for several additions to St Michael's Hospital but may well be better
remembered as secretary of the Ontario
Association of Architects from 1935 to
1945, in which role he was tireless in the
interests of the profession and of education
at a critical time in the history of the School
of Architecture.
1895 Fern Avenue school
1895 St Ann's separate school, Boulton
      Avenue

**Irving, William** 1830–83
Born at Edinburgh, Scotland, son of John
Irving, a contractor and stone-carver, he
arrived in Toronto in 1852 and trained under Joseph Sheard, whose daughter Mary
he married in 1857. It appears that he was
his father-in-law's partner in all but name
before he succeeded to the practice in 1862.
Although he had no other partners, there
is evidence of his working in close co-
operation with James Grand and W.G.
Storm on a few isolated projects. E.J. Lennox was one of his pupils.
1867 Golden Lion, store for Robert Walker,
      King Street East
1871 A.R. McMaster and Brother ware-
      house, Front Street West
1874 Ontario Bank additions, Wellington
      and Scott streets
1878 Dominion Bank building, King and
      Yonge streets

**James, Arthur H.**
**James, John King**
The James brothers emigrated from England and were based in New York. The
Toronto Board of Trade building of 1889 is
one of the first projects on which they
collaborated, but by 1892 they had gone
their separate ways.

**Jarvis, [Edgar] Beaumont** 1864–1948
The eldest son of Edgar John Jarvis of Glen
Hurst, which is now on the grounds of
Branksome Hall girls' school, Jarvis
attended Upper Canada College. Research
has failed to reveal where he did his architectural training. In 1889 he joined Wilm
Knox and John Elliot in a partnership that
lasted less than a year, that year coinciding,
however, with their winning the competition to design the Confederation Life building. He left the firm to practise on his
own before the excavation of the site was
completed.
*Knox, Elliot & Jarvis* 1889–90: see Knox
*Beaumont Jarvis*
1895 Columbus Greene house, now Kappa
      Alpha, St George Street
1897 Chapel at Loretto Abbey, Wellington
      Street West

**Johnston, John** fl 1846–9
Coming to Toronto from New York in
1846 with at least twenty years' experience
there and in England, he designed few
buildings during his short stay but was one
of the city's earliest lithographic artists,
an active member of the Toronto Society
of Arts, and one of the committee of three
architects who judged proposals for
rebuilding St James' Cathedral in 1849.

**Jones, Chilion** 1835–1912
Member of a leading Brockville family and
trained probably as a civil engineer, he
first appeared in Toronto in 1857 in partnership with Robert Messer. The next year
they joined forces with Thomas Fuller,
but within a matter of months Messer had
left for Brazil. In August 1859 Fuller &
Jones secured first place in competition for
designs for the main Parliament building
in Ottawa. Both partners moved to Ottawa
during 1860. Later Jones became a contrac-

tor for railway, canal, and harbour works. Related to him were Bernal Jones, who for years was with Darling & Pearson before establishing his own practice in Kitchener, and Hugh G. Jones of Montreal, who was one of the associated architects for the present Toronto Union Station.

**Kauffmann, William** c 1823–75
His birthplace in Marbach, Wurttemburg, and his training at a German school of architecture and civil engineering made Kauffmann exceptional in the ranks of Toronto architects when he arrived from Rochester, NY, in 1855. His Rochester partner, Josiah Bissell, played no known part in their Toronto commissions. Kauffmann appears to have been the first architect in this city to use structural iron in a major way and designed several important buildings during the first decade of his practice in Canada.
*Kauffmann & Bissell* 1854–6
1855 Rossin House, King and York streets
1856 Masonic Hall (Canada Permanent building), Toronto Street
*William Kauffmann*
1861 Royal Insurance building, Yonge and Wellington streets
1862 Bank of Toronto, Wellington and Church streets
1863 Store alterations for Thomas Haworth, King Street East
1864 *Globe* building, King Street East
1865 Court House and Jail for the County of Peel, Brampton
1870 High school, Jarvis Street

**Kennedy, Thomas** c 1849–1916
From a base in Barrie he and his partners were exceptional among out-of-town architects in securing several commissions in Toronto during the 1880s. In 1882–9 they had a branch office in the city, latterly supervised by William Holland, who was then resident here. Kennedy seems to have been responsible for all designs, however, and continued to live in Barrie. He was a founding member of the Ontario Association of Architects.
*Kennedy, McVittie & Holland* 1881–3
1883 St Joseph's Roman Catholic Church, Leslieville

*Kennedy, Gaviller & Holland* 1884–5
1885 Orient Hall Masonic Lodge, Queen Street East
*Kennedy & Holland* 1885–9
1887 Lakeview House, now Hotel Winchester, Parliament Street
1887 Cyclorama, Front Street
1889 St Mary's Separate School, Adelaide Street West

**Knox, Wilm** 1858–1915
A Glaswegian by birth, he acquired his architectural training in the Edinburgh office of Moffett & Aitken. In 1886 a world tour he was making was cut short when he reached Chicago and saw the innovations being made in building design there. Working in the office of Burnham & Root, he met John Elliot and they opened a Toronto office together in mid-1888. Beaumont Jarvis was taken into the partnership in 1889, shortly before the firm won the prestigious competition to design the Confederation Life building. In 1892, attracted by the preparations for the Columbian Exhibition in Chicago, both Knox and Elliot returned there to assist Henry Ives Cobb. A year later Knox moved to Cleveland, and when Elliot joined him soon after, their partnership was revived and continued until Knox's death.
*Knox, Elliot & Jarvis* 1889–90
1889 Theodore Heintzman house, Annette Street
1890 Confederation Life building, Richmond and Yonge Streets
*Knox & Elliot* 1890–2
1890 Harbord Street Collegiate
1891 Disciples of Christ Church, Cecil Street
1892 E.F. Blake house, now Celebrity Club, Jarvis Street

**Lalor, George Hughes** c 1852–81
Was a student in the office of James Grand in 1871, when the latter died suddenly. Lalor and Henry James (d 1893) took over the practice and were partners for two years. In 1873 they were the architects for the Union Block at Adelaide and Toronto Streets. Later the same year the new partnership of Lalor and Charles Martin designed the Grand Opera House on Adelaide

Street West in conjunction with a New York architect, Thomas R. Jackson.

**Lane, Henry Bowyer Joseph** c 1818–unknown

Probably born on Corfu in the Ionian Islands, where his father was stationed with the British Army, he received part of his education at Blundell's School, Tiverton. His architectural training took place in England before 1841, when he emigrated to Cobourg, Upper Canada. Two years later he moved to Toronto, where, enjoying the patronage of the Boulton family, to whom he was related through marriage, he had an enormously successful practice until his abrupt return to England in 1847. His last known address, four years later, was Birchfield near Birmingham.

1843 Little Trinity Church, King Street East
1844 Second City Hall and Market House, Front Street East
1844 Church of St George the Martyr, John Street
1844 Osgoode Hall, west wing and alterations
1846 Holy Trinity Church, Trinity Square
1846 The Home Wood, house for G.W. Allan, Wellesley Street East

**Langley, Charles** 1870–1951

The son of Henry Langley, he began practice in the twentieth century but is remembered as the first graduate of the School of Architecture of the University of Toronto in 1892 and the generous donor of drawings, mostly of churches designed by his father, to the Metropolitan Toronto Library and Ontario Archives.

**Langley, Henry**, RCA 1836–1907

Son of a Toronto shoemaker, he was educated at the Toronto Academy before beginning a seven-year apprenticeship with William Hay. After Hay's departure from Toronto in 1862, his former partner, Thomas Gundry, and Langley began a very successful practice together. After Gundry died in 1869, Langley practised alone until 1873, when he took his brother Edward (a builder) and his nephew, Edmund Burke, into partnership. Langley's reputation as a

designer of churches ensured for their firm a large share of such commissions throughout Ontario. Edward withdrew from the partnership in 1884, as did Burke in 1892, when he assumed the practice of the late W.G. Storm. During the balance of Langley's career he worked with his son Charles. Drawings for a majority of Langley's work are to be found in the Langley Collections in the Metropolitan Toronto Library and Ontario Archives, and in the Horwood Collection at the Ontario Archives.

*Gundry & Langley* 1862–9: see Gundry

*Henry Langley* 1869–73
1870 Metropolitan Methodist Church, Queen Street East
1871 Eighth Post Office, Adelaide Street East at head of Toronto Street
1871 Bank of British North America, Wellington Street East at Yonge
1872 Necropolis chapel and lodge, Winchester Street

*Langley, Langley & Burke* 1873–84
1873 St James' Cathedral spire, pinnacles, and side porches
1874 Jarvis Street Baptist Church
1877 William McMaster house, Bloor Street East
1877 Old St Andrew's Presbyterian (now United) Church, Jarvis and Carlton streets
1878 Enlargement of John Macdonald warehouse, Wellington Street East
1878 Horticultural Pavilion, Allan Gardens
1881 McMaster College, Bloor Street West

*Langley & Burke* 1884–92
1886 Robert Simpson house, Bloor Street East
1889 Trinity Methodist (now Trinity–St Paul's United) Church, Bloor and Major streets

*Langley & Langley* 1892–1907

**Langton, William** 1854–1933

Born at Peterborough, Canada West, he was the son of John Langton, first auditor-general of Canada and vice-chancellor of the University of Toronto, 1856–60. He was educated at Upper Canada College and is first listed as an architect in 1888 directories. His works are not numerous; the best known of them may be the Toronto Golf Club (1912). Langton was influential, however, on city planning at the turn of the century. He headed the Ontario Association of Architects in 1902 and was first president of the Arts and Letters Club in 1908.

**Law, Frederick Charles** 1841–1922
English-born and a former commander in the Royal navy when he arrived in Toronto in 1874, he served as secretary to five lieutenant-governors, the first of whom was his father-in-law, John Willoughby Crawford. Architecture seems to have been an avocation; only one important building, the Church of Our Lady of Lourdes, Sherbourne Street (1886), can be attributed to Law. It was designed during or shortly after a period he spent in the offices of Darling & Curry.

**Lennox, Edward James** 1855–1933
A Torontonian by birth, he attended the Grammar and Model schools. His professional training came during five years in the office of William Irving and as a student in the architectural drawing classes at the Mechanics' Institute, where he received first prize and a diploma in 1874. His professional debut coincided with his formation in 1876 of a partnership with William Frederick McCaw. After the firm was dissolved in 1881, Lennox had no other partners during his long career before his son Edgar Edward joined him in practice in 1929. His brother Charles (1862–1949) was a mainstay in E.J.'s office for almost thirty-five years, until 1915, but their association appears never to have been formalized as a partnership.

  Lennox was one of Toronto's most influential architects. His designs had a progressive and robust spirit that owed much to the work of H.H. Richardson but also exhibited marked originality. Some of Lennox's drawings are in Ontario Archives, while others related to the third City Hall are held in the City of Toronto Archives.
*McCaw & Lennox* 1876–81
1876 Landscape plan for Queen's Park
1878 Bond Street Congregational Church, Dundas and Bond streets
1879 Hotel for Edward Hanlan, Toronto Island

*E.J. Lennox* 1881–1929
1884 Manning Arcade, King Street West
1885 Victoria Orange Hall, Queen and Berti streets
1888 Dr G.R. McDonagh house, Church Street
1889 Third City Hall, Queen Street West
1891 Toronto Athletic Club, College Street
1908 Casa Loma stables, Walmer Road
1910 Restoration after fire, west wing of Parliament buildings, Queen's Park
1910 Casa Loma, Austin Terrace
1915 Lenwil, Lennox's own house, Austin Terrace

**Marani, Cesare** 1864–1934
He was an instructor in the course in architecture in the School of Practical Science, 1890. There are no buildings to his credit, but that deficiency was more than made up by the achievements of his son, F.H. Marani, in this century.

**Miller, George Martell** 1854/5–1933
Born in Port Hope and educated at the School of Practical Science, University of Toronto, he worked for Charles Walton in 1883–5. In practice on his own by 1886, he designed a number of important buildings and was also the supervising architect for the construction of Massey Hall. Many of Miller's drawings are held in the Thomas Fisher Rare Book Library, University of Toronto.
1888 Parkdale Collegiate Institute, Jamieson Avenue
1888 Gladstone Hotel, Queen Street West at Gladstone Avenue
1890 W.D. Matthews house, St George Street at Hoskin Avenue
1893 Massey Hall, supervising architect
1898 Havergal College, Jarvis Street
1901 Annesley Hall, Victoria College, Queen's Park
1908 Lillian Massey Building, Queen's Park at Bloor Street West

**Mundie, William** c 1811–58
Born in Scotland, he came to Canada about 1850 and settled in Hamilton. As the outstanding landscape gardener of his time in Canada, he was much sought after. Important commissions in Toronto required

him to live here for a few years between 1853 and 1856, when he returned to Hamilton. His grandson was architect William B. Mundie of Chicago, the partner from 1891 to 1903 of William Le Baron Jenney.

1853  Normal School grounds
1853  Drainage and site preparation for new Parliament buildings and governor's residence, University (later Queen's) Park
1856  Toronto General Hospital grounds
1856?Greenhouses at Woodlawn for the Honourable J.C. Morrison, Yonge Street, Yorkville
1857  Design for University Park
1857  Brock's Monument grounds, Queenston

**Parmentier, André** 1780–1830
He was born at Enghien, Belgium, into a family prominent in horticulture; Potage Parmentier is named for one of its members well known as a proponent of the potato. André emigrated to the United States in 1824 to become that country's earliest professional landscape gardener. From his nursery in Brooklyn he executed commissions from the Carolinas to Canada, including several on estates such as Hyde Park along the Hudson River. One of his last was a plan for the grounds of Upper Canada College at York.

**Paull, Almond E.** 1824–1902
**Paull, Herbert G.** 1858–1948
Father and son came to Canada from Cornwall, England, in 1870. From 1877 until 1888 they were in partnership together. Both subsequently practised on their own. The Salvation Army Temple, now demolished, at Albert and James streets (1885) was erected to plans prepared by Herbert G. Paull, and he secured the fourth premium for his design entered in the Toronto Court House competition the following year.

**Pearson, John** 1867–1940
Soon after his arrival in Toronto from England in 1889, he joined the staff of Darling & Curry and worked on the plans for the Victoria Hospital for Sick Children. So marked was his talent that three years

later the firm took him into partnership along with the equally youthful and able Henry Sproatt. From 1892 to 1895 Pearson spent some time in Newfoundland helping to rebuild St John's after a major fire. His major contribution to Canadian architecture, however, was made in the twentieth century, with many bank buildings and the reconstruction of the Parliament buildings to his credit.
*Darling, Curry, Sproatt & Pearson* 1892: see Darling
*Darling, Sproatt & Pearson* 1893–6: see Darling
*Darling & Pearson* 1896–1932, 1936–8: see Darling
*Darling, Pearson & Cleveland* 1933–5

**Pilkington, Robert** 1765–1834
A British Army engineer in Canada from 1793 until 1803, he occasionally prepared plans and estimates for both Simcoe and Russell. In the 1830s he was inspector of fortifications in the British army, with the rank of major-general.
1797  Barracks for Queen's Rangers, Fort York
1800  Lieutenant-governor's house, Fort York

**Post, Albert Asa** 1850–1926
Having begun his practice in Whitby, his birthplace, he moved to Toronto in 1886, the move coinciding with a commission to build a new spire on St Basil's Church on St Joseph Street. From 1891 to 1896 the firm he established with Arthur W. Holmes enjoyed a substantial Roman Catholic patronage. In 1895 Post left Toronto to live in Buffalo, although for some years afterwards he was still undertaking work in Canada
*Post & Holmes* 1891–6
1891  St Michael's College School, St Clair Avenue
1894  St Michael's Hospital wing, Bond Street

**Radford, Edward** 1831–1920
**Radford, George Kent** 1827–1908
These brothers were trained in England and were civil engineers like their father, William Radford, and an elder brother. Appar-

ently Edward and George had some interest in architecture as well. They were in practice together in London during 1853 before George emigrated and settled in Toronto. When Edward followed, they revived their partnership, which George combined with a post as manager of the Toronto Waterworks company. Although the Radfords achieved some notice by winning second prize in the Quebec Custom House competition, they will be remembered chiefly for their designs for St Paul's Anglican Church on Bloor Street in Yorkville of 1858. That same year George returned to England, where he remained for about a decade until coming to the United States in the late 1860s to work for the landscape architects Olmsted & Vaux; he was Vaux's partner from 1874 to 1892. Edward left Toronto in 1861/2 for Cincinnati, where he worked for the architect William Tinsley until returning to England in 1864.

**Ridout, Thomas** 1828–1905
Eldest son of Thomas Gibbs Ridout, cashier of the Bank of Upper Canada, he trained as a civil engineer at King's College, London. In any architectural history of Toronto he appears, if only briefly, as the partner of F.W. Cumberland. Later in the 1850s he was associated for a short time with Sandford Fleming and Collingwood Schreiber. From 1875 until retirement Ridout was a public servant in the Department of Railways and Canals at Ottawa.
*Cumberland & Ridout* 1850–2: see Cumberland

**Roberts, David, Sr** 1810/11–81
A civil engineer who emigrated from Mountmellick, [Queen's] County Laoighis, Ireland, to the United States in 1842 and settled in Toronto two years later, he was an expert millwright, metal-founder, and designer of stationary steam-engines, which soon brought him the valuable patronage of Gooderham & Worts. He may also have had some architectural training. Although in the early 1860s he retired to Elgin County to farm, he appears to have kept his hand in as a consulting engineer.
1845 Gooderham & Worts distillery
    additions

1859 Gooderham & Worts new steam-mill
    and distillery
1863 Gooderham & Worts new malt house
    (with Gundry & Langley)
1864 Toronto General Hospital, heating
    and ventilating
1870 Toronto Sugar Refinery cribwork,
    foot of Peter Street

**Roberts, David, Jr** 1845–1907
Son and namesake of the preceding civil engineer, he studied under his father and at Bryant and Stratton's Mercantile College, Toronto (1864–5), before entering the office of a Toronto architect, thought to be Gundry & Langley but not confirmed at present. Roberts formed a brief partnership with George Shaw in 1868–9. After this, apart from having associates on a few projects, he practised on his own. The Gooderhams' commissions gave him exceptional scope to enrich Toronto's streetscapes, which he did with considerable skill.
1875 Grandstands for Woodbine Riding
    and Driving Park
1881 Toronto Grape Sugar Co Works, foot
    of Princess Street
1886 Lombard Street firehall
1889 George Gooderham house, St George
    and Bloor streets
1889 Thorncrest, house for G.P. Magann,
    foot of Dowling Avenue
1891 George H. Gooderham house, Jarvis
    Street
1892 Gooderham (Flat-Iron) Building,
    Wellington and Front streets East

**Rogers, Thomas** 1778/82–1853
Born in England and trained there as an architect, he emigrated prior to 1825, settling in Kingston, Upper Canada, where he was responsible for several buildings and public works. His talents were much in demand in York before John G. Howard and Thomas Young arrived and provided the architectural design, construction supervision, and surveying services needed by the emerging city.
1829 Parliament buildings, Front between
    Simcoe and John streets
1829 Central School house additions, Jarvis
    and Lombard streets

1831 St James' Church, King and Church
streets

**Rolph, Ernest** 1871–1958
A member of Toronto's Rolph family of
printers and engravers, he studied with
David Roberts, Jr, and then in 1894 took a
draughtsman's position with Darling,
Sproatt & Pearson, where presumably the
seed was planted that resulted six years later
in the formation of Sproatt & Rolph. The
work of this distinguished firm was entirely
in the twentieth century.

**Sheard, Joseph** 1813–1883
Born at Hornsea, Yorkshire, and trained as
a wheelwright, he immigrated to York,
Upper Canada, in 1833. After working
several years as a carpenter, Sheard became
a builder and then, about 1846, an architect. Notwithstanding a lack of formal
training, he was very successful until retiring in 1862 in favour of his son-in-law,
William Irving. He then served as one of
the commissioners inquiring into problems
connected with the construction of the
Ottawa Parliament buildings, and devoted
more time to his duties as a city alderman.
A veteran of civic politics from 1849, he
was elected mayor of Toronto in 1871–2.
1852 William Cawthra house, Bay and
King streets
1854 John, Phoebe, and Victoria Street
schools
1854 St Michael's Cemetery deadhouse,
Yonge Street
1854 Primitive Methodist Church, Alice
Street
1856 Oliver Mowat house, Jarvis Street
1856 Romain buildings, King Street West
1859 Givens, Louisa, and Palace Street
schools
1861 Ontario Bank, Wellington and Scott
streets

**Sheard, Matthew** 1840–1910
Eldest son of architect Joseph Sheard, he
was a student in his father's office. Afterwards he practised in New York, Chicago,
Milwaukee (1871), and Ottawa (1871–6)
before returning to Toronto in 1877–8. For
twenty years, until 1884, Sheard had an
Ottawa-based partnership with Henry H.

Horsey, another of Joseph Sheard's students, although the partnership must have
been a loose arrangement that permitted
Matthew to pursue commissions elsewhere
without necessarily involving Horsey.
Sheard's Toronto practice was carried on in
his own name.
1878 *Evening Telegram* building, King and
Bay streets
1885 Ontario College of Pharmacy, Gerrard
Street East

**Siddall, John Wilson** 1861–1941
English-born and -trained, he came to Canada in 1891 to work for Knox & Elliot
in connection with the Confederation Life
building. In 1892, when both partners
in the firm returned to Chicago, Siddall in
partnership with Fred S. Baker succeeded
Knox & Elliot. From 1895 until his retirement in 1938, Siddall practised alone.
1895 Holy Blossom Synagogue (now St
George Greek Orthodox Church),
Bond Street
1901 St Lawrence Market rebuilding

**Simpson, Henry** 1864–1926
Born in Toronto and apprenticed to E.J.
Lennox, he went to New York in 1887 to
further his training but was back in Toronto by late 1888. During his subsequent
practice here he had brief partnerships with
Charles J. Gibson, 1888–90; James A. Ellis,
1897–8; and Robert Young, 1908.
1891 Cooke's Presbyterian Church, Queen
Street East
1892 Bethany Chapel, University Avenue
1898 Metallic Roofing Co showroom, King
Street West
1904 J.H. McGregor house, Crescent Road

**Smith, [Ralph] Eden** 1858–1949
Smith was an Englishman from a well-to-
do background who had architectural training before immigrating to Canada in 1885.
En route here he was persuaded to try
homesteading near Minnedosa, Manitoba,
which was a failure. In 1888 he moved
to Toronto and worked for four years as a
draftsman for Strickland & Symons. He
opened his own office in 1892 and from
1895 to 1899 was associated with Eustace
Bird, with offices in Toronto and Barrie.

For much of the period from 1896 to 1915 Smith shared offices in Toronto with architect James P. Hynes, a close friend, but his sons were his only partners during the two decades before his retirement in 1920.

Eden Smith was the first president of the Architectural Eighteen Club in 1900 and a founding member of the Arts and Letters Club in 1908.

The decision to terminate this history of Toronto building and its architects at 1900 is irrevocable, but Eden Smith suffers particularly from it since much of his most important work was done in the twentieth century. He revolutionized house design in Toronto (designing some 2,500 residential units in his thirty-three years of practice), several branch libraries, and quite a few fine churches. The Toronto Housing Company's terraces on Bain and Sumach streets (1914) are still models of their kind. The distinguished editor of the *Architectural Review*, Dr Nikolaus Pevsner, considered the Studio Building on Severn Street an outstanding building for its day (1913). Eden Smith was largely responsible for the layout and for the design of many of the houses in Wychwood Park.

1892 St John the Evangelist Anglican Church, Portland Street
1893 St Thomas's Anglican Church, Huron Street
1899 St Hilda's College, Trinity Park, Queen Street West

**Smith, James Avon**, RCA 1832–1918
From his birthplace in Macduff, Banffshire, Scotland, he emigrated to Canada in 1851 and apprenticed to William Thomas. In 1858–60 Smith practised with a partner, John Bailey, and then for a decade by himself before taking his former student, John Gemmell, into partnership in 1870. This firm existed for forty-five years. Smith's own career as an architect lasted for a remarkable fifty-seven years, during which, it was said, he had been involved with the building of over ninety of Toronto's churches! He was also an active member of the Ontario Society of Artists, a charter member of the Royal Canadian Academy in 1880, its treasurer 1880–7, and secretary-treasurer 1887–1910.

*James Smith 1860–70*
1862 Elm Street Methodist Church
1867 Northern Congregational Church, Church Street above Wood
*Smith & Gemmell 1870–1915*
1871 Royal Canadian Bank, Front Street East
1873 Knox College, Spadina Crescent
1874 National 'Reform' Clubhouse, Bay Street
1877 St James' Square Presbyterian Church, Gerrard Street
1878 Church of the Redeemer, Bloor Street at Avenue Road
1878 O'Keefe Lager Brewery, Gould and Victoria streets
1879 Warring Kennedy house, St George and Bloor streets
1886 St Paul's Methodist (United) Church, Avenue Road at Webster Avenue

**Sproatt, Henry**, LLD (Toronto) 1866–1934
A son of Charles Sproatt, a land surveyor and civil engineer, he received some of his training in A.R. Denison's office, followed by a period in New York City and travelling in Europe. He became a partner in Darling, Sproatt & Pearson, 1893–6. With Ernest Rolph, Sproatt will be remembered for the National Club on Bay Street (1906), designed during a short association with S.G. Curry, and for Hart House at the University of Toronto (1911).

**Stewart, William** 1832–1907
Son of a builder and cabinet-maker in York, Upper Canada, who was a strong supporter of William Lyon Mackenzie, Stewart attended the Model School and also graduated from the Normal School. It is not known with whom he trained in Toronto before departing to work from 1857 to 1872 in St Paul, Minnesota, Cincinnati, Ohio, and Covington, Kentucky. Returning to Toronto in 1872, he teamed up three years later with W.R. Strickland. Before they went their own ways in 1881, they had developed a large practice specializing in factories, schools, heating, and ventilation. Stewart moved to Hamilton in the mid-1880s, where he spent the rest of his life.

*William Stewart* 1872–5
1873  Walker House Hotel, Front and York streets
*Stewart & Strickland* 1875–81
1875  Holy Blossom Synagogue, Richmond Street East
1876  City Hall renovations and additions, Front Street East
1878  Police Station and Firehall, Dundas Street East
1878  Several buildings, Industrial Exhibition (CNE) grounds

**Storm, William George**, RCA 1826–92
In 1830 Storm came with his parents to York, Upper Canada, from his birthplace at Burton-upon-Stather, Lincolnshire. His father was a builder, and William turned naturally to architecture as a profession. In 1844 he joined the office of William Thomas, whose ability and experience were unmatched at that time in Toronto. At the end of Storm's apprenticeship in 1848 he worked for Frederic Cumberland, whose partner he became four years later. They formed an ideal pair, with Cumberland the engineer and man-of-affairs complementing Storm, whose talents as a designer and delineator have been underrated. Soon they had surpassed all others, including William Thomas, to become the leading firm in Toronto. While Storm was unable to maintain this position when the partnership was formally dissolved in 1863, he continued to make a creditable showing in the face of impressive competition. Most of his drawings from this period are in the Horwood Collection, Ontario Archives.

Although Storm had not been prominent in efforts prior to the 1880s to form and sustain an architects' association, the first meeting of the Architectural Guild was held in his office in October 1887. This led two years later to the founding of the Ontario Association of Architects, of which he was chosen the first president. It was a richly deserved honour. He was also a charter member of the Royal Canadian Academy, established in 1880.
*Cumberland & Storm* 1852–63: see Cumberland
*William G. Storm* 1864–92
1865  Great Western Railway station, foot of Yonge Street

1866  Osgoode Hall cast-iron fence
1873  Wellesley School, Wellesley and Bay streets
1874  St Andrew's Presbyterian Church, King and Simcoe streets
1880  Osgoode Hall wing for law school
1881  Protestant Episcopal Divinity School (Wycliffe College), College Street west of Queen's Park
1883  Mrs William Cawthra house, Jarvis and Isabella streets
1889  Sir William Mulock house alterations, Jarvis and Gloucester streets
1889  Victoria College, Queen's Park

**Strickland, Walter Reginald** 1841–1915
A member of the literary Strickland family of Lakefield, he trained under his brother-in-law, Kivas Tully. He opened his office in 1871, practising on his own during the intervals between his partnerships with William Stewart (1875–81) and William L. Symons (1887–98). He was a founder member of the Architectural Guild in 1887.
*W.R. Strickland*
1872  Iron-front wholesale warehouses, 45–9 Front Street East
*Stewart & Strickland* 1875–81: see Stewart
*Strickland & Symons* 1887–98
1887  Consumers' Gas purifying and retort houses, now Canadian Opera Company buildings, Front Street East
1887  St Simon's Anglican Church, Howard Street
1889  Upper Canada College, Deer Park, supervising architects
1889  St Matthew's Anglican Church, First Avenue
1893  Second Union Station additions, Front Street West

**Symons, William Limbery** c 1865–1931
English-born, at Stoke Gabriel, Devon, he immigrated to Canada with his parents and acquired his architectural training here, probably with Walter R. Strickland, since the notation 'turned architect' beside his name in the 1887 minute book of the Architectural Draughtsmen's Club coincided with the formation of their partnership. Symons appears to have been the designer in the firm.

In the twentieth century he had a large domestic practice, advised Queen's University on the layout of its campus, and was architect to the Canadian Medical Health Commission during the First World War, responsible for designing hospitals like that on Christie Street. From 1925 until his death he lived in New York City, where he was retained by J. Pierpont Morgan as a consultant in the restoration of Trinity Church, Broadway, designed in 1839 by Richard Upjohn.

*Strickland & Symons* 1887–98: see Strickland

**Taylor, Edwin** fl. 1858–60
English-born and said to have been a pupil of Sir Joseph Paxton, Taylor carried out the landscaping of the University Park in 1859, after the death of William Mundie, who had prepared earlier designs; Taylor also laid out the Horticultural (now Allan) Gardens. He seems to have left Toronto by the time the latter grounds were opened in September 1860.

**Thomas, Cyrus Pole** 1833–1911
Third son of architect William Thomas, he came to Canada with his parents in 1843 and five years later, at fifteen, was among the staff in his father's office. He and his brother, William Tutin, were taken into formal partnership by their father in 1857. The following year Cyrus opened the firm's Halifax-office and was well placed to secure commissions when a large fire occurred in that city in 1859. He remained in Halifax until late 1862 and then moved to Montreal, where he was joined in 1864 by William Tutin Thomas. They practised together for two years and then separately until 1869, when Cyrus moved to Chicago. Once again, he was lucky to be on hand when a major fire occurred. He remained in Chicago until 1896, then returned to Toronto. While here he designed the St George Apartments at St George and Harbord Streets (1899), one of the earliest such structures in the city. Moving to Cambridge, Massachusetts, in 1900, he missed Toronto's greatest fire by four years.

**Thomas, William** c 1799–1860
Raised in Chalford, Gloucestershire, he apprenticed 1812–19 to John Gardiner, a carpenter and joiner. He spent most of the 1820s working in Birmingham and the

1830s in Leamington, where he became both a speculative builder and an eclectic designer of some talent. Bankruptcy in 1840 may have led him to make up his mind to move to Toronto three years later.

Canada West was entering a boom period, and there was a shortage of architects in the city. Those on hand included John G. Howard and Thomas Young, who were long-established, and the well-connected Henry Bowyer Lane. In spite of this competition Thomas soon became the city's leading architect and remained so until about 1850. He was then overtaken by ill health and by younger architects, most of whom were newly trained in the styles fashionable in Victorian Britain. In 1857 Thomas took his sons, William Tutin and Cyrus, into partnership. His death from diabetes came three years later.

That Thomas remained on good terms with both Howard and Young is evidence of his amiability. He was the president of the Toronto Society of Arts in 1847 and 1848, and president of Canada's first architects' organization, the Association of Architects, Civil Engineers and Public Land Surveyors, established in 1859.

*William Thomas* 1843–57
1844 Adelaide Buildings, King Street East
1845 Commercial Bank, Wellington Street West
1845 St Michael's Cathedral, Bond and Shuter streets
1845 Bishop's Palace, Church Street
1847 Knox's Church, Queen Street West
1848 Oakham House, Thomas's own home, Church and Gould
1848 Jennings Church, Richmond and Bay
1849 St Lawrence Hall, King and Jarvis
1855 Zion Congregational Church, Bay and Adelaide streets
1857 Cooke's Presbyterian Church, Queen and Mutual streets
*William Thomas & Sons*, 1857–60
1858 Don Jail, Gerrard Street East

**Thomas, William Tutin** 1829–1892
English-born and eldest son of architect William Thomas, he followed in his father's footsteps, and probably began his architectural studies with him soon after the family arrived in Toronto in 1843. It is surprising that the senior Thomas waited until 1857 to

take his sons, William Tutin and Cyrus Pole, into formal partnership. When he died in 1860, William Tutin carried on the practice in Toronto and saw the Don Jail completed before he moved to Montreal in 1864. He was quite successful there, remaining for the rest of his life.

1862  St Michael's College wing, St Joseph and Bay streets
1864  Unexecuted design for St Michael's Cathedral spire (sent from Montreal)

**Townsend, [Samuel] Hamilton** 1856–1940

From Brantford, Canada West, but educated at the Model School in Toronto, Towsend trained with W.G. Storm, 1874–6, following which he had a three-year partnership with Herbert Hancock (c 1836–80). He left Toronto in the mid-1880s to travel in the United Kingdom and on the Continent, much of the time on a 'penny-farthing' bicycle, but then resumed his practice here. It was largely a residential one and included many South Rosedale houses on streets like Cluny Avenue and Chestnut Park. He retired about 1916. Townsend was a founder member of the Architectural Guild in 1887 and president of the Ontario Association of Architects in 1898. A keen sailor, he designed his own boat, the *Wah-Wah*, which won the Royal Canadian Yacht Club's Prince of Wales Cup in 1897.

**Tully, John Aspenwell** 1818–86

Born and educated in Ireland, where he had some professional training, he was the elder brother of Kivas Tully. Arriving in Toronto in 1843, John entered the office of J.G. Howard to continue his apprenticeship. By 1846 he had qualified as a land surveyor and an architect, and practised as such without enjoying the same success as his brother. He left in 1855 or 1856 for Chicago, where he worked for or was in partnership with several architects, then had his own office until he settled in New Mexico in 1879. Tully was the secretary of the Association of Architects, Civil Engineers and Provincial Land Surveyors of Canada in 1860–1.

1855  Hughes Terrace, King Street West
1856  John O'Donahue houses, Shuter Street
1859  House of Refuge, Industrial Farm, Broadview Avenue

**Tully, Kivas** 1820–1905

Born at Garyracum, [Queen's] County Laoighis, Ireland, he trained with the civil engineer W.H. Owen of Limerick and, before immigrating to Canada in 1844, acquired some experience under George Wilkinson, architect in Ireland for the Poor Law commissioners. Tully was in private practice in Toronto from 1844 to 1868, when he was appointed the senior architect and engineer of the Ontario Public Works Department. From then until his retirement in 1896 he oversaw the design, construction, alteration, and maintenance of many provincial public buildings. Even longer was his appointment, lasting from 1852 to his death, as engineer to the Board of Toronto Harbour Commissioners. Tully was a founding member of the Canadian Institute in 1850 and was active as a Toronto school trustee, councillor, and alderman.

1845  Bank of Montreal, Yonge and Front streets
1845  Custom House, Front and Yonge streets
1848  St Catharines Town Hall, later Lincoln County Court House
1851  Trinity College, Queen Street West
1857  Victoria Hall, Cobourg
1861  Queen's Wharf lighthouse, now at Fleet Street and Lakeshore Boulevard

**Waite, Richard Alfred** 1846–1911

Contrary to a popular notion that he was an 'English' architect, Waite came to the United States from England as a boy and was trained in the New York City office of John Kellum. By 1874 he had opened an office in Buffalo. In 1880, when he was invited to be one of the judges in the competition for the new Parliament buildings, he was already the architect for the *Mail* building (then under construction) and no stranger to Toronto. Subsequently, he designed several other buildings in this city and in Montreal.

1880 *Mail* building, King and Bay streets
1880 Western Assurance Building, Wellington and Scott streets
1886 Ontario Parliament buildings, Queen's Park
1888 Canada Life building, King Street West
1889 Canadian Bank of Commerce, King and Jordan streets

**Walton, Charles Albert** 1845–1908
A Yorkshireman born in Leeds, he came to Canada in 1856 and apprenticed with William Kauffmann for five years. This was followed by a decade spent in Montreal, Albany, Detroit, and Chicago before he returned to Toronto in 1876. A brief partnership with William Storm in 1877 preceded his practising on his own until his death thirty years later.
1883 Toronto Arcade building, Yonge Street
1885 Caledonia Club curling rink, Mutual Street

**Wickson, [Alexander] Frank** 1861–1936
Attended Jarvis Collegiate, Upper Canada College, and the Ontario School of Art before apprenticing in the office of Smith & Gemmell. Later he was on the staff of Darling & Curry before forming a partnership with Norman B. Dick. After Dick's early demise in 1895, Wickson worked by himself for a decade, then entered into partnership with Alfred H. Gregg in 1904, which lasted until Wickson's death.
*Wickson & Gregg* 1904–36
1905 Berkeley Street Firehall
1905 Warehouse at 70 Wellington Street West

**Willmot, Mancel** 1855–1934
Born in Yorkville village, he apprenticed under W.G. Storm in 1874–5. Apart from a few years in the early 1880s spent in Winnipeg, he practised largely but not exclusively in the Yorkville area of Toronto.
1877 Yorkville Public School, Cottingham Street
1889 Yorkville Firehall (except tower), Yorkville Avenue

**Windeyer, Richard Cunningham**, ARCA, OSA c 1830–1900
English by birth, he trained in the ordnance department at Woolwich, England, and in the office of architect Jonathan B. Snook of Brooklyn, New York. He moved back and forth among Canada, the United States, and England from 1854 to 1862, when he finally settled in Montreal. Nine years later he moved to Toronto. His partners here were William Malsburg (1871–2), Joseph Savage (1873–5), a stepson, John Falloon (1885–7), and his own son Richard (1893–6).
1873 Toronto Custom House, Front and Yonge streets
1874 All Saints' Anglican Church, Sherbourne and Dundas streets
1885 St Alban the Martyr Anglican Cathedral, Lowther and Howland avenues (partly constructed)

**Wright, Charles Henry Challenor** 1864–1944
Almost always referred to by the initials of his given names, he was an instructor in the School of Practical Science, 1890, and professor and head of the School of Architecture, 1901–34.

**Young, Thomas** 1805–60
Studied with architect Charles Heathcote Tatham in London, England, and then worked for the builder Joseph Bramah and Sons before emigrating. He settled in York, Upper Canada, in 1832/4. Until his appointment in 1837 as architect for King's College, Young was better known as a teacher of drawing and as an artist. During the 1840s a number of court houses, jails, and churches in many parts of the province, in addition to the university, were built to his plans. Although he won the 1843 competition to design a column to replace the damaged monument to General Sir Isaac Brock at Queenston, Young's scheme was never built. With Daniel McDonald he was the contractor for the 1844 City Hall, which seems to have contributed to his bankruptcy soon after. Near the end of his life he was reduced to the modest role of

clerk of works for William Thomas & Sons on the construction of the Don Jail.
1839 St James' Anglican Cathedral, King Street East
1842 King's College, University [Queen's] Park

1850 Anatomical School (later Moss Hall), University of Toronto, University Park
1854 St Patrick's Market, Queen Street West

# Appendix B

## Builders and Contractors

It is paradoxical that although contractors and master tradesmen were many times more numerous than architects in nineteenth-century Toronto, they are much less well known as individuals. In spite of the large enterprises these builders created to bring alive the architects' plans – some like John Ritchey and John Worthington gave work to hundreds of men and were the largest employers in the city – they have been neglected by most biographers. Although the newspapers of the day reprinted word for word the speeches of political figures and reported at length on fires, accidents, and performances by visiting entertainers, the activities of these entrepreneurs went largely unnoticed.

At least as early as the 1840s, all building projects of any size required the skills of more than a dozen recognized trades. Typically these were grouped for purposes of costing and tendering as follows:

1 excavator, bricklayer, mason, and stonecutter
2 carpenter, joiner, blacksmith, and founder
3 slater and tinsmith
4 plumber, gas-fitter, and bell-hanger
5 plasterer
6 glazier, painter, and stainer.

Since wages and materials for the structural trades in the first two groups made up most of the construction costs, it was from the ranks of these trades that almost all major builders came. They would invariably have their own businesses, based on their trades, and would contract for work on behalf of men they employed directly. What appears to have set them apart from other master craftsmen, however, was their ability when it was to their advantage to contract for the whole of the work to be done on a job and then to subcontract some of it to others. This involved not only a greater risk but required more organization and supervision.

Sometimes builders would put in both whole and trade tenders for the same job, hopeful of getting some business at least, or would form joint ventures with other builders to submit tenders for the whole work. Often they would act as subcontractors. Many had profitable related enterprises such as stone and slate quarries, millwork shops, and builders' supply yards. Others, like John Harper and Joseph Sheard, who later became architects, might provide designs and plans.

The great variety of their activities and the differences in scale between major builders and those who made their living putting up small houses, one at a time, discourage further generalization. Unfortunately, even for the largest builders, business records and papers seldom survive, making it that much more difficult to understand their operations in detail. The following biographies, some all too brief, present Toronto builders of the nineteenth century as a related group for the first time.

**Allan, William**
A Kingston contractor, he built the York Town Hall and Market of 1831.

**Brown and Love**
(Frederick D. Brown; Henry G. Love)
Both partners had previous experience as builders in England. Their firm was organized in 1875 to take over the business of Benjamin Walton when he retired from contracting to give more time to the development of his slate quarries.
1876 Consumers' Gas offices, 19 Toronto Street
1878 Building and Loan Chambers, 13–15 Toronto Street
1878 Dominion Bank, King and Yonge streets
1880 *Mail* building, King and Bay streets
1884 Manning Arcade, King Street West
1888 Canada Life building, King Street West
1889 Bank of Commerce, King and Jordan streets
1889 George Gooderham house, St George and Bloor streets
1890 Confederation Life building, Richmond and Yonge streets

**Burke, William** See Smith, Burke & Co

**Dinnis, Richard** b 1834
He was a carpenter from Falmouth, England, who immigrated to Toronto in 1856. After working for William H. Pim for two years, he joined Worthington Bros and gained experience on many of their jobs in Canada and Ohio. He started his own building business in 1872, and won the contract for carpentry for the third City Hall of 1889 at Queen and Bay streets.

**Elliott & Neelon**
(John Elliott, d 1891; Sylvester Neelon, 1824–97)
This partnership was apparently formed to bid for the masonry contract on the third City Hall, which Elliott and Neelon won in 1889. After Elliott's death Neelon carried on until architect E.J. Lennox took the work out of his hands in 1893.

**Farquhar, James** d 1890
English born and a mason by trade, he worked for John Worthington on the building of Brock's Monument at Queenston during the 1850s. Later, in partnership with his nephew George Farquhar, he had stone quarries, lime works, and a contracting and builders'-supply business. James Farquhar's sons, Ewart and Charles, worked for their father for a time before establishing in 1873 their own contracting company, which specialized in street paving.

**Farquhar, William**
In the 1860s he was a partner of David Ramsay in a stonecutting business at the foot of Church Street. Ramsay & Farquhar had the contract in 1867 for the cut stonework for the Golden Lion, Robert Walker's store on King Street East. During the 1870s William Farquhar was in partnership with Alexander Manning and others as W. Farquhar & Co to build the Parliamentary Library in Ottawa.

**Forbes, Duncan** See Metcalfe, Wilson & Forbes

**Ford & Hayden**
(John Ford; William Hayden)
Ford, a carpenter, came to York from

Edinburgh in 1819. He submitted plans in 1826 for the new Parliament buildings, although his proposal was not awarded the first premium. In the 1830s he styled himself an architect. His partner, William Hayden, who was also a carpenter, owned land in Yorkville and is remembered by Hayden Street, south of Bloor between Yonge and Church streets.

1824 Home District Court House and Jail, King Street, York
1826 Gore District Court House and Jail, Hamilton

**Harper, John** 1806–88
Born in Belfast, Harper came to York in 1817 with his parents and later followed his father into the building business. During the late 1850s he began calling himself an architect and in 1867 formed a partnership with his son George (1843–1910) that lasted until 1881, when the elder Harper retired. He was an alderman on the first council for the city of Toronto in 1834. The list of buildings that follows refers to Harper's work as a builder; some of his projects as an architect are shown in Appendix A under his son's name.

1834 Canada Company office, Frederick Street
1840 Officers' Quarters (Stanley Barracks), New Garrison
1842 Victoria Row, King Street East
1844 Terrace of four houses for Captain Dick, Front Street West (later the core of the Queen's Hotel)
1845 St Michael's Cathedral, Bond and Shuter streets
1846 Mental Asylum, Queen Street West (foundations)
1846 Holy Trinity Church, Trinity Square
1855 Toronto General Hospital, Spruce Street (foundations)

**Hayden, William** See Ford & Hayden

**Kennedy, McArthur & Co**
(Duncan Kennedy, d 1833/4; Peter McArthur)
Duncan Kennedy, a master builder, arrived in Canada in the early 1820s. Peter McArthur was his partner on the construction of Brock's Monument and also on the construction of the Bank of Upper Canada

when Kennedy's original partners, Francis Hall and John Kidd, left for Nova Scotia to work on the Shubenacadie Canal. Kennedy incurred a large loss on the bank contract. In 1831–3, shortly before his death, he and McArthur superintended the construction of the York Town Hall and Market and the completion of the Parliament buildings.

1824 Brock Monument, Queenston
1825 Bank of Upper Canada, York

**Love, Henry G.** See Brown & Love

**Lucas, Henry** 1846–1926
A native of Portsmouth, England, he learned his trade of bricklaying while working for his father, a large contractor and builder. He arrived in Canada in 1871, was in partnership with his brother John from 1874 to 1878, and then operated a business on his own.

1887 Barber and Ellis Co warehouse, Bay Street
1888 Toronto Club, Wellington and York streets
1889 Victoria Hospital for Sick Children, College Street
1893 Fred Victor Mission, Jarvis and Queen streets

**Manning, Alexander** 1819–1903
Leaving Dublin, Ireland, at a young age and immigrating to Toronto in 1834, Manning apprenticed as a carpenter. During the 1840s he worked in partnership with Robert Petch, also a carpenter, and on his own. His interests broadened in the 1850s and 1860s into railway building, and Manning became a major developer and owner of property. In the 1870s he was a contractor on the Welland and Cornwall canals and a partner in William Farquhar and Co, which had the contract to build the Parliamentary Library in Ottawa. He served several years on Toronto City Council and was mayor of the city in 1873 and again in 1885. At his death his were the largest individual property taxes in Toronto.

1845 Firemen's Hall and Mechanics' Institute, Court Street, (with Robert Petch)
1847 Stores for A.V. Brown, Yonge Street

**McArthur, Peter** See Kennedy, McArthur and Co

## McBean & Withrow

(John McBean; James Withrow, 1804–64)
Little is known about McBean, a carpenter,
before his partnership with Withrow in
the late 1840s. By 1852, however, he was
sufficiently well established to take over
the contract to complete Trinity College
when Metcalfe, Wilson & Forbes failed.

Withrow, who was also a carpenter,
came to York from Nova Scotia in 1833.
His son, John Jacob Withrow, followed
in his father's footsteps as a builder and
contractor but is better remembered as a
long-time president of the Canadian National Exhibition.

1847  Knox's Church, Queen Street West
      (carpentry)
1849  Store for Dr Christopher Widmer,
      Church Street

## McDonald & Young

(Daniel McDonald; Thomas Young, c
1805–60)
A partnership between Daniel and James
McDonald, as carpenters and builders, existed at the same time as Daniel's in 1844–5
with the sometime architect Thomas Young
to construct the City Hall on Front Street.
The McDonalds were partners again in
the 1860s.

## Metcalfe, Wilson & Forbes

(James Metcalfe, 1822–86; Alexander Wilson, d 1851/2; Duncan Forbes, d 1885/6)
This firm, or, as it was sometimes known,
'the Company,' was very successful at
the mid-century but failed in March 1852,
soon after the death of partner Alexander
Wilson.

Metcalfe was a native of Cumberland,
England, who came to Canada in 1843.
After his financial failure he went to Australia, returning to Toronto in 1858 by
way of California, where, it is said, he became very rich and was known henceforth
as 'California' Metcalfe. He served in the
House of Commons from 1867 to 1878 as
the member for York East, was a vice-president of the Royal Canadian Bank, and
laid out Prince Arthur Avenue in Yorkville.

Duncan Forbes later established a substantial roofing business. His son John Colin
(1846–1925) and grandson Kenneth (1892–
1980) became outstanding portrait painters.

1847  Knox Presbyterian Church, Queen
      Street West (cut stone)
1848  Jennings Church, Richmond and Bay
      streets
1849  St Lawrence Hall, King Street East
1850  St James' Cathedral, King Street East
1850  Lodge and farm buildings, Mental
      Asylum, Queen Street West
1851  Trinity College, Queen Street West
1851  Seventh Post Office, Toronto Street
1851  Normal School, Gould Street

## Neelon, Sylvester  See Elliott & Neelon

## Netting, George

1856  John O'Donohue houses, Shuter
      Street

## Petch, Robert

Petch was a carpenter and joiner who,
according to an 1832 newspaper, also kept
a hearse available.

1818  Methodist Church, King and Jordan
      streets
1832  Methodist Church, Adelaide and Toronto streets
1845  Fire Hall and Mechanics' Institute,
      Court Street (with Alexander
      Manning)

## Pim, William Henry  1807–60

Born at Croydon, Middlesex, he apprenticed for seven years with a builder in Hemel Hempstead. After emigrating in 1832,
he settled near Cayuga, Upper Canada,
where he combined building with farming.
He is listed as a carpenter in a Toronto
directory of 1846–7 and in the 1850s had
his own company. The Pim Papers in the
Metropolitan Toronto Library provide an
unmatched record of the business of one of
the city's larger firms of carpenters and
joiners.

1853  Warehouse and engine stable, Ontario,
      Simcoe and Huron Rail Road, Queen's
      Wharf, Toronto
1853  Ontario County Court House,
      Whitby
1853  Mechanics' Institute, Church Street
      (carpentry)
1856  Sword's Hotel additions, Front Street
      (carpentry)
1857  Pendarves, house for F.W. Cumberland, College Avenue

1858  St Stephen's Church, Bellevue Avenue
      at College Street
1858  University College west wing
      (carpentry)

## Plenderleith, John

1856  House of Providence, Power Street
      (carpentry)
1856  Gould Street Presbyterian Church
      (carpentry)
1864  *Globe* building, King Street East
      (carpentry)
1869  Holy Trinity Church reredos

## Priestman, Matthew

He was contractor in 1829 for the Parliament buildings, Front Street West, and the main building at Upper Canada College, begun that year. When he failed, his contracts were completed by others.

## Ritchey, John  1796–1866

Ritchey came to Canada from Ireland in 1819. During the 1840s he was the leading builder in Toronto and the first to introduce slate roofing on Toronto buildings. About 1850 Metcalfe, Wilson & Forbes seem to have underbid him consistently and secured most of the large contracts. Ritchey went on to become one of the city's largest property owners and developers. He was a member of Toronto City Council most years from 1837 to 1850.

1829  Osgoode Hall east wing
1831  St James' Church, King Street East
1833  King's College entrance gates and
      lodge, Queen Street West
1839  St James' Cathedral, King Street East
1841  St Paul's Anglican Church, Bloor
      Street East, Yorkville
1842  King's College, University (Queen's)
      Park
1843  Bank of Upper Canada porch, Adelaide Street East
1843  Little Trinity Church, King Street
      East
1844  Church of St George the Martyr,
      John Street
1844  Osgoode Hall, west wing and
      alterations
1845  Bank of British North America, Wellington Street East at Yonge
1845  Bank of Montreal, Yonge and Front
      streets

1846  Mental Asylum, Queen Street West
1848  Royal Lyceum Theatre, King Street
      West
1851  York County Court House, Adelaide
      Street East
1855  Ritchey's Terrace, Adelaide Street
      West

## Smith, Burke & Co

(G.B. Smith; William Burke, 1822–99)
The firm operated a planning mill and sash factory but acted occasionally – notably in connection with the Crystal Palace – as a general contractor. Burke, who later operated as a dealer in builders' supplies, was the father of prominent architect Edmund Burke (1850–1919).

1858  Crystal Palace, King Street West
1859  Gooderham & Worts steam-mill and
      distillery (carpentry)

## Smith, William  d 1819

A native of Nottinghamshire, he was in Cape Breton as early as 1774 in connection with unspecified public works and remained there until shortly before coming to Upper Canada about 1790. He visited York in 1793 and moved his family from Niagara to the townsite the following year. As one of the first carpenter-builders in town he erected many structures, including the Don Bridge at King Street (1802). Smith may have built St James' Church (1805), but original sources show that it is less likely he was involved in constructing the house of William Jarvis (1798) or the lighthouse on Gibraltar Point (1808), as some have claimed.

## Snarr, Thomas  c 1816–93

Born in England, he came to Toronto about 1841. He was a mason who was one of the crew on the construction of the Mental Asylum. From the mid-1850s he had his own business and seems to have preferred to bid on the masonry work rather than on general contracts. In 1861 he represented St David's Ward on Toronto City Council.

1854  John, Phoebe, and Victoria Street
      schools (masonry)
1856  St Michael's College, Clover Hill
      (masonry)
1856  Consumers' Gas Works additions

1857 Model School, Gould Street (masonry)

**Stephenson & Co, Edward**
The firm was in business during the 1860s and was the successor to Thomas Storm's business on his death in 1871.
1871 Trust and Loan Company office, Toronto and Adelaide streets
1873 St James' Cathedral spire, King Street East
1876 Consumers' Gas offices, 19 Toronto Street (carpentry)
1877 William McMaster house, Bloor Street East

**Storm, Thomas** 1801–71
A native of Winteringham, Lincolnshire, he apprenticed as a carpenter and joiner, then became a master builder at Burton-upon-Stather. Immigrating to Toronto in 1830, he had a partnership with Richard Woodsworth and Alexander Hamilton for the construction of buildings at the New Garrison, and later was a partner of Sheldon Ward until the latter's death in a scaffolding accident in 1845, which almost claimed Storm and his son William as well. It is fortunate for Toronto architecture that the son was spared. The elder Storm, after being bankrupted in 1848, continued as a builder until his death, when his business was taken over by E. Stephenson & Co.
1840 New Garrison
1843 Kearnsey House for William Proudfoot, Yonge and Dundonald streets
1856 Holy Trinity parochial school (carpentry)
1856 John Robertson house, John Street
1857 Model School, Gould Street (carpentry)
1862 Bank of Toronto, Wellington and Church streets (carpentry)
1863 Gooderham & Worts malt-house

**Tate, George**
1858 Don Jail, Gerrard Street East

**Turton, Joseph**
A mason, Turton was originally a subcontractor for Matthew Priestman on the building of the Parliament buildings in 1829. When Priestman failed, Turton took over a portion of his contract and completed the east wing. A newspaper of 1833 reported that a block of buildings erected (and owned) by Turton on King Street west of Bay was a handsome and convenient structure intended as offices for professional men.

**Wagner, Jacob P.**
He and his brother George came from Rochester, New York, as contractors for the Rossin House. Jacob remained in Toronto afterwards and for over thirty years was a builder as well as a manufacturer of sashes, doors, and shutters.
1855 Rossin House, King and York streets
1865 St Michael's Cathedral spire, Bond Street
1867 Golden Lion, store for Robert Walker, King Street East (carpentry)

**Walsh, James**
1856 St Michael's College, Clover Hill (carpentry)
1865 Rossin House, King and York streets, rebuilding after fire

**Walton, Benjamin** 1819–85
Born in Huddersfield, Yorkshire, and a mason by trade, he arrived in Toronto in 1844. He may have worked for either John Ritchey or Metcalfe, Wilson & Forbes, since he did not become a prominent builder until they were no longer active. In 1875, after a quarter of a century as a contractor, he decided to concentrate his attention on his slate quarries at Melbourne in Quebec. His business was taken over by Brown & Love.
1853 Mechanics' Institute, Church and Adelaide streets (masonry)
1856 University College (foundations)
1856 Gould Street Presbyterian Church, Victoria and Gould streets
1857 Osgoode Hall, central section, including Great Library
1871 Bank of British North America, Wellington Street East at Yonge
1873 Custom House, Front and Yonge streets

**Wilson, Alexander** See Metcalfe, Wilson & Forbes

**Withrow, James** See McBean & Withrow

**Worthington Brothers**
(John Worthington, 1818–73; James Worthington 1822–98)
John Worthington, elder brother and senior partner in the firm, was born in Whitby-rocks, Staffordshire. Orphaned at twelve, he apprenticed as a stonemason and worked at his trade for a few years in London before coming to Toronto in 1841. Leaving to work on Kingston City Hall, he rose quickly to be a foreman. At the conclusion of that job he was asked by John Ritchey to return to Toronto as masonry foreman on the building of St George's Church and the additions to Osgoode Hall. In 1848 Worthington formed his own business, enjoying modest success until chosen in 1853 as contractor for Brock's Monument.

By 1855 his firm was employing 350 men; he owned stone-quarries in Ohio and was a partner with F.W. Cumberland in establishing the Toronto Patent Pressed Brick Company at Yorkville, where Ramsden Park is today. He was responsible also for developing the lime-kilns and other works at Limehouse, near Georgetown. At the conclusion of the large and profitable university contract in 1860, John withdrew from the firm to pursue railway building in Canada and the United States and to give attention to his extensive quarry operations.

James Worthington, who entered into partnership with his brother c 1856, continued a few years longer as a building contractor in Toronto until he too was attracted by larger and more lucrative contracts on the intercolonial and Canadian Pacific Railways.

*John Worthington*
1853 Brock's Monument, Queenston
1855 Zion Congregational Church, Bay and Adelaide streets
*Worthington Bros*
1856 House of Providence, Power Street
1856 Holy Trinity parochial school (masonry)
1856 University College
1856 Sword's Hotel additions, Front Street West (masonry)

1856 Masonic Hall, Toronto Street
1857 Cooke's Presbyterian Church, Queen and Mutual streets (masonry)
1860 St James-the-Less, Parliament Street
*James Worthington*
1861 Ontario Bank, Wellington and Scott streets
1862 Bank of Toronto, Wellington and Church streets (masonry)
1863 Warehouse for John Macdonald, Wellington Street East
1864 *Globe* building, King Street East (masonry)

**Yorke, Lionel** 1834–89
Born in Wisbech, Cambridgeshire, he learned his trade in England. Emigrating in 1859, he went first to the United States and came the following year to Peterborough, Canada West. After a decade there as a builder and quarry owner he moved to Toronto and was soon a major contractor, erecting 'more churches than any other builder in the city,' as his obituary noted. He also continued to be a supplier of stone from quarries he owned at the Forks of the Credit.
1868 Government House, King and Simcoe streets
1871 Eighth Post Office, Adelaide Street East
1871 A.R. McMaster & Brother warehouse, Front Street West
1874 All Saints' Anglican Church, Sherbourne and Dundas streets
1874 St Andrew's Presbyterian Church, King and Simcoe streets
1877 Old St Andrew's Presbyterian (now United) Church, Jarvis and Carlton streets
1878 Church of the Redeemer, Bloor Street at Avenue Road
1881 Protestant Episcopal Divinity School (Wycliffe College), College Street, west of Queen's Park
1883 Mrs William Cawthra house, Jarvis and Isabella streets
1883 Toronto Arcade, Yonge Street
1885 Bank of Montreal, Yonge and Front streets
1886 Ontario Parliament buildings, Queen's Park

# Appendix C

## The Origin of Street Names in Toronto

This list has been prepared from Williamson's map of 1878 and the street directories of 1890 and 1900. Only streets of the eighteenth and nineteenth centuries are listed, with 1900 as a terminal date. Omitted from the following lists are streets whose names are merely descriptive, like Lakeshore, or geographic, like Madeira, or those, like Harbord, whose origins are obscure or unknown.[1] Needless to say, the list is not a complete one, even for the nineteenth century, because the reasons for naming streets are seldom given on maps or in by-laws.

Just as the social history of a people may be read in its architecture, the history of a city may be read in the names of its streets. Names like Simcoe, Russell, Baldwin, and Osgoode take us back to the very foundation of the city, and others like Brulé, Seneca, and Huron recall the remote past of people who knew well the village at the end of 'le passage de Toronto' centuries before the settlement at York.

From Simcoe's arrival in 1793 our street names have fallen into many patterns. In the days of York they indicated quite unmistakably our loyalty to the Crown and the royal family. The English queens of the nineteenth century were all there; the royal dukes were not forgotten, and our affection for the Hanoverian sovereigns did not preclude the naming of streets after their ancestral estates in Germany.

This was particularly true of the early days in York, but the British connection was never lost. Colonial secretaries, British prime ministers, governors general, and lieutenant-governors were recorded with few exceptions, along with British heroes like Nelson, Havelock, Gordon, Napier, and Wellington and the battles they fought. So strong is the British element in our street names that it comes as a shock to find that Alderman Steiner had sufficient influence to name one after Chancellor Bismarck (made more palatable later, it is true, by Asquith), and someone with a catholic taste in princes gave us Czar and Sultan streets.

There is no evidence that the ties with Britain ever weakened in Toronto, but we find less and less indication of colonial dependence as the village became town and the town city. Pride in the city is clearly shown by the numerous streets called after mayors, aldermen, property owners, and public-spirited persons whom the city desired to honour, but Sir Wilfrid Laurier, prime minister of Canada 1896–1911, stands alone in the almost unbroken chain of colonial secretaries, and only Brown and McGee of the Fathers of Confederation are remembered.

Lawyers rank below wives, daughters, and aldermen in the number of streets honouring members of their profession, and the medical list is more impressive than lengthy, with names like Macaulay, Baldwin, and Widmer going back to the eighteenth century. The church is represented by two Roman Catholic bishops (Power of Toronto and Macdonell of Kingston), two Anglican bishops (Strachan of Toronto and Stewart of Quebec), and by Church of England parsons Darling of Holy Trinity, Maynard of Little Trinity (who was also a master of Upper Canada College), Charles Winstanley, and Addison, who was chaplain to the Legislative Assembly. Three Ontario premiers come down to us in streets named after Blake, Mowat, and Whitney.

The brewers rate four in Bloor, Doel, Davies, and O'Keefe, and universities three, Oxford, Cambridge, and Harvard. They are followed by a most exclusive list: architects two (Howard and Langley), cab-drivers two (Paterson and Hazelton), a carpenter (Hayden), a biscuit-maker (Christie), a broker (Phipps), a brick-maker (Pears), a jeweller and watch-maker (Jordan), and a university president (McCaul).

There were street names, long gone, that recall a frontier town with few pretensions to culture. Rabbit Lane and Fish Lane aptly suggest their proximity to woods and lake, but alleys like Whiskey, Grog, and Deadbeat could not have represented the most desirable residential districts.

Research has shown that many streets of 1878 (Williamson's map) disappeared before the city directory of 1890, and some between 1890 and 1900. Still more have been lost in this century. In most cases one can only regret their absence and deplore the substitution that was made. Ann, it will be remembered, was changed to Granby at the whim of the people on the street, and the name of that Rousseau who acted as pilot when Lieutenant-Governor Simcoe and Mrs Simcoe made their historic entry into the harbour of Toronto is no longer on the map of the city except, rather obscurely, in St John's Road. These are but two of many. Almost as regrettable as the loss of a historic name are the misspellings, of which Cuttle, Givens, and Orde provide examples.

Street names we have been unable to identify are not listed, nor are those where the origin seems at first sight so obvious. It would not be difficult to write 'Kintyre, Mull of, Scotland,' and it would be tempting to identify 'Knox, the Scottish reformer, 1505–72,' but it would be embarrassing if later research proved Kintyre and Knox to have been aldermen from Wards 2 and 4 respectively. If the writer should seem to show undue timidity in making such decisions, he would point to Bellwoods, which conjures up a memory of bells heard in a wood. In reality the word is an unromantic combination of the names of two Toronto aldermen.

This study of street names has been prepared because such a list has appeared only twice, in part, in print: in the *Landmarks of Toronto* (1894) and in the pamphlet by Mary Hoskin Jarvis. It is hoped that it may give citizens, especially schoolchildren, a new interest in their city and those who made it what it is; and that the examples it offers, of how we once honoured the great and the humble and those who served their city well in politics, the professions, and trade, may set a precedent for the naming of new streets. This is an area in which, today, we show little imagination or realization of the history, dignity, and reputation of Toronto among the cities of the world. When one looks back on the last sixty years of Canadian history, the great events that took place in that time, and those who took part in them on our behalf, one wonders how names like Radio Valve Street could find a place on the map of Toronto.

1 SOURCES: John Ross Robertson *Landmarks of Toronto* s 1 516; T.A. Reed's own handwritten and typewritten lists; Mary Hoskin Jarvis 'Streets of Toronto,' in *Transaction* 28 of the Women's Canadian Historical Society (1934); also city directories, the Registry Office, the City Hall, Osgoode Hall, the Royal Canadian Military Institute, and the press of the nineteenth century

*Abbey Lane* Russell Abbey, the home of the Hon Peter Russell, which once stood at the corner of Palace and Princess streets. *See* Russell.

*Abbs* A market gardener, James Abbs, in the old village of Parkdale

*Abell* John Abell, manufacturer of agricultural implements, located in the vicinity

*Aberdeen* The earl of Aberdeen, governor general of Canada 1893–8

*Addison* Probably the Rev Robert Addison, 1755–1829, first rector of Niagara and chaplain to the Legislative Assembly

*Adelaide* The dowager queen of William IV. Until 1842–3 Adelaide Street was called Newgate Street, probably because when laid out in 1797, the block south of Adelaide between Church and today's Toronto Street was reserved for a jail. Newgate Prison in London was recalled by the name.

*Admiral* Admiral Augustus W. Baldwin, 1776–1866, a member of the same family as Hon W.W. Baldwin. *See* Baldwin.

*Afton* Probably the 'Sweet Afton' of Robert Burns

*Agnes* Probably a friend or member of the Macaulay family. *See* Macaulay.

*Albany* Leopold, duke of Albany (1853–84), youngest son of Queen Victoria

*Albert* Albert, prince consort, husband of Queen Victoria. Albert Street was previously Macaulay Lane.

*Alexander* Alexander Wood, who purchased twenty-five acres lying north of Carlton Street from Mrs Mary Elmsley in 1826. *See* Wood.

*Alice* Probably a friend or member of the Macaulay family. *See* Macaulay.

*Allen* Thomas Allen, alderman 1877–9, 1883–6, 1890–1, 1895–7

*Alma* The battle of the Alma in the Crimean War, 1854; part of a subdivision of military names. *See* Trafalgar, Waterloo.

*Amelia* The wife of John Scadding, who bought two hundred acres in this area from the Simcoe estate of Castle Frank. *See* Scadding.

*Ancroft* Anthony Croft, owner of property on Maple Avenue, in the same vicinity

*Anderson* A property owner in the district. Anderson Street is now Dundas between University Avenue and McCaul Street.

*Ann* Ann, widow of Andrew McGill, who later married Rt Rev Dr John Strachan. In 1834 Dr Strachan purchased twenty-five acres north of Gerrard Street of which he and his wife deeded certain portions to the city in the same year. The name superseded the original St Anne Street in 1843. Now Granby. *See* McGill, Strachan.

*Anne* Anne, daughter of Dr James Macaulay, who married Dr Peter Diehl in 1829. Unfortunately for the memory of Anne, the street was later renamed Alice and, finally, Teraulay. *See* Macaulay.

*Argyle* The duke of Argyle, father of the marquis of Lorne, governor general of Canada 1878–83. *See* Lorne.

*Armstrong* James Armstrong, property owner in the district

*Arthur* Arthur, duke of Connaught (1850–1942), third son of Queen Victoria, a visitor to Toronto in 1870

*Augusta* A female member of the Denison family (*see* Denison) or Charlotte Augusta, only daughter of George IV (*see* Charlotte).

*Austin* James Austin, who came to Canada from Ireland in 1828 and as a youth was employed by William Lyon Mackenzie in the printing business. Later, with the Hon John Ross, he founded the Dominion Bank, of which he became the first president, 1871–9. In 1866 Austin purchased considerable land on Davenport Road from the Baldwin Estate and built his own home there.

*Badgerow* George Washington Badgerow, the county attorney c 1890, admitted as a student at Osgoode Hall in 1866, called to the bar in 1871

*Bain* The family of that name, residents in the district

*Baldwin* Dr W.W. Baldwin, owner of the country house on the hill called Spadina. *See* Admiral, Heyden, Phoebe, Robert, St George, Spadina, Sullivan, Walmer, Willcocks.

*Balmoral* The royal residence in Scotland

*Balmuto* A friend of Arthur R. Boswell, QC, mayor of Toronto 1883–4. *See* Boswell.

*Bartlett* A property owner of that name in the district

*Barton* Edward W. Barton, broom manufacturer and alderman, old St Stephen's Ward, 1884–8

*Bathurst* Henry, third earl Bathurst, secretary for War and the Colonies 1812–27. This name applied to the present street south of Queen (then Lot) when given in 1837. The northern section was known as Crookshank's Lane, after the Hon George Crookshank, who owned a large estate there. *See* Crookshank.

*Battye* A property owner of that name

*Baxter* John Baxter, resident of York in 1830, alderman and councilman for St Patrick's Ward intermittently between 1860 and 1890

*Bay* Named in 1797 when the boundaries of the Town of York were enlarged for the first time. Obvious relationship with the bay, but possibly part of deliberate geographic aphorism. *See* Yonge, York.

*Beachell* William Beachell, who was connected with the Grand Trunk Railway

*Beaconsfield* Benjamin Disraeli, Lord Beaconsfield, prime minister of Great Britain 1868, 1874–80

*Beatrice* A daughter of E.O. Bickford of Gore Vale. *See* Gore Vale.

*Beaty* James Beaty, QC, mayor of Toronto 1879–80

*Bedford* The duke of Bedford, the head of the Irish branch of the family of Hon Peter Russell, who received an original grant of land in this vicinity. *See* Russell.

*Bell* John Foli Bell, admitted as a student to Osgoode Hall in 1864, a solicitor

*Bellair* Walter Bellairs, nephew of Walter McKenzie of Castle Frank. His house was on the north side of Yorkville, west of Yonge and nearly opposite Bellair. Bellairs was a well-known man about town.

*Bellevue* The home of George Taylor Denison, who owned 150 acres as early as 1817. Bellevue Avenue was one of the roads to the family homestead at Denison Square. *See* Denison.

*Bellwoods* William Bell, alderman, St Stephen's Ward, 1881–3, 1888–91; Ward 5, 1892–3; and collector, St Stephen's Ward, 1884–6. John Woods, alderman, St Stephen's Ward, 1882; St Mark's Ward, 1885–6. Bellwoods Avenue was formerly Strachan Street. Its name was changed in 1882.

*Belmont* Belmont, England, the birthplace of John Sheppard, a property owner in the vicinity

*Berkeley* John Small's home, Berkeley House. John Small was first clerk of the Executive Council of Upper Canada 1793–1831. He was born in Berkeley, Gloucestershire, in 1746. His house stood at the southwest corner of Berkeley and King streets from 1796 to 1926. Berkeley Street was formerly Parliament Street. The name was transferred when the road from the Parliament buildings to Castle Frank was opened up. *See* Coxwell.

*Bernard* Bernard Saunders, alderman, St Paul's Ward, 1883–1900 with few interruptions; executor of the Noah L. Piper Estate, through which the street ran from Avenue Road to near Bedford Park

*Berczy* Charles Albert Berczy (1794–1858), born at Newark (Upper Canada), postmaster of Toronto

*Berryman* Dr Charles Berryman, a well-known practitioner in Yorkville, who was instrumental in getting the village incorporated and succeeded James Severn, the first reeve

*Beverley* Beverley House, home of Sir John Beverley Robinson, 1791–1863; the attorney-general, built on the southeast corner of Queen and John streets. *See* Robinson.

*Binscarth* After the family of William Bain Scarth, born 1837 in Scotland. His father, James Scarth, was a descendant of the family of the Scarths of Binscarth, Orkney Islands. *See* Scarth.

*Bishop* Dr John Strachan, 1778–1867, first bishop of Toronto, 1839–67. *See* Strachan.

*Bismarck* The German chancellor's name was given by Alderman H.L. Steiner (1880–1, 1883–6, 1899) to the former Jarvis Street, Yorkville. Changed to Asquith Avenue during First World War. *See* Steiner.

*Blake* Probably the Hon Edward Blake (1833–1912), premier of Ontario 1871–4

*Bleecker* Charlotte Bleecker Powell, daughter of Grant Powell, who married John Ridout, registrar of Deeds 1855–94. *See* Sherbourne.

*Blevins* John B. Blevins, city clerk 1885–1900 and alderman for St David's Ward 1864–84

*Blong* Henry Blong, a butcher in the district. The name appears in the directory of 1866.

*Bloor* Joseph Bloor, 1788–1862, a brewer who lived at 100 Bloor Street. Bloor and Sheriff Jarvis laid out the village plots for the town of Yorkville, just north of Bloor. For many years Bloor was the northern limit of the city proper. It was formerly known as St Paul's Road, Sydenham Road, and Toll-Gate Road, the latter after the toll-gate that stood at the corner of Yonge Street.

*Bond* Thomas Bond, who appears in the directory of 1837 as 'Thos. Bond, brick maker, Lot Street.' J.G. Howard's diary for 1845 mentions the drawing of plans and specifications for sewers on Church and several short streets contracted for by Thomas Bond in 1845–8.

*Booth* George S. Booth, alderman 1889–90, who was a coppersmith.

*Borden* Esther Borden Lippincott, daughter of Captain Richard Lippincott, an officer in the Revolutionary War and early settler in York. She married George Taylor Denison. *See* Denison.

*Boswell* Arthur R. Boswell, QC, mayor of Toronto 1883–4. *See* Balmuto.

*Boultbee* Alfred Boultbee, who practised law in Newmarket for twenty-five years before moving to Toronto, member of Parliament for North York in 1871, for East York in 1878

*Boulton* Probably W.H. Boulton, mayor 1845–6, 1847, 1858. *See* D'Arcy, Emily, Grange, Henry.

*Boustead* James B. Boustead, councilman, St David's Ward, 1865, and St James' Ward, 1866; alderman, St James' Ward, intermittently from 1869 to 1891; Ward 3, 1896

*Bowden* John B. Bowden, a contractor

*Bracondale* The suburban village of Bracondale, northwest of Bathurst and Dupont, which took its name from the estate of Robert John Turner, a solicitor from Yarmouth, England, who settled here, practised law, and became accountant-general of the Court of Chancery. He died in 1872. *See* Turner.

*Brant* Joseph Brant, born 1742 on the Ohio River, a chief of the Mohawk tribe who settled in this province and in 1786 visited England to raise funds to build the first Episcopal church in Upper Canada. He died in 1807.

*Breadalbane* Probably John Campbell, second marquis of Breadalbane, 1796–1862

*Bright* John Bright, son of James Bright, a resident of the east end, whose father, also a resident of York, fought under Brock at Queenston Heights

*Brock* General Sir Isaac Brock (1769–1812), administrator of Upper Canada, who fell at Queenston Heights. Now part of Spadina Avenue south of Queen. Brock Street was formerly Broadway Place.

*Brookfield* Brookfield House, the home of Sophia Denison, widow of Captain John Denison. *See* Denison.

*Brown* The Hon George Brown (1818–80), journalist and statesman, editor of the *Globe*. Elected to the Legislative Assembly 1851, appointed to the Senate 1871

*Brunswick* Caroline of Brunswick-Wolfen-büttel (1768–1821), wife of George IV. *See* Caroline.

*Buchanan* Sir James Buchanan Macaulay (1793–1859), born at Newark (Niagara) Upper Canada, son of Dr James Macaulay. The street was on a subdivision of his Wykeham Hall estate. *See* Macaulay.

*Buller* Charles Buller, 1806–48, an Englishman who was secretary to Lord Durham in 1838

*Bulwer* Probably the English statesman and author Edward George, Earl Lytton, secretary for the Colonies 1858–9 and author under the name Bulwer-Lytton of many popular novels from 1827 to 1873. *See* Lytton.

*Caer Howell* Caer Howell in Montgomeryshire, Wales, the family seat of Hon William Dummer Powell, chief justice of Upper Canada 1815–25. Later incorporated in Elm Street, which was always distinguished for its horse chestnuts and a solitary elm. *See* Elm Street.

*Cambridge* The English university of that name; next to it was Oxford Street. Renamed Nassau Street about 1860

*Cameron* John Hillyard Cameron, lawyer and MP (1817–76). Educated Upper Canada College; 1860 treasurer of the Law Society of Upper Canada. One of the founders of Trinity College, of which he was chancellor in 1864

*Campbell* Probably William Campbell, who purchased a large section of land in this district, the western section of Davenport Road. *See* Edwin, Royce.

*Carlaw* Major John A. Carlaw (b 1840), cashier of the Grand Trunk Railway in Toronto and property owner in the district

*Carlton* Guy Carleton Wood, son of Dr George Wood, United Empire Loyalist of Cornwall. Named by his sister Ann McGill, wife of Rev Dr John Strachan. The present spelling is Carlton. *See* Ann.

*Carling* Hon John Carling (1828–1911), brewer and politician. Federal minister of Agriculture 1867–71. Entered his father's business and succeeded him as president of Carling's Breweries

*Carlyle* William Carlyle, alderman for St Thomas' Ward 1879–90

*Caroline* Named by Gov Simcoe after Caroline, Princess of Wales, later Queen of George IV. At present part of Sherbourne Street, south of Queen. *See* Brunswick.

*Carr* Probably John Carr, city councillor, alderman, clerk and commissioner, 1847–73. Carr Street was originally Elizabeth Street, part of Bellevue Estate owned by Colonel George Denison. The name was changed in 1870. John Carr resided at 21 Denison Avenue in 1873.

*Carroll* Dr John A. Carroll, alderman for St Matthew's Ward, 1884

*Casimir* Col Sir Casimir Gzowski (1813–98), the street being in the vicinity of his home 'The Hall,' now Alexandra Park, Bathurst and Dundas streets

*Catharine* Catharine, Mrs Stephen Heward, the street named by her father, Hon George Crookshank. *See* Crookshank.

*Cawthra* William Cawthra (1801–80), who, in 1847, purchased a block on Jarvis Street from S.P. Jarvis.

*Cecil* First after Col Givins's daughter Cecilia, and later renamed Halton Street after one of his sons. Col Givins had accompanied Gov Simcoe to Canada and for many years was superintendent of Indian Affairs. *See* Givens.

*Cedar* A cedar swamp on the west side of Dundas, north of Queen

*Centre* Why 'Centre' is obscure, but it was located on the property of the Rev Thomas Raddish, of whom little is known beyond the fact that he was the nominee for the rectorship of York. He returned to England after a few months. He conveyed his large lot to Chief Justice Elmsley, who in turn sold it, in part, to Alexander Wood and John Beverley Robinson.

*Chapel* The Roman Catholic Chapel, afterwards St Paul's Church, Power Street, to which the street led. After St Basil's Church was built at Clover Hill, that part of Bay Street east of St Michael's College today was called Chapel Street.

*Charles* Rev Charles Winstanley, who owned property on the street in the 1840s

*Charlotte* Charlotte Augusta (1796–1817), only daughter of George IV and Queen Caroline, who married Leopold of Saxe-Coburg in 1816. She died in childbirth in 1817. *See* Augusta, Claremont, Leopold.

*Christie* William Christie (1829–1900), a baker of that district. His bakery was moved later to Yonge Street.

*Christopher* Christopher Robinson (1837–1923), son of Chief Justice Robinson, born at Thorah, Upper Canada, editor and publisher. *See* Robinson.

*Church* From the fact that since 1797 land had been set aside there for a church. St James' Church (now the cathedral) was built in 1805.

*Churchill* The 'Church on the Hill' built by Richard Lippincott Denison of Dovercourt. *See* Denison.

*Cibola* Probably after the legendary 'seven cities of Cibola' in Mexico. A boat called Cibola once plied regularly between Niagara-on-the-Lake and Toronto.

*Clandeboye* The county seat in Ireland of the marquis of Dufferin and Ava, governor general of Canada 1872–9. *See* Dufferin.

*Claremont* Claremont House, near Esher, England, built for Lord Clive, afterwards the home of Princess Charlotte, daughter of George IV. *See* Charlotte.

*Clarence Square* Laid out and named in 1837, a few months before the death of William IV, who had been Duke of Clarence before his accession

*Clarke* Edward F. Clarke, mayor of Toronto 1888–91

*Clinton* Probably Henry Clinton (1811–64), secretary for the Colonies 1852–4. He visited Canada in 1860.

*Close* P.G. Close, alderman 1873–8 and 1880

*Coatsworth* Emerson C. Coatsworth, city commissioner of Toronto from 1873 to 1903, when the office was abolished. *See* Virgin.

*Colborne* Sir John Colborne (1778–1863), first Baron Seaton, lt-gov of Upper Canada 1828–36. Formerly Market Lane. *See* Seaton.

*Collachie* Angus MacDonell (d 1804), son of Allan MacDonell of Collachie. Treasurer of the Law Society of Upper Canada 1801–4. He was drowned in the loss of the *Speedy* on Lake Ontario.

*College* Its original use (1829) was as a private avenue of approach to King's Col-

lege, but it was leased by the Univeristy of Toronto, along with the University Avenue, as public streets (c 1888). College Avenue is now College Street. *See* University.

*Collier* An official in the Canada Company, *or* Frank Collier Draper (1837–94), chief of police and son of Chief Justice Draper. F.C. Draper reorganized the police force about 1870. *See* Draper.

*Conduit* Probably a street of that name running between Regent Street and Bond Street in London

*Constance* The daughter of Col Walter O'Hara, who was captain in the 47th Regiment during the Peninsular War. *See* O'Hara.

*Coolmine* From the Kirkpatrick family, originating with Alexander Kirkpatrick of Coolmine, Co Dublin (1749–1818). His grandson, George B. Kirkpatrick, born 1835, was director of Surveys of the province of Ontario.

*Cooper* George Cooper, a property owner in the district

*Court* The police or magistrates' court was in a building on the north side

*Coxwell* Charles Coxwell Small (1746–1831), son of Mayor John Small of Berkeley House, and clerk of Common Pleas 1825–64. *See* Berkeley.

*Crawford* Joshua Crawford, who filed a plan in 1856. In 1887 this name was changed to Elliot Street. The present Crawford Street was named after Hon Thomas Crawford, Speaker of the Legislative Assembly.

*Crocker* James Crocker, alderman 1875–89

*Crookshank* Hon George Crookshank (1773–1859), deputy commissary-general from 1796 until the end of the War of 1812, and a member of the Legislative Council of Upper Canada. *See* Bathurst, Wilton.

*Cumberland* The birthplace of James Wallace, one of the early councillors of Yorkville

*Curzon* The street in London of the same name

*Cuttle* Thomas Cuttell, printer in this district and resident of Trinity Square in 1873

*Czar* The Russian ruler, named at a time when that country was held in high esteem. Czar Street is now Charles Street West. *See* Sultan.

*Dale* The residence of Dr John Hoskin, KC 1836–1921). *See* Devonshire Place, Hoskin.

*Dalhousie* The marquis of Dalhousie, governor general of Canada 1820–8

*Danforth* Asa Danforth (1746–1836), contractor for the construction of this road between York and the Bay of Quinte in 1799

*D'Arcy* D'Arcy Boulton (1785–1846), builder of the Grange, now part of the Art Gallery of Ontario. *See* Boulton.

*Darling* Rev W.S. Darling (1818–86), rector of the Church of the Holy Trinity, Father of Frank Darling, architect

*Dartnell* Georgina Dartnell, wife of Col Frederick Wells (1822–77), son of Hon J. Wells and veteran of the Crimean War. *See* Wells.

*Davenport* Residence of Col the Hon Joseph Wells (1773–1853), on the hill to which it led. Originally, Davenport Road was the 'new road to Niagara.' In 1844 and 1852 called 'Plank Road.' *See* Wells.

*Davies* Thomas Davies, brewer, alderman 1873–4, 1881–4, 1889, 1893, 1895–6, 1898–9

*Dean* Harriet Dean, daughter of Joseph K. Dean (1810–71) and wife of George Gooderham. *See* Matilda, Mill.

*Defoe* D.M. Defoe, alderman 1884

*Defries* Robert Defries, brewer, and other members of the well-known family of that name, long resident in the east end of the city

*De Grassi* Alfio De Grassi, merchant, insurance agent, and prominent Mason in the 1870s

*Denison* The street was one of the roads to the Denison house at Denison Square owned by George Taylor Denison and, after his decease, by his son Lt.-Col. Robert Brittain Denison (1821–1900). *See* Augusta, Bedford, Bellevue, Borden, Brookfield, Churchill, Dewson, Dovercourt, Esther, Fennings, Lippincott, Major, Ossington, Robert, Rolyat, Rusholme.

*Derby* Probably the earls of Derby in Lancashire.

*Devonshire Place* The birthplace of Dr John Hoskin, member of the Board of Trust-

ees of University of Toronto in 1889, when the street was laid out. *See* Dale, Hoskin.

*Dewson* Mary Ann Dewson, wife of George Taylor Denison II (1816– 73). *See* Denison.

*Doel* W.H. Doel of Broadview Avenue, son of John Doel (1790–1871), brewer at northwest corner of Adelaide and Bay streets.

*Don Mills* Because of its proximity to the River Don. There were several mills in the vicinity.

*Dorset* Dorset House, Wellington Street, home of George Ridout (1791– 1871), second son of Hon Thomas Ridout. *See* Sherbourne.

*Douro* After one of the duke of Wellington's titles; now part of Wellington Street. *See* Wellington.

*Dovercourt* Dover Court was the name of the estate owned by Richard Lippincott Denison. Its name is derived from his mother's family home, Dover Court, near Harwich in the county of Essex. *See* Denison.

*Dowling* Col Dowling, who married the sister of Col A.R. Dunn, VC. *See* Dunn.

*Draper* William Henry Draper (1801–77), politician and jurist, chief justice of Upper Canada 1863–9. *See* Collier.

*Drumsnab* The home of Frank Cayley (1807–90), at 5 Drumsnab Road

*Dublin* Original name of township of York

*Duchess* The duchess of York, daughter-in-law of George III and eldest daughter of the king of Prussia. The first Duchess Street was laid out by Gov Simcoe in 1793. It later became Duke Street, and a second Duchess, the one we know today as Richmond east of Jarvis, was laid out in 1797 one block north.

*Dufferin* The marquis of Dufferin and Ava, governor general of Canada 1872–8. *See* Clandeboye.

*Duke* The duke of York, son of George III, one of the streets in the town of York laid out by Gov Simcoe in 1793, being the northern boundary. Duke is now King Street. *See* Frederick.

*Dundas* Sir Henry Dundas, first Viscount Melville, Home Secretary 1791–4. Like Yonge Street, Dundas Street was laid out by Gov Simcoe, who intended that it

join the provincial capital at York with
the Thames River on the west and the
mouth of the River Trent on Lake Ontario on the east. Within Toronto's
boundaries, Dundas Street today is
formed from a series of earlier streets,
including St Patrick, Anderson, and Agnes
Streets west of Yonge; Crookshank Street,
Wilton Avenue, Wilton Crescent, and
Beech Street between Yonge Street and the
Don River.

*Dunedin* The Gaelic name of Edinburgh

*Dunn* John Henry Dunn (1792–1854), re-
ceiver-general of Canada, father of Col
A.R. Dunn, VC, who fought at Balaclava.
*See* Dowling.

*Dupont* George Dupont Wells (1814–54),
son of Col the Hon J. Wells of Davenport, County York. *See* Wells.

*Durham* John George Lambton, first earl of
Durham (1792–1840), governor general
of Canada 1838. Durham Street is now
Shanly Street. *See* Lambton.

*East* After its location, north to Eastern
Avenue just east of the Don River;
changed to Water Street in 1876

*Eastern* Formerly South Park Street, since it
was part of an area set aside for the
government park or reserve for public
buildings. *See* Park.

*Edgar* Edgar John Jarvis of Rosedale (b
1835), nephew of the original owner. *See*
Jarvis.

*Edward* Probably after a friend or member
of the Macaulay family. *See* Macaulay.

*Edwin* A member of the family of William
Campbell, a large landowner in the Davenport district. *See* Campbell.

*Elgin* The earl of Elgin, governor general
of Canada 1847–54

*Elizabeth* Elizabeth Hayter, wife of Dr
James Macaulay, surgeon of the Queen's
Rangers and deputy inspector-general
of Hospitals, 1813–22. This street ran
through the southern part of a large
property owned by him in 1799 and later
laid out in building streets and lots as a
remote suburban district for working
people, whence it became known as Macaulay Town. *See* Macaulay.

*Elliot* Thomas E. Elliot, alderman of St
Matthew's Ward 1884–6

*Ellis* John Ellis, JP, a landowner in the
district

*Elm Ave* An avenue in Rosedale named by
Edgar Jarvis and planted with elm trees.
*See* Jarvis.

*Elm St* After a legendary ancient landmark,
a solitary elm tree that once stood near
the corner of Yonge and Elm streets

*Elmsley* Hon John Elmsley (1801–63), son
of Chief Justice John Elmsley. *See* Alban,
Surrey.

*Ernest* Ernest Albert MacDonald, alderman
for St Matthew's Ward, 1886– 7, 1889,
1890, 1896, and mayor 1900

*Esplanade* After the road skirting the har-
bourfront behind the stores on Front
Street

*Esther* Esther Borden Lippincott, who became the wife of George Taylor Denison
1. Esther Street is now Augusta Avenue.
*See* Denison.

*Euclid* The Greek mathematician

*Evans* George M. Evans, alderman of St
Patrick's Ward, 1879–83

*Farley* William Farley, alderman of St Andrew's Ward, 1874

*Farquhar* The family of that name who
were contractors in the district

*Fee's* Probably Joseph Fee, groceryman and
large property owner in the district

*Fennings* John Fennings Taylor (1817–82),
author, appointed chief clerk of the Legislative Assembly of Upper Canada in
1836. Senate of Canada 1867. *See*
Rolyat.

*Fermanagh* The birthplace in Ireland of Col
Walter O'Hara. *See* O'Hara.

*Fort Rouillé* The Dufferin Street Fort
Rouillé, built 1750–1

*Foster* Joseph Foster, who owned property
on Elizabeth Street c 1861

*Foxley* Foxley Grove, the home of Judge
Samuel Bealey Harrison (1802–67), an
eminent legal authority. His gardens and
orchards were the admiration of the
community. *See* Harrison.

*Frankland* Henry Robert Frankland, butcher
and cattle exporter, alderman for Ward
1, 1895, 1898–9; later collector of Inland
Revenue for the Toronto Division;
County Police magistrate and director of
the Canadian National Exhibition

*Frankish* Charles Frankish, a property
owner in the district

*Franklin* Probably Sir John Franklin, the
Arctic explorer, 1786–1847

*Fraser* The Hon C.F. Fraser (1839–94), member of the Ontario Cabinet, 1890. He was one of the originators of the Ontario Catholic League.

*Frederick* Frederick, duke of York, son of King George III. One of the streets laid out by Gov Simcoe in 1793. *See* Duke.

*Frizzell* Rev William Frizzell, minister of Queen Street East Presbyterian Church, who died in 1910

*Front* Probably because it was the first and foremost street facing the lake, or 'fronting' it, when York was laid out in 1793 by Gov Simcoe. It was thus the southern boundary. East of the market Front Street was originally called Palace Street, since it led to the Parliament buildings and the reserve where the governor's residence was to be erected.

*Fuller* Valancy England Fuller, son of Thomas Brock Fuller (1810–84), first bishop of Niagara, who purchased four acres in the vicinity in 1878

*Funston* J.J. Funston, a large property owner in the district

*Galley* Edward Galley, builder and alderman for St Thomas' Ward, 1885–7

*Galt* John Galt (1779–1830), the secretary of the Canada Company, *or* his son, Sir A.T. Galt (1817–93), one of the Fathers of Confederation

*Garnet* Col Garnet Joseph Wolseley (1833–1913), later Viscount Wolseley, assistant quartermaster-general in Canada in 1861. In 1895 commander-in-chief of the British army. *See* Wolseley.

*Garrison* After its proximity to the old army garrison where the troops of York were billeted. Garrison Street was changed to Mitchell Avenue, 1882–3.

*Geoffrey* The son of Col Walter O'Hara. *See* O'Hara.

*George* George, Prince of Wales, son of George III. The boundaries of the town laid out by Gov Simcoe in 1793 were George, Adelaide, Berkeley, and Front.

*Gerrard* A friend of Captain John McGill, receiver-general 1813–22

*Gilead* Probably biblical. 'Is there no balm in Gilead?' (Jer 8:22)

*Givens* James Givins (1759?–1846), who accompanied Governor Simcoe to Upper Canada, attained the rank of colonel,

and for many years was superintendent of Indian Affairs. His log house, built about 1800, stood at the head of Givens Street until 1891. The original spelling was Givins. *See* Cecil, Halton.

*Gladstone* The prime minister of Great Britain, the Hon William Ewart Gladstone, 1809–98

*Gordon* Charles George Gordon (Chinese Gordon) (1833–85), governor general of the Soudan and hero of Khartoum, *or* the family name of the marquesses of Huntly. *See* Huntley.

*Gore Vale* From Duncan Cameron's house, built c. 1820 and named after Sir Francis Gore, lieutenant-governor of Upper Canada 1806–17. Duncan Cameron was a member of the Executive Council of Upper Canada and warden of St. James', 1811–12. A later owner of the property was E.O. Bickford. *See* Beatrice, Grace.

*Gould* Nathaniel Gould, a director of the British American Land Co and a Montreal friend of Captain John McGill

*Goulding* William Goulding, carpenter, who resided at No. 1 in 1890. Goulding Street was formerly Renforth Place.

*Grace* The daughter of E.O. Bickford of Gore Vale. *See* Gore Vale.

*Graham* Alderman Graham, St Stephen's Ward 1887–91; Ward 5, 1892, 1895, 1899; elected to Board of Control (by fellow aldermen) 1897

*Grand Opera House* The Opera House on the corner, which was built in 1874, burned 1879. This is a lane on the south side of Adelaide between Bay and Yonge.

*Grange* The Grange, residence of D'Arcy Boulton, son of Mr Justice Boulton. *See* Boulton.

*Greenwood* A gardener of that name in the district

*Grenville* Probably the English statesman Richard Temple Grenville, first duke of Buckingham, 1776–1839

*Grosvenor* Probably the English Whig Robert Grosvenor, first marquis of Westminster, who laid out Belgravia in London in 1826

*Grove* Foxley Grove, the home of Hon S.B. Harrison, of which it and Foxley Street were a part. *See* Harrison.

*Guelph* After the British royal family

*Gwynne* Dr William Gwynne (1806–75), who owned two hundred acres west side of Dufferin Street, south of Queen. *See* Huxley, Spencer, Springhurst, Tyndall.

*Hagerman* Christopher Alexander Hagerman (1792–1847), born in Adolphustown, Upper Canada, the son-in-law of Dr James Macaulay. Attorney-general; judge of the Court of Queen's Bench 1840; regarded as one of the pillars of the Family Compact

*Hallam* Probably John Hallam (1833–1900), born in Chorley, Lancashire, who resided at Linden Villa, Isabella Street, and was chairman of Parks and Gardens. He was alderman for St Lawrence Ward 1870–2, 1876–83, 1888–91, and for Ward 2, 1892–9. In 1882 Hallam secured the passage of the Public Library Act. *See* Linden.

*Halton* Halton, the fifth son of Col Givins. The original name was Cecil Street, after Col Givins's daughter Cecilia. *See* Givens.

*Hamilton* Probably William Hamilton, Jr, city councilman 1865 and alderman 1870–5

*Hammersmith* The western metropolitan borough of London, near the birthplace of Joseph Williams, a farmer who named several streets in Toronto on land formerly owned by him. *See* Kew.

*Hanlan's* Edward Hanlan (1850–1908), champion sculler of Canada, United States, and England, 1879

*Harbour* After its location near the harbour

*Harman* Samuel Bickerton Harman (1819–92), city treasurer 1874–88; assessment commissioner 1874–5; mayor 1869–70; chairman, Board of Evaluators, 1873

*Harrison* The Hon Samuel Bealey Harrison (1802–67) of Foxley Grove, judge of County Court. *See* Foxley, Grove.

*Harvard* Probably the university of that name

*Hastings* Thomas Hastings, alderman 1883–6

*Havelock* General Sir Henry Havelock, 1795–1857

*Hayden* William Hayden, a carpenter of Yorkville on Yonge Street, south of Bloor, who bought six acres from Mrs Mary Elmsley in 1829. He was the contractor for the jail and Court House in 1824.

*Hayter* Elizabeth Hayter, wife of Dr James Macaulay. *See* Macaulay.

*Hazelton* Joseph Hazelton, cab-driver of Yorkville and later owner of an extensive livery business, *or* George Hazelton White, a landowner whose mother was a Miss Hazelton

*Hector* A Christian name in the family of Frank Turner, CE. *See* Turner.

*Henry* William Henry Boulton (1812–74) of the Grange. From 1844 to 1853 he represented Toronto in the Legislative Assembly of Canada. *See* Boulton.

*Hepbourne* Susan Maria Hepbourne, wife of Richard Lippincott Denison. *See* Denison.

*Herrick* Dr George Herrick, born in Ireland in 1789, who emigrated to York in 1838 and opened an office at 42 Lot Street. He remained a bachelor and an eccentric all his life but was well liked as a teacher and highly respected as a specialist in the diseases of women and children.

*Hewitt* William Hewitt, hardware merchant, Adelaide and Yonge streets

*Heyden* Lawrence Heyden (1804–68), a well-known Toronto barrister and a relative of the Baldwins. He was clerk to the Court of Common Pleas and later clerk in the High Court. *See* Baldwin. The later spelling was Hayden, and the street is now called Sussex Avenue.

*Hogarth* George Hogarth, who resided at No 66 and owned considerable property in the vicinity

*Homewood* The Home Wood, residence built in 1847 on the present site of Wellesley Hospital for George William Allan (1822–1901), who gave Allan Gardens to the city; later the home of Benjamin Homer Dixon (1819–99), consul-general for the Netherlands, who changed the spelling to Homewood

*Hoskin* Dr John Hoskin, 1836–1921, chairman of the Board of Trustees of the University of Toronto 1904–5, and in 1906 chairman of Board of Governors. *See* Dale, Devonshire.

*Howard* Allen Maclean Howard, clerk of the Division Court. Howard Street was originally East Street.

*Howard Park* John George Howard (1803–

90), architect, who donated High Park in the same district to the city of Toronto. *See* Sunnyside.

*Howland* Sir William Pierce Howland (1811–1907), Lt-Gov of Ontario 1868–73; in the plan of 1857 Howland Avenue is called Pierce Street, second name of Sir William. *Or:* W.H. Howland, mayor of Toronto 1886–7; the Howland Syndicate owned the block Bloor to Dupont and Howland to Bathurst

*Hunter* Thomas Hunter, alderman for St John's Ward 1884–7 and one of the promoters of the baseball stadium south of Queen Street East, near Broadview Avenue

*Huntley* The Moss Farm or Mossfield near Huntly in Aberdeenshire, Scotland, birthplace of Col William Allan, second postmaster and collector of customs in York. Col Allan was one of the signatories to the surrender of York to the Americans in April 1813. Formerly Bridge Street. *See* Gordon, Moss Park.

*Huxley* Thomas Henry Huxley (1825–95), English biologist. President of the Royal Society 1883–5. So named by Dr Wm Gwynne. *See* Gwynne.

*Indian* After the old Indian trail that ran close to the Humber River and was laid out by J.G. Howard

*Ingham* Joshua Ingham, alderman 1887

*Inkerman* The Crimean battle of 1854

*Irwin* John Irwin, born in Ireland 1824, immigrated to Toronto in 1850. He was proprietor of the General Wolfe Hotel at the corner of Church and King streets. For a time Irwin was an alderman for St John's Ward, and he was reputed to be the last man to hitch a horse to a steam fire-engine.

*Isabella* Mrs Isabella Roaf, daughter of Dr James Richardson, who opened up the street

*James* Dr James Macaulay, surgeon of the Queen's Rangers. *See* Macaulay.

*Jameson* Robert Sympson Jameson (d 1854), attorney-general 1833, vice-chancellor of Upper Canada 1837–54, who owned property there. He was the husband of Anna Brownell Jameson, noted woman of letters (*Winter Studies and Summer Rambles in Canada*; *Characteristics of Women,*

etc), who resided in York in 1836–7. *See* Maynard.

*Jarvis* Samuel Peters Jarvis (1792–1857), who opened up and named Jarvis Street from Queen to Bloor. His father, William Jarvis, was appointed registrar of Upper Canada in 1792. The lower part of Jarvis Street was originally New Street (1797), and afterwards Nelson Street. *See* Edgar, Elm Ave, Meredith, Mutual, Nanton, Orde, Rosedale.

*Jefferson* Probably Thomas Jefferson (1743–1826), third president of the United States 1801–9

*John* Lt-Col John Graves Simcoe (1752–1806), first Lt-Gov of Upper Canada 1791–6. *See* Simcoe.

*Johnson* A carter who owned a row of houses on the street

*Jones* John Jones, alderman 1884–8

*Jordan* Jordan Post, jeweller, who owned land between Yonge and Bay streets in 1802. *See* Melinda.

*Keele* William Keele, solicitor, who owned property in Toronto Junction

*Kenilworth* The Scottish castle made famous by the novel of that name by Sir Walter Scott

*Kent* Edward Augustus, duke of Kent (1767–1820), fourth son of George III and father of Queen Victoria. Kent Street was formerly Surrey Street.

*Ketchum* Jesse Ketchum (1782–1867), an American philanthropist who came to Canada in 1799. He amassed a great fortune from leather, particularly through sales to the Canadian government. His generosity extended to the various religious denominations in Toronto and to the gift of the land for the Jesse Ketchum School, Jesse Ketchum Park in Yorkville, and Knox Church, which once occupied a site bounded by Bay, Yonge, Richmond, and Queen. *See* Rose, Temperance.

*Kew* Kew Gardens in England. The street was named by Joseph Williams, who was born there, immigrated to Canada in 1853, and owned a large farm in the eastern section of Toronto that he sold later for building purposes. *See* Hammersmith.

*King* After the sovereign, George III; one of

the streets laid out by Gov Simcoe in 1793. This King Street was changed to Palace as early as 1797. The present King Street was formerly Duke.

Lambton John George Lambton, first earl of Durham. *See* Durham.

Lamport Henry Lamport, whose parents came to Canada from France in 1800. He prospered as a merchant in Vittoria, Norfolk Co, but moved to Toronto, where he became the owner of considerable farm property in what is now Rosedale. His house was on Jarvis Street at the corner of Earl Street. Lamport was the grandfather of former Mayor Allan Lamport.

Langley Henry Langley (1836–1907), architect

Lansdowne The marquis of Lansdowne, governor general of Canada 1883–8

Laurier Sir Wilfrid Laurier (1841–1919), prime minister of Canada 1896–1911

Leader The *Leader*, Tory paper from 1852 to 1878. Originally, Leader Lane ran from Colborne Street to King Street. The southern part of Leader Lane to Wellington Street was originally Berczy Street, and later, on the completion of the Toronto Exchange in 1855, 'Change Alley.

Lennox Joseph Lennox, a property owner in the district

Leopold Leopold of Saxe-Coburg, who married Charlotte Augusta, only daughter of George IV, in 1816. *See* Charlotte.

Leslie The Leslie family of Leslieville, an eastern suburb of Toronto

Lewis Catherine Lewis, wife of John Saulter, who owned a farm here (*see* Saulter), *or* after Lewis Bright, who settled in York in 1802 and whose descendants lived in the vicinity

Linden Linden Villa, residence of John Hallam, alderman and merchant of Toronto. *See* Hallam.

Lindsey Charles Lindsey, city registrar and son-in-law of William Lyon Mackenzie. He was editor of the *Leader* and purchaser of the Foxley Estate. *See* Mackenzie.

Lippincott Esther Borden Lippincott, wife of George Taylor Denison and daughter of Captain Richard Lippincott. *See* Denison.

Lisgar Sir John Young (1807–76), Baron Lisgar, governor General of Canada 1869–72

Little Arthur Prince Arthur, duke of Connaught (1850–1942), seventh child of Queen Victoria. The name was changed to Hickson in 1890. *See* Prince Arthur.

Lobb James Lobb, who was alderman in 1880, 1881, 1884

Logan The Logan family, in the 1850s market gardeners in the district

Logie Probably James Logie, born in Elgin, Scotland, 1863, who immigrated to Toronto in 1889. Logie was connected with the E.B. Eddy Company for twenty years.

Lombard After the celebrated financial street in London. Lombard Street was originally March Street after the earl of March, second title of the duke of Richmond, and later Stanley Street, after George Stanley, fourteenth earl of Derby, Colonial minister 1841–5.

Lorne The marquis of Lorne, 1845–1914, afterwards ninth duke of Argyll, governor general of Canada 1878–83, who was received here on his first visit to Toronto in September 1879. This was a short street between Bay and York, now the site of the Union Station. *See* Argyle.

Louisa Probably a friend or member of the Macaulay family. Was formerly Macaulay Lane. *See* Macaulay.

Lovatt Thomas Lovatt, a large property owner in the district now part of South Regent Park

Lumley M. Lumley, wholesale clothier, now Euclid Avenue

Lynd Dr Adam Lynd, a resident of the village of Parkdale and mayor of Parkdale 1887–8

Lytton Edward George, Baron Lytton (1803–73). *See* Bulwer.

Macaulay Dr James Macaulay (1759–1822), born in Scotland, an early medical practitioner and large landowner in York. He was also surgeon with the Queen's Rangers under Lt-Col Simcoe until the regiment disbanded. The district between Queen and Yonge and Bay and College streets was known as Macaulay Town, and the original residence Teraulay Cottage stood on the site of Holy

Trinity Church. *See* Agnes, Alice, Anne, Buchanan, Edward, Elizabeth, Hagerman, Hayter, James, Louisa, Teraulay, Vanauley.

*Macdonell Sq* Alexander Macdonell (1762–1840), first Roman Catholic bishop of Kingston, whose diocese included most of Upper Canada. The square surrounded lands granted in 1837 for a Roman Catholic church and presbytery, and is today the site of St Mary's Church on Bathurst Street. *See* Stewart.

*Mackenzie Cres* William Lyon Mackenzie (1795–1861), mayor 1834, named by his son-in-law, Charles Lindsey, who purchased the old Foxley property. *See* Lindsey.

*Macpherson* Senator Sir David L. Macpherson (1818–96) of Chestnut Park. In 1880 he was appointed Speaker of the Senate; associate in railway construction with Casimir Gzowski.

*McCaul* Dr John McCaul (1807–86), first president of the University of Toronto (1853–80); formerly William Henry Street, after William Henry Boulton (1812–74)

*McFarren's*: Andrew McFarren, grocer, wine, flour, and feed merchant in the district in 1873

*McGee* Thomas D'Arcy McGee (1825–68), one of the Fathers of Confederation. McGee Street was formerly D'Arcy Street.

*McGill* Ann McGill, wife of Rev Dr John Strachan. Not to be confused with McGill Square. The residence of Captain John McGill, receiver-general 1813 –22, stood in McGill Square on a grant of land received in 1799, on the present site of the Metropolitan Church. *See* Ann, Gerrard, Gould, Mutual, Shuter, Strachan.

*McMaster* Senator, the Hon William J. McMaster (1811–87), born at Rathnally, Ireland. Settled in York, Upper Canada, 1833. First president of the Bank of Commerce. The bulk of his estate went to McMaster University. *See* Rathnally.

*McMurrich* William B. McMurrich, mayor of Toronto 1881–2

*Madison* James Madison (1751–1836), fourth president of the United States 1809–17, the street being named by S.H. Janes, who laid out the district

*Maitland* Sir Peregrine Maitland (1777–1854), lieutenant-governor of Upper Canada 1818–28. *See* Richmond.

*Major* Major Robert Brittain Denison (1821–1900). *See* Denison.

*Manning* Alexander Manning, mayor of Toronto 1873 and 1885

*Maria* Maria Willcocks, who was left property here in 1822 by her cousin Elizabeth Russell, stepsister of the Hon Peter Russell. Maria Street is now Soho Street. *See* Russell, Willcocks.

*Mark* Mark Defries, son of Richard Defries, gardener, Kingston Road

*Market* After the market to which it led. Market Street is now Wellington Street.

*Markham* Probably a Captain Markham of the 32nd Regiment

*Marion* Probably the grandmother of John F. McCrae, Marion Munro, wife of David McCrae, who in the 1890s developed this district (*see* Marmaduke), *or* Marion, the wife of Col Walter O'Hara, who was a captain in the 47th Regiment during the Peninsular War (*see* O'Hara)

*Marlborough* The seventh Duke of Marlborough, John Winston Spencer Churchill (1822–83), Lord-Lieutenant of Ireland 1876–80

*Marmaduke* Marmaduke McCrae. The street was named by his great-grandson John F. McCrae, real-estate agent and owner of considerable property in the vicinity. *See* Marion.

*Massey* Hart A. Massey (1823–96), founder of the Massey Harris Company, philanthropist. *See* Vincent.

*Matilda* Probably after a member of the Gooderham family. *See* Dean.

*Maynard* Rev George Maynard, a master of Upper Canada College, 1836–56, who received property in this vicinity under the will of Vice-Chancellor R.S. Jameson. *See* Jameson.

*Melbourne* Probably William Lamb, second Viscount Melbourne (1779–1848) and a favourite of Queen Victoria

*Melady* P. Melady, drygoods merchant

*Melinda* Melinda, the wife of Jordan Post (1767–1845), York's leading clock-maker and jeweller who owned property there. *See* Jordan.

*Melita* A Christian name in the family of Frank Turner, CE, *See* Turner.

*Mercer* Andrew Mercer (1778–1871), who owned property in this street. He came to York, Upper Canada, in the year 1800 and amassed a great fortune. He died intestate, and out of the funds taken over by the Crown, the Mercer Reformatory was built. His house stood at Bay and Wellington.

*Meredith* E.A. Meredith, LLD (1817–98), principal, McGill University, 1846–1853, under-secretary of State for Canada 1878, and husband of Fanny Jarvis, daughter of Sheriff Jarvis. The street was named by the Jarvis family. *See* Jarvis.

*Metcalfe* Probably Sir Charles, first Baron Metcalfe (1785–1846), governor of Canada 1843–5

*Mill* After the old Gooderham and Worts windmill, which stood on the bayshore just east of Parliament Street and was for many years a famous landmark. *See* Dean, Trinity.

*Millicent* The daughter of Elmes Henderson, who opened this street through property he owned there

*Mincing Lane* After the ancient street of that name in London, England

*Minto* The earl of Minto, governor general of Canada 1898–1904

*Mitchell* John E. Mitchell, alderman 1880–1, 1884–5

*Monck* Lord Monck (1819–94), governor general of Canada 1861–8

*Morris* James H. Morris, alderman, St Andrew's Ward, 1880

*Morrison* Angus Morrison, mayor of Toronto 1876–8

*Morse* George D. Morse, a cattle-dealer who drowned in the Don River

*Moss Park* Moss Park was the estate of William Allan and the Hon G.W. Allan. It received its name from the birthplace of William Allan near Huntly in Aberdeenshire in Scotland. *See* Huntley.

*Mountstephen* George Stephen (1829–1921), born in Banffshire, Scotland; later Baron Mount Stephen, financier. He was president of the CPR from 1881 to 1891.

*Mowat* Hon Oliver Mowat, premier of Ontario, 1872–96

*Mulock* Sir William Mulock, KCMG (1844–1944), born at Bond Head, chief justice of Ontario, chancellor of the University of Toronto 1924–44

*Munn* George Munn, a carter in the vicinity. Munn Lane was changed to Mincing Lane

*Munro* George Monro, mayor of Toronto 1841. Present spelling is Munro

*Murray* Maiden name of Mrs William Powell, wife of Hon William Powell, chief justice of Upper Canada 1815–25. *See* Powell.

*Muter* Lt-Col Robert Muter of the Royal Canadian Regiment, who married a daughter of John Hillyard Cameron. Muter Street is now Palmerston Avenue.

*Mutray* Col Murray (or Moutray), born in Ireland, who served with the 7th Regiment of Fusiliers on the peninsula and who lived for some time on the street bearing his name

*Mutual* Probably from the fact that it was once a 'mutual' road surveyed between the park lots owned by the Jarvis and McGill families. *See* Jarvis, McGill.

*Nanton* Augustus Nanton, barrister, admitted as a student to Osgoode Hall in 1846, called to the bar in 1852, who married a daughter of Sheriff W.B. Jarvis. *See* Jarvis.

*Napier* Sir Charles Napier (1782–1853), the hero of Sind, *or* after the three brothers known as 'the Wellington Colonels,' of which he was one

*Nassau* Almost certainly named for the eldest son of Ogle R. Gowan, first Grand Master of the Grand Orange Lodge of British North America and later an official with the city of Toronto, who lived at the corner of Augusta Avenue. His son was named in honour of William of Orange, a member of the house of Nassau.

*Nelson* Horatio, Viscount Nelson (1758–1805). Nelson Street is now that part of Jarvis Street south of Queen.

*New Fort* After Stanley Barracks (1840). *See* Stanley.

*Niagara* After the original path along the east bank of the old Garrison Creek, made by the troops from old Fort York on their journey around the head of the Lake to Niagara

*Nina* The daughter of Col Frederick Wells, wife of the Rev Adam Uriah de Pencier, bishop of New Westminster. *See* Wells.

*North* That part of Bay Street between St Mary's and Bloor that ran north to what was then the northern city limits, Bloor Street

*Northcote* Sir Stafford Henry Northcote (1818–87), British statesman

*Northern* After its location, running north from the Northern Railroad

*Northumberland* Probably the dukes of Northumberland. *See* Percy.

*O'Hara* Col Walter O'Hara (1784–1874), captain 47th Regiment, Peninsular War, who came to Canada in 1831 and became adjutant-general of forces in Upper Canada. In 1840 he purchased 420 acres. *See* Constance, Fermanagh, Geoffrey, Marion, Roncesvalles, Ruth, Sorauren, West Lodge.

*O'Keefe* Eugene O'Keefe (1827–1913), founder of O'Keefe Breweries: came to Upper Canada from Bandon, Co Cork, in 1832; in 1909 appointed papal chamberlain of the Roman Catholic Church

*Olive* Olive Grove, the home of William Campbell, the proprietor of the Ontario House, and later of J.S. Howard, postmaster of York, treasurer of the counties of York and Peel. Now Balmoral Avenue at Yonge

*Ontario* 'So called from the end of the old trail to the Carrying Place to Lake Ontario' (T.A. Reed)

*Orde* Lewis Ord, a government official who in 1860 owned property on the street. He married Sarah, the daughter of W.B. Jarvis and Mary Powell. *See* Jarvis, Powell.

*Orford* A family of that name, resident in the district

*Osborne* The Rev A. Osborne, rector of St Saviour's Church, East Toronto, 1903–9

*Osgoode* The Hon William Osgoode (1754–1824), first chief justice of Upper Canada 1792–4

*Osler* After a member of the Osler family, probably E.B. Osler, who was MP for West Toronto in 1896

*Ossington* Ossington House, near Newark in Nottinghamshire, England, was the family seat of the Denison family. *See* Denison.

*Oxford* After the English university. Next to it used to be Cambridge Street. For a time c 1870 Oxford Street was called Augustus Street.

*Palmerston* Lord Palmerston, prime minister of England 1855–8

*Pape* After the family of Albert Pape or John Pape, market gardeners for three generations in that vicinity

*Pardee* Hon T.B. Pardee, Ontario minister of Crown Lands 1873–88

*Park* After the area that was originally the government park or reserve for public buildings

*Parliament* After the first Parliament buildings, on Front Street between Berkeley and Parliament streets

*Paterson* George Paterson, a cab-driver of the district known as Cabbagetown

*Pears* Leonard Pears, brick-maker of Yorkville, who used clay found where Ramsden Park is today. Later the family had brickyards on Eglinton Avenue on the present site of Eglinton Park, known as Pears Park until the 1950s.

*Pearson* Pearson Brothers, real-estate brokers, who opened up this district

*Peel* Sir Robert Peel, the English statesman (1788–1850), under-secretary for the Colonies under Lord Liverpool 1810–12 and prime minister 1841–5

*Pelham* Probably George Pelham (1766–1827), bishop successively of Bristol, Exeter, and Lincoln, *or* John Thomas Pelham (1811–94), bishop of Norwich

*Percy* Probably after the dukes of Northumberland, whose family name is Percy. *See* Northumberland.

*Peter* The Hon Peter Russell, president and administrator of the province 1796–9 and owner of the farm Petersfield, to which the road led. *See* Russell.

*Phipps* A broker of that name

*Phoebe* Phoebe Willcocks, cousin of Hon Peter Russell; she became the wife of Dr W.W. Baldwin in 1803. *See* Baldwin, Willcocks.

*Piper* Noah Piper, a hardware merchant, and Harry Piper, alderman and zoo proprietor; originally Murray Street

*Poplar Plains* From the fact that the table land above the present winding street was formerly called Poplar Plains

*Portland* The third duke of Portland (1738–

1809), home secretary 1794–1801, who was responsible for designating York as the seat of government for Upper Canada, contrary to Simcoe's recommendations for an inland site safer from attack. There seems to be no connection between Portland and the trio of Bathurst, Brock, and Tecumseh, for whom the flanking streets were named and who were linked through the War of 1812.

*Poucher* John Poucher, builder and landowner in the district and valuator for the city of Toronto

*Poulett* Charles Poulett Thomson, first Baron Sydenham of Kent and Toronto, governor general of Canada 1839–41 and a one-time resident of Toronto. *See* Sydenham.

*Powell* After the Powell family (originally Ap Howell), connected with the Jarvis family, who laid out Rosedale. Mary Powell, granddaughter of Chief Justice William Dummer Powell, married Sheriff William B. Jarvis and lived in Rosedale. *See* Caer Howell, Jarvis, Murray, Rosedale, St Patrick, William.

*Power* Bishop Michael Power, first Roman Catholic bishop of Toronto, 1842–7

*Price* After the property of Miss Sarah Price of Thornwood (near the corner of Price and Yonge), so called because her father, Joseph Price, from Thornwood in Essex, willed ten acres to his daughter in 1846. *See* Thornwood.

*Princess* Originally Princes, after the various princes who were members of George III's family. Princes Street was the second most easterly of the streets running north and south as laid out by Governor Simcoe in 1793.

*Prince Arthur* Arthur, Duke of Connaught (1850–1942), who first visited Canada in 1870 and became governor general of Canada 1911–16. *See* Little Arthur.

*Queen* Queen Victoria (1819–1901). So named about 1843. Queen Street was formerly Lot Street because of the 'park lots' abutting it and extending north to Bloor Street. Lot became the northern limit of the town in 1797, as it grew beyond the original boundary of Duchess.

*Queen's Park* After Queen Victoria and

dedicated by Albert Edward, Prince of Wales (later Edward VII) in 1860, during his visit to Toronto in the name of his mother, 'for the recreation of the citizens.' Formerly University Park

*Radenhurst* John Radenhurst (1795–1853), who for many years was chief clerk in the surveyor-general's office.

*Rains* Rains was a Christian name in the family of Frank Turner, CE. *See* Turner.

*Rathnally* From the estate of W.J. McMaster, whose birthplace was Rathnally in Ireland. *See* McMaster.

*Rebecca* After the Rebeccaites, of South Wales, who in 1843 destroyed the tollgates and bars. Rebecca was so called because it was originally a lane to avoid the toll-gate at Ossington and Queen streets. 'Rebecca ... let thy seed possess the gate' (Gen 24:60).

*Regent* The street of that name in London, England, *or* the Prince Regent, who became George IV

*Reid* John Reid, a painter and councilman

*Reynolds* William Reynolds, born 1818, who was a baker in the vicinity of Yonge and Bloor streets c 1843 and a member of a well-known Yorkville family

*Richmond* The duke of Richmond, governor general of Canada 1818–19 and father-in-law of Sir Peregrine Maitland, lt-gov of Upper Canada 1818–28. Richmond Street was formerly (until about 1840) Hospital Street because, when laid out in 1797, the block south of Richmond between Church and Yonge was reserved for a hospital. In 1820 the first general hospital was built elsewhere. *See* Maitland.

*Ritchie* John Ritchey, the builder in 1829 of the east (first) wing of Osgoode Hall and later one of the city's largest property owners. He was a member of City Council most years between 1837 and 1850.

*River* After the Don River, which it parallels

*Riverdale* After the Don River, which flows through it

*Robert* Hon Robert Baldwin (*see* Baldwin), *or* Col Robert Denison (*see* Denison)

*Robinson* Sir John Beverley Robinson (1791–1863), first chancellor of Trinity

College, 1853, near which the street was situated. *See* Beverley, Christopher, Sayer.

*Roden* Ephraim P. Roden, public school trustee 1874–97 and employee of the city engineer's department 1883

*Rolyat* From John Fennings Taylor the elder (1801–76), son-in-law of John Denison. Rolyat is Taylor reversed. Appointed assistant clerk of the Legislative Council by Gov Sydenham 1841; master of Chancery 1843; clerk, by Lord Elgin, 1850; and Lt-Col by Lord Elgin, 1853. *See* Fennings.

*Roncesvalles* After the battle in Spain in 1813, the street so named by Col Walter O'Hara, who fought there. *See* O'Hara.

*Rose* Sir John Rose (1820–88), minister of Finance in the first Dominion Cabinet 1867, *or* Anna, daughter of Jesse Ketchum (1782–1867), who married Walter Rose, a private banker (*see* Ketchum)

*Roseberry* The marquis of Rosebery, prime minister of Great Britain 1894–6; British foreign secretary 1886 and 1892–4

*Rosedale* The residence of William Botsford Jarvis, sheriff from 1827 to 1856, who purchased this land in 1824 from J.E. Small, builder of the original house there in 1821. Reputedly received its name in 1827 from Mary Powell when she came as the bride of Sheriff Jarvis to discover the hillsides covered with wild roses. *See* Jarvis, Powell.

*Ross* Hon John Ross, QC (1818–71), born in Co Antrim, Ireland, educated in the district school Brockville. He was a member of the Legislative Council of Canada 1852–62, a senator, and in 1869 Speaker of the Senate. Married Augusta, daughter of the Hon Robert Baldwin. *See* Baldwin.

*Rowanwood* The residence of James Grant Macdonald; situated north of Sir David Macpherson's Chestnut Park

*Royce* The Royce family, whose farm adjoined Davenport. William Campbell, who purchased large sections of land in the district, married a Royce. *See* Campbell.

*Runnymede* The name given by John Scarlett to his house on Dundas Street in 1838

*Rush* The town on the Irish Sea, fifteen miles from Dublin, *or* Frank Rush, a grocer on Queen Street

*Rusholme* The estate Rusholme, owned by Col George Taylor Denison II (1816–73), adjoined Dover Court, the estate of his brother Richard Lippincott Denison. *See* Denison.

*Ruskin* John Ruskin (1819–1900), art critic and writer

*Russell* Probably Hon Peter Russell (1733–1808), president and administrator of the province 1796–9. *See* Abbey Lane, Bedford, Maria, Peter, Russell Hill.

*Russell Hill* The Hon Peter Russell *See* Russell.

*Ruth* Probably after a member of the O'Hara family. Ruth Street is now Fern. *See* O'Hara.

*St Alban* An expression of the religious zeal of the Hon John Elmsley, who in the 1830s became a convert to the Roman Catholic Church. *See* St Joseph, St Mary, St Thomas, St Nicholas, and St Charles. St Alban Street is now Wellesley Street West. *See* Elmsley.

*St Andrew's* After the patron saint of Scotland

*St Anne's* From its proximity to St Anne's Anglican Church

*St Charles' See* St Alban

*St David* After its location in old St David's Ward

*St George* After Laurent Quetton St George (1771–1821), an early trader at York and Niagara and a partner of John Spread Baldwin, brother of Dr W.W. Baldwin. *See* Baldwin.

*St Joseph* After the convent of the Sisters of St Joseph on the Elmsley estate. *See* St Alban.

*St Lawrence* After its location in old St Lawrence Ward

*St Mary's See* St Alban.

*St Nicholas See* St Alban.

*St Patrick* After the ward of the same name. St Patrick Street was formerly William Street and, before that, Dummer Street, both after Hon William Dummer Powell, chief justice of Upper Canada 1815–25. *See* Powell

*St Patrick Market* After its location in St Patrick's Ward

*St Thomas See* St Alban.

*Sackville* The street of that name in Dublin, Ireland, Sackville Street was formerly Pine Street.

*Salem* Salem, Massachusetts

*Salisbury* The marquis of Salisbury, prime minister of Great Britain 1885, 1886–92

*Sarah* Sarah Ellerbeck Playter, wife of John Playter (b 1774). The land around this street was part of the original grant in 1793 to the Playter family. It is now Cambridge, north of Danforth. Playter Boulevard and Playter Crescent are nearby.

*Saulter* John Saulter, farmer on east bank of the Don River. *See* Lewis.

*Saurin* James Saurin McMurray (1840–95), barrister and alderman; secretary to the Hon George Brown at a conference in Washington. DC, in 1872. At the time of his death he was vice-consul to Norway and Sweden. His father was Archdeacon McMurray (1810–94). Now Afton Avenue

*Sayer* The maiden name of Mrs Christopher Robinson, mother of Chief Justice Sir John Beverley Robinson, who laid out and named the street, now Chestnut Street. *See* Robinson.

*Scadding* John Scadding (1754–1824), who came to Canada with Gov Simcoe in 1793 and returned to England with him. In 1818 he emigrated with his family and settled on his grant of two hundred acres on the east bank of the Don River. The street is now the southern end of Broadview Avenue. *See* Amelia.

*Scarth* After the family of William Bain Scarth, born 1837 in Scotland, manager of the Scottish Ontario and Manitoba Land Company, which developed an extensive tract in this vicinity. *See* Binscarth.

*Scollard* Maurice Scollard of the Bank of Upper Canada, whose name appears in the directory of 1833–4

*Scott* Chief Justice Thomas Scott, chief justice of Upper Canada 1804–24, through whose estate the street extended

*Seaton* Lord Seaton, who, as Sir John Colborne, was lt-gov of Upper Canada 1828–36 and the founder of Upper Canada College. *See* Colborne.

*Selby* Prideaux Selby, receiver-general of Upper Canada from 1808 until his death in 1813

*Shaftesbury* The seventh earl of Shaftesbury (1801–85)

*Shanly* Walter Shanly, general manager of Grand Trunk Railroad, *or* Francis Shanly, architect and city engineer 1875–80. Both were sons of James Shanly, who came to Canada in 1836. Shanly was formerly Durham Street.

*Shaw* Major-General Aeneas Shaw (d 1815), an officer of the Queen's Rangers under Simcoe during the Revolutionary War. His log cabin, called Oakhill after the ancestral home in Scotland, was built in 1793. It was succeeded in 1797 by a larger house, which stood for over eighty years northwest of old Trinity College.

*Sheppard* Harvey Sheppard's iron-work establishment, where he made axes and adzes

*Sherbourne* Sherbourne House, residence of Thomas Gibbs Ridout (1792–1861), cashier of the Bank of Upper Canada 1822–1861 and half-brother of Samuel Ridout, sheriff of the Home District 1815–17. The Ridouts' home in England was at Sherborne, Dorsetshire. Sherbourne Street was formerly Caroline Street, after the Princess of Wales, daughter-in-law of George III, and was also long known as Allan's Lane. *See* Bleecker, Dorset.

*Shuter* John Shuter, a director of the British American Land Co and a Montreal friend of Captain John McGill, receiver-general in 1813–22. There is a Shuter Street in Montreal, transferred to the city of Montreal by the estate of his son Joseph in 1873, forty years after the naming of the Toronto Street. *See* McGill.

*Simcoe* John Graves Simcoe (1752–1806), first lt-gov of Upper Canada, 1791–6. Simcoe Street was formerly, until 1842–3, called Graves Street. The original Simcoe Street, named in 1837, is now Richmond Street west of Spadina. *See* John.

*Smith* Probably a John Smith who had property there c 1884

*Soho* The district in London

*Sorauren* After the battle in Spain in 1815,

the street so called by Col Walter O'Hara, who fought at the battle. *See* O'Hara.

*Spadina* Spadina, the country home of Dr W.W. Baldwin, to which it was the approach. The name is derived from Espadinong, an Indian word meaning a little hill. *See* Baldwin.

*Sparkhall* Cubett Sparkhall, born in Norfolk, England, in 1821, who immigrated to Canada in 1832 with his mother. In 1839 he opened a butcher shop.

*Spencer* Herbert Spencer (1820–1903), the English philosopher. So named by Dr William Gwynne. *See* Gwynne.

*Springhurst* After the numerous springs in the vicinity. So named by Dr William Gwynne. *See* Gwynne.

*Sproat* Charles Sproatt, city engineer 1883–90 and father of architect Henry Sproatt

*Stanley* Lord Stanley of Preston, governor general of Canada 1888–93. Also Stanley Barracks, built 1840, first called New Fort, renamed 1893. *See* New Fort.

*Steiner* N.L. Steiner, alderman 1880, 1881, 1883–6, and 1899. *See* Bismarck.

*Stewart* Charles James Stewart (1775–1837), Anglican bishop of Quebec. When the street was named in 1837, Toronto was in the diocese of Quebec. *See* Macdonnell.

*Strachan* The Hon and Rt Rev Dr John Strachan (1778–1867), bishop of Toronto 1839–67, founder of Trinity College in 1851. *See* Ann, Bishop.

*Strange* Maxwell Strange, an auctioneer, who first appears in the directory of 1837

*Sullivan* Hon Robert Baldwin Sullivan (1802–53), justice of the Queen's Bench in 1848, nephew of Dr W.W. Baldwin, and mayor of Toronto 1835. *See* Baldwin.

*Sultan* Probably after the sultan of Turkey, named at a time when that country was much in the public eye. *See* Czar.

*Summerhill* After the estate of Charles Thompson, who bought the stage service in 1840 from William Weller, and later of Dr Larratt William Smith, QC (1820–1905), vice-chancellor of the University of Toronto 1873

*Sunnyside* From 'my new villa, Sunnyside, on the Lake Shore Road.' Sold by John G. Howard to George H. Cheney, merchant, for £1,200 in 1853. This would appear to be a summer cottage or a speculation, because Colborne Lodge (1836) continued to be the Howard home. *See* Howard Park.

*Surrey* Probably Surrey Park, the home in England of Captain Benjamin Hallowell, RN, father of Mary, wife of Chief Justice Elmsley, who owned property here. *See* Elmsley.

*Sword* In 1856 P. Sword was proprietor of Sword's Hotel, later the Queen's, which stood on that site until Sept 11 1927, when it was replaced by the present Royal York Hotel, which opened two years later.

*Sydenham* Charles Poulett Thomson, first Baron Sydenham of Kent and Toronto (1799–1841), governor general of Canada 1839–41. *See* Poulett.

*Symes Place* An A. Symes built houses in the area.

*Tate* A Mr Tate, contractor for the Grand Trunk Railroad

*Taylor* The Taylor family, who owned the Taylor Paper Mills in the Don Valley

*Tecumseth* Sometimes spelled Tecumseh; he was a famous Indian chief and an ally of General Sir Isaac Brock.

*Temperance* Named by Jesse Ketchum, who built a temperance hall there. He was a leading temperance advocate. *See* Ketchum.

*Teraulay* A combination of the names of Elizabeth Hayter and her husband, Dr James Macaulay, or solely from the Macaulay property, Ter Auly, land of Aulay. Dr Macaulay's house on the site of the Church of the Holy Trinity was called Teraulay Cottage. *See* Macaulay.

*Theatre Lane* From the fact that it once led to the Royal Lyceum Theatre

*Thornwood* Birthplace in Essex, England, of Jos Price, who owned from Yonge Street east to the Don and south from the CPR tracks to Rowanwood. *See* Price.

*Tinning* Richard Tinning owned a sawmill and built houses on this street around 1852.

*Toronto* From an Indian word that some claim to mean 'the meeting place of the waters.' Correct or not, no more poetic derivation has been suggested

*Trafalgar* The naval battle of 1805

*Trinity* After Trinity Church, the first city parish cut off from the original parish of York (St James) in 1843. The church was built in the same year on King Street East at Trinity (near Parliament). Trinity Street was formerly Windmill Street because it led to the windmill of Worts and Gooderham. *See* Mill.

*Turner* Frank Turner, CE, who subdivided Bracondale, the home of his father Robert J. Turner, a solicitor from Yarmouth, England. Turner Avenue was originally West Street, and it is now Whittaker. *See* Bracondale, Melita, Rains, Yarmouth.

*Tyndall* John Tyndall, the natural philosopher (1820–93). So named by Dr William Gwynne. *See* Gwynne.

*University* Originally (1829) College Avenue, it was laid out as a private tree-lined street from Queen Street to the future King's College (1843). In 1888 it was leased by the University of Toronto as a public street. *See* College.

*Vanauley* Probably, a combination of the names Vankoughnet and Macaulay. *See* Macaulay, Vankoughnet.

*Van Horne* Sir William Cornelius Van Horne, born in Illinois in 1843, who became president of the Canadian Pacific Railroad. He refused a knighthood in 1891 and 1892, and finally accepted in 1895.

*Vankoughnet* Philip Vankoughnet, QC (1823–69), minister of Agriculture 1856, chancellor of Upper Canada 1862–7, and chancellor of Ontario 1867–9. *See* Vanauley.

*Vermont* For the first state received into the American union after the adoption of the federal constitution

*Verral* George Verral, alderman 1884–91, 1892–3

*Victoria* Queen Victoria; formerly known as Upper George Street. *See* George.

*Vincent* Anna Vincent Massey, wife of Chester D. Massey and mother of the Rt Hon Vincent Massey, CH. *See* Massey.

*Vine* After its location through an old vineyard

*Virgin* Named after a Mr Virgin by his close friend, Emerson Coatsworth. *See* Coatsworth.

*Walker* The family of Walter Walker, a carriage-maker and old resident who owned property here fronting on Yonge Street (1888)

*Walmer* Walmer, in England, was the birthplace of James McQueen Baldwin, who was born there in 1860; the street was named by his father Robert Baldwin. *See* Baldwin.

*Walton* Matthew Walton, in 1827, bought six acres here and laid it out in town lots. In 1834 he was appointed chamberlain of the city but held office only a few weeks.

*Wardell* O. Wardell, an auctioneer

*Waterloo* The battle of 1815

*Waverley* Probably after Sir Walter Scott's novel

*Wellesley* The duke of Wellington, formerly Arthur Wellesley. Was first Frank Street (after Castle Frank); then Charles Street after Charles Scadding, son of John Scadding, who bought the two hundred acres of Castle Frank property; then, and finally, Wellesley. *See* Wellington.

*Wellington* The duke of Wellington. Formerly called Market Street because it gave a direct approach to the market from the west in 1837. *See* Douro, Wellesley.

*Wells* Col the Hon J. Wells of Davenport, who came here in 1821. *See* Dartnell, Davenport, Dupont, Nina.

*West Lodge* West Lodge was the residence of Col Walter O'Hara. *See* O'Hara.

*West Market* After its location bordering the west side of St Lawrence Market

*White's Place* George White, tassel-maker, of 57 Sherbourne Street in the same district

*Whiteside* Thomas R. Whiteside, appointed collector of taxes in 1886. Circa 1897–9 the system of appointing multiple tax collectors, one for each ward, was consolidated by the appointment of one tax collector with assistants.

*Whitney* Sir James Pliny Whitney (1843–1914), DCL, LLD, KCMG, born at Williamsburg, Upper Canada, educated at Cornwall Grammar School, prime minister of Ontario 1905–8

*Wickson* John Wickson, a butcher of Yorkville. Wickson Avenue is now called Alcorn Avenue.

*Widmer* Dr Christopher Widmer (1780–1858), who was one of the first qualified medical practitioners in York. He was a member of the Upper Canada Medical Board from its inception in 1819 until his death, and its chairman from 1853. He was also one of the founders of the York General Hospital (c 1818), the property of which was subdivided and this street opened.

*Willcocks* Col William Willcocks (1736–1853), judge of the Home District 1802, in whose name a large piece of property here was patented in 1798. His daughter Phoebe married Dr W.W. Baldwin. *See* Baldwin, Maria, Phoebe.

*Wilkins* Thomas Wilkins, a large property owner, founder of Wilkins Smallware, and builder of many houses in the vicinity of the Church of the Holy Trinity

*William* Hon William Dummer Powell (1755–1834), chief justice of Upper Canada 1815–25. *See* Powell.

*Wilmot* Samuel Wilmot, deputy-surveyor in 1811

*Wilson* Sir Adam Wilson, KC (1814–91). In 1859 he was the first popularly elected mayor of Toronto and became chief justice of the Court of Queen's Bench in Ontario 1884–7. He was knighted in 1887.

*Wilton* After Sarah Lambert, who married the Hon George Crookshank, originally from Wilton, Conn. *See* Crookshank. Wilton Street was later called Crocker Avenue after James Crocker, alderman for St Stephen's Ward 1875–89. *See* Crocker.

*Withrow* John J. Withrow, of Withrow and Hillock, lumber dealers. Withrow was alderman 1873–8, a founder of the CNE, and its president 1879–1900.

*Wolseley* Col Garnet Joseph Wolseley (1833–1913), later Viscount Wolseley, who came to Canada in 1861 as assistant quartermaster-general. In 1870 he commanded the force sent west to the Red River to quell the Riel insurrection. Wolseley Street was formerly Monck Street. *See* Garnet.

*Wood* Alexander Wood in 1826 purchased from Mrs Mary Elmsley twenty-five acres lying north of Carlton Street. *See* Alexander.

*Woodbine* Name of the residence of Joseph Duggan, proprietor of Woodbine Park Hotel; subsequently, the grounds of the race course

*WoodGreen* WoodGreen Methodist Church, founded in 1875. It was given the combined name in honour of Rev Dr Enoch Wood, president of the Toronto Annual Conference, and Rev Anson Green, who conducted the opening services.

*Woodlawn* An estate of that name was owned by Mr Justice Joseph Curran Morrison (1816–85). Born in Ireland, he came to Canada in 1832 and was educated at Upper Canada College.

*Worts* James Worts of Gooderham and Worts. *See* Gooderham.

*Wyatt* Charles Burton Wyatt, third son of James Wyatt (1748–1822?), architect. In 1804 he was appointed surveyor-general of Upper Canada. He moved to York after a runaway marriage that alienated his father. He returned to England in 1807 after a 'series of collisions' with Lt-Gov Francis Gore (1806–17).

*Yarmouth* After Yarmouth, England, birthplace of Robert Turner, a major property owner in the Davenport Road district who immigrated to Canada about 1840. *See* Turner.

*Yonge* Named by Gov Simcoe after Sir George Yonge, MP for Honiton, England, and secretary of State for War 1782–94. One of the first streets laid out by Gov Simcoe, it extended in 1794 from York at Bloor Street to Lake Simcoe. Originally Toronto Street south of Lot (Queen) Street. *See* Bay, York.

*York* The western boundary of the town of York when its boundaries were enlarged for the first time in 1797. The next two streets east of York Street having the same alignment were called Bay and Toronto (the latter soon renamed Yonge, after its northerly extension), providing a neat geographic aphorism: York, Bay (of) Toronto.

*Yorkville* After the village of Yorkville, which extended from Sherbourne Street to a point opposite old McMaster University, and from Bloor Street north to approximately the CPR tracks. Yorkville was annexed in 1883.

# Bibliography

## Collections of Papers, Photographs, and Drawings

METROPOLITAN TORONTO LIBRARY, BALDWIN ROOM

Robert Baldwin Papers
W.W. Baldwin Papers
John Elmsley Letter Book
J.G. Howard Papers and Collection of architects' drawings
William Jarvis Papers
Langley Collection of architectural drawings
William H. Pim Papers
Peter Russell Papers
D.W. Smith Papers
Strachan Papers

ONTARIO ARCHIVES

Baldwin Papers
J.C.B. and E.C. Horwood Collection of architectural drawings and
related materials
Langley Collection of architectural drawings

MCGILL UNIVERSITY, MCCORD MUSEUM

Notman Photographic Archives

PUBLIC ARCHIVES OF CANADA

National Photography Collection

## Eighteenth- and Nineteenth-Century Newspapers and Magazines

*British Colonist*
*British Canadian*
*Builder* (London, England)
*Canadian Architect and Builder*
*Canadian Correspondent*
*Canadian Freeman*
*Canadian Illustrated News*
*Canadian Review*
*Christian Guardian*
*Church*
*Colonial Advocate*
*Courier of Upper Canada*
*Daily Colonist*
*Dominion Illustrated*
*Examiner*
*Globe*
*Herald*
*Illustrated London News* (London, England)
*Leader*
*Loyalist*
*Mail and Empire*
*Morning Star*
*North American*
*Observer*
*Patriot and Farmers' Monitor*
*Star*
*Telegram*
*U.E. Loyalist*
*Upper Canada Almanack*
*Upper Canada Gazette* (or *American Oracle*)
*York Gazette*

## Books and Articles

Publications of a general nature, such as biographical collections, encyclopaedias, atlases, etc (unless containing substantial text), are not listed. Publishers are not designated for any works previous to 1940.

Adam, G. Mercer *Toronto, Old and New* Toronto 1891
André, John *William Berczy* Published by the author 1967
André, John, Stephen A. Otto, and Douglas Richardson *William Kauffmann,*

*1821/2-1875* Society for the Study of Architecture in Canada, Selected Papers, 1982

Armstrong, C.H.A. *The Honourable Society of Osgoode Hall* With an essay on 'The History and Architecture of the Fabric' by E.R. Arthur. Toronto: Clarke, Irwin 1952

Armstrong, F.H. 'The First Great Fire of Toronto, 1849' *Ontario History* 53 (1961) 201–21

– 'The Rebuilding of Toronto after the Great Fire of 1849' *Ontario History* 53 (1961) 233–49

– *Toronto in Transition: The Emergence of a City, 1828–1838* PH D diss, Toronto 1965

*Art Work on Toronto* Toronto 1898

Arthur, Eric R. *From Front Street to Queen's Park* Toronto: McClelland and Stewart 1979

Barnett, W.E., and others *St Lawrence Hall* Toronto: Thomas Nelson & Sons 1969

Bethune, A.N. *Memoir of the Right Rev. John Strachan, First Bishop of Toronto* Toronto 1870

Bissell, Claude T., ed *University College, a Portrait, 1853–1953* Toronto: University of Toronto Press 1953

Bland, John 'Osgoode Hall' R.A.I.C. JOURNAL (July 1959)

Bonnycastle, Sir Richard H. *The Canadas in 1841* London 1841–2

– *Canada and the Canadians in 1846* London 1846

Bouchette, Joseph *The British Dominions in North America* London 1832

Bridle, Augustus *The Story of the Club* Toronto 1945

Brown, Donald A. *Fort Rouillé Excavation, Summer 1982* Toronto: Learnx Press 1983

Bull, William Perkins *Spadunk; or, From Paganism to Davenport United* Toronto 1935

Card, Raymond *The Ontario Association of Architects, 1890–1950* Toronto: University of Toronto Press 1950

Careless, J.M.S. *Toronto to 1918* Toronto: James Lorimer and Company and the National Museums of Canada 1984

*City of Toronto Illustrated* Toronto, Sept 1888

Clarke, C.K. *A History of the Toronto General Hospital* Toronto 1913

Colgate, William *Canadian Art* Toronto: Ryerson Press 1943

Collard, Edgar A. *Canadian Yesterdays* Toronto: Longmans Green 1955

Colvin, H.H. *A Biographical Dictionary of British Architects, 1600–1840* London: John Murray 1978

*Commemorative Biographical Record of the County of York, Ontario* Toronto 1907

Cruikshank, E.A., ed *The Correspondence of the Honourable Peter Russell* 3 vols. Toronto 1932–6

– *The Correspondence of Lieut. Governor John Graves Simcoe* 5 vols. Toronto 1923–31

Curry, S.G. 'Architecture: Looking Back' *Construction* (June 1929)

Dendy, William *Lost Toronto* Toronto: Oxford University Press 1978

De Volpi, Charles P. *Toronto, A Pictorial Record* Toronto: Dev-Sco Publications 1965

Dickens, Charles *American Notes and Pictures from Italy* London 1842

Dufferin and Ava, Marchioness of *My Canadian Journal* London 1891

Fidler, Isaac *Observations on the Professions, Literature, Manners and Emigration in the United States and Canada* London 1833

Firth, Edith G., ed *The Town of York, 1793–1815* Toronto: University of Toronto Press 1962

– *The Town of York, 1815–1834* Toronto: University of Toronto Press 1966

Firth, Edith G. *Toronto in Art* Toronto: Fitzhenry and Whiteside 1983

– 'Prologue to Toronto' *Canadian Collector* (May–June 1984)

Galt, John *Autobiography* London 1833

Gentilcore, R. Louis, and C. Grant Head *Ontario's History in Maps* Toronto: University of Toronto Press 1984

Gowans, Alan *Looking at Architecture in Canada* Toronto: Oxford University Press 1958

– *Building Canada, An Architectural History of Canadian Life* Toronto: Oxford University Press 1966

Grant, G.M., ed *Picturesque Canada* Toronto 1879

Guillet, E.C. *Early Life in Upper Canada* Toronto: Ontario Publishing Co 1933; repr University of Toronto Press 1963

– *Toronto: From Trading Post to Great City* Toronto: Ontario Publishing Co 1934

– *Pioneer Inns and Taverns* 4 vols. Published by the author 1954–8

Halpenny, Francess G., gen ed *Dictionary of Canadian Biography* 9 vols published to present. Toronto: University of Toronto Press 1966–

Hamilton, James Cleland *Osgoode Hall: Reminiscences of the Bench and Bar* Toronto 1904

Heriot, George *Travels through the Canadas* London 1807

*Historical Atlas of the County of York* Toronto 1878

*History of Toronto and County of York, Ontario* 2 vols. Toronto 1885

Hitchcock, H.R. *Early Victorian Architecture in Britain* 2 vols. New Haven: Yale University Press 1954

Hopkins, J. Castell *Toronto, an Historical Sketch* Toronto 1893

Howard, John G. *Incidents in the Life of J.G. Howard, Esq., of Colborne Lodge, High Park* Toronto 1885

Hubbard, R.H. 'Canadian Gothic' *Architectural Review* (August 1954)

Humphries, Charles W. 'The Capture of York' *Ontario History* 51 (1959) 1–21

*Illustrated Toronto: The Queen City of Canada* Toronto 1890

Innis, Mary Quayle, ed *Mrs. Simcoe's Diary* Toronto: Macmillan 1965

Jameson, Anna *Winter Studies and Summer Rambles in Canada* London 1838

Langton, John *Early Days in Upper Canada: Letters of John Langton* Ed W.A. Langton. Toronto 1926

Lownsborough, John *The Privileged Few* Toronto: Art Gallery of Ontario 1980

Lizars, K.M. *The Valley of the Humber* Toronto 1913

MacDonald, Edith *Golden Jubilee, 1869–1919: The Fiftieth Anniversary of the T. Eaton Co.* Toronto 1919

Macmurchy, Angus, and T.A. Reed *Our Royal Town of York* Toronto 1929

MacRae, Marion, and Anthony Adamson *The Ancestral Roof* Toronto: Clarke, Irwin 1963

– *Hallowed Walls* Toronto: Clarke, Irwin 1975

– *Cornerstones of Order* Toronto: Clarke, Irwin 1983

MacTavish, Newton *The Fine Arts in Canada* Toronto 1925

McEvoy, H. *The Province of Ontario: Gazeteer and Directory* Toronto 1869

McHugh, Patricia *Toronto Architecture, A City Guide* Published by the author 1985

Martyn, Lucy Booth *Toronto, 100 Years of Grandeur* Toronto: Pagurian Press 1978

– *Aristocratic Toronto* Toronto: Gage Publishing 1980

Masters, D.C. *The Rise of Toronto, 1850–90* Toronto: University of Toronto Press 1947

Meredith, A.G. *Mary's Rosedale and Gossip of Little York* Toronto 1928

Middleton, Jesse Edgar *The Municipality of Toronto: A History* 3 vols. Toronto 1923

– *Toronto's Hundred Years* Toronto 1934

Mosser, Christine, ed *York, Upper Canada, Minutes of Town Meetings and Lists of Inhabitants, 1793–1823* Toronto: Metropolitan Toronto Library Board 1984

Mulvany, C. Pelham *Toronto, Past and Present* Toronto 1884

O'Brien, Roberta M. *The Prehistory of South Central Ontario* Toronto: Ontario Ministry of Culture and Recreation 1980

Pearson, W.H. *Recollections and Records of Toronto of Old* Toronto 1914

*Picturesque Toronto* Toronto 1885

Reed, T.A. 'The Historic Value of Street Names' Ontario Historical Society *Papers and Records* 1929

– *A History of the University of Trinity College, 1852–1952* Toronto: University of Toronto Press 1952

– 'The Story of Toronto, 1871–1958' Ontario Historical Society, *Papers and Records* 1934

– 'Records of Toronto' Toronto Historical Society, *Papers* 1934

– 'Toronto's Early Architects' R.A.I.C. *Journal* (Feb 1950)

– A History of the Church of Holy Trinity, 1871–1910. Ms, 1955

– Four volumes of photographs with notes. Baldwin Room, Metropolitan Toronto Library

– A Toronto Bibliography. Ms, Ontario Archives

Rempel, John I. *Building with Wood* Rev edn. Toronto: University of Toronto Press 1980

Roberton, T.B. *The Fighting Bishop* Ottawa 1926

Robertson, John Ross *Landmarks of Toronto* 6 vols. Toronto 1894–1914
– *What Art Has Done for Canadian History* Toronto 1917
– Four volumes of photographs. Baldwin Room, Metropolitan Toronto Library
Robinson, Blackett C. *History of York County (Including Toronto)* 2 vols. Toronto
      1885
Robinson, Percy J. *Toronto during the French Régime* Toronto 1933; repr University
      of Toronto Press 1964
Rochefoucauld-Liancourt, Duke de la *Travels through the United States of North
      America, the Country of the Iroquois, and Upper Canada, 1795–97* London 1799
Scadding, Henry *Toronto of Old: Collections and Recollections* Toronto 1873
– *History of the Old French Fort at Toronto and Its Government* Toronto 1887
Scadding, Henry, and Charles Dent *Toronto Past and Present* Toronto 1884
Selz, Peter and Mildred Constantine *Art Nouveau* New York: Museum of Modern
      Art 1959
Shuttleworth, E.B. *The Windmill and its times* Toronto 1924
Spendlove, F. St George *The Face of Early Canada* Toronto: Ryerson Press 1958
Sylvester, Alfred *Sketches of Toronto* Toronto 1858
Taylor, C.C. *Toronto Called Back, from 1892 to 1847* Toronto 1947
Thompson, Austin Seton *Spadina, a Story of Old Toronto* Toronto: Pagurian Press
      1975
– *Jarvis Street, a Story of Triumph and Tragedy* Toronto: Personal Library Publishers
      1980
Timperlake, J. *Illustrated Toronto, Past and Present* Toronto 1876
*Toronto, Photographs in Black and White* New York 1891
*Toronto Illustrated* Toronto 1893
Trollope, Anthony *North America* New York 1862
Walker, Frank N. 'Doorways That Welcome' *Canadian Banker* (Spring 1959)
Wallace, W. Stewart *A History of the University of Toronto* Toronto 1926
Walling, H.F., ed *Toronto in the Camera* Toronto 1868
Yeigh, Frank *Ontario's Parliament Buildings, 1792–1892* Toronto 1893

## Directories, Handbooks, Almanacs, and Yearbooks

1833–1900 York and Toronto City Directories
1834 Swift's Almanac
1851 The Canada Directory
1858 Descriptive Catalogue of the Provincial Exhibition
      The Handbook of Toronto. By a member of the Press (G.P. Ure)
1860–1900 Nelson and Sons, Handbooks
1874 The Toronto Illustrated Almanac for the Year 1874
1898 Fraser's Official Guide Book of Canada
      Official Guide and Souvenir of Toronto

# Index

References to illustrations are by page number followed by illustration number, and follow all references to the text proper within each subsection. Illustration numbers appear in bold-face; main appendix entries for individual architects, builders, and contractors are in italics.

Adelaide Buildings 146, **4.110**. *See also* Thomas, William 261

Aitkin, Alexander 6, 16, 21, 32, 33; his plan of York Harbour 13, **2.3**

Albert Buildings 146, **4.110**

Allan, William 51, 56; his residence Moss Park 65, **3.39**

Allan, William, contractor *266*

Allegheny County Court House. *See* Pittsburgh Court House

Angell, Edward 75, *241*

Argus Corporation building. *See* Post Office (1851)

Armouries 188; 209, **5.80**. *See also* Fuller, Thomas 247

Art Nouveau 189

Arts and Crafts movement 189

Austin, James. *See* Spadina (1866)

Baby, James 8

Badgley, Sidney Rose *241*; Massey Hall 215, **5.89**

Bagot, Sir Charles 98

Baldwin, William Warren 33, 50–1, 68, 74, 75, 80, 90, 237, *241*; residence at Front and Bay 45; 38, **3.7**; Spadina (first house, 1818) 43, 45; (second house, 1836) 38, **3.6**

Bank of British North America (1845) 84, **4.21**. *See also* Howard, John George 251; Ritchey, John 269

Bank of British North America (1871) 171, **5.19**. *See also* Langley, Henry 254; Walton, Benjamin 270

Bank of Commerce (1867) 154, **4.123**

Bank of Commerce (1889) 176. *See also* Waite, Richard Alfred 262–3

Bank of Commerce (1898) 218, **5.94**. *See also* Darling, Frank 244

Bank of Montreal (1845) 85, **4.22**. *See also* Ritchey, John 269; Tully, Kivas 262

Bank of Montreal (1885) 225; 185, **5.39–41**; 206, **5.77**. *See also* Darling, Frank 244; Yorke, Lionel 271

Bank of Nova Scotia 218, **5.96**. *See also* Darling, Frank 244

Bank of Toronto (1862) 155, **4.124**. *See also* Kauffmann, William 253; Storm, Thomas 270; Worthington Brothers 271

Bank of Toronto (1912) 210. *See also* Bird, Eustace Godfrey 242

Bank of Upper Canada 61, 75, 80; 58, **3.31**; 59, **3.33**. *See also* Kennedy, McArthur & Co 267; Ritchey, John 269

Barnum House at Grafton, Ontario 39
Bartlett, William Henry, his drawing of
    Ontario House 48, **3.21**
Beikie, John, residence of 26, **2.13**
Bellevue. *See* Denison, George Taylor
Bennett, John 32
Benvenuto 200–1, **5.65–8**
Berczy, William 75, 230, *241*; Russell
    Abbey 24
Berkeley House. *See* Small, John
Beverley House. *See* Robinson, John
    Beverley
Bird, Eustace Godfrey *242*
Bishop's Palace 152; 96, **4.42**. *See also*
    Thomas, William 261
Board of Trade building 184, 188; 206,
    **5.77**. *See also* Brown, [John] Francis 242;
    James, Arthur H. & John King 252
Bouchette, Joseph 15, 16
Boultbee, Alfred E. *242*
Boulton, D'Arcy Jr, his residence the
    Grange xv; 54, **3.27, 28**
Boulton, H.J., his residence Holland
    House 48, **3.20**
Boulton, William Henry 101
Brock, Sir Isaac 50
Brown, A. Page. *See* Benvenuto
Brown, George 124
Brown, [John] Francis *242*
Brown and Love *266*
Brown Brothers book bindery and
    stationery warehouse 146, **4.110**
Brulé, Etienne 3, 4
Brunel, Alfred *242*
Burke, Edmund 238, *242–3*; 240, **A.1**;
    Robert Simpson Store 213, **5.84, 85**
Burke, William. *See* Smith, Burke & Co
Burnham, Daniel Hudson 157

Campbell, Sir William, his residence
    Campbell House xv, 61; 44, **3.15**
Campbell House. *See* Campbell, Sir
    William
Canada Company building. *See* Quetton St
    George, Laurent
Canada Life building 176. *See also* Waite,
    Richard Alfred 262–3
Canada Permanent Building. *See* Masonic
    Hall
Canadian Imperial Bank of Commerce. *See*
    Bank of Commerce
Cane, James, his plan of Toronto 81, **4.18**

Capreol, F.C., residence of 84, **4.23**
Carleton, Sir Guy 10, 11, 15, 16
Cartwright, Richard 30–1
cast iron, its use in architecture 176, 188–9
Castle Frank. *See* Simcoe, John Graves
Cawthra, John, shop of 146, **4.110**
Cawthra, William. *See* Cawthra House
Cawthra House xvi; 112, **4.65**. *See also*
    Sheard, Joseph 258
Cayley, Francis, his residence Drumsnab
    66, **3.44**
Chadwick, [William Craven] Vaux *243*
Chewett, James Grant 51, *243*
Chewett, William 51; his plan and
    drawings of Maryville Lodge 22–3,
    **2.7–9**
Chicago Exhibition 202, 210
Chicago Movement 157, 163, 169
Church at York 35–6
Church of the Redeemer 220, **5.99**. *See also*
    Smith, James Avon 259; Yorke, Lionel
    271
City Hall (1831) 62, 117, 124, 125; 63,
    **3.37, 38**. *See also* Chewett, James Grant
    243; Allan, William 266
City Hall (1844) 124, 227; 87, **4.26**. *See
    also* Lane, Henry Bowyer Joseph 254;
    McDonald & Young 268; Stewart,
    William 259–60
City Hall (1889) 157, 169, 175, 176,
    189, 224, 230; 190–3, **5.46–52**. *See also*
    Dinnis, Richard 266; Elliott & Neelon
    266; Lennox, Edward James 255
City Hall (1961) 226–7, 228, 229, 230
City Jail. *See* Jail (1858)
Cochrane, John 84, **4.21**; 96, **4.42**; 122, **4.78**
Colborne, Sir John 74, 93
Colborne Lodge 71, **4.5, 6**. *See also*
    Howard, John George 251
Collier Street, houses on 227, **5.104**
Commercial Bank x, 100, 152; 83, **4.19,
    20**; 84, **4.23**. *See also* Thomas, William
    261
Confederation Life building 207, **5.78**. *See
    also* Brown and Love 266; Gray, James
    Wilson 248–9; Knox, Wilm 253
Connolly, Joseph 93, *243*; St Mary's
    Church 186, **5.42, 43**; St Michael's
    Cathedral 94–5, **4.39, 40**; St Paul's Church
    (1887) 187, **5.44, 45**
Consumers' Gas offices 179, **5.29**. *See also*
    Brown and Love 266; Dick, David

Brash 245; Stephenson & Co, Edward 270

Coronelli 6; his map of North America 4, 1.2

County of York Court House. See Court House (1851)

Court House (1824) 61; 46, 3.16, 17. See also Baldwin, William Warren 241; Ewart, John 247

Court House (1851) 144; 113, 4.66, 67. See also Cumberland, Frederic William 243–4; Ritchey, John 269

Crookshank, George, residence of 26, 2.13

Crystal Palace (first, 1858) 178; 204, 5.72. See also Fleming, Sir Sandford 247; Smith, Burke & Co 269

Crystal Palace (second) 204, 5.73

Cumberland, Frederic William xi, xii, 108, 130, 131, 136, 144, 145, 237, 238, 243–4; Chapel of St James-the-Less 134, 4.95; Edinburgh Life Assurance building 84, 4.23; houses for J. Lukin Robinson 132, 4.92; Mechanics' Institute 115, 4.69; Normal School 110, 4.61; Osgoode Hall 102, 4.48; 106, 4.55; Pendarves 150, 4.117; Post Office (1851) 127, 4.85; second Court House (1851) 113, 4.66; St James' Cathedral (1850) 129, 4.86; University College 139, 4.99

Curry, [Samuel] George 175, 238, 244; 240, A.1

Custom House 85, 4.22; 173, 5.21. See also Walton, Benjamin 270; Windeyer, Richard Cunningham 263

Danforth, Asa 31

Darling, Frank 130, 175, 238, 239, 244–5; Bank of Commerce (1898) 218, 5.94; Bank of Montreal (1885) 185, 5.39–41; Bank of Nova Scotia 218, 5.96; Toronto Club 218, 5.95; Trinity College gates 126, 4.83

Davenport. See Wells, Joseph

Deane and Woodward. See Oxford Museum, England

Denison, Arthur Richard 238, 244–5

Denison, George Taylor, his residence Bellevue 40, 3.8

Dick, David Brash 151, 238, 245; Consumers' Gas offices 179, 5.29; Sword's Hotel 133, 4.93; University College 140, 4.101; University of Toronto Library 199, 5.64

Dick, Norman Bethune 245; 240, A.1

Dickens, Charles 68

Dinnis, Richard 266

Disciples Church. See West Presbyterian Church

Dominion Bank 179, 5.30. See also Browne and Love 266; Irving, William 252

Don Jail. See Jail (1858)

Dorchester, Lord. See Carleton, Sir Guy

Douville, sieur 7, 8

Draper, William Henry, residence of 30

Drumsnab. See Cayley, Francis

Dufaux, Joseph 7

Duggan, George & Thomas 36

Durand, George F. 245; Upper Canada College (1889) 195, 5.56

Durham, Lord 114, 116

Eaton store 212, 5.86

Edinburgh Life Assurance building 84, 4.23. See also Cumberland, Frederic William 243–4

Edwards, Robert James 245; 240, A.1

eighth Post Office. See Post Office

Elgin, Lord 116

Elizabeth Street, stores on 109, 4.57

Elliot, John Harlock 245–6

Elliot and Sons 198

Elliott & Neelon 266

Ellis, James Augustus 246

Elmsley, John 33; his residence Elmsley House 20, 56, 61

Elmsley House. See Elmsley, John

Engelhardt, Heinrich Adolph 246

[Enoch Turner] Schoolhouse 88, 4.30

Ewart, John 61, 74, 80, 100, 101, 239, 247; Osgoode Hall 103, 4.49; second jail (1824) 47, 3.18; St Andrew's Church (1830) 47, 3.19; Upper Canada College (1829) 64, 3.40

Excelsior Life Building 170, 5.17

Farmers' Market 123, 4.81

Farquhar, James 266

Farquhar, William 266

Fénelon, Abbé 5, 90

first City Hall. See City Hall (1831)

first Court House. See Court House (1824)

first jail. See Jail (1799)

Fitz-Gibbon, James 90

flat-iron building. *See* Gooderham Building
Fleming, Sir Sandford 237, *247;* Crystal
    Palace 204, **5.72**
Forbes, Duncan. *See* Metcalfe, Wilson &
    Forbes
Ford & Hayden *266–7;* jail (1824) 47, **3.18**
Foresters' building. *See* Temple Building
Fort Rouillé xvi–xvii, 6, 7, 8; 9, **1.3, 4**
Fort Toronto 7, 8; 4, **1.1**; 9, **1.3**
Fort York xv–xvi, 230; officers'
    quarters 41, **3.10**
fourth City Hall. *See* City Hall (1961)
fourth jail. *See* Jail (1858)
Fowler, Charles xiv, 93, 98; his drawing
    for a University of King's College at
    York 99, **4.45**
Fowler, Joseph Ades *247*
Fuller, Thomas *247;* Armouries 209, **5.80**;
    St Stephen's-in-the-Fields 135, **4.96**

Galerie des Machines, Paris 188
Galt, John 68, 73
Ganatsekwyagon (Canatehekiagon) 5, 6; 4,
    **1.2**
Garrison Church. *See* St John the
    Evangelist Anglican Church
Gearing, Joseph, residence of 161, **5.7**
Gemmell, John 175, *247*; 240, **A.1**
Gerrard Street, houses on 65, **3.42**; 150, **4.118**
Gibraltar Point lighthouse 43; 37, **3.3**
Gibson, Charles J. *248;* house for John
    Miller 214, **5.88**; McLaughlin Flour
    Mills 162, **5.9**
Gillespie, John: his sketch of the Wellington
    Hotel 49, **3.22**; his painting of the first
    City Hall 63, **3.38**
Givens, Philip 230
Givins, Angelica 56
Givins, James 33; residence of 43, 56; 38,
    **3.5**. *See also* Berczy, William 241
Glennon, James 33
*Globe*, offices of 53, **5.24**
Golden Griffin 158, **5.1**
Golden Lion 158, **5.2**; 159, **5.3**. *See also*
    Farquhar, William 266; Irving, William
    252; Wagner, Jacob P. 270
Gooderham, George 210
Gooderham and Worts distillery 161, **5.8**.
    *See also* Roberts, David Sr 257; Smith,
    Burke & Co 269
Gooderham Building 196, **5.57**. *See also*
    Roberts, David Jr 257

Gooderham house. *See* York Club
Gordon, Henry Bauld 175, *248*; 240, **A.1**
Gore, Sir Francis 45, 50
Gouinlock, George Wallace 188, *248*;
    Temple Building 208, **5.79**
Goulstone, George T. *248*
Government House 20; 19, **2.5**
Graham, William 27, 28
Grand, James *248*; Toronto Exchange 119,
    **4.71–3**
Grand Opera House 172, **5.20**
Grange. *See* Boulton, D'Arcy Jr
Grant, Alexander, residence of 76, **4.10**
Grasett, Dr Henry James 131, 137
Gray, James, his drawing of York 37, **3.4**
Gray, James Wilson *248–9*
Greenshields, J.H., store of 168, **5.15**
Gregg, Alfred Holden *249*
Gregg, William Rufus *249*; 240, **A.1**
Gropius, Walter 163
Gundry, Thomas 93, 237, *249*;
    Oaklands 149, **4.115**; St Michael's
    Cathedral spire 94, **4.38**; warehouse of
    John Macdonald 149, **4.116**
Gwynne, Charles William, residence of 77,
    **4.11**
Gzowski, Sir Casimir 137; residence
    of 181, **5.34**

Hahn, Gustav 189, 198; 206, **5.76**
Hale, Elizabeth F. 24
Half Way House 26, **2.13**; 78, **4.14**
Hall, Francis 75, 80, *249*; his design for a
    Province House at York 52, **3.23**
Harbord Street Collegiate 212, **5.87**. *See
    also* Knox, Wilm 253
Harper, George Robinson *249–50*; Oak
    Hall 205, **5.74**; police court, station, and
    fire hall 172, **5.28**
Harper, John *267*
Haworth, Thomas, store of 155, **4.125**. *See
    also* Kauffmann, William 253
Hay, William 90, 130, 237, 239, *250*;
    Oaklands 149, **4.115**; St Basil's Church
    and St Michael's College 120–1, **4.75–7**;
    Toronto General Hospital 115, **4.68**;
    Trinity College chapel 127, **4.84**;
    Yorkville Town Hall 148, **4.113, 114**
Hayden, William. *See* Ford & Hayden
Hayter, Elizabeth 68
Head, Sir Edmund xii, 144, 145
Helliwell, Grant 175, 238, *250*

Hennepin, Father xvii
Holbrook and Mollington 185, **5.39–41**
Holland, William *250*
Holland House. *See* Boulton, H.J.
Holmes, Arthur W. *250*; St Mary's
  Church spire 186, **5.42, 43**
Holy Blossom Synagogue 217, **5.92, 93**.
  *See also* Siddall, John Wilson 258
Holy Trinity. *See* Trinity Church (1846)
Home District Court House and Jail. *See*
  Court House (1824), Jail (1824)
Home District Grammar School 35, 36
Horwood, John Charles Batstone *250–1*
Howard, John George 6, 74, 80, 101,
  131, 237, 239, *251*; Bank of British
  North America (1845) 84, **4.21**; building
  of A.V. Brown, grocers 84, **4.21**;
  Colborne Lodge 71, **4.5, 6**; design for a
  public building on King Street 70, **4.3**;
  George Keith and Son store 110, **4.60**;
  Kearnsey House 109, **4.58**; King's
  College gates 160, **5.5**; Mental
  Asylum 91, **4.34, 35**; plan for a dentist's
  surgery 72, **4.7**; St Andrew's Church
  spire 47, **3.19**; third jail (1838) 79, **4.16**;
  three designs for a house 72, **4.8**
Howland, [William] Ford *252*
Hughes Brothers, shop of. *See* Golden
  Griffin
Hunter, Peter 20, 28
Huron Indians 3, 5
Hutchison and Co building 118, **4.70**
Hynes, James Patrick *252*
Hynes Brothers 106, **4.55**

Independent Order of Foresters' building.
  *See* Temple Building (1895)
Iroquois League 3, 5
Irvine, Robert: his painting of three houses
  at York 26, **2.13**; of the Gibraltar Point
  lighthouse 37, **3.3**
Irving, William 238, *252*; Dominion
  Bank 179, **5.30**; Golden Lion 159, **5.3**;
  A.R. McMaster warehouse 171, **5.18**;
  Ontario Bank 153, **4.119–21**

jail (1799) 18, **2.6**
jail (1824) 61; 46, **3.16, 17**; 47, **3.18**. *See also*
  Baldwin, William Warren 241; Ewart,
  John 247; Ford & Hayden 266–7
jail (1838) 79, **4.16**. *See also* Howard, John
  George 251
Jail (1858) 146, **4.109**; 147, **4.111, 112**. *See*

*also* Tate, George 270; Thomas,
  William 261
James, Arthur H. & John King 184, 252;
  Board of Trade building 206, **5.77**
James and James. *See* Board of Trade
  building
Jameson, Anna xii, 62, 67, 73, 74
Janes, S.H. *See* Benvenuto
Jarvis, [Edgar] Beaumont *252*; Loretto
  Abbey chapel 216, **5.91**
Jarvis, Samuel P. 74, 137
Jarvis, William 17, 20, 27, 68; plan for his
  residence 26, **2.12**
Jenney, William Le Baron 157
Jennings Church 96, **4.43**. *See also* Metcalfe,
  Wilson & Forbes 268; Thomas,
  William 261
Johnston, John 131, 239, *252*; his
  engraving of Knox's Church 97, **4.4**
Jones, Chilion *252–3*
Jordan's Hotel 30, 56, 62

Kane, Paul 74
Kauffmann, William 237–8, *253*; Bank of
  Toronto (1862) 15, **4.124**; Masonic
  Hall 133, **4.94**; Rossin House 132, **4.90**;
  Royal Insurance building 154, **4.122, 123**
Kearnsey House 109, **4.58**. *See also*
  Howard, John George 251; Storm,
  Thomas 270
Keith, George, and Son, store of 110,
  **4.60**
Kennedy, McArthur & Co *267*
Kennedy, Thomas *253*
King Edward Hotel 219, **5.97**
King Street, shops on 65, **3.41**
King's College 98, 100, 125, 137; 99,
  **4.46**. *See also* Young, Thomas 263–4;
  Ritchey, John 269
King's College gates 160, **5.5**. *See also*
  Howard, John George 251
Knox, Wilm *253*; Confederation Life
  building 207, **5.78**; Harbord Street
  Collegiate 212, **5.87**
Knox College 220, **5.100**. *See also* Smith,
  James Avon 259
Knox's Church 97, **4.44**. *See also* Fleming,
  Sir Sandford 247; McBean & Withrow
  268; Metcalfe, Wilson & Forbes 268;
  Thomas, William 261

Laforce, René-Hippolyte, his map of Fort
  Rouillé 9, **1.4**

Laing, David 57
Lalor, George Hughes *253–4*
Lane, Henry Bowyer Joseph 80, 90, 100,
    101, *254*; Church of St George the
    Martyr 86, **4.24**; Holy Trinity Church
    (1846) 89, **4.32**; Little Trinity Church
    (1843) 88, **4.28, 29**; Osgoode Hall 103,
    **4.49**; second City Hall (1844) 87, **4.26**;
    sketch of the Grange 54, **3.27**
Langley, Charles 239, *254*
Langley, Henry 93, 238, 239, *254*; 240,
    **A.1**; Bank of British North America
    (1871) 171, **5.19**; eighth Post Office
    (1871) 170, **5.16**; John Macdonald
    warehouse (enlargement) 149, **4.116**;
    Metropolitan Church (1870) 221, **5.101,
    102**; Necropolis chapel and lodge 167,
    **5.12**; St James' Cathedral spire 128, **4.88**
Langton, Hugh xii
Langton, John xii, 144–5
Langton, William xi, 144, *254–5*; 240, **A.1**
Latham, Jacob, residence of 76, **4.10**
Law, Frederick Charles *255*
Lawrence, Joseph 73
Le Corbusier 163, 226
legislative buildings. *See* Parliament
    buildings
Lennox, Edward James 169, 210, *255*;
    Excelsior Life Building 170, **5.11**;
    Manning Arcade 183, **5.38**; Dr G.R.
    McDonagh house 203, **5.71**; third City
    Hall (1889) 190, **5.46**; Toronto Athletic
    Club 195, **5.55**; Victoria Orange
    Hall 182, **5.37**
Little Trinity. *See* Trinity Church (1843)
Loretto Abbey 216, **5.91**. *See also* Jarvis,
    [Edgar] Beaumont 252
Love, Henry G. *See* Brown and Love
Lowther Avenue, houses on 87, **4.27**
Lucas, Henry 267

McArthur, Peter. *See* Kennedy, McArthur
    and Co
McBean & Withrow *268*
McCaul, Dr John 145
Macaulay, James 68; his residence Teraulay
    Cottage 80, 82; 89, **4.31**
McConkey, George S., restaurant of 182,
    **5.35**
McDonagh, G.R., residence of 203, **5.71**.
    *See also* Lennox, Edward James 255
McDonald & Young *268*. *See also* Young,
    Thomas 263–4

Macdonald, John: his residence Oaklands
    149, **4.115**; his warehouse 149, **4.116**. *See
    also* Gundry, Thomas 249; Langley,
    Henry 254; Worthington Brothers 271
Macdonald, Sir John A. 124
MacDougall, Peter, residence of 49, **3.22**
McGill, Ann xiii
McGill, John 28, 33, 51
Mackenzie, Alex 175
Mackenzie, William Lyon 17, 39, 43, 68,
    98, 101, 114; residence of 69, **4.1, 2**
McLaughlin Flour Mills 162, **5.9**. *See also*
    Gibson, Charles J. 248
McMaster, A.R.: residence of 214, **5.90**;
    warehouse of 171, **5.18**; 206, **5.77**. *See
    also* Irving, William 252; Yorke,
    Lionel 271
Magann, G.P. *See* Thorncrest
Maitland, Sir Peregrine 36, 57
Mann, Gother 11, 16, 28; his plan of
    'Toronto' 12, **2.2**
Manning, Alexander 267
Manning Arcade 183, **5.38**. *See also* Brown
    and Love 266; Lennox, Edward
    James 255
Manufacturers' Building 188
Marani, Cesare 239, *255*
markets: first 61; second 62; Farmers'
    123; St Patrick's 120. *See also* City Hall
    (1831)
Marshall, Robert, bookstore of 168, **5.14**
Marshall Field store 169
Marther, Samuel 24
Maryville Lodge. *See* Smith, D.W.
Masonic Hall 133, **4.94**; 170, **5.17**. *See also*
    Kauffman, William 253; Worthington
    Brothers 271
Massey Hall 215, **5.89**. *See also* Badgley,
    Sidney Rose 241; Miller, George
    Martell 255
Massey house. *See* McMaster, Arthur R.
Mechanics' Institute 115, **4.69**. *See also*
    Cumberland, Frederic William 243–4;
    Pim, William Henry 268–9; Walton,
    Benjamin 270
Mental Asylum 101; 91, **4.34, 35**. *See also*
    Harper, John 267; Howard, John
    George 251; Metcalfe, Wilson &
    Forbes 268; Ritchey, John 269
Metcalfe, Wilson & Forbes 130, 268
Methodist Church (1818) 36
Methodist Church (1832) 46, **3.16**; 113,
    **4.67**. *See also* Petch, Robert 268

Methodist Church (1844) 86, **4.25**
Metropolitan Church (1870) 56, 225; 221, **5.101, 102**. *See also* Langley, Henry 254
Miles, Abner 17
Millen, Robert, residence of 55, **3.30**
Millen Cottage. *See* Millen, Robert
Miller, George Martell *255*
Miller, John, residence of 214, **5.88**. *See also* Gibson, Charles J. 248
Minerva Building. *See* McMaster, A.R., warehouse of
Mississauga Indians 5
Model School 117; 110, **4.61**. *See also* Cumberland, Frederic William 243–4; Snarr, Thomas 269–70; Storm, Thomas 270
Moore, Henry 230
Morris, William 189
Moss Park. *See* Allan, William
Mundie, William *255–6*

Necropolis chapel and lodge 167, **5.12**. *See also* Langley, Henry 254
Neelon, Sylvester. *See* Elliott & Neelon
Netting, George *268*
new fort. *See* Stanley Barracks, hospital at
Normal School 117; 110–11, **4.61–3**. *See also* Cumberland, Frederic William 243–4; Metcalfe, Wilson & Forbes 268; Mundie, William 255–6

Oak Hall 178, 184; 205, **5.74**. *See also* Harper, George Robinson 249–50
Oakham House 92, **4.36, 37**. *See also* Thomas, William 261
Oaklands 149, **4.115**. *See also* Gundry, Thomas 249; Hay, William 250
Old Mill 5
Ontario Bank 153, **4.119–21**. *See also* Irving, William 252; Sheard, Joseph 258; Worthington Brothers 271
Ontario House 49, **3.21, 22**; 118, **4.70**
Osgoode, William 16
Osgoode Hall xvii, 61, 100, 108, 114; 102–7, **4.47–57**. *See also* Baldwin, William Warren 241; Cumberland, Frederic William 243–4; Ewart, John 247; Lane, Henry Bowyer Joseph 254; Ritchey, John 269; Storm, William George 260; Walton, Benjamin 270
Oxford Museum, England 139, **4.100**

Page and Steele. *See* Renaissance Centre
Paisley Shop 78, **4.15**
Paris Exposition 178
Parliament buildings (1796) 27–30, 39, 56
Parliament buildings (1820) 30, 61
Parliament buildings (1829) 30, 62, 100; 60, **3.34–6**. *See also* Priestman, Matthew 269; Rogers, Thomas 257–8; Turton, Joseph 270
Parliament buildings (1886) 169, 175–6; 194, **5.53**. *See also* Darling, Frank 244; Gordon, Henry Bauld 248; Lennox, Edward James 255; Waite, Richard Alfred 262–3; Yorke, Lionel 271
Parliament Street, Victorian houses on 177, **5.26**
Parmentier, André *256*; Upper Canada College grounds 64, **3.40**
Paull, Almond E. & Herbert G. *256*
Payson, Ephraim 27–8
Pearson, John 130, 152, *256*
Pendarves 150, **4.117**. *See also* Cumberland, Frederic William 243–4; Pim, William Henry 268–9
Petch, Robert *268*
Petun Indians 3
Phillpotts, George, his plan of York 57; 42, **3.12**
Pilkington, Robert 20, *256*; his plan for Government House 18, **2.5**
Pim, William Henry *268–9*
Pittsburgh Court House 169, 190
Plenderleith, John *269*
police court, station, and fire hall 172, **5.28**. *See also* Harper, George Robinson 249–50
police station and fire hall 174, **5.24, 25**. *See also* Stewart, William 259–60
Portneuf, sieur de 7
Post, Albert Asa *256*
Post Office (1851) 117, 131, 144, 178; 127, **4.85**; 170, **5.17**. *See also* Cumberland, Frederic William 243–4; Metcalfe, Wilson & Forbes 268
Post Office (1871) 131; 170, **5.16, 17**. *See also* Langley, Henry 254; Yorke, Lionel 271
Priestman, Matthew *269*
Prince George, the. *See* Rossin House
Proudfoot, William. *See* Kearnsey House

Queen's Hotel. *See* Sword's Hotel
Queen's House at Greenwich, England 108

Queen's Wharf lighthouse 156, **4.126**. *See also* Tully, Kivas 262

Quetton St George, Laurent 35, 36, 39, 50, 56; residence of (Canada Company building) 34, **3.1**. *See also* Harper, John 267

Radford, Edward & George Kent *256–7*; St Paul's Anglican Church (1858) 135, **4.97**

Raffeix, Pierre 5

Red Lion Inn 39, 43; 34, **3.2**

Renaissance Centre 220, **5.99**

Revell, Viljo 226–7, 230

Richardson, Henry Hobson 157, 163, 169, 175

Ridout, John 137

Ridout, Thomas (surveyor-general) xi, 137

Ridout, Thomas (architect) 130, 131, *257*

Ripley, William Honeywood 80

Ritchey, John 74, 101, *269*; Ritchey's Terrace 132, **4.91**

Ritchey's Terrace. *See* Ritchey, John

Robert Simpson store 188; 213, **5.84, 85**. *See also* Burke, Edmund 242

Roberts, David Jr 210, *257*; George Gooderham house (York Club) 197, **5.60–2**; Gooderham (flat-iron) Building 196, **5.57**; Thorncrest 203, **5.69**

Roberts, David Sr *257*; Gooderham and Worts distillery 161, **5.8**

Robinson, Christopher 24

Robinson, J. Lukin, houses for 132, **4.92**. *See also* Cumberland, Frederic William 243–4

Robinson, John Beverley 51, 80; his residence Beverley House 77, **4.12**

Rochefoucauld-Liancourt, duc de la 17

Rogers, Thomas 62, *257–8*; Parliament buildings (1829) 60, **3.34**

Rolph, Ernest *258*

Rolph, John 74

Romanticism 75, 152

Root, John Wellborn 157

Ross, Mitchell and Company building 154, **4.123**

Rossin House 144; 132, **4.90**. *See also* Kauffmann, William 253; Wagner, Jacob P. 270; Walsh, James 270

Rousseau dit Saint-Jean, Jean-Bonaventure 8

Rousseaux St John, Jean-Baptiste 8, 16

Royal Canadian Bank 178; 205, **5.75**. *See also* Smith, James Avon 259

Royal Insurance building 154, **4.122, 123**. *See also* Kauffmann, William 253

Royal Lyceum Theatre 74. *See also* Ritchey, John 269

Russell, Peter 16, 20. *See also* Russell Abbey

Russell Abbey 24, 27, 31; 25, **2.11**. *See also* Berczy, William 241

St Andrew's Presbyterian Church (1830) 75; 46, **3.16**; 47, **3.19**; 227, **5.103**. *See also* Ewart, John 247; Howard, John George 251

St Andrew's Presbyterian Church (1874) 167, **5.13**. *See also* Storm, William George 260; Yorke, Lionel 271

St Anne's Anglican Church x. *See also* Howland, [William] Ford 252

St Basil's Roman Catholic Church 120–1, **4.75–7**. *See also* Hay, William 250; Post, Albert Asa 256

St George Greek Orthodox Church. *See* Holy Blossom Synagogue

St George the Martyr, Anglican Church of 80; 86, **4.24**. *See also* Lane, Henry Bowyer Joseph 254; Ritchey, John 269

St James' Anglican Cathedral (1839) 62, 82, 131; 63, **3.38**. *See also* Young, Thomas 263–4

St James' Anglican Cathedral (1850) xi, 35, 62, 75, 117, 131, 136–7, 144, 152, 178, 225; 128, **4.88, 89**; 129, **4.86, 87**. *See also* Cumberland, Frederic William 243–4; Langley, Henry 254; Metcalfe, Wilson & Forbes 268; Ritchey, John 269; Stephenson & Co, Edward 270

St James' Anglican Church (1831) 57, 61, 62, 82, 137; 46, **3.17**; 70, **4.3**. *See also* Ritchey, John 269; Rogers, Thomas 257–8

St James' Parochial School 115, **4.69**

St James-the-less, Chapel of 152; 134, **4.95**. *See also* Cumberland, Frederic William 243–4; Worthington Brothers 271

St John the Evangelist Anglican Church 211, **5.83**. *See also* Smith, [Ralph] Eden 258–9

St Lawrence Hall x, xii, 117, 124–5, 144, 224; 122–3, **4.78–80**. *See also* Metcalfe, Wilson & Forbes 268; Thomas, William 261

St Lawrence Market. *See* City Hall (1844)

St Mary's Roman Catholic Church 186, **5.42, 43**. *See also* Connolly, Joseph 243; Holmes, Arthur W. 250

St Michael's Roman Catholic Cathedral 56, 90, 93; 94–5, **4.38–41**. *See also* Gundry, Thomas 249; Harper, John 267; Thomas, William 261; Thomas, William Tutin 261–2; Wagner, Jacob P. 270

St Michael's College 120–1, **4.75–7**. *See also* Hay, William 250; Snarr, Thomas 269–70; Thomas, William Tutin 261–2; Walsh, James 270

St Patrick's Market 120, **4.74**. *See also* Young, Thomas 263–4

St Paul's Anglican Church (1858) 117, 152; 135, **4.97**. *See also* Radford, Edward & George Kent 256–7

St Paul's Methodist (United) Church (1886) 189, 198; 206, **5.76**. *See also* Smith, James Avon 259

St Paul's Roman Catholic Church (1822) 90. *See also* Ewart, John 247

St Paul's Roman Catholic Church (1887) 90; 187, **5.44, 45**. *See also* Connolly, Joseph 243

St Stephen's-in-the-Fields Anglican Church 135, **4.96**. *See also* Fuller, Thomas 247; Pim, William Henry 268–9

Sanford, W.E. 184

Scadding, Henry, residence of 90

Scadding, John, residence of 53, **3.26**

Schoolhouse, the Enoch Turner 88, **4.30**

second City Hall. *See* City Hall (1844)

second Court House. *See* Court House (1851)

second jail. *See* Jail (1824)

second Union Station. *See* Union Station (1873)

Selby, Prideaux 51

Selkirk, Lord 17

Seneca Indians xvi, 5

seventh Post Office. See Post Office (1851)

Severn, John, brewery of 70, **4.4**

Shaw, Aeneas 33

Shaw, John 169, 175

Sheaffe, Sir Roger 50

Sheard, Joseph 238, *258*; Cawthra House 112, **4.65**; Ontario Bank 153, **4.121**

Sheard, Matthew *258*

Siddall, John Wilson *258*; Holy Blossom

Synagogue 217, **5.92, 93**

Simcoe, Elizabeth Posthuma 6, 14, 15–16, 223; her sketch of Castle Frank 19, **2.4**

Simcoe, John Graves xv, 7, 8, 10, 11, 14–16, 17, 20, 21, 24, 27, 28, 30–1, 43, 82, 93, 125, 223; his residence Castle Frank 20; 19, **2.4**

Simpson, Henry *258*

Simpson store. *See* Robert Simpson store

Sinclair's Hotel 74–5

Small, Charles 24

Small, John 20; his residence Berkeley House 21, 24; 25, **2.10**

Smith, Burke & Co *269*

Smith, D.W., his residence Maryville Lodge 20–1; 22, **2.7**; 23, **2.8, 9**

Smith, Goldwin, his residence the Grange xv; 54, **3.27, 28**

Smith, James Avon 238, 239, *259*; 240, **A.1**; Church of the Redeemer 220, **5.99**; Knox College 220, **5.100**; Royal Canadian Bank 205, **5.75**; St Paul's Methodist (United) Church 206, **5.76**

Smith, [Ralph] Eden 258–9; St John the Evangelist Anglican Church 211, **5.83**

Smith, Samuel 57

Smith, William *269*

Snarr, Thomas *269–70*

Soane, Sir John xiv, 57; his plan for Government House 42, **3.13**

Soho Street, houses on 203, **5.70**

Spadina (first house, 1818, and second house, 1836). *See* Baldwin, William Warren

Spadina (third house, 1866) 242; 180–1, **5.31–3**

Sproatt, Henry *259*

Spruce Street, houses on 172, **5.27**

Stafford, Obadiah, residence of 76, **4.10**

Stanley Barracks, hospital at 79, **4.17**

Stephenson & Co, Edward *270*

Stewart, William *259–60*; police station and fire hall 174, **5.24, 25**

Storm, Thomas *270*

Storm, William George 108, 144, 151, 175, 238, 239, *260*; 240, **A.1**; Osgoode Hall 103, **4.48**; 106, **4.55**; St Andrew's Presbyterian Church (1874) 167, **5.13**; Victoria College 199, **5.63**; Wellesley School 166, **5.11**

Strachan, John xiii, 35, 36, 50, 51, 56, 61, 62, 74, 82, 90, 93, 114, 125, 137, 151; residence of 44, **3.14**

Strickland, Walter Reginald 238, *260*;
  second Union Station (1873)
  211, **5.82**
structural steel, its use in architecture
  184–8
Stuart, George Okill 35, 36
Sullivan, Louis 157, 158, 169
Sword's (Queen's) Hotel 133, **4.93**
Sydenham, Lord 116
Symons, William Limbery *260–1*

Talbot, Thomas 14
Tate, George *270*
Taylor, Edwin *261*; University College
  grounds 139, **4.99**
Tecumseh Wigwam 53, **3.25**
Teiaiagon (Toioiugon) 5, 6, 8; 4, **1.1**, 2; 9,
  **1.3**
Temple Building 188–9; 208, **5.79**; 209,
  **5.81**. *See also* Gouinlock, George
  Wallace 248
Teraulay Cottage. *See* Macaulay, James
third City Hall. *See* City Hall (1889)
third jail. *See* Jail (1838)
third Union Station. *See* Union Station
  (1914)
Thomas, Cyrus Pole 238, *261*
Thomas, William 90, 93, 124, 237, 239,
  *261*; Adelaide Buildings 146, **4.110**;
  Bishop's Palace 96, **4.42**; Commercial
  Bank 83, **4.19**, 20; Don Jail (1858) 147,
  **4.111**; Jennings Church 96, **4.43**; Knox's
  Church 97, **4.44**; Oakham House 92,
  **4.36**, 37; Ross Mitchell and Company
  building 154, **4.123**; St Lawrence
  Hall 123, **4.80**; St Michael's
  Cathedral 94–5, **4.38–41**
Thomas, William Tutin 93, 238, 239,
  *261–2*
Thomson, David 28
Thorncrest 203, **5.69**. *See also* Roberts,
  David Jr 257
Tiers, Daniel 35, 39, 43
Tom Taylor and Co, building of 184
Toronto Athletic Club 194–5, **5.54**, **55**. *See
  also* Lennox, Edward James 255
Toronto Carrying Place 5, 11; 4, **1.1**
Toronto Club 218, **5.95**. *See also* Darling,
  Frank 244; Lucas, Henry 267
Toronto Custom House. *See* Custom
  House
Toronto Exchange 117; 118–19, **4.70–3**.
  *See also* Grand, James 248

Toronto Exhibition building. *See* Crystal
  Palace
Toronto General Hospital 62, 98; 115,
  **4.68**. *See also* Harper, John 267; Hay,
  William 250; Mundie, William 256;
  Roberts, David Sr 257
Toronto Purchase 8, 10; 12, **2.1**
Toronto (York): fire of 1849 117, 124;
  Georgian architecture 35; growth 20,
  31–2, 57, 61, 67, 68, 73; health
  conditions 33; layout 6, 11, 16–17;
  incorporation 62, 67, 68; raid of 1813
  45, 50–1, 56; rebellion of 1837 114;
  social life 24, 33, 34; slavery 27;
  transportation 31; Victorian architecture
  198, 202
Toronto (York) and area, maps of 4, **1.1**; 9,
  **1.3**, 4; 12, **2.1**; 13, **2.2**, 3; 40, **3.9**; 41, **3.11**;
  42, **3.12**; 81, **4.18**; 164–5, **5.10**
Townsend, [Samuel] Hamilton 238, *262*
Trinity Church (1843) 80; 88, **4.28, 29**. *See
  also* Lane, Henry Bowyer Joseph 254;
  Ritchey, John 269
Trinity Church (1846) 80, 82, 90; 89, **4.32,
  33**. *See also* Harper, John 267; Lane,
  Henry Bowyer Joseph 254;
  Plenderleith, John 269
Trinity College (1851) xi, 117, 130,
  225; 126–7, **4.82–4**. *See also* Darling,
  Frank 244; Hay, William 250; Metcalfe,
  Wilson & Forbes 268; Tully, Kivas 262
Tully, John Aspenwell 238, *262*
Tully, Kivas xi, 130, 131, 237, 239;
  Bank of Montreal (1845) 85, **4.22**;
  Queen's Wharf lighthouse 156, **4.126**;
  Trinity College (1851) 126, **4.82**
Turner, Enoch 88
Turton, Joseph *270*

Union Station (1873) 211, **5.82**. *See also*
  Strickland, Walter Reginald 260
Union Station (1914) 210
University College xii, 75, 100, 117,
  144–5, 151, 224; 138–9, **4.98–9**;
  140–3, **4.101–8**. *See also* Cumberland,
  Frederic William 243–4; Dick, David
  Brash 245; Pim, William Henry 268–9;
  Walton, Benjamin 270
University of Toronto Library 199, **5.64**.
  *See also* Dick, David Brash 245
Upper Canada College (1829) 61; 64, **3.40**.
  *See also* Ewart, John 247; Parmentier,
  André 256; Priestman, Matthew 269

Upper Canada College (1889) 195, **5.56**.
  *See also* Durand, George F. 245;
  Strickland, Walter Reginald 260

van der Rohe, Mies 163, 226
Vanier, Georges 230
Victoria College 199, **5.63**. *See also* Storm,
  William George 260
Victoria Orange Hall 182, **5.37**. *See also*
  Lennox, Edward James 255

Wagner, Jacob P. *270*
Waite, Richard Alfred 175–6, *262–3*;
  Canada Life building 176; Canadian
  Bank of Commerce 176; Ontario
  Parliament buildings (1886) 194, **5.53**
Walker, Robert, store of. *See* Golden Lion
Walsh, Edward 24, 28; his painting of
  York 25, **2.11**; his plan for a House of
  Assembly 29, **2.14**
Walsh, James *270*
Walton, Benjamin *270*
Walton, Charles Albert *263*
Ware, William R. 188
Washburn, Simon 90
Webb Zerafa Menkes Housden partnership.
  *See* Renaissance Centre
Wellesley School 166, **5.11**. *See also* Storm,
  William George 260
Wellington Hotel 49, **3.22**
Wellington Street, number 70, warehouse
  at 219, **5.98**. *See also* Wickson,
  [Alexander] Frank *263*
Wells, Joseph, his residence Davenport 55,
  **3.29**
Wesleyan Methodist Church. *See* Methodist
  Church (1832)
West Presbyterian Church 148, **4.112**
White, John 24
Whitfield, Edwin, his painting of
  Toronto 112, **4.64**
Wickson, [Alexander] Frank *263*;
  Wellington Street, number 70,
  warehouse at 219, **5.98**
Williams, George, his plan of York 40, **3.9**
Willing and Williamson, store of. *See*
  Haworth, Thomas, store of
Willmot, Mancel *263*

Wilson, Alexander. *See* Metcalfe, Wilson &
  Forbes
Windeyer, Richard Cunningham *263*;
  Toronto Custom House 173, **5.21**
Withrow, James. *See* McBean & Withrow
Wood, Guy Carleton xiii
Woodsworth, Richard 86, **4.25**
Worthington, John 137, 144, *271*
Worthington Brothers *271*
Worts, James 74
Wright, Charles Henry Challenor 239,
  *263*
Wright, Frank Lloyd 157, 176, 178
Wyatt, C.B. 21

Yonge and Marlborough streets, toll-gate
  at 160, **5.6**
York, England, cathedral at 93
York, maps of. *See* Toronto (York) and
  area, maps of
York, Town of. *See* Toronto (York)
York Chambers 47, **3.18**
York Club 176; 196–7, **5.58–62**. *See also*
  Brown and Love 266; Roberts, David
  Jr 257
York County Court House. *See* Court
  House (1851)
York Hospital 30
York Hotel. *See* Jordan's Hotel
York Market. *See* Market
York Town Hall and Market. *See* City Hall
  (1831)
Yorke, Lionel *271*
Yorkville Town Hall 117; 148, **4.113, 114**.
  *See also* Hay, William 250
Young, Thomas 80, 98, 100, 131, 239,
  *263–4*; his drawing of the Parliament
  buildings (1829) 60, **3.34**; his plan of the
  Court House Square 46, **3.16**; his
  proposal for City Hall 63, **3.37**; King's
  College 99, **4.46**; his sketch of Upper
  Canada College (1829) 64, **3.40**; St
  James' Anglican Cathedral (1839) 63,
  **3.38**; St Patrick's Market 120, **4.74**. *See
  also* McDonald & Young 268

Zion Congregational Church 76, **4.9**

# Picture Credits

Abbreviations for frequently cited sources have been used in the paragraphs below as follows: City of Toronto Archives (CTA); McGill University, Montreal (MCG); Metropolitan Toronto Library, Baldwin Room (MTL); Ontario Archives, Toronto (OA); Panda Associates, Toronto (Panda); Public Archives of Canada, Ottawa (PAC); Toronto Camera Club (TCC). In many cases the reference number assigned by the source is included also. Any errors or omissions are unintended and regretted.

FOREWORD

John A. de Visser, Toronto

CHAPTER ONE

**1.1** Robinson *Toronto during the French Régime*; **1.2** PAC NMC-8473; **1.3** Robinson *Toronto during the French Régime*; **1.4** British Library, ms add 57707(10)

CHAPTER TWO

**2.1** MTL, Indian Treaties, Copy Book of Deeds; **2.2** PAC C-15979; **2.3** Public Record Office, London; **2.4** OA, Simcoe Collection 132; **2.5** PAC C-16016; **2.6** PAC C-16017; **2.7** MTL, D.W. Smith Papers B 15-87; **2.8** MTL, D.W. Smith Papers B 15-90; **2.9** MTL, D.W. Smith Papers B 15-88; **2.10** John Songhurst, Toronto; **2.11** University of Michigan, Clements Library; **2.12** MTL, Wm Jarvis, Estimates; **2.13** Private collection; **2.14** PAC C-70866; **2.15** MTL, D.W. Smith Papers B 9-311

CHAPTER THREE

**3.1** MTL T-10080; **3.2** MTL T-11063; **3.3** Art Gallery of Ontario; **3.4** PAC C-2046; **3.5** Robertson *Landmarks* I. opp 21; **3.6** MTL T-11128; **3.7** MTL T-11124; **3.8** MTL T-11190; **3.9** PAC C-15981; **3.10** Stan Peavoy, TCC; **3.11** Griffith Taylor *Topographical Control in Toronto*; **3.12** PAC C-96380; **3.13** Soane Museum, London; **3.14** MTL T-11528;

**3.15** Panda; **3.16** Toronto Registry Office; **3.17** Royal Ontario Museum, Sigmund Samuel Collection; **3.18** Panda; **3.19** MTL T-10706; **3.20** MTL T-11149; **3.21** PAC C-6658; **3.22** N.P. Willis *Canadian Scenery*; **3.23** MTL, Wm Allan Papers; **3.24** MTL T-12306; **3.25** MTL T-11087; **3.26** Robertson *Landmarks* I. 195; **3.27** Art Gallery of Ontario; **3.28** O.J. Eaton, TCC; **3.29** MTL T-11544; **3.30** MTL T-11422; **3.31** MTL T-30675; **3.32** Dudley Witney; **3.33** OA D-112; **3.34** PAC C-1667; **3.35** OA S-1354A; **3.36** MTL T-31255; **3.37** CTA PT-169C-6; **3.38** Royal Ontario Museum, Sigmund Samuel Collection; **3.39** MTL T-11101; **3.40** PAC C-1668; **3.41** MTL T-12659; **3.42** K.B. Jackson, Toronto; **3.43** Eric Arthur; **3.44** MTL T-11172

CHAPTER FOUR

**4.1** Panda; **4.2** Panda; **4.3** MTL T-11956; **4.4** MTL T-10907; **4.5** Page Toles, Toronto; **4.6** MTL T-11342; **4.7** MTL, Howard Papers III. 254; **4.8** MTL, Howard Papers III. 96; **4.9** MTL T-14089; **4.10** MTL T-12246; **4.11** MTL T-11251; **4.12** MTL T-11468; **4.13** K.B. Jackson, Toronto; **4.14** Fred Coates, Scarborough; **4.15** Panda; **4.16** Robertson *Landmarks* I. opp 87; **4.17** K.B. Jackson, Toronto; **4.18** CTA; **4.19, 20** OA D-284, 285; **4.21** MTL T-10463; **4.22** O.J. Grainger, Toronto; **4.23** MTL T-12834; **4.24** MTL T-10720; **4.25** MTL T-10700; **4.26** MTL T-11787; **4.27** Panda; **4.28** Panda; **4.29** Panda; **4.30** Panda; **4.31** MTL; **4.32** MTL; **4.33** T. Eaton Co Archives; **4.34** MTL T-10968; **4.35** Panda; **4.36** Panda; **4.37** Eric Arthur; **4.38** MTL, Langley Collection 99; **4.39** CTA SC-497-75; **4.40** Panda; **4.41** Panda; **4.42** Panda; **4.43** MTL T-10833; **4.44** MTL T-10256; **4.45** OA, Horwood Collection (411); **4.46** University College Archives; **4.47** Panda; **4.48** Panda; **4.49** PAC PA-122978; **4.50** Panda; **4.51** Panda; **4.52** Panda; **4.53** Panda; **4.54** Panda; **4.55** OA, Horwood Collection (747)2; **4.56** Panda; **4.57** Panda; **4.58** MTL T-11441; **4.59** Panda; **4.60** Panda; **4.61** PAC PA-122980; **4.62** Panda; **4.63** Panda; **4.64** MTL T-10276; **4.65** MTL T-11171; **4.66** Panda; **4.67** MTL T-12418; **4.68** MTL T-30148; **4.69** MTL T-13074; **4.70** PAC PA-122974; **4.71, 72, 73** MTL, Langley Collection 177; **4.74** MTL T-11575; **4.75** MTL, Langley Collection 169; **4.76** Panda; **4.77** Panda; **4.78** Panda; **4.79** MTL T-17182; **4.80** MTL T-12103; **4.81** MTL T-11558; **4.82** PAC PA-122986; **4.83** Panda; **4.84** Mr and Mrs Derrick Leach, Toronto; **4.85** Panda; **4.86** PAC Merrilees box 9127; **4.87** MTL T-10740; **4.88** CTA SC-497-72; **4.89** Panda; **4.90** MTL T-12706; **4.91** PAC PA-122994; **4.92** OA, Horwood Collection (94)2; **4.93** MTL T-11052; **4.94** O. Thompson *Toronto in the Camera* (1868); **4.95** Panda; **4.96** MTL T-10812; **4.97** OA, Merrilees Collection 103; **4.98** OA, Horwood Collection (107a); **4.99** National Gallery; **4.100** Sir Kenneth Clark *The Gothic Revival*; **4.101** Panda; **4.102** MTL T-30148; **4.103** MTL T-13141; **4.104** MTL T-13133; **4.105** MTL T-13066; **4.106** Panda; **4.107** Panda; **4.108** University of Toronto Archives; **4.109** Panda; **4.110** PAC PA-122984; **4.111** Panda; **4.112** MTL T-10837; **4.113** MTL T-12173; **4.114** John Songhurst, Toronto; **4.115** Panda; **4.116** Panda; **4.117** Panda; **4.118** Page Toles, Toronto; **4.119, 120** anon student, School of Architecture, Toronto; **4.121** MCG, Notman Collection; **4.122** Eric Arthur; **4.123** MTL T-12853; **4.124** MCG, Notman Collection; **4.125** MCG, Notman Collection

CHAPTER FIVE

**5.1** MCG, Notman Collection; **5.2** O.J. Grainger, Toronto; **5.3** MTL T-12617; **5.4** MTL T-12668; **5.5** MTL T-12970; **5.6** MTL T-12119; **5.7** MTL T-11228; **5.8** Panda; **5.9** MTL T-12447; **5.10** PAC NMC 43223; **5.11** OA, Horwood Collection (660)17; **5.12** Panda; **5.13** Panda; **5.14** MTL T-12330; **5.15** Panda; **5.16** Panda; **5.17** Panda; **5.18** *Monetary Times* Toronto 1872; **5.19** Panda; **5.20** *Canadian Illustrated News*; **5.21** C.P. Mulvaney *Toronto Past* *and Present*; **5.22** Panda; **5.23** John Songhurst, Toronto; **5.24, 25** Panda; **5.26** Panda; **5.27** Eric Arthur; **5.28** Mike Filey; **5.29** Consumers' Gas Co; **5.30** MTL T-31084; **5.31** Private collection; **5.32, 33** Panda; **5.34** MTL T-11257; **5.35** Ontario Association of Architects; **5.36** Panda; **5.37** Panda; **5.38** Panda; **5.39** Panda; **5.40** Ruth Gillespie, TCC; **5.41** Robert Hill; **5.42, 43** Panda; **5.44, 45** Panda; **5.46** Boris Spremo; **5.47** CTA A-77-8; **5.48** CTA 9.2.3G-42; **5.49** Panda; **5.50** Panda; **5.51** CTA 1985-111-16; **5.52** Panda; **5.53** MCG, Notman Collection; **5.54** MCG, Notman Collection; **5.55** *Canadian Architect and Builder*; **5.56** OA, Durand accession; **5.57** Robert Hill; **5.58** OA D-612; **5.59** Panda; **5.60, 61, 62** Panda; **5.63** W.H. Carre and Co *Art Work on Toronto* (1898); **5.64** MCG, Notman Collection; **5.65** Miss L. Janes, Toronto; **5.66** MTL T-11352; **5.67** Miss L. Janes, Toronto; **5.68** MTL T-10498; **5.69** G. Mercer Adam *Toronto, Old and New*; **5.70** Morley Markson, Toronto; **5.71** Panda; **5.72** G.P. Ure *Handbook of Toronto*; **5.73** John Songhurst, Toronto; **5.74** Eric Arthur; **5.75** MCG, Notman Collection; **5.76** Fiona Spalding-Smith; **5.77** John Easton, Toronto; **5.78** W.H. Carre and Co *Art Work on Toronto*; **5.79** W.H. Carre and Co *Art Work on Toronto*; **5.80** Panda; **5.81** Panda; **5.82** MTL T-12193; **5.83** Panda; **5.84** Panda; **5.85** Robert Simpson Co Archives; **5.86** T. Eaton Co Archives; **5.87** W.H. Carre and Co *Art Work on Toronto*; **5.88** Panda; **5.89** OA, Merrilees S 17392; **5.90** Panda; **5.91** Panda; **5.92** CTA SC-497-26; **5.93** Panda; **5.94** Panda; **5.95** Panda; **5.96** OA D-584; **5.97** King Edward Hotel; **5.98** Panda; **5.99** Robert Hill; **5.100** MCG, Notman Collection; **5.101** O.J. Grainger, Toronto; **5.102** Eric Arthur; **5.103** MTL T-10308; **5.104** Morley Markson, Toronto

EPILOGUE

**6.1** CTA 1985-123-4; **6.2** CTA 1985-123-1

APPENDIX A

**A.1** MTL T-31524; **A.2** Thomas McIlwraith

FRONT COVER

PAC C-21429

BACK COVER

OA D-610

# Toronto, No Mean City

*Third Edition*
Eric Arthur
*Revised by Stephen A. Otto*

Eric Arthur fell in love with Toronto the first time he saw it. The year was 1923; he was twenty-five years old, newly arrived to teach architecture at the University of Toronto. For the next sixty years he dedicated himself to saving the great buildings of Toronto's past. *Toronto, No Mean City* sounded a clarion call in his crusade. First published in 1963, it sparked the preservation movement of the 1960s and 1970s and became its bible. Now a new edition, prepared by Stephen Otto, updates Arthur's classic to include information and illustrations uncovered since the appearance of the first edition. Among these are some of the earliest photographs ever taken of Toronto, recently unearthed in a British library, and the architect's drawings for King's College, commissioned in 1829.

Those who have long depended on Arthur's book as the basic reference work on the development of Toronto's cityscape will find its reliability reinforced in Otto's judiciously revised text, a fuller section on Toronto's architects, and an added appendix on builders and contractors. Those new to the subject will delight in this anecdotal account of the city's rich architectural heritage. All will find the compact format attractive and easy to use.

ERIC ARTHUR was, at his death in 1982, professor emeritus in the School of Architecture, University of Toronto. Appointed Companion of the Order of Canada in 1968, he was the recipient of numerous other honours and awards for distinguished service to the arts and architecture in Canada. He was the author of many books, including *Iron: Cast and Wrought Iron in Canada from the Seventeenth Century to the Present* (1982, with Thomas Ritchie) and *The Barn: A Vanishing Landmark in North America* (1972, with Dudley Whitney).

STEPHEN OTTO has a distinguished record in heritage conservation, as initiator of the Ontario Bicentennial celebrations, director of the Ontario Heritage Foundation, member of the Toronto Historical Board, and head of the Ontario government's heritage-conservation programs. It was through his initiative that the superb Horwood Collection of architectural drawings was presented in 1979 to the Ontario Archives.